# Six Decades of Adventure in Space and Time

A social, cultural and screen history of *Doctor Who*

Frank Danes was born in Wembley in 1965 and was educated in Worthing, Sussex and the Universities of Kent and Oxford. He taught English and English Literature for thirty years in seven secondary schools. In 2017 he left full-time teaching to become a full-time writer. Frank lives in Ely, Cambridgeshire with his wife, three children and two Daleks.

Also by Frank Danes:

*Victorian Literature: Teachers' Guide*
*Fifty Years in Time and Space*
*The Canterbury Tale –*
    *Doctor Who* short story in *Temporal Logbook II*
*The Little Book of Spelling, Punctuation and Grammar*
*Get It Right!*

OCR GCSE guides:

*Macbeth*
*Romeo and Juliet*
*The Merchant of Venice*
*Much Ado about Nothing*
*Animal Farm*
*Pride and Prejudice*
*Great Expectations*

OCR A level guides:

*Women in Literature*
*Dystopia*
*The History Boys*
*The Merchant's Prologue and Tale*
*A Streetcar Named Desire.*

Frank Danes

# Six Decades of Adventure in Space and Time

A social, cultural and screen history of
*Doctor Who*

Unauthorised

**BWCC**

Published in 2018 by Bedford Who Charity Con (Books)
(formerly St Mark's Press)
20 Close Road
Pavenham, Bedfordshire MK43 7PP
www.bedfordwhocharitycon.co.uk

There are some corners of the universe which have bred the most terrible things. Things which act against everything we believe in. They must be fought.

Cover illustration by Roger Langridge

Cover design by Zoe French

Parts of this book, now completely revised and updated, previously appeared in *Fifty Years in Time and Space: A Short History of* Doctor Who by Frank Danes (St Mark's Press, Bedford, 2013, 2014).

Hate
is always foolish
and
Love
is always wise.

*– The Doctor*

For Emma
and
For Simon

# Contents

# Foreword

This book is a history of the British Broadcasting Corporation's television programme *Doctor Who*. It is also intended as an introduction to the programme for those who enjoy it but aren't over-familiar with it, such as viewers who have enjoyed the revived series which debuted in March 2005 but haven't seen much of the original show, which ran on BBC 1 from 1963-1989. It's also intended for viewers in the United States and other countries who are familiar with the post-2005 run but are less familiar with the original show: France, Germany, China, Mexico and so on. It is, I hope, the only one volume history of *Doctor Who* you will ever need.

*Six Decades in Space and Time* explains the history of *Doctor Who*: from its inception as a family show intended to bridge a gap in Saturday afternoon programming on the BBC in the early 1960s, to its return as an unexpected smash hit in 2005. I have chronicled the major back stage decisions that were made as the show evolved and devolved over the course of six decades, and have tried to demonstrate how the show was shaped by the changes in British and Western culture and ideology. I've also done my best to chronicle the experience of watching the show when it was first shown. Parts of this story were told in my previous book *Fifty Years in Time and Space: A Short History of* Doctor Who[1] but have been extensively revised in the light of five more years of revelations about the show's history and, of course, five more years (more or less) of production of the show.

The book isn't an episode guide and some *Doctor Who* television stories are covered in detail, others skipped (well, there are about 280 of them to date...). Interested readers can find story details in one of the many guides to the show online or in printed form. I have, however, provided details of episodes as an appendix and have scored them shamelessly according to my own preferences, for what

---

[1] St Mark's Press, Bedford, 2013 and 2014

these are worth. I hope that readers who are unfamiliar with all of the *Who* might thus be given some idea of which stories might be worth viewing. On the other hand, what do I know anyway: lots of people love the stories I have only rated at one star.

*Six Decades in Space and Time* should also be of interest to the *Doctor Who* fan who is, like me, steeped in the show's history and reads anything about it she can get her hands on. It is, inevitably, a personal reading of the show: any book which wasn't would be dry as dust and there is no such thing as an objective analysis of a media text anyway. Having said that, I do apologise to any readers who might be hurt that I have been less than generous to their favourite periods of *Doctor Who*. We *Who* fans are all friends, I hope, and should respect each other's differences with the tolerance shown by the Doctor herself. Himself. Do please disagree with my opinions and, as I have said, what do I know anyway.

So. I have apparently been watching the show since I was born in 1965 – on a Saturday, in fact, and just in time to watch "Galaxy Four" episode two. Some of my earliest memories are of watching the programme: I remember my twin brother and I putting our hands over the screen when the Yeti appeared in the London Underground[1], prompting yells of "Get those twins away from the television!" from my elder brothers. I must have seen "Seeds of Death" in 1968 although I have no memory of it, as I thought the Silurians in "Doctor Who and the Silurians" (1970) were Ice Warriors. I must also have seen "The Evil of the Daleks" in 1967, as I was not only able to remember the Daleks when they reappeared in "Day of the Daleks" (1972) but was able to correct a nursery worker at my pre-school when she erroneously called the Marx toy Dalek, which graced our playgroup, a "robot". My brother and I went down the road to watch the programme in colour in the early seventies, at a time when a colour television cost something in the region of £2000 in today's money; we would return to tell our father, who watched the programme in black and white, what colour the monsters had been (usually green). I co-edited a fanzine in the

---

[1] "The Web of Fear"(1968)

1980s, did some professional writing, got a degree in English and American Literature and taught English in secondary schools for thirty years. I've always been a *Doctor Who* fan even as I have become (in 1970's script editor Terrance Dicks' words) older, fatter, greyer, but not noticeably wiser.

## A note on language

Stephen Moffat established that a Time Lord can change her gender when she changes her face, most notably when The Master became Missy and, of course, when Jodie Whittaker was cast as the thirteenth Doctor in 2017. Choosing a pronoun for the Doctor has thus become problematical and controversial, as she can be he or she, depending on the incarnation. To avoid clumsiness, I've used the pronoun "he" when writing about male Doctors and "she" when writing about the thirteenth Doctor. As thirteen of the Doctor's screen incarnations – including the War Doctor (John Hurt) – have been male, and one female, I've used the pronoun "he" when referring to the Doctor as a single being across all of her or his incarnations. Opting for "he" thus does not indicate that the author is a sexist pig, but is a point about language to avoid confusions between the first twelve (thirteen?) and the thirteenth (fourteenth?) Doctor, and to avoid clumsy "he or she", "she or he", "she/he", "he/she" or "s/he" references in the text.

How important are gender differences to the individual Time Lord anyway? The programme itself draws a bit of a veil over this, and, perhaps considering the audience and time slot, does not specify the precise nature of a Time Lord's primary sexual attributes. "The Pilot" (2017) confirms for the first time that there is a toilet on the TARDIS[1], although the Doctor's surprise at Bill asking where she

---

[1] This revelation finally silences hilarious jokes aired since the series began, and once referenced by Peter Davison, asking if the TARDIS has a loo. These jokes were very funny as the improbability of the characters' lives in a science fiction show was indicated by their lack of need of a lavatory, although such wags never asked, say, where the toilet was in the

can find it suggests he doesn't use it himself. Bill has to explain quietly, "I've had a shock. I need to use your toilet". There are some good jokes about the Doctor's physical nature in the post-2005 series. When Rose tells Jackie that the Doctor has two hearts, her mother asks "He hasn't got two of anything else, has he?" ("The Christmas Invasion" (2005)). Rory's suspicion that the Doctor might have fathered Amy's child ("The Almost People" (2011)) suggests that humans and Time Lords might be genetically and genitally compatible. The tenth Doctor has more sexuality than his fellows and beams that he "snogged Madame de Pompadour" ("The Girl in the Fireplace" (2006)); the eighth Doctor kisses Grace twice in the 1996 TV movie but the eleventh Doctor squirms with embarrassment when Amy and River Song try, on separate occasions, to engage him in a clinch.

## A note on season numbering

The original run of *Doctor Who* numbered its seasons from 1-26[1] between 1963 and 1989. The number of seasons is itself impressive – by comparison, the original series of *Star Trek* (1966-1969) only

---

police station in *Z Cars* (BBC, 1962-1978). When the original series aired, drama series tended not to dwell on the toilet of their characters, not least to keep up a good pace which would be spoiled if characters had to pause for a comfort break before leaping into squad cars or running back to the TARDIS. Similar hilarious jokes were made about the lack of bathrooms on the Starship Enterprise. *Babylon 5* answered the question when a character asks Security Chief Garibaldi where the bathroom is, and is told to avoid the one that's "for methane breathers only" (*Babylon 5,* "Midnight on the Firing Line", 1994).

[1] In fact, they were called "series" at the time, and a new season was labelled *New Series* in the BBC listings magazine *Radio Times* when it appeared each year. As *Doctor Who* as a whole was also called "a series", as in the American term "mini-series" for a show with a finite run (e.g. the original BBC *House of Cards* in the 1990s), "series" is a hopelessly ambiguous term. "Season" is an American term for a year's run of new episodes and has been sensibly adopted by the Brits.

ran for three seasons – even if the quality of the stories was highly variable. When *Doctor Who* was revived in 2005, the BBC opted to start numbering the seasons again from the beginning: thus Christopher Eccleston's season was season 1, David Tennant's first season was season 2 and so on. This was a deliberate attempt by the BBC to show that post-2005 *Doctor Who* was a new show and not in any way linked with the wobbly-setted, cardboard monstered, critically derided final episodes of the 1986-1989 seasons, absolutely not. It was a decision made for good reasons. Market research had suggested that children saw *Doctor Who* as an old show for their parents: would they really watch it if they thought they had to catch up on 26 years of backstory in order to understand it, let alone enjoy it? Thus Russell T Davies and the BBC cleared the decks and started numbering the new seasons from 1. Peter Capaldi completed season 10 in 2017 and Jodie Whittaker's season in 2018 is season 11.

But nothing is ever simple with Doctor *Who*, which has ambiguity hardwired into its fictional and factual narrative. Although the BBC presented post-2005 *Doctor Who* as a new show, it clearly was a continuation of the original run, via the 1996 TV movie with Paul McGann[1]. Russell T Davies assured fans, in *Doctor Who Magazine*, that the Doctor as played by Christopher Eccleston really was the same character who had met the Drahvins[2] and had been a member of the Prydonian chapter of Time Lords[3] in the original series. The TARDIS was still a police box; the Doctor still had two hearts and could change his form; he still expressed a preference for the planet Earth and travelling with human sidekicks (often female, sometimes male, usually good looking).

The re-tooled *Who* thus was and was not part of the narrative of the original series. There was a break with the past, as represented in

---

[1] A back-door pilot in an attempt to launch a new series made for American television. It did well in the UK but bombed in the States. New Paul McGann series was there none.
[2] In "Galaxy Four" (1965)
[3] See "The Deadly Assassin" (1976)

the numbering of the seasons. However, the American dramatist and writer Harlan Ellison, who loved *Doctor Who*, expressed extreme impatience with the new numbering and said that, if the new show continued the old one, then what was all this goddam nonsense about the first season when it was obviously the twenty seventh.

In agreement with Harlan Ellison that there is one show called *Doctor Who* and not two separate shows, this book numbers seasons consecutively from 1963: Christopher Eccleston's first season is season 27 and Jodie Whittaker's first season is season 37. However, I've put the revised season numbers in brackets where relevant, so season 37 is referenced as season 37 (season 11). This numbering is as pernickety as it is absolutely vital.

Finally, the Doctor is always the Doctor whichever body he inhabits. I haven't followed the recent practice of capitalising incarnations as the Fifth Doctor or the Thirteenth Doctor as there is no such character as the Thirteenth Doctor. He or she is always the Doctor so the incarnation number doesn't deserve a capital letter and is written without one in this book, as the thirteenth Doctor. So there.

# An Introduction:
# *Doctor Who* and Television in the United Kingdom

Television in the United Kingdom is an entirely different beast from American television, and it was so in 1963 when *Doctor Who* was first broadcast. The show has always been made by the BBC, the British Broadcasting Corporation, which, probably uniquely in the world, is a publicly-owned, government-supported organisation paid for by British taxpayers through the television licence fee.

The BBC started its life in 1922 as the British Broadcasting Company Ltd, exclusively licensed by the General Post Office on behalf of Bonar Law's Conservative government to produce programmes for the new medium of radio. The service was financed not by direct taxation but by payment of a radio licence: if you wanted to own a radio set in Britain, you had to pay an annual licence fee of ten shillings, equivalent to something like £27 today. This was the origin of the present day, somewhat eccentric, system of funding for the BBC. Television has long since replaced radio as the most successful popular medium, and the radio licence is now (obviously) called the television licence, but the principle is the same. If you want to watch TV in the UK, you have to pay a television licence of £150.50 a year. The licence fee goes directly to the BBC to make programmes not just for television, but also for radio: in fact, it funds 11 television channels, 18 national radio channels, numerous local radio channels, BBC iPlayer (the online service for BBC programmes) and the BBC World Service, the BBC news version of Voice of America.

The British Broadcasting Company Ltd became a public service corporation, the British Broadcasting Corporation, in 1927. Sir John Reith, the BBC's first Director General, was determined that the BBC should be a public service corporation rather than a commercial company, and the government agreed. The BBC was to

15

be funded by the licence fee and was not to run advertisements. In fact, there were no adverts at all on British television until ITV, independent television, came along in 1955: this was funded by ads and always had more money than the BBC, something obvious in the production values of many of its dramas.[1]

Until 1955, though, the BBC had a monopoly on television production in the United Kingdom.[2] There was only one channel: BBC. Its Director General Sir John Reith, a Scottish Calvinist, insisted on high moral aims for the new service and declared that the BBC's brief was to "inform, educate and entertain". Instead of giving the public what they wanted, it was to give them something better than that.

This somewhat paternalistic ethos held the BBC in good stead in the Second World War. Its news broadcasts were second to none, acclaimed worldwide and widely seen as trustworthy. The prevailing wisdom was that, if you heard it on the BBC, it must be true. The BBC broadcast clandestine messages to resistance groups in Nazi-occupied Europe[3]; German citizens put their ears to muted radio sets in 1944-5 to find out what was actually going on, although Goebbels

---

[1] In fact, the BBC took the ban on advertisements so seriously that it refused to allow commercial products to be named on screen for fear of advertising. In the 1970s, the children's magazine programme *Blue Peter*, which often featured *Doctor Who*, always called Sellotape "sticky tape" when it showed its audience how to do some junk modelling (a cardboard Dalek and a *Doctor Who* miniature theatre featured over the years). Sitcoms showing characters eating cornflakes would blank out the word Kellogg's from the cereal box, substituting some bland and absurd label like Sunshine. By the 1990s, the policy became a little less hysterical and Kellogg's and other brand names were allowed to appear, unmolested.

[2] And, surprisingly, on radio production until 1973, when the new Independent Broadcasting Authority licensed commercial stations to begin broadcasting. Illegal, "pirate" radio stations like Radio Caroline had broadcast from ships near the British coastlines from 1964

[3] Directly inspired by European resistance groups, plucky resistance fighters pitted against a vastly superior and better equipped fascist war machine appeared in *Doctor Who* in the 1964 story, "The Dalek Invasion of Earth" and its movie version, *Daleks: Invasion Earth, 2150 A.D.* Terry Nation, who had lived through the German bombardment of Swansea, based much of his work on the horrors of World War II. See Chapter 2.

declared such treachery was to be severely punished[1]. It was the BBC which broke the news of the concentration camps to a horrified mass audience. The highly respected reporter Richard Dimbleby entered Belsen concentration camp with British troops in 1945. In his report, he said, "This day at Belsen was the most horrible of my life." Mindful of the excesses of anti-German propaganda in the First World War, the BBC at first refused to believe it or to broadcast it. Dimbleby immediately got on the phone to London and shouted that, if they didn't broadcast it at once, he would resign. The BBC gave way.

Such was the status of the BBC in the 1940s, 1950s and early 1960s. Modern politicians of left and right have attacked the BBC for political bias: Prime Minister David Cameron called it "The British Bolshevik Corporation" and half joked in the 2015 election campaign that he would close it down when the Conservatives won. The truth is, of course, that the BBC holds the government of the day to account, and governments often don't like this. Tony Blair's Labour government savaged the BBC in 2003 over its accusations that its dossier justifying war against Iraq was "sexed up"; the row became so serious that it ended with the resignation of the then Director General Greg Dyke, himself a Labour supporter. Yet in the early 1960s, the BBC was still seen as the responsible voice of the establishment.

As far as *Doctor Who* was concerned, Reith's "educate, inform, entertain" mantra (often referred to as "Reithian values") influenced the programme as originally conceived by Sydney Newman. The show was to go forwards, backwards and sideways in time, and the Doctor and his companions were to meet real characters from history. The children in the audience were to be educated as well as thrilled, and the first Doctor met Robespierre, Nero, Marco Polo and Kublai Khan among others. The Doctor's original companions were his granddaughter Susan and two of her schoolteachers. Kim Newman aptly described the choice as reflecting the "slightly bossy"

---

[1] In a typically revolting phrase, Goebbels pronounced the BBC, "Jew radio".

BBC of the time[1]: Barbara taught history and represented the historical side of the show, so she was able to fill in background details about the Aztecs and the French Revolution, both visited in *Doctor Who*'s first season. Ian was a science teacher who was intended to fulfil the same role for science. However, by the time the first episode was finally made, Ian instead tended to be utterly disbelieving and bewildered when confronted by scientific marvels beyond his own time. "I don't believe it!" he declares on first entering the TARDIS, and his role in the show is instead to handle the rough stuff which the Doctor, conceived in some original documents as virtually senile, was unable to do. Ian and Barbara become symbolically representative as the science and history sides of the show. As the Doctor became more of a genial know-all in the first ten years of the series, and particularly as played by Jon Pertwee, Barbara and Ian's conceived roles as talking encyclopaedias – never fully developed in the programme itself – was quickly assumed by the Doctor.

Sydney Newman declared that on no account was the show to feature BEMs – "bug-eyed monsters" – but was to be far more intelligent and philosophical in its approach to history. An early and abandoned script by Malcolm Hulke concerned a parallel Earth on the other side of the sun; the time travellers were to explore and deduce its differences from our Earth in the story[2]. Remarkably enough, child (and adult) viewers found the science fiction adventure stories more fun than the historicals, and children, quick to spot sneaky attempts to educate them, preferred the Daleks to Richard the Lionheart. Robert Holmes, who wrote some of the show's best adventures from 1969-1986, once said that he had always suspected *Doctor Who* had been conceived as a way to teach

---

[1] Kim Newman, *Doctor Who*, BFI 2005, p.12
[2] Gerry Anderson (of *Thunderbirds* fame) produced a film with a very similar premise, *Doppleganger*, in 1969. Intended as a pilot for a series, an astronaut finds himself back at home and much relieved after many years lost in space. Or does he? Groping in the dark for his light switch, he finds it is on the other side of the door from where he thought it was. He is on a parallel Earth on the other side of the sun, the mirror image of our own. Had Anderson glimpsed Hulke's original premise?

kids history and it was a good thing that sci-fi eventually won out. The purely historical adventures were phased out with Patrick Troughton's second story, "The Highlanders" in 1966-7, not to return until "Black Orchid" in 1982, featuring Peter Davison as the Doctor. Newman was furious with Verity Lambert for introducing the Daleks in 1963 and William Russell, who played Ian, one of the Doctor's original companions, said the regular cast much preferred making the historical to the science fiction stories. But the viewers disagreed.

The BBC, then, was completely unlike the American networks of the 1960s. *Star Trek* was made by Desilu, an independent, private production company. Gene Roddenberry, the show's creator, worked with Desilu to produce the pilot episode "The Cage" in 1965 and tried to sell it to NBC, a television network similar to ITV in the UK. NBC rejected the pilot and it wasn't until a year later that a re-tooled *Star Trek*, now starring William Shatner as the gallant Captain Kirk, was bought and screened by NBC[1]. *Doctor Who*, by contrast, was made in-house by the BBC, in BBC studios crewed by BBC salaried employees, videoed and filmed by BBC paid cameramen. Even the special effects from 1963-1989 (the show's original run) were produced by the BBC's in house Visual Effects Department, and private companies were only occasionally used by the BBC when their own people were too busy. Shawcraft, a company which began as a boat builders, built the Daleks for their first appearance in December 1963; the dinosaurs in "Invasion of the Dinosaurs" (1974) were provided by an external effects company. Barry Letts had wanted the BBC chaps who had been so successful

---

[1] *Star Trek* arrived in the UK in 1969 after NBC had cancelled the show. It was screened as a summer replacement for *Doctor Who* after Patrick Troughton had spun away into the void at the end of "The War Games" (1969) and before Jon Pertwee took the show into colour. The BBC re-edited *Star Trek* to begin with the title sequence. The teaser followed, then the episode's title, and a right old mess was made of the original. *Star Trek* was enormously popular as a (perceived) high budget, colour show and *Doctor Who* suffered in the early 1970s from endless gibes about its comparative cheapness, not least because it was still primarily made on video when *Star Trek* was made on glorious film.

with the Drashigs[1] to handle the dinosaurs and was furious when the private effects company turned in rubber monsters worked as rod puppets.

When *Doctor Who* finally went off the air in 1989, not with a bang but a whimper, conditions of production had changed enormously at the BBC. The corporation had been under attack for ten years from the radical Conservative governments of Margaret Thatcher. Suspicious of public companies and perceiving the BBC as biased to the left and Labour, legions of Conservative MPs suggested selling off the BBC as other nationalised industries and QUANGOs[2] had been sold off to the private sector (railways, water, electricity, gas, British Airways, British Telecom etc.). The BBC responded to such pressure by reorganising itself in a way likely to please a Conservative government, raising its own money by selling programmes and merchandising through BBC Enterprises (latterly, BBC Worldwide) and commissioning programmes from private production companies. There were several attempts to revive *Doctor Who* as an independent production, made by private companies and sold back to the BBC (a la *Star Trek* and NBC). Terry Nation, who created the Daleks, and Gerry Davies, who co-created the Cybermen, headed separate bids. None got anywhere, although the BBC told anyone who asked that *Doctor Who* would probably, eventually, return but made by an independent production company. This was almost certainly an inexactitude to quieten fans: the BBC was weary of the programme and wanted to dampen down expectations and negative publicity.

That this euphemistic formula actually became reality is something of an ironic twist. The 1996 TV movie with Paul McGann (imaginatively titled *Doctor Who*) was made by Universal,

---

[1] In "Carnival of Monsters", 1973.

[2] Quasi-Autonomous Non Governmental Organisation, such as The Milk Marketing Board. Financed by public money and with members appointed indirectly by the government, Quangos functioned in effect as private companies. Most were abolished by Conservative governments, sold off wholesale to private enterprise or had their functions subsumed into central or local government.

an American company, for screening on the new Fox TV network in the USA and the BBC in the UK. The programme was managed by the triumvirate of Fox-Universal-the BBC and it is something of a miracle that it was ever made at all. Some would say that three parents are bound to create a monstrous child and the TV movie was a bit of a disaster, which is not kind. Paul McGann was applauded for his dashing performance as the Doctor but the script was described by Terrence Dicks[1] as "incoherent crap". The movie was conceived as a back-door pilot for a new television series and McGann signed a five year contract. It performed well in the UK but bombed in the US against the final episode of the ratings giant *Roseanne* and no new series was forthcoming. As plans for the series included Cybermen who were sort of galactic raiders like the Reavers in *Firefly* (Mutant Enemy, 2002-3), that might perhaps have been just as well.

The single fact that *Doctor Who* was made by the BBC explains its longevity. The show celebrated its fifty-fifth year in 2018, which sees the first full series with the thirteenth lead actor to play the Doctor, Jodie Whittaker, the first woman to play the role in a radical and exciting piece of casting. Had ITV made the show, it's unlikely it would have lasted past its second or third year. Relying on advertising revenues for their income, commercial television companies make more money on advertising in a highly viewed show. When the ratings fall off, the income dries up and the company unceremoniously takes an axe to the offending programme. As viewing figures for the early seasons of *Who* began to dip, a commercial company would have almost certainly pulled the plug. Proof positive is in Fox's decision not to commission another movie or series after the McGann film flopped on its American network. But the BBC is, or at least was, a different beast in the 1960s. It was a publicly owned corporation committed to public service broadcasting, giving the public not just what they wanted but something better. So *Doctor Who* was renewed year after year in the 1960s because it was felt that it had a big enough

---

[1] Script editor of *Doctor Who* from 1969-1974

audience to justify recommissioning it. Viewing figures for "The War Games" in 1969 dipped to three million, yet the show was renewed for 1970 when, now in colour with Jon Pertwee, it renewed its vigour and chart position and was a tremendous success. When the show first faced cancellation after 1963, it wasn't until the end of season seven in 1970: Pertwee's successful first season. The show was renewed largely because the BBC couldn't find a satisfactory replacement for it. Then viewing figures held steady and continued to rise and there was no thought of cancelling it until Michael Grade arrived from ITV in the 1980s. He brought with him the thought process of commercial television and axed programmes which were perceived to be performing badly. One show to be unceremoniously dumped was *The Tripods* (1983-4). This mini-series was conceived in the *Doctor Who* mould and directed by such *Who* stalwarts as Christopher Barry, who directed "The Dead Planet" back in 1963. Based on the science fiction trilogy by John Christopher, *The Tripods* was due to run for three seasons. One episode was shot at the castle home of Conservative minister and diarist Alan Clark, who was rather taken with the lead actress. Grade axed the show after two series, leaving one book undramatised and the story hanging in mid-air. Pre-Grade, the BBC would have continued with the series for reasons of artistic integrity: to complete the story. Grade axed it because of perceived low viewing figures. Fans of the books and show reacted with dismay and some bewilderment: cancelling a show conceived to run for three years after only two was something new and unwelcome, but this was the brash and brave new world Grade ushered in. He cancelled *Doctor Who* at the end of Colin Baker's first season (1985) on the outrageous grounds that he personally hated it[1]. Declining viewing figures were cited as a justification, as was the need to use the show's budget to finance

---

[1] In 2013, a member of the House of Lords asked Grade, a fellow peer, if he would have axed *Doctor Who* if he had known that John Hurt was to play a future Doctor. Grade nodded vigorously. This contradicted his praise for Christopher Eccleston's single season as the Doctor in 2015 but demonstrated that his hostility to the show was consistent over twenty eight years.

the new BBC soap *EastEnders* (1985-present) and the new breakfast service. BBC accounting didn't work in this way, but Grade languidly offered it as an excuse. *Doctor Who* had been cancelled, but the BBC said it was only being rested. Bad publicity and a threat by *Who* fans to march on Parliament persuaded a reluctant BBC, which now hated the show, to recommission it for a much reduced run of 14 episodes a season from 1986. Richard Marson writes[1] that BBC executives couldn't face the thought of photos appearing in the national press of Daleks and monsters outside the Houses of Parliament demanding a new series. The BBC's attitude to the programme in 1985 was summed up by Jonathan Powell, the Controller of BBC 1, who, when interviewed by Richard Marson, said of *Who* producer John Nathan-Turner, "I just wanted him to fuck off and take his fucking programme with him."[2] Crushed by the mighty weightings juggernaut of *Coronation Street,* against which it competed on ITV, stripped of film for its exterior scenes (which had always improved the show's look), and cut down to 25 minutes from season 22's 45 minutes, *Who* began to look distinctly wobbly in execution and in confidence. Season 22 had experimented with 45 minute episodes when Grade cancelled the show, the new length an attempt to give the programme the dramatic heft of serious dramas. From 1986, it was back to 25 minutes, when ITV was drawing huge audiences with its two hour, filmed episodes of *Inspector Morse.* Even BBC executives made unfavourable comparisons between *Who* and the new American series *Star Trek: The Next Generation,* which had a budget about five times *Doctor Who*'s, and sneakily insinuated that the BBC could never match the Americans' production values and surely it was time to put it out of its misery...

*Doctor Who* returned in 2005 when it was commissioned by people who had grown up enjoying the programme as children. Looking for a successful family show for Saturday evenings, BBC One controller Lorraine Heggessey thought, why not do something

---

[1] In *The Life and Scandalous Times of John Nathan-Turner* (Miwk Publishing, 2013)
[2] Op cit pp. 230-231

like *Doctor Who*? In fact, why not just do *Doctor Who*? Thirteen years on from its relaunch, the programme continues to do well and the main threat to its survival are not so much artistic as political. From 2005-2010, *Doctor Who* was made when Britain was governed by the Labour governments of Tony Blair and Gordon Brown and Labour has always been much more well disposed towards the BBC than the Conservatives, disputes over the Gulf War notwithstanding. The Conservatives were returned to power in 2010 in coalition with the Liberals; won the 2015 general election with a small majority and scraped back into government in 2017 with the support of the Northern Ireland's Democratic Unionist Party. The Conservatives have been hostile to the BBC since Mrs Thatcher's time, and the Coalition government (2010-2015) enacted some policies which were strongly antipathetic to the BBC. The licence fee was frozen and the existence of the BBC itself was again questioned as its Royal Charter, which granted it the right to broadcast as a public body, came up for renewal. The impacts of these changes on *Doctor Who* were obvious, if denied. Matt Smith's final season was split into two and screened over two years; Peter Capaldi's seasons were one episode shorter per year; only three new episodes were screened in 2009 and there was no series at all in 2016. Jodie Whittaker's first season only had ten episodes. An increase in the running time of each episode – from 45 to 50 minutes – isn't wonderful as compensation. All this is very frustrating for merchandisers, who justifiably complain that it is impossible to sell merchandise when the show is off the air; and indeed, *Doctor Who* toys have generally disappeared off the shelves of Britain's supermarkets since about 2010.

The Conservative governments of 1979-1997 encouraged the BBC to generate more of its own income and the BBC agreed. BBC Enterprises, which had long been selling programmes abroad and granting merchandising licences, became BBC Worldwide and ramped up its production with the enthusiasm of a megalomaniac computer planning to take over the world. The success of post-2005 *Doctor Who* was such that each episode was paid for five times over

The *Doctor Who* display in Toys R Us, Cambridge, 2007.

in merchandise and overseas sales. Not that *Doctor Who* itself saw much of this money: Worldwide's profits were fed back into the common BBC pot and *Doctor Who* had to wait in line for its share. A deal with the Canadian Broadcasting Company financed part of the budget for the David Tennant serials. The Conservative coalition government, however, decreed after 2010 that Worldwide had become too successful, and it was jolly rotten for private media companies which were not partly bankrolled by the taxpayer to have to compete with the BBC and Worldwide. Thus Worldwide was told not to make excessive profits and its remit was severely limited. The BBC's website, which provided a free library of services and programme information, was similarly hacked back for fear that it would swamp such frail organisations as News International.

The Conservatives' hostility to the corporation reached a peak in 2015 with the appointment of the free marketeer John Whittingdale as Culture Secretary. Again, the existence of the BBC was called into question. Ideas were floated including axing all BBC services except BBC 1 and some radio stations. Whittingdale did not last long in his post – former chair of the BBC governors and ex-Conservative cabinet minister Chris Patten described him as a free market obsessive – and Theresa May sacked him in 2016 when she became Prime Minister. The atmosphere calmed a little, and the prevailing policy appeared to be that all BBC programmes, including *Doctor Who*, should be put out to tender to independent production companies: the BBC should become a platform for private companies' work. BBC programmes began to carry the tag "BBC Studios production" in anticipation of being sold off or continuing to be made in-house. All this has been thrown into doubt following the referendum of 2016, in which British voters opted to leave the European Union (although if 600,000 people had voted the other way, the UK would be staying in), and the Conservative government lost its parliamentary majority in the 2017 general election. Theresa May's government has rather more on its hands at time of writing than a free market restricting of the BBC. It seems that, for the time being, the BBC is safe enough and *Doctor Who* will continue to be made, at least until the Conservatives make such a success of Brexit that they have time again to look at the bête noir broadcaster. It has been suggested that Labour could probably win a general election by warning that the Tories will axe *Doctor Who* but that is by the way.

# 1

# Genesis of a Classic

As with any human endeavour, several stars had to come into alignment before *Doctor Who* could reach British television screens on 23rd November, 1963. There was a gap in the Saturday afternoon schedule, for one thing. The BBC sport magazine programme *Grandstand* had a huge audience and the corporation wanted to keep hold of it over the half hour break before *Juke Box Jury*, a popular panel show whose guests commented on and rated records in the top forty[1]. Then as six decades later, the BBC was in fierce competition with ITV for Saturday evening ratings. What could plug the gap?

The answer came initially from the BBC's new Head of Drama, a feisty Canadian called Sydney Newman. He had arrived at the BBC in 1962 from ABC television, one of the ITV franchises, where he had created *Armchair Theatre* and *The Avengers* – in its pre-fantasy days starring Ian Hendry, back when Steed was an occasional character played by Patrick Macnee[2]. Newman had also created three science fiction series for ITV: these were the three *Pathfinders* series by Malcolm Hulke, who went on to write some of *Doctor Who*'s best scripts in the 1970s. Newman praised what worked well at the BBC and ruffled feathers in shaking up the organisation where necessary. He completely overhauled the BBC script unit, whose in-house writers wrote the drama output for television, and established the model for a production team which would be adopted by the new *Doctor Who* series: a producer would oversee all aspects of production and a story editor (later, a script editor) would commission and edit the scripts from BBC staffers and freelance

---

[1] Carole Ann Ford, who played Susan, appeared as one of the contestants once *Doctor Who* had become an established hit.

[2] Newman said in the 1980s that he didn't give a damn about *The Avengers*' wildly popular re-incarnation as a fantasy show, starring Patrick Macnee, Honor Blackman and, later, Diana Rigg and Linda Thorson.

writers.

The story of *Doctor Who*'s genesis is beautifully told in *An Adventure in Space and Time,* Mark Gatiss's 2013 film which chronicles the origin of the series, focusing on William Hartnell's three years as the original Doctor.  There is a wonderful scene in which Brian Cox as Newman is discussing the Saturday gap with Mervyn Pinfield, among others, and Newman suggests science fiction.  "Is it really that popular?" someone asks.  "I like it," the cigar wielding, loud-checked-jacket wearing Newman beams, his eyes gleaming with possibilities.

## Bull, Frick and Newman

So: not another adaptation of Dickens, but a new science fiction serial.  What about a science fiction anthology show?  Cogitating possibilities, Newman drew on the work of the wonderfully named Donald Bull and Alice Frick, who had reported before his appointment on the viability of making programmes in the science fiction genre.  The BBC had had previous success here and wanted to explore its possibilities further: Nigel Kneale's three *Quatermass* series in the 1950s had been tours de force, iconic science fiction serials which had emptied the pubs of viewers rushing home to catch the latest instalment[1].  Bull and Frick reported in late 1962 and suggested adapting some literary science fiction by such writers as John Wyndham, whose short story "Dumb Martian" had recently been televised successfully.  They advised against some types of science fiction adventure as too fanciful and difficult to realise.

Sydney Newman and Donald Wilson, the Head of the Script Department, considered this original report, and a follow-up report

---

[1] Kneale had a certain degree of disdain for *Doctor Who* itself, thinking the premise was a terrible idea and the sort of thing which one should think of only to reject at once. He also noted that the programme shamelessly pillaged his plots on occasions: for example, there are marked similarities between *Quatermass and the Pit* (1958/9) and "The Daemons" (1971), both serials hinging on the manipulation of humankind's development by alien intervention.

by Frick and John Braybon. Newman came up with the basic premise for his science fiction series. It was to be about a traveller who was able to move about in space and backwards, forwards and sideways in time. Eschewing the usual criteria for a hero, Newman decreed that the hero, or anti-hero as he quickly became, was to be a crotchety old man, at least 350 years old.[1] He was to travel with human companions who were to be points of identification for the audience: a heroic male, a young woman and a teenager. The hero shouldn't have a name but a title: Doctor. One story about the show's development at this point has it that Hugh David, one BBC writer who did some initial work on the series, was discussing the programme with another writer in a restaurant. He wrote "Doctor…" on a piece of paper and, wondering what his name should be, added: "who?" In fact, the programme's title appears with the question mark – *Doctor Who?* or, more usually, *Dr Who?*[2] – on several early documents. It was thus quickly established that a central dramatic drive of the new series should be the mystery around the Doctor's character: who is he and where does he come from? This question was endlessly deferred as the Doctor and his companions found themselves faced with the far more urgent question of surviving from week to week, and was only finally answered in Patrick Troughton's last story, "The War Games" (1969).

Having established the basics, Newman handed the show over to other writers to develop. These included Donald Wilson and Mervyn Pinfield, who became the show's associate (aka executive) producer: the crew on the first season story "The Sensorites" (1964) named the bald, bewhiskered aliens "Mervyns" because they said they looked like him. David Whitaker was appointed as *Doctor Who*'s first story (script) editor and Newman brought a former colleague over from ABC Television to act as producer. This was the twenty-eight year old Verity Lambert, whose appointment raised eyebrows and some hackles at the male-dominated BBC. Gatiss makes much of the

---

[1] See *The Making of Doctor Who*, Malcolm Hulke and Terrence Dicks, London, 1972, p.3

[2] For example, on some of Raymond Cusick's design sketches for early serials.

radicalism of the series in *An Adventure in Space and Time* (2013): Lambert is referred to as "a pushy Jewish bird"; Waris Hussein, the first director of the show, is Asian and gay. Newman himself, the Creator, was Canadian; Anthony Coburn, the first writer, was Australian. Australian MPs rightly lauded the series' Australian heritage in a debate celebrating the show's fiftieth anniversary in 2013.

Once the series had been commissioned in early 1963, its details were quickly fleshed out. Some early ideas for the Doctor were that he was to be virtually senile, bewildered by his surroundings and completely unable to comprehend his space machine. His eyes were to blaze with anger and suspicion if he suspected his human companions of interference. Some of these elements survived into the finished programme, or at least the pilot: here, the Doctor addresses Ian contemptuously as "Schoolmaster" and is scornful of Ian and Barbara's incomprehension when they enter the TARDIS. The Doctor's selfishness and lack of heroism in "The Daleks" (1963-4) is also a remnant of the initial character treatment, although he was starting to move in the direction of heroism as early as the middle of that serial.

Several ideas were discussed for the Doctor's – Dr Who's? – space machine. An invisible sphere was suggested but then discarded because it was difficult to realise and, anyway, couldn't have been seen on screen. Someone suggested that a craft that sophisticated would have to be disguised if the primitive natives of planet Earth weren't to investigate it. This idea quickly developed into the notion that it could disguise itself wherever it goes, although the notion of building a new prop for every serial was quickly squashed on cost grounds. Why not have its disguise mechanism broken in the first story? Then viewers could have the fun of seeing an everyday object in fantastic settings. Perhaps influenced by C.S. Lewis's wardrobe as a gateway into another world (from *The Lion, the Witch and the Wardrobe* (1950)), the space machine's exterior would be a similar  large box: a police box, then as familiar on British streets as, say, post boxes are today.

Just to show that there are still a few police boxes in use: this one was built in the 1990s and stands proudly outside Earl's Court Underground station in London

## Doctor Who? Dr Who?

The series was commissioned for an initial run of thirteen 25 minute episodes. David Whitaker started to commission scripts. BBC staff writer Anthony Coburn was to write the first serial and the characters started to take shape. Verity Lambert and David Whitaker tried to make it clear that "Doctor Who" was the name of the programme and not the name of the character: the "Who" suffix was a question about the character's origins. Had they stuck with the question mark on the name of the series – *Doctor Who? / Dr Who?* – (which strangely became a feature of the costumes for Doctors four to seven, long after the Doctor's origins as a Time Lord had been established) – they might have pre-empted the confusion about the Doctor's name which has dogged the programme ever since. William Hartnell's credit on the end titles was always given as "Dr Who", with the abbreviated form of "Doctor" implying that the next word was his name; the character was called "Dr Who" in scripts and stage directions but not in dialogue. The Doctor's granddaughter's name does indeed seem to be "Susan", but the first story's script indicates that she borrowed her surname, Foreman, from the gates of the scrapyard where the TARDIS first landed. These bear the legend –

I.M.Foreman
Scrap Merchant
76, Totter's Lane

Both programme and the Doctor (Doctor Who?… sorry) were to revisit the scrapyard several times over the years[1] and it has been suggested that the owner's name is a pun on the Doctor's purpose: I. M. Foreman = "I am for Man", with "Man" being a relatively acceptable name for the human race until the end of the 1970s or so[2]. It has also been suggested that this is an interpretation too far.

Ian addresses the Doctor as "Doctor Foreman" in episode two, "The Cave of Skulls": "Eh? Doctor who? What is he talking about?" Hartnell soliloquises. This was the first auto-referential use

---

[1] The Doctor mentions his original landing on Earth in "a totter's yard" in "Logopolis" (1981), which prompted Tom Baker to query, of the script, "What's all this whippet shit about Totter's Yard?". The junkyard pops up again in "Attack of the Cybermen" (1984), and "Remembrance of the Daleks" (1988) and "The Day of the Doctor" (2013). Facinating fact: a "totter" is a dealer in junk. Who knew?

[2] Note on apparently sexist language: the words "man" and "woman" both come from the Old English "man", meaning, human being. Hence the third Doctor's usage of the word "Man" to mean "the human race" when negotiating a peace with the Sea Devils in 1973 (the Chief Sea Devil is unconvinced that humans would share the planet: "And Man would agree to that?"). In Old English, "man" did not indicate gender. The prefix "wif" (woman) had to be added to "man" to indicate a female human being: so, *wifman* translates as "woman". "Man" also originally required the prefix "waepen" to indicate a male human being: so *waepenman* meant, male human being or, literally, a human being with a weapon i.e. penis. Old English speakers clearly enjoyed a saucy pun. Thus, when Captain Kirk declares in the opening narration of *Star Trek* (1966) that the Enterprise's mission is "To boldly go where no man has gone before", he probably intends to mean, "where no human being has ever gone before." However, as Captain Kirk was a sexist, womanising beast, he probably did just mean "man".

of the programme's name in dialogue; later in the second episode, when Barbara refers to him as "Doctor Foreman", Ian corrects her: "That's not his name. Who is he? Doctor who?" The character was colloquially called "Doctor Who" but fans and the production team knew he was just "The Doctor". Sort of. This point was lost on the makers of the two Peter Cushing Dalek films (*Dr Who and the Daleks* in 1965 and *Daleks: Invasion Earth 2150 A.D.*, 1966) where the character, now a human scientist who has invented the TARDIS, introduces himself as "Dr Who" and is addressed as such by other characters. His granddaughters are thus presumably called, Susan Who and Barbara Who. Similarly, the ghastly 1960s *TV Comic* strip, which began in 1964, usually called him "Dr Who". Production teams have been somewhat confused about the matter as well and this usage bled into the television programme's continuity, which went a bit pear shaped in "The War Machines" (1966): new script editor Gerry Davis failed to edit lines where the megalomaniac computer WOTAN demands: "Dr Who is required. Bring him here."

For the rest of the classic series (1963-1989), the production teams thereafter used "Who" as a joke. Mostly. Sort of. The Doctor adopts the alias "Doktor von Wer"[1] to pass himself off as a German in "The Highlanders" (1966-7); Jon Pertwee's sprightly Edwardian roadster Bessie, introduced in 1970, has the number plate "Who 1" (changed to "Who 7" at Sylvester McCoy's suggestion for its appearance in the 1989 story "Battlefield") and there are many quips of the "What Doctor? Doctor who?" variety along the way. Passing himself off as his android double, the Doctor warns the android Sergeant Benton to beware of the real article in 1976's "The Android Invasion": "We don't know who's who."[2] In a bid to please the fans (it did), producer John Nathan-Turner changed the actor's credit from "Dr Who" or "Doctor Who" to "The Doctor" for Peter Davison's run in 1981, and thus it remained until Sylvester McCoy wandered across a field to the TARDIS at the end of "Survival" (1989).

---

[1] German: literally, "Doctor of Who"
[2] This was apparently an ad-lib by Tom Baker.

It all got more complicated with the show's post-2005 revival. Christopher Eccleston was credited as "Doctor Who" in the programme's titles, presumably to match the new series with the colloquial naming of the character as the series was re-launched: no point in confusing people. Steven Moffat returned to the question in Matt Smith's second series (2011): "Silence Will Fall" when the ultimate question is asked, which Dorium reveals is, "Doctor who?" In the 2012 series, Moffat played around with the Doctor's title and name again as Matt Smith whirls around the TARDIS console, asking himself (or calling himself?) "Doctor Who?" Moffat said firmly in 2016 that the Doctor's name *was* Doctor Who, and justified his point by reference to Bessie's number plate, Doctor von Wer and the question marks which Doctors four to seven sported on their costumes. The academic and fan writer Martin Wiggins once argued that Bessie's number plate was a joke by the production team and shouldn't be taken seriously, thus voicing the spirit with which many fans had viewed, with increasing embarrassment, the hilarious references to "Who is Who?" Moffat settled the question once and for all with Missy emerging from the TARDIS, pretending to be the Doctor, in "The Doctor Falls" (2017): "I am that mysterious adventurer in all of time and space known only as Dr Who... He says, I'm the Doctor, and they say, Doctor who?" The Doctor (Peter Capaldi) says nothing to this, thus leaving traditionalist fans a chance to cling to the increasingly tattered belief that he is just called the Doctor, and that "Who" is a nickname, a mistake... oh dear.

## *TARDIS* gets her first crew

Verity Lambert considered actors to play the Doctor. Hugh David, a writer and actor who had done some initial work on the programme, was considered but ruled himself out: he didn't want to return to acting in a long running series. Lambert thought of Cyril Cusack and Michael Hordern but her final choice was William Hartnell. Hartnell was in his fifties and had had a distinguished film career, turning in outstanding performances as the gangster Dallow in *Brighton Rock* (1947), and *The Yangtse Incident* (1957), of which a critic had written that Hartnell, even when silent and filmed from the back, acted everyone else off screen. Hartnell had become somewhat stuck in a rut playing tough sergeants and army types in films like *Carry on Sergeant* (1958) and television series like *The Army Game* (ITV, 1957 to 1961); he had dismissed the latter as "rubbish". Verity Lambert had been struck by Hartnell's performance as the talent scout in the film *This Sporting Life* (1963). Here, the character's air of slight incompetence and pathos touched her and seemed exactly right for the Doctor: at least, as the early treatment notes had conceived him.

Lambert and Hussein invited Hartnell to lunch. Accounts of what happened at their first meeting differ. Hussein has said that Hartnell was bemused, asking, "I don't know quite what you people want from me. What do you want from me?" Lambert said that she handed Hartnell the script for the first episode "and he just loved it". The Doctor was cast and BBC noted in the *Radio Times* that "this [was] Mr Hartnell's first role for the BBC".

The companions were also cast. William Russell, an experienced television actor who had found fame in *The Adventures of Sir Lancelot* (ITV, 1956-7), was to be Ian Chesterton; Jacqueline Hill was to play Barbara Wright; Carole Ann Ford was to play Susan. As the Doctor had been partly conceived as an elderly anti-hero, the role of dashing young hero was to be taken by Ian: he could handle the rough and tumble of their adventures which the Doctor's age and temperament precluded. In 1974, producer Barry Letts made a similar decision in casting Ian Marter as the dynamic young naval lieutenant Harry Sullivan before casting the fourth Doctor, reasoning that if an older actor were cast (Graham Crowden was under consideration), Harry could handle the rough stuff.

The companions of 1963 were worlds away from the capable Clara or Bill of the revived series. Ian Chesterton is a square jawed, decent Englishman who speaks with a received pronunciation (or BBC) accent. He is a science teacher at Susan's school; Barbara is a history teacher, the companions thus representing the two aspects of the new series: science (fiction) and history. As we have already noted, using teachers as identification points was old fashioned even in 1963; even by the end of Hartnell's run, the companions became a modern mini-skirted secretary, Polly, and the cockney sailor Ben Jackson. Ian is obviously heroic, taking charge of the travellers' attempts to escape "The Cave of Skulls" (1963) in the first story and trying to organise the Thals into a fighting force against the Daleks in the second.[1] Barbara is highly intelligent and resourceful and not the screaming stereotype which, in lazy writing about *Doctor Who*, later companions were said to become. She often defies the Doctor. In the first story, the Doctor wants to abandon an injured caveman to his death so that they can escape to the TARDIS: Barbara insists on helping him ("They must be out of their minds!" the Doctor exclaims, incredulously); in the second, Barbara insists on their moral duty to help the Thals when the Doctor implies it is none of their business. By the time of "The Aztecs" (1964), Barbara embraces the persona of the goddess Yetaxa in a bid to stop the Aztecs' practice of human sacrifice, defying the Doctor who tells her it is wrong and futile ("You can't rewrite history. Not one line"[2]).

Susan was conceived by Sydney Newman as a point of audience identification for younger, or teenage, viewers. It was Anthony Coburn who scripted her as the Doctor's granddaughter, perhaps inspired by Little Nell's relationship with her grandfather in

---

[1] When I showed an episode of "The Daleks" to a year seven class (of 11 and 12 year olds) in 2006, most of them, accustomed to the heroic David Tennant and Christopher Eccleston, assumed that Ian was the Doctor.

[2] This was the series' first attempt to deal with the paradoxes of time travel. It seemed at this point that events before 1964 were "history" and could not be changed, while events after 1964 were fair game and could be changed. The point wasn't cleared up until "The Fires of Pompeii" in 2008, which established that there were some fixed points of time which couldn't be altered, like the eruption of Vesuvius in AD 79. Otherwise, says the Doctor, history can be "rewritten" – and his use of the word deliberately echoes Hartnell's line back in "The Aztecs" in 1964.

Dickens's novel *The Old Curiosity Shop* and certainly motivated by a need to sidestep any prurient questions about why a young girl should be travelling with a much older man. She is nominally fifteen and a student at Ian and Barbara's Cole Hill School. Kim Newman has noted that the school itself is another sign of the series' radicalism: it is either a comprehensive or a secondary modern, and is thus closer to many of the viewers' own school experience than the private or boarding schools of such other popular, contemporary icons as *Whacko!* or the *St Trinian's* film series. Carole Ann Ford said that character was sold to her as being an *Avengers* type lady, but there were to be no signs of Cathy Gale's leather suits or high kicking action and Ford left the series after a year. She gives a wonderful and convincing performance as a brave and intelligent young woman. Indeed, the first two seasons are notable for the outstanding performances of their principals, who never send the series up and always play it straight: something essential if the "preposterous" (to use a contemporary viewer's word) situations are to be sold to the viewers. Verity Lambert criticised some later (presumably the McCoy) eras of the show for not taking themselves seriously and thereby ruining the illusion.

### For children or adults?

*Doctor Who* was never conceived as a children's programme, although it has been often identified as such. Writing in *The Daily Sketch* in the early 1970s, Gerald Garrett described it as "the children's own programme which adults adore"[1]; actor Frazer Hines created gasps of dismay at a 1980 convention when he said he thought it was a children's programme. Sidney Newman never identified it as such in the early 1960s; nor is there anywhere in the show's original documentation which says it is intended for children. Its scheduling suggests it was intended to keep hold of the

---

[1] From *The Daily Sketch*; quoted on the back covers of original Target *Doctor Who* novelisations, e.g. *Doctor Who and the Doomsday Weapon*, Malcolm Hulke, London, 1974.

family audience from *Grandstand* and hold it over for *Juke Box Jury* and was thus a family programme. It never patronised children, which accounts for its popularity with them. It is presumably the place that science fiction holds in the British psyche which partly accounts for *Doctor Who*'s identification as a children's programme: many are sniffy about science fiction and think it not respectable as a genre or "childish", thus it must be for children. These are not cultural assumptions in America, where science fiction is taken somewhat more seriously. No-one dismissively assumed that *Star Trek* (1966-69), for example, was a children's programme, even though it was popular with children. Why, I myself had a Captain Kirk's Space Communicator set in 1975, of which I was very proud. This device was nothing like the communicators in the show, but two blue plastic globules linked by a string and thus a variation on that perennial toy, the two cans linked by a string.

Nevertheless, many within the BBC assumed the programme was for children even at its conception: the Children's Department was miffed that the show was to be made by the Drama department, thus affording it arguably greater kudos, and not by the Children's Department. It responded by eyeing the programme with suspicion. One of the earliest criticisms of the programme's violence was by the BBC Children's Department, which objected strongly to Susan threatening Ian with a pair of scissors and using them to slash at her bed, presumably as an Ian substitute, in "The Brink of Disaster" (the third story, 1964). This was actually a fair point: Daleks firing fantasy ray guns was one thing, real violence in the form of possessed teenagers wielding sharp scissors at tea time something quite different. For children or adults? Why not for both? Steven Moffat rightly said, "If you like it, it's for you" in an attempt to settle the question once and for all.

Verity Lambert was horrified to learn that the new, technically complex series was not to be allocated studio space at the gleaming new BBC Television Centre but in the ancient studios at Lime Grove, where lights were worked by sliders on the walls and the cameras were so ancient that zooms could only be accomplished by physically trundling them towards the actors. Were the forces of suspicion at the BBC, dubious about and jealous of the favour *Doctor Who* enjoyed with Sydney Newman, flexing their muscles? Lambert protested, but got nowhere. *Doctor Who* was to be made at Lime Grove on a tiny budget and production teams struggled throughout the show's original run with trying to make science fiction on the money usually allocated to a cop show[1]. The designers discovered that a full scale police box prop wouldn't fit into the lifts at Lime Grove. The prop had to be scaled down: the larger props used in the 2005 revival are much closer to the original police box size. Considering the restrictions, the standard of the finished programmes was miraculous: the journey across Asia to Cathay (in "Marco Polo", 1964) was achieved in a tiny studio and so impressed some visiting Walt Disney executives that they wanted to adapt that serial into a film (nothing came of it).

Peter Brachacki was assigned to design the first episode and was responsible for the look of the TARDIS interior, a design as identifiable and iconic as the Daleks or K9 to the series' imagery. The original set introduced the roundelled walls which have featured in every subsequent redesign to the present day. Brachacki reasoned that, if the TARDIS was to have only one operator, all the controls would need to be readily accessible: hence the hexagonal control console which, again, has been a staple of the TARDIS's interior. There is an annoying continuity mistake in "Journey's End" (2010), when the Doctor explains that six Time Lords would have originally piloted a TARDIS, and he and his companions grin and gurn as they take a panel each to fly the TARDIS. Brachacki also included two huge roundelled doors which usually opened immediately onto the

---

[1] *Doctor Who* fared better than *Blake's 7*, the BBC's other seventies sci-fi show, which had an even smaller budget. The set of the Liberator, the flagship spacecraft, had plastic bins for consoles and tessellated ashtrays for its teleport's walls. It regularly raided *Doctor Who*'s costume cupboard to clothe its characters. Mat Irvine, a special effects designer who worked on both series, gleefully recalled that the special effects budget for *Blake's 7* was £50 an episode.

exterior, visible from the control room. Stepping outside the TARDIS, the police box doors usually shut in unison with the much larger interior doors: a magical and extraordinary image for the original viewers. The TARDIS interior of the film *Dr Who and the Daleks* (1965) was, by contrast, a dull affair, a tangled mess of wires which abandoned the hexagonal console and the distinctive wall circles. The huge doors were replaced by the white interior doors of the police box, a design poached for the new TARDIS interiors from "Rose" (2005) onwards.

Although the TARDIS's control room was a wonder of design for the original viewers, Waris Hussein was recorded as saying that the designer had apparently thrown some flats together in five minutes and pushed off. Hussein was very angry about it but there was no time to redesign the set. The cameras rolled on "An Unearthly Child" in September 1963, mere months after the programme had been conceived.

There is some argument about whether the first version of "An Unearthly Child" is a pilot or whether, as William Russell has said, "That was no pilot – that was an attempt to get it right first time!" Most recently, Graeme Burk[1] has argued that it was always intended as a pilot. If it worked, it would be broadcast as a first episode and, if it didn't, it would be changed and re-shot. Burke writes that some early documentation about the series specifically referred to it as a pilot, and making a pilot was standard BBC practice in the 1960s: for example, Verity Lambert's next show, *Adam Adamant Lives!*[2] began its screen life as a pilot. Waris Hussein, the director, agrees with William Russell that there was no pilot but the original version of episode one was intended to be the screened one. On the other hand, we might argue that William Russell's remark (it was not a pilot, but an attempt to get it right first time), indicates that the unscreened version of "An Unearthly Child" was both a pilot *and*

---

[1] See Sydney Newman (with contributions from Graeme Burk), *Head of Drama*, Toronto, 2017, pps. 457-458

[2] Also created by Sydney Newman.

intended as a broadcast episode: as Graeme Burk argues, pilots which went well were actually aired.

This unscreened episode features a much more aggressive and alien Doctor and a much stranger Susan. Susan tells her teachers that she was born in the forty-ninth century (in the second, broadcast recording, this becomes, "I was born in another time, another world") and there are two fluffed attempts at entering the TARDIS when the interior doors fail to shut properly. Perhaps some of the problems stemmed from the difficulties of recording such a technically demanding and new type of programme on only two cameras at Lime Grove. Sydney Newman saw the finished episode, took Hussein and Lambert out to dinner and told them he should sack the pair of them. Instead, he told them to re-record the episode and to make it better.

Re-shooting episode one, "An Unearthly Child", gave Verity Lambert and story editor David Whitaker a chance to iron out the difficulties of the first attempt. The Doctor's costume was tweaked and his abrasiveness softened in the first step towards making him a more heroic character – a process fully accomplished by the end of the first season. He patronises Ian and Barbara but is no longer contemptuous and scornful. Susan was similarly softened and became much more like a human teenager than the pilot's extraordinarily alien girl. The new episode was shot on four cameras, not two, and the entrance into the TARDIS went smoothly. The *Radio Times*, the BBC's listing magazine, unobtrusively publicised the new series with a small write up on its Saturday page, illustrated with a picture of Hartnell as the Doctor, and listed it each week as "An Adventure in Space and Time". The first episode was broadcast on Saturday 23rd November, 1963 at 5.15 p.m..

# 2
# Into the Time Vortex

Sydney Newman had stipulated that *Doctor Who* stories should go forwards, backwards and sideways in time. Future – or science fiction – stories should thus alternate with historical stories set in Earth's past. Newman always felt that children should *learn* something from television and criticised *Doctor Who* in the 1980s as being nothing more than escapist froth[1]. His view fulfilled the edict of Lord Reith, the BBC's first Director General, that the corporation should inform as well as entertain and, unlike its commercial rivals, give the public not what they wanted but something better. As Robert Holmes (script editor 1974-1977) noted, part of the original brief for *Doctor Who* was to teach children history: fortunately, as he went on to observe, the entertainment principle quickly dominated. The first Doctor thus encounters such historical figures as Marco Polo, Kublai Khan, the Emperor Nero, Robespierre, Napoleon, Richard the Lionheart and Wyatt Earp. More liberties were taken with historical accuracy when Dennis Spooner took over from David Whitaker as story editor: Spooner had a somewhat cavalier attitude towards historical fact and turned the dial up on the humour. Noting that viewers apparently preferred the science fiction stories, the production team phased out the historicals after "The Highlanders" (1966), the story which introduced Jamie McCrimmon (Fraser Hines) as a companion. The next straight historical story was Terence Dudley's "Black Orchid" in 1982, set in the 1920s and featuring Peter Davison's fifth Doctor: Christopher Bidmead, who favoured hard science fiction, noted that he'd rejected Dudley's script when he had been script editor of the previous season and opined that "Black Orchid" should never have been made.

---

[1] See Sydney Newman (with contributions from Graeme Burk) *Head of Drama*, Toronto 2017.

Dennis Spooner's light-hearted approach to history culminated in "The Time Meddler" (1965). The story is noteworthy on several levels. An historical setting and plot – hairy Viking invaders (with names like Sven) raid a Saxon village – are enlivened by science fiction elements: the Time Meddler himself, who wants to help King Harold win the Battle of Hastings by supplying him with atomic bazookas. This jolly idea is worlds away from the serious tone of "Marco Polo" only a year earlier and typical of Spooner's quirky sense of humour. Writing alternative episodes of "The Daleks' Masterplan" (1965-6) with Terry Nation, Spooner ensured that he left the Doctor and his companions in as impossible a situation as possible at the end of his episodes before handing over to Terry Nation. Nation replied in kind and both authors scratched their heads over the problem the other had set.

The Meddling Monk is another member of the Doctor's race, the first (after Susan) to be encountered in the series. In a cliffhanger which must have been totally unexpected to the original viewers, companions Vicky and Stephen enter a tomb and find themselves inside another TARDIS. The Monk himself is delightfully played by actor Peter Butterworth, who had seen distinguished war service as a serial escaper from German prisoner of war camps. He returned as the Monk in "The Daleks' Masterplan" (1965-6) and became a regular in the *Carry On* films, memorably playing Detective Constable Slowbotham, in *Carry On Screaming* (1966)[1], Brother Belcher in *Carry On Up the Khyber* (1968) and Mr Fiddler in *Carry on Camping* (1969).

"The Time Meddler" was the first of the pseudo-historicals, stories set in Earth's past but enlivened by a science fiction element. This imaginative fusion resulted in some of the series' best loved stories

---

[1] *Carry on Screaming* also stars Kenneth Williams as Dr Watt, a zombie type who has young women kidnapped to turn them into tailors' dummies (shades of the Autons in *Doctor Who* three years later). When he introduces himself to Harry H. Corbett's Detective Sergeant Bung, the latter replies, "Doctor who?" "No," says Watt, "Who's my uncle. I haven't seen him in ages." Jon Pertwee also turns up as a relatively mad scientist.

(such as "The Talons of Weng-Chiang" in 1977). Meetings between the Doctor and famous historical figures were, however, phased out by the end of Hartnell's run. Writing "The Time Warrior" in 1974, Robert Holmes agreed to set the story in medieval times on the specific condition that he didn't have to include any real figures from the period. Re-launching the show in 2005, Russell T. Davies re-launched the pseudo-historical. Reflecting the script writers' background in English literature, there was an emphasis on the Doctor meeting writers: Christopher Eccleston's Doctor meets Charles Dickens, David Tennant's Doctor meets William Shakespeare and Agatha Christie. Other characters were those children might know from their history lessons: the tenth Doctor encounters Queen Victoria and Queen Elizabeth I; Matt Smith's Doctor meets Van Gogh, knows Winston Churchill well and has met him off screen before the events of "Victory of the Daleks" (2010). Others were less well known: Madame du Pompadour is "The Girl in the Fireplace" (2006) and Queen Nefertiti travels with the eleventh Doctor in "Dinosaurs on a Spaceship" (2012). Davies' and Moffat's resurrection of the pseudo-historicals is one of many examples of the revised series' looking to the Hartnell era for inspiration: from 2005, the Time Lords have gone and the ninth, tenth and eleventh Doctors wander in time and space without them in the background – as had the first and second Doctors until "The War Games" (1969)[1]. Matt Smith's Doctor reboots the universe and even the Daleks forget who the Doctor is in the 2012 season, thus recreating the original scenario of other characters having no idea who he is and giving Moffat a chance to air the "Doctor who?" jokes again. The jokes culminated, of course, in Moffat firmly declaring that the Doctor's name was, in fact, "Doctor Who".

---

[1] The Time Lords and Gallifrey return in "The End of Time" (2009-2010) only to disappear and reappear again at various points in the eleventh and twelfth's Doctors' timelines.

## Episode to story titles

*Doctor Who* stories had individual episode titles until the penultimate serial of season three, "The Savages" (1966), when they were given an overall title and episode numbers. The titling of individual episodes was in keeping with the programme's original premise that this was a *continuing* "adventure in space and time": one story led directly into the next and viewers had no idea when one story was to end and another to begin. Thus original viewers of "The Daleks" would have suspected that the story was to end at the conclusion of its fourth instalment: the Doctor and his companions have escaped with the Thals from the Dalek ambush, say farewell to the latter and wish them luck, and prepare to leave in the TARDIS. Only then does the Doctor realise that the Daleks have taken the ship's fluid link and they cannot leave: they must return to the city to retrieve it. Only then do the viewers realise that the story is not over after all. This continuous story telling meant that there were no gaps between stories. From the 1970 series onwards – Pertwee's first season – time appears to pass between stories, creating convenient gaps for fans of the show to imagine that the Doctor has other adventures in them, often writing such adventures themselves, not least in order to plug continuity gaps left by the televised series.

The practice of naming individual stories was also presumably abandoned because it became too difficult, or too tedious, to think of a new title every week. Some are simply variations on each other and near synonyms, as in the third story's two episodes, "The Edge of Destruction"/"The Brink of Disaster" (1964). Russell T Davies again looked to the original Hartnell episodes for inspiration in the 2005 revival: stories, even of two or three part stories, were to have individual episode titles. The solitary exception, in the revived series (2005 onwards) is "The End of Time" parts one and two.[1] This was

---

[1] Programme historians note that the twelve years from "Rose" to "The Doctor Falls" in the revived series is the same as the twelve year distance between "An Unearthly Child" and "The Brain of Morbius". This thought makes some of us feel very old.

the Christmas special of 2009-2010, which saw David Tennant's Doctor regenerate into Matt Smith's; episode one was broadcast on Christmas Day 2009 and episode two on New Year's Day 2010. The insistence on "episode one" was presumably to encourage turkey-stuffed, groggy and boozed-up British viewers that the story hadn't finished on Christmas Day and they should tune in again next week.

## An Unearthly Child

The first *Doctor Who* serial combines science fiction and history. Episode one introduces us to the Doctor (his first words: "What are you doing here?") and to the TARDIS. Susan explains, "I made up the name from the initials: Time and Relative Dimension in Space." This explanation was fine for the ephemeral medium of television, when programmes would be shown once or at the most twice and then forgotten, and Anthony Coburn could hardly have been aware that he was sparking one of the show's first continuity controversies. Was Susan a solar engineer who had worked on the Time Lords' first time and space machines and had named them? Did she win a Gallifreyan competition and the prize was to name the time ships? Was the fourth word "dimension" or "dimensions"? Susan says "dimension"; so do Paul McGann in the TV movie (1996) and Christopher Eccleston in "Rose" (2005: he was apparently ad-libbing; the script said "dimensions"); most recently, Peter Capaldi's Doctor uses the word "dimension" when he explains the TARDIS's acronym. Classic era Doctors other than Hartnell say "dimensions". Perhaps Susan's claim that she "named" the TARDIS is evidence of the original conception that the Doctor built it (as Patrick Troughton once says, although the tenth Doctor tells Rose, "They were grown, not built" and Jack Harkness tries to grow one on his desk in *Torchwood*): this was a hint picked up by the makers of the 1965 film *Dr Who and the Daleks* in which Dr Who [sic], played by Peter Cushing, proudly informs Roy Castle's Ian that the TARDIS is "my greatest invention" ("What, a police box?" Castle replies dopily).

It's not even clear whether the time and space machine is "the

TARDIS" or *Tardis*. Calling the time-ship *Tardis*, without the definite article, implies that this is the ship's name in the way that other ships are called *Hispaniola* or *Bismarck*. David Whitaker's novelisation of "The Dead Planet" has the TARDIS called *Tardis*[1]. Even as late as 1992, Barry Letts' scripts for the BBC Radio 4 plays "The Paradise of Death" named the ship *Tardis*; a fan at the studio recordings spotted this was a mistake and got the "the" re-inserted[2]. The haziness over the name may partly be because it is usually called "the Ship" rather than "the TARDIS" or even "*Tardis*" by the crew in season one. The first Doctor calls it "the ship" in the 2017 Christmas special "Twice Upon A Time"[3], much to the twelfth Doctor's (Peter Capaldi's) amusement.

"The War Games" in 1969 finally and firmly establishes that TARDISes were built by the Time Lords and the Doctor stole one because he was bored, which contradicts what Susan said six years previously: but this was in the days before home video, DVDs and cable television repeats and perhaps no-one could really remember. Terrence Dicks once said that *Doctor Who* script editors' attitude to the programme's continuity was the same as the definition of history in the book *1066 and All That* (1930): "what you can remember". There is, of course, a world of difference between writing and producing a television programme under pressure, and analysing it at leisure as a fan or a critic; there was never much intention of getting *Doctor Who*'s internal continuity absolutely right in its original run. Speaking in the 1970s, producer Graham Williams said that, if he had to make a choice between telling a good story and contradicting something Patrick Troughton had said ten years ago, he would always opt for telling the good story. Only in the post-

---

[1] There were similar wobbles in James Blish's 1960s novelisations of the original *Star Trek* adventures, where the Enterprise was regularly named *Enterprise* in italics.

[2] Private information given to the author. (This radio show starred Jon Pertwee, with Elisabeth Sladen and Nicholas Courtney reprising their roles as Sarah Jane Smith and the Brigadier.)

[3] The first Doctor was played by David Bradley in 2017; Hartnell himself had died in 1975.

2005 revival, when the fans *were* the writers and producers, did internal continuity across the show's six decades become fun to reference accurately.

Episode two of *Doctor Who*, "The Cave of Skulls" establishes that the TARDIS's chameleon circuit (called such in the novelisations, but never on screen in the original series) has broken: the Doctor tuts, "It's still a police box. Why hasn't it changed? Dear dear dear. How very disturbing." Barbara works out that the TARDIS should "[disguise] itself wherever it goes" and Susan confirms that's right. Why then does it adopt the form of a London police box when it lands in a 1963 junkyard? As Ian says in "An Unearthly Child", "What's it doing here? These things are usually on the street." Shouldn't the TARDIS have become an old wardrobe or something (or would that be too close to *The Lion, the Witch and the Wardrobe*?) to blend in with the other junk? Or was the chameleon circuit already starting to malfunction? It chose a contemporary London artefact, but one from the wrong place. Presumably Anthony Coburn had forgotten that the police box form was supposed to blend in with its surroundings (it didn't) and the circuit wasn't supposed to break until the end of episode one. Those as wants to can already have continuity fun with the first few minutes of *Doctor Who*.

The second, third and fourth parts of the first story are set on prehistoric Earth. A stone age tribe has lost the secret of fire: the ice age is coming and without fire, they will die. The cavemen didn't speak in the original script but do in the finished version. Coburn gives them a pleasingly poetic speech style to contrast with the time travellers': recalling cooked meat, Horg says, "I remember how the meat and fire join together." Eloquent cavemen was not to everyone's taste and a contemporary critic confessed himself puzzled about the well-chiselled 1960s looks of a stone age tribe which speaks perfect English. He would have perhaps preferred the production team to pull out a few teeth and restore the original script's grunts for verisimilitude, but he did hit on a perennial problem in science fiction television: all the aliens speak contemporary English. This was recognised as a dramatic necessity and makers of the original series quietly ignored it: *Star Trek*'s team issued all Star Fleet personnel with a universal translator as a get-out clause. In "The Masque of Mandragora" (1976), the hypnotised Sarah asks the Doctor how she is able to understand Renaissance Italian. This witty, auto-referential reference to a question the series had always quietly avoided immediately alerts the Doctor to the fact that she has been turned against him: only a hypnotised companion would ever question the conventions of the show. "It's a Time Lord gift I let you share," he later explains. Perhaps this telepathic gift isn't always effective, as the Doctor can only speak "a little" Tibetan to K'anpo Rinpoche in "Planet of the Spiders" (1974), or perhaps Hinchcliffe and Holmes had forgotten what Letts and Dicks had established two years earlier, which seems much more likely. Realising that twenty first century audiences were much more likely to scoff at the convention, and anxious to avoid any ridicule that had dogged the original series in its final years, Russell T Davies addressed the issue in the revived series' second story, "The End of the World" (2005). Conversing with her first aliens in the far future, Rose asks the Doctor why they all speak English. "You hear English," the Doctor explains. He goes on to say that the TARDIS translates for her. This isn't quite what the Doctor said in "The Masque of Mandragora" but Davies makes it clear that the Doctor is an essential part of the telepathic circuit in David Tennant's first story "The Christmas Invasion" (2005). The humans are only able to hear the Sycorax's speech as gibberish until the Doctor awakens from his regeneration trauma coma (an awakening brought about by smelling Jackie's nice hot cup of tea in a pleasingly British moment). When Rose hears the Sycorax leader speaking English, she knows that the Doctor and the TARDIS are translating for her and that the Time Lord has recovered. Continuity for Russell T Davies, as for Terence Dicks, remained "what you can remember". However, Dicks was working in an age where stories were shown once or twice at the most: Davies access to home video, VHS and DVD. Fans endlessly re-watched the show and Davies' knowledge of internal continuity was, like most fans', very good indeed. He, and all the writers on the post-2005 series, could make references to past stories which fans, with their shared access to the archive, had a good chance of getting. These references pleased the fans but were unnoticed by the general viewer and didn't interfere with the story telling.

If language was one problem for the Tribe of Gum, as they were called in the script but not on screen, costuming was another. Derek Newark, who played Za, recalled that he was asked if he was a hairy man at his audition.

"Pardon?"

"Are you a hairy man?" Newark paused and then asked if they wanted him to strip off. It was then explained that, if he was to play a primitive human being, excessive body hair might be an advantage. Carole Ann Ford recalled[1] that the animal skins they were given to wear were full of insects.

On 23rd November 1963, the attention of the world was focussed on the assassination of President John F. Kennedy rather than on the new science fiction serial which debuted quietly that Saturday evening. Those who watched it said it made a stir. Sixth Doctor Colin Baker was a law student at the time; coming home to his digs, he caught the opening minutes as he came up the stairs and said he was still standing in the same place, transfixed, twenty five minutes later. Another viewer told me said he had been similarly transfixed as a child, there being nothing like *Doctor Who* on British television in 1963 (*Lost in Space* and *Star Trek* didn't exist). Knowing that its first broadcast had been completely overshadowed by Kennedy's assassination, the BBC demonstrated its faith in *Doctor Who* by repeating "An Unearthly Child" on Saturday 30th November, 1963 immediately before the second episode, "The Cave of Skulls". Six million people watched the first story. In today's multi-channel age, this would be considered a very high, if not, spectacular, figure: in 1963, it wasn't bad but neither was it an unbounded critical success. Verity Lambert was preparing to wind up the series after the third

[1] In the 1973 *Radio Times Doctor Who Tenth Anniversary Special*

serial "The Edge of Destruction" (1964), thus completing the BBC's initial order of thirteen episodes. Some elements in the BBC, such as the Children's Department, would have been happy to see the new series go. Some had been shocked by the violence of the first story: Ian observes that all the skulls in "The Cave of Skulls" have been split open and Kal is mauled by an (unseen) sabre toothed tiger. My mother turned the television off at this point, concerned at the effect on my brothers aged three, five and seven. It soon went on again and, somewhat to her amusement, most of my family was glued to the programme for the next fifty-five years. Concerns and complaints about the series' violence were an immediate feature of reaction to *Doctor Who* and dogged the series throughout its run. John Nathan-Turner (producer 1980-89) said that, in his prayers at night, he asked that anti-sex and violence campaigner Mrs Mary Whitehouse had watched the programme and disliked it, as her protests always put another two million on the viewing figures. Certainly, *Doctor Who*'s depiction of violence and peril helped to contribute to the ambivalent position it held in the BBC and led some in the corporation to dislike it heartily: if it was a children's programme, why was it made by the Drama department? And if it was for children, why was it so horrific?

**Enter the Daleks**

In creating the series, Sydney Newman had specified that the science fiction stories were not to contain "Bug Eyed Monsters" or BEMs. Perhaps he intended them to be thoughtful, imaginative explorations of existing science along the lines of some of John Wyndham's stories. Anthony Coburn's second script for the series, "The Masters of Luxor", was such a tale. It was never made. David Whitaker had commissioned a story from Terry Nation, who was best known as a comic writer for Tony Hancock but who had contributed a script to the BBC's anthology science fiction series *Out of the Unknown*, which Whitaker had seen and liked. Nation turned in a seven part tale introducing some strange creatures called

Daleks. It has been said that Lambert and Whitaker didn't much like it but had no other script ready to go into production. "The Daleks" (aka "The Mutants") it had to be for story two.

In 1963, the designer assigned to each serial was responsible for virtually all the designs, bar costume and visual effects. Staff designer Raymond Cusick was not only responsible for the very effective petrified jungle sets in the second story, but also for the Daleks' city and the Daleks themselves. When the four travellers enter the city in "The Dead Planet" (1963), episode one of the story, it is clear that it is not built for human beings: floors, walls and corridors are made of metal and the doors are far too small for even average sized people to go through with comfort. This was the series' first alien environment and it was wonderfully effective. Cusick also designed the Daleks from a somewhat sketchy description in Nation's script. Nation had been inspired by watching the Georgian State dancers, who wore long dresses and appeared to glide across the floor: he wanted the Daleks to move like that. The script stipulated they were to be hideous machine-like creatures without human features; the eye was on a flexible shaft, arms with mechanical grips carried strange weapons. One BBC staffer blithely suggested spraying cardboard tubes silver and bedecking an actor with them. A designer other than Cusick produced some sketches along these lines: they looked ridiculous[1].

Up to this point, alien creatures in films and on television, however brilliantly designed, had always, clearly been actors in suits. Steven Moffat said that this problem had been solved precisely once, in Cusick's Daleks. Cusick was determined to break up the human form entirely and himself produced two designs. He sketched an actor sitting in a chair and drew the basic shape around him. When Barbara asks Ian if he thinks there might be someone inside them, this might be an auto-referential joke to the actor inside the prop: such was the strangeness of the movement that many viewers assumed the Daleks must be radio controlled, complete machine

---

[1] See *Nothing At The End of the Lane*, issue 4, Autumn 2015

creations, as Barbara herself at first thought[1]. Cusick explained that he demonstrated the movement to someone by pushing along a salt or pepper cellar, although, contrary to legend, a condiments set had not inspired the actual design.

Four Daleks were made. The job was contracted out to the firm Shawcraft as BBC departments were over-stretched with other shows. Shawcraft was responsible for many of the creations of the show's early years, including the Slyther and the Mechonoids. In an attempt to make the Daleks easier to build, Raymond Cusick had broken the base down into a series of studded panels. He had originally wanted a smooth, sloped cone. Once the Daleks were finished, Shawcraft asked why he hadn't wanted a cone rather than a panelled base? It would have been so much easier to build. The four Daleks had sink plungers at the end of their arm-stick. This was, it seems, an attempt to save money and the production team got away with it for the first Dalek story: as the Daleks continued to return, the plungers became increasingly ridiculed and *Doctor Who* fans tired of explaining that it wasn't really a sink plunger at all honestly, it was actually a highly sophisticated alien probe... Even by the end of Hartnell's time, plungers were quietly acknowledged as Not Quite the Thing and were sometimes exchanged for flame throwers and locating instruments. The revived series after 2005 featured Daleks with cutting tools, strange pine-cone shaped arm tips and so on, but the basis sucker shape remained, as did the ubiquitous jokes, which remained hilarious to all Whovians who heard them, of Daleks unblocking lavatories and so on.

The Daleks arrived at the rehearsal room and William Russell said the cast all laughed at them, thinking them ludicrous. Hartnell was unhappy about being cut by one of the Daleks' shoulder bands if it slid past him, and sellotape was applied to some of the supposedly sharp edges. One of the crew noted that this made not a blind bit of difference, but it was important to keep the show's star happy. The

---

[1] Catherine Tate, who played Donna Noble in the 30th (4th) season, said she was astonished when she discovered that actors inhabited the Dalek casings: she too had always assumed they were radio controlled.

Dalek operators rehearsed in the bases without the top half. Once camera rehearsals began and the Daleks were completed, director Christopher Barry found it impossible to tell which Dalek was which and which actor was inside each one (apparently a perennial confusion with Dalek stories, as some of the studio footage from "Death to the Daleks" (1974) reveals). He opted to tape numbers onto the domes and then was able to issue clear directions: "Dalek one – go left; Dalek two, circle right" and so on. The reels of sellotape used to stick on the numbers were jammed into the Daleks' shoulder collars. Numbers and reels are clearly visible in BBC publicity shots for the serial and some illustrators for early books and comic strips about the Daleks assumed that the numbers were part of the design and that the sellotape reel must be a speaker for the Dalek voice. Both features were erroneously retained in some drawings, notably in *The Dalek Book* (1964). Perhaps Mike Tucker and his team remembered the numbered Daleks when they came to revamp the beasts for the revived series' episode *Dalek* (2005) as all bronze Dalek domes carry an identification symbol under the eye stick.

Nation's script immediately chimed with the popular imagination and viewing figures for "The Daleks" rose from six million for "An Unearthly Child" to nine million for this second story. They peaked at ten million for the third story "The Edge of Destruction", perhaps as a result of word of mouth recommendations that this new show was worth watching. Certainly, the Daleks ensured *Doctor Who*'s success and the BBC commissioned another batch of thirty or so episodes: enough to take the show through to the end of its first season.

The radioactive, ashen forest in "The Dead Planet" chimed with contemporary terrors about nuclear war. It was broadcast only a year after the Cuban missile crisis, the point at which humanity had come closest to a nuclear holocaust, a war in which "the fruits of victory would turn to ash in our mouths" as an American diplomat had told the United Nations. The flesh and blood part of the Daleks was a hideous mutation created by years of radiation poisoning: the result of the neutronic war with the Thals "many centuries ago". Susan is terrified at having to encounter the Thals as the Daleks assure her they must be "disgustingly mutated". In fact, the mutation cycle has gone full circle and they are tall, attractive and mostly blond humanoids. Presumably the Thals mutated more quickly because they stayed out in the open: the embittered Daleks, by contrast, retreated into their city, built themselves travel and survival machines and, in a horrifying twist to viewers who feared radiation sickness, became dependent on the radiation that would kill the Thals. Nuclear holocaust was a theme that haunted Nation and he returned to it in his 1970s series *Survivors* and in the first series of *Blake's Seven* (1978). As a boy, he had been terrified of the bombing of Swansea, his home city, and appalled by reports of the use of the atom bomb on Hiroshima and Nagasaki at the end of the Second World War: hence the central theme of his work, the terrifying misuse of advanced technology, so common to post-War science fiction[1].

The Second World War had ended only eighteen years before the Daleks' first appearance and it is very quickly apparent that they are Nazis in armoured pepperpots. They use Susan to get them the Thals' anti-radiation drug and then refuse to let the time travellers have any – "Let them die", one Dalek grates – thus, like the Nazis, treating people as means and not as ends. The Daleks are interested in leaving their city and colonising the rest of the planet: they need *lebensraum*[2] and cannot see why they should share their world with a supposedly inferior species. When the drug is demonstrated to be poison for them, they determine to explode another neutron bomb to increase the radiation levels on which they have become dependent:

---

[1] See, for example, John Wyndham's novel *The Day of the Triffids* (1951). Strange green lights appear in the sky and everyone who looks at them goes blind, allowing the Triffids to take over. The hero, Bill Masen, speculates that the lights were a super weapon – an extrapolation from atomic bombs. Hideous mutations resulting from nuclear radiation is the basis of Wyndham's *The Chrysalids* (1955). With all this dystopia around, plus Wyndham's penchant for high adventure, it's little wonder that David Whitaker tried to get him to write for *Doctor Who*.

[2] German, "living space": Hitler, 1938.

they will then be able to colonise the rest of the planet. By happy coincidence, the bomb will also kill all the Thals. The Doctor protests that the plan is "sheer murder" and a Dalek corrects him: "No. Extermination." The word is a clear reference to the Nazis' so-called "final solution" and it is a neat piece of irony that the supposedly inferior species in fact resembles the Nazi Aryan ideal – an apt comment on the absurdity of racism. If viewers hadn't got the point yet, the story's second director, Richard Martin, makes it clear by ending the scene quoted above with the Daleks lining up, raising their sucker sticks in salute and chanting their war cries in unison. Daleks also gave Nazi salutes in their second story, "The Dalek Invasion of Earth" (1964). Referencing the appeasers of Hitler in the 1930s, and perhaps glancing at conscientious objectors in the war itself, Ian attempts to convince the pacifist Thals to fight the Daleks. They refuse until he proposes to exchange one of their females for the TARDIS's missing component: perhaps the Daleks would like to experiment on her. One of the Thals knocks Ian down, thus proving his point that sometimes evil must be fought if it is to be defeated. This tenet of the Just War philosophy runs through the series like a golden thread and is the bedrock of the Doctor's strength and heroism. As the second Doctor says in "The Moonbase" (1967); "There are some corners of the universe that have bred the most terrible things. They must be fought."

The fifth episode of *Doctor Who*, "The Dead Planet", ends with Barbara, separated from her friends (a common trope!) and exploring the city on her own. She comes to a door at the end of a corridor – a dead end – and hears a noise. Turning round, she sees something which terrifies her and screams. The end credits roll. The something is obviously a Dalek: what the viewers see is the alien point of view as it trundles towards her, its sucker stick clear on the right of the shot. (This shot was virtually repeated in "Dalek" (2005): Rose is trapped by the closed bulkhead and we see her from the Dalek's point of view as it advances.) We don't see a whole Dalek because Shawcraft hadn't finished them, but contemporary accounts say viewers were excited and astonished. Nation has said that his phone didn't stop ringing on the night "The Dead Planet" was shown, with people demanding, "What the hell was it?" They had to wait till next week to find out and the viewing figures inexorably rose.

Sydney Newman was furious when he saw some of the early episodes of "The Daleks" and summoned Verity Lambert for a dressing down. Lambert recalled that he hated the Daleks, thinking them the worst kind of science fiction cliché, and he raged at her: "Jesus, bug eyed monsters" – the very thing he had stipulated must not appear in the show. Lambert defended herself: "They are not! They are survivors of an atomic war." "Uh huh," Newman replied, unconvinced. It says much for Newman's good grace and strength of character that when he saw the viewing figures, he apologised to Verity Lambert. She recalled that he said, you guys obviously understand *Doctor Who* much better than I do, so go ahead and do your own thing. Here was a creator willing to pass on his baby to someone else who could do it better: something of a contrast to *Star Trek* creator Gene Roddenberry, who continued to offer suggestions and storylines to his successors long after he had moved on as executive producer of the franchise and long after they were welcome[1]. Newman congratulated Verity Lambert on the second Dalek story and said he had loved it.

Britain apparently went Dalek crazy in 1964. Quick to cash in on the Daleks' success, Britain's manufacturers rushed out "robot action" battery operated Daleks, Dalek slippers, Dalek wallpaper and turned the water pistol into "Dr Who's Anti-Dalek Fluid Neutraliser". The BBC meanwhile gave two of its Daleks props away to a Dr Barnardo's children's home and said, at first, that it had no plans to bring the creatures back. In the face of endless enquiries and petitioning from the press and from children, and belatedly awakening to a cash cow when they eventually saw one, the BBC confirmed that the Daleks would return at some point. Raymond Cusick had been largely responsible for the Daleks' success with his superb, iconic design but it was Terry Nation who

---

[1] At least according to William Shatner: *Star Trek Movie Memories* (1995).

One of the best of the sixties Dalek toys:
the splendid Codeg clockwork Dalek

co-owned the copyright with the BBC and coined in the royalties, earning enough to buy himself an agreeable Elizabethan country house where he installed four of the beasts. As a BBC staff designer who received a salary in place of royalties, Cusick made not a penny. Eventually, the BBC recognised that he had played some part in the Daleks' success and gave him a one-off payment of a few hundred pounds, which Cusick considered derisory. Later in the 1960s, the children's BBC magazine programme *Blue Peter* showed viewers how to make their own model Dalek and one of the presenters remarked that whoever had designed the originals deserved a *Blue Peter* badge. These were given out as rewards for success, endeavour or for appearing on the show: 1980s companion Ace wore one on her bomber jacket. Cusick wrote in, said he had designed them, and duly received his. Cusick's cause was championed by fans from the late 1980s onwards, who accepted that the Daleks' success was attributable to his design even more than Nation's scripts: if the BBC had gone with actors wearing cardboard tubes, the Daleks, and probably the show, would have disappeared without trace. Cusick's contribution to the success and longevity of the series was lauded by Jeremy Bentham in *Doctor Who: The Early Years[1]*, one of the first books to publish the original designs of the Daleks as they evolved from a rather spindly, post-shaped creature to the familiar pepperpot. Cusick became a regular interviewee on BBC DVDs and was invited by new series designer Edward Thomas to the *Doctor Who* studios in Cardiff to inspect the new Daleks in 2005.

The production team were keen to capitalise on the success of the Daleks and one monster after another was created, at least partly in the hope that they would emulate the merchandising success of Terry Nation's creations. High hopes were pinned on the Voord (a man in a rubber suit), the Zarbi (a giant ant-like creature) and the Chumblies (a trundling meringue-shaped robot) but nothing much came of them, although the Zarbi and their Vortis companions the Menoptra[2] did merit a badge each – now hotly sought by collectors and a snip at £85 apiece on eBay. The Mechonoids, spherical robots introduced in "The Chase" (1965), were, in effect, redesigned Daleks: hideous machine creatures moving around on a round base, arms with mechanical grips for hands and all. Small toys were made of them and they featured in the Dalek strip in the comic *TV21[3]*, but they never reappeared in the series and the toys quickly vanished from toyshops (but you can occasionally get an original 1960s Mechonoid toy from eBay for around £200 – original price, five old pence. Hurry while stocks last.)

---

[1] Published by W H Allen in 1986
[2] Lepidoptera is Latin for the order of insects which includes butterflies and moths, so men+optera means, butterfly men. Come on, keep up.
[3] This was a vehicle for Gerry Anderson's series, including *Stingray* and *Thunderbirds*. Anderson thought *Doctor Who* was dreadful but that the Daleks were excellent. Wishing he had invented them, he had them imported into *TV21*.

# Now on the Big Screen – In Colour!

British cinema, ever keen to capitalise on small screen successes, approached the BBC with a view to making a film of the first Dalek serial. This approach was fronted by Milton Subotsky and Max J. Rosenberg, producers of horror films which rivalled the more famous (and equally cheap and cheerful) output of Hammer studios. They created a company called Aaru productions to make the first *Who* feature film.

It was common practice in the 1950s and 1960s to turn television programmes into cinema films. Television was ephemera and programmes were usually only shown once, or twice at the most, and then never seen again. Films, however, could be seen as many times as an audience member could stump up the admission fee. Moreover, films could reach a wider, more international audience than the original programme: Hammer films had remade the first two 1950s *Quatermass* serials as films, changing Quatermass from a thoughtful English academic to an American bully played by Brian Donlevy. This was a precondition for stateside sales, and Kneale commented that they changed "my troubled professor into a screaming, shouting person" and that he hadn't liked the first two *Quatermass* films at all[1].

Furthermore, feature films could be made in colour at a time when television was emphatically small screen and black and white. Acknowledging the equal appeal of the Doctor and the Daleks to the public, "The Dead Planet" became *Dr Who and the Daleks* for the film. The movie's poster announced the title with *Dr Who and the* in a small font but *DALEKS* shouted in giant capitals along the bottom width of the poster. The illustration replicated this wording by

---

[1] As a result, the degree of Kneale's creative control over the final *Quatermass* film increased from zero to considerable when he wrote the screenplay for *Quatermass and the Pit* (1967), an adaptation of his original 1958-9 BBC television serial. Quatermass was now played by the Scottish actor Andrew Keir, familiar to *Doctor Who* fans as Wyler in the second *Dr Who* movie, *Daleks: Invasion Earth 2150 A.D.*.

showing the new TARDIS crew cowering in apparent awe as giant, colourful Daleks sweep past them. The poster also made a simple and direct appeal to those who had enjoyed the black and white serial, proclaiming that it was "NOW ON THE BIG SCREEN – IN COLOUR!" All very true and exciting, but Whovians generally consider the movie vastly inferior to the thoughtful, original serial. Subtlety and pace was out: colour and B-movie excitement was in and big, big, big. As were the Daleks themselves, now some six feet in height and apparently controlled by an actor or extra standing up, rather than sitting down. They were built by Shawcraft and voiced by the actors who provided the TV series' Dalek voices, impressively matching the ring-modulated frequency of the originals. Big Daleks looked impressive and frightening ("Beware these Men of Steel!" warned the trailer... men?) but the redesign was questionable as the original, five foot high Daleks had seemed much more alien. It was easier to imagine that the film Daleks were operated by a human actor. By 1965, jokes about sink plungers had somewhat worn down believability in the Daleks, and almost all the film Daleks sported impressive pincers or grabbers – which didn't actually pinch or grab anything much.

Subotsky appears to have had some thoughts about using the television cast, but they were busy making the television series itself. The film was duly recast. Subotsky has explained that they had to use an internationally recognised star if the film was sold abroad and Peter Cushing was cast as Dr Who (sic). The script stuck closely to Nation's original but crammed seven episodes into 79 minutes: terribly short by today's standards but the right length for Saturday morning at the children's pictures. The film, unlike the series, is specifically aimed at children. The Doctor is much more of an amiable old buffer than Hartnell's edgy and unpredictable original; Susan (often "Susie") becomes a twelve year old granddaughter, Barbara another granddaughter and the gallant Ian Chesterton a bumbling oaf played by Roy Castle. The film is exciting and the story sweeps along, although the heavy eye make up of the Thals excited some comments: presumably the fascist

Daleks thought this was another sign of their decadence. The extras for these perfect physical specimens were Covent Garden porters, who apparently were not happy about being asked to shave off their body hair to reveal their rippling torsos. The violence of the original was toned down: in the original serial, a Thal is killed when he tries to cross a bottomless cavern in a cave under the Dalek city. In the film version, he falls onto a convenient ledge. The ending was simplified: instead of the Daleks' power failing and killing the lot of them, the Doctor and his companions run between the Daleks, who fire and miss but hit each other and blow up. This brings about the end of the whole race. There is a wizard sequence where Ian calls on the Daleks to exterminate him and they fire at him, he ducks, and their impressive control desk blows up. Director Gordon Flemyng said that this control panel prop was held together by taught elastic, which was let fly when the Daleks' guns hit it: they had one chance to get it right and did so, so the sequence we have was the first take.

*Dr Who and the Daleks*, made quickly with a main eye on profit, capitalised effectively on Dalekmania and a sequel was commissioned. This was 1966's *Daleks: Invasion Earth 2150 A.D.*. Peter Cushing's Doctor introduced viewers to the idea that another actor could play the part, which perhaps eased the production team's fears when, in 1966, they had to consider whether to replace the ailing William Hartnell or end the series. I watched *Dr Who and the Daleks* for the first time in 1973, when it premiered on BBC 1 as part of the "High Adventure" early evening film series. I remember looking through the *Radio Times* and being surprised and aggrieved to find that the Doctor was not being played by Jon Pertwee; although I had watched other Doctors, I could barely remember them and had been mystified by finding some old bloke with long hair pretending to be the Doctor in an old annual. Reviewing the film in 1977, the *Radio Times* film critic Philip Jenkinson wrote, "*Star Wars* it ain't, but they must have spent a few quid on the cardboard and papier mâché."

David Whitaker adapted "The Daleks" (1963-4) for the first (and best) *Doctor Who* novelisation. This included the third version of the introduction of the TARDIS crew, if we include "An Unearthly Child" and the human inventor Dr Who of the film. *Doctor Who*[1] (1964) is told in the first person by Ian Chesterton, now an ex-schoolmaster who has tried, and failed, to get a job as a rocket scientist. Returning from his job interview, he stops his car at last in a thick fog and encounters Barbara, who has been involved in a road accident. The driver of the other vehicle, a military truck, is dead and Barbara's passenger, Susan English (not Foreman), has disappeared. Barbara has been giving Susan some private coaching at her flat and has insisted on driving her home in the fog, ignoring Susan's protests. Ian is alarmed to hear someone strike a match so near to a car accident: this is the Doctor, who has come to investigate. Ian observes that the match never seems to burn down. "Just a little invention of mine," the old man observes. Ian is surprised to find a police box in the middle of Barnes Common[2] and the adventure at that point more or less follows the script of "The Daleks" although, as it is written from Ian's point of view, much is left out. Whitaker's writing is excellent and the prose is worthy of John Wyndham. *Doctor Who* aficionados in 1964 thus had three versions of "The Daleks" to choose from: the original television serial (which, admittedly, they could only access in memory), the Aaru film and the novel.

---

[1] The title of Whitaker's first novel is actually *Doctor Who*. It was retitled *Doctor Who and the Daleks* when it was reissued by Target books in 1973, but the original strapline read, "In An Exciting Adventure With the Daleks". Historians have mistakenly assumed that the title of the first novel is *Doctor Who in An Exciting Adventure with the Daleks* when it, like the Paul McGann TV movie (1996) and the series itself, was actually called, baldly, vanilla-ly, *Doctor Who*. It is vital that we are precise when considering this important point.

[2] Mark Gatiss wittily references the opening of the novel in his film *An Adventure in Time and Space* (2013): on a foggy night, a car pulls up next to a police box on Barnes Common. It is Bill Hartnell (David Bradley) who is driving, rather than Ian Chesterton, but fans appreciated the joke.

## The Brink of Disaster

If the film could afford a much larger budget than the television series, the television series was running out of money by the end of the second story. David Whitaker wrote a two episode filler "The Edge of Destruction"/"The Brink of Disaster", set entirely on board the TARDIS and featuring only the regular cast. This is as tense and strange as it is slow: the TARDIS is apparently infiltrated by a strange force which causes the travellers to lose touch with their surroundings. Ian and Barbara think they are once again teaching at Cole Hill School and Susan threatens to slash Ian to ribbons with a pair of scissors. The Children's Department duly protested and perhaps got its way: such "real" violence is absent from the first couple of years of the original series, although the show continued to get into trouble with viewers of a sensitive or nervous disposition. A mother wrote to the *Radio Times* in 1967 to protest about Polly's screams of terror as she was dragged to the operating table to be transformed into a fish person: a gauzy creation of sequins and body stocking which made the Menoptra look flawless in execution and design. Her child was to go into hospital to have her tonsils removed on the Monday after the offending episode aired. Polly was traumatised at having to have an injection. Did not the programme makers realise that they would upset unnecessarily children who had to have injections and operations? This was all very fair in its way, although the correspondent about "The Underwater Menace" (1967) might have made a more germane point about that story by saying it was crappy. Complaints about the series' violence dogged the original series for the whole of its run until 1976, when Mrs Whitehouse's campaign (of which more later) caused the BBC to change the series radically away from violence and horror at the end of Tom Baker's third season.

The first season, meanwhile, continued with a journey across thirteenth century Europe in "Marco Polo" (1964), notable for effective shooting of this epic journey in a tiny studio and for Polo's voice-over narrating their voyage and stating his irritation with the

Doctor. The science fiction/historical/science fiction pattern continued. After reaching Cathay, the crew hunted for the six Keys of Marinus in an eponymous adventure. Again scripted by Terry Nation, this was sub-standard peril-of-the-week fare and very much in the vein of 1930s and 1940s cinema adventure serials like *Flash Gordon*, which had some influence on the serial adventure format of the Hartnell stories. It was again designed by Raymond Cusick, charged to create a different environment for each episode on a tiny budget. On the DVD release of the story, he was asked, "Are you proud of your work on 'The Keys of Marinus'?" Cusick replied musingly, "Am I proud of my work on 'The Keys of Marinus'?" He paused. "No."

## Temporal paradox

John Lucarotti, who had written the acclaimed "Marco Polo", turned in another intelligent and thoughtful script with the next story, "The Aztecs". Barbara is mistaken by the Aztecs for the reincarnation of the goddess Yetaxa, a role she embraces in an attempt to make the Aztecs abandon their barbaric practice of human sacrifice. The Doctor protests and argues, "You can't change history. Not one line." This is one of the first attempts in the series to grapple with the complications and ambiguities of time travel. The Doctor argues that history is fixed, has happened and cannot be changed. Barbara ignores him, even to the extent of half seeming to believe in her new persona. "Not Barbara," she corrects the Doctor. "Yetaxa." Her *idees de grandeur* meet their come-uppance: the human sacrifice she saves is most indignant at being denied his moment of glory and the Aztecs continue in their bloodthirsty ways. History absorbs her attempt to change it and she becomes part of established events. This was an idea the series returned to in "Day of the Daleks" (1972), in which a band of guerrillas from the future arrive back on Earth during the Doctor's twentieth century exile, determined to assassinate Sir Reginald Styles. Styles, they argue, was responsible for the world war which led to the Dalek invasion: having invited the peace delegates to his country house for final negotiations, he exploded a bomb which killed the lot of them and plunged the world into war. All but one of the guerrillas, Shura, return with the Doctor to the Dalek-ruled Earth of the future and the Doctor realises the truth: Shura, left alone and determined to finish the mission, detonated the bomb which kills Styles and the delegates. "You're trapped in a temporal paradox," the Doctor sternly announces. "Styles didn't cause that explosion and start the wars. You did it yourselves." The guerrillas, like Barbara, attempt to change history but become part of its inexorable pattern and flow.

The original production team realised that time travel paradoxes were something to be handled very carefully and the 1960s stories tend to avoid them. If the Doctor cannot change history – presumably defined as events before 1964, when "The Aztecs" was made – why, they asked, is he able to change events in the future or on different planets? As a time traveller, he lives outside time: past and future are alike to him, so, if he can't change historical events, surely he shouldn't be able to change future ones either? In "Day of the Daleks", Jo asks the Doctor why, if the guerrillas can't kill Styles on their first attempt (he's out of the country), don't they just reset their time machines to the previous evening and have another go? "That's the Blinovitch Limitation Effect," the Doctor explains. He is about to explain what this is but he and Jo are called away by the guerrillas before he gets a chance to do so. Script editor Terrance Dicks cheerfully explained that this was because the Blinovitch Limitation Effect didn't bear close scrutiny and was inserted to plug a plot hole which the viewers might have worked out for themselves. Blinovitch himself is described by the Doctor in one of the Target novelisations[1] as a great bear of a man, a Russian whose time travel experiments eventually resulted in him regressing himself to babyhood.

The question asked – and avoided – by the original production team was eventually answered in James Moran's 2008 story "The

---

[1] Note on terminology: a novel is an original story; a "novelisation" is an adaptation of a script into a novel. It might be an ugly portmanteau word but you get used to it.

Fires of Pompeii". In 79 AD, Donna insists that the Doctor must save the Pompeiians before Vesuvius erupts and is upset when he refuses. He explains that there are such things as fixed points in time which cannot be changed: one is Pompeii's destruction by Vesuvius. Other points in time are fluid and can be changed. Viewers thus had to wait forty four years before the first Doctor's objections to Barbara changing history were properly explained. This is part of the fun of sticking with *Doctor Who*, particularly with our contemporary production teams' keenness to extrapolate and develop good ideas from the original, and particularly the black and white, stories.

"The Aztecs" is the first story to feature romance for the Doctor. Hartnell, unlike the tenth Doctor, was no inveterate snogger, but he shares a cup of chocolate with an elderly Aztec lady, Cameca. As every Key Stage Two pupil knows from their history project, the Aztecs were one of the first people to discover the blessings of chocolate (although pupils don't learn it was considered an aphrodisiac), and Cameca explains that the sharing of the drink signals their engagement. Ian, much amused, congratulates the Doctor on the news. The Doctor seems unfussed about his impending nuptials, perhaps suggesting that Time Lords and human beings are genetically and genitally compatible (something certainly assumed by Rose, Martha, Amy and Rory in the revival). Even Susan muses on the type of man she would like to marry, determined to choose for herself, and anticipating her romance and marriage with David Campbell, one of the freedom fighters in series two's "The Dalek Invasion of Earth" (1964).

Rather to the BBC's surprise – and the surprise of its own production team – *Doctor Who* completed its first season of 42 twenty five minute episodes with the last episode of "The Reign of Terror", set during the French revolution, airing on 12th September, 1964. Season one amounted to about 15 ½ hours of television, plus the opening and closing titles. To put this in perspective, a modern season of 13 episodes clocks in at about nine hours of television (minus the titles)[1]. The original cast of the show spent five days rehearsing each episode, usually in a rented church hall, recorded it on the Saturday, and had Sunday off: an exhausting schedule which necessitated several companions for the Doctor, so that an episode could concentrate on the storyline of one companion and give another a week's holiday. The cast recorded the first show of the new season, "Planet of Giants", and had took four week break. Season two started on 31st October, 1964.

---

[1] Fans of the revived series have watched in some dismay as the number of episodes was steadily cut, from thirteen 45 episodes for Christopher Eccleston in 2005, to twelve for Peter Capaldi in 2015, to ten for Jodie Whittaker in 2018. Then there are the years with only few episodes screened (2009, 2012 and 2013) or (like 2016) only a Christmas special. Old hands like me think this is nothing, and remember the fifteen year gap between seasons (1989 to 2015); we keep our traps shut out of superstitious dread that criticising the paucity of episodes will create a karmic nemesis that will take *Doctor Who* off our screens again, for good…

# 3

# Doctor Who? Wanderers in the Fourth Dimension

Season one concluded with the familiar pattern of alternating science fiction and historical stories. "The Sensorites" (1964) is a slightly dated affair and the humans' rocket ship seems to have come out of a 1940s film serial; its twenty eighth century crew wear buttoned shirts and jackets with rocket logos. The starship Enterprise it ain't. The Sensorites themselves are effective designs; they joined the Zarbi and Menoptra, equally impressive creations from season two's "The Web Planet" (1965), in the first *Doctor Who* annual, largely written by story editor David Whitaker. The publishers also wanted to include the Daleks but Terry Nation was using them in their own series of annuals, independent of the Doctor. Jacqueline Hill (Barbara) is absent from much "The Sensorites" as she was on holiday. It was common practice in the 1960s to write out characters from individual episodes when the actor needed a break or was unwell: an absolute necessity when *Doctor Who* ran for forty-odd weeks of the year and the cast made one episode a week. Hartnell hurt his back when filming season two's "The Dalek Invasion of Earth" (1964): the episode was speedily rewritten to render the Doctor unconscious, so that he could be played by an extra with his back to the camera. In "The Celestial Toymaker" (1966), the Doctor is rendered invisible and only his pre-recorded voice is heard: Hartnell was on holiday.

Season one concluded with Dennis Spooner's first story for the series, "The Reign of Terror". Set in the French revolution, it sees Barbara and Susan carted off to the guillotine and is inflected more towards humour – Spooner's preference – than some of the earlier historicals. Spooner took over from Whitaker as story editor from the third story, "The Rescue" (1965).

Sydney Newman had stipulated in 1963 that *Doctor Who* stories should go forwards, backwards and sideways in time. Forwards and backwards was fine, but what did "sideways" mean? It seemed to indicate unfamiliar dimensions and was not realised until the first story of season two, "Planet of Giants" (1964). The TARDIS crew arrive back on contemporary Earth but are only one inch high. As far as plot goes, that's basically it. The idea for the story was in the earliest of the programme's pre-production documents, before the show's name was even fixed, and survived into execution long after other similarly daft story ideas had been thrown out. There were at least two attempts at writing the script: the one that was eventually made was scripted by academic Louis Marks[1] and sadly betrayed the limitations of the original notion. Once he has shrunk them to miniscule size, what was the writer supposed to do with the time travellers for ninety-odd minutes? Marks's solution is to have them clamber into cracks between pavements that become trenches and avoid giant cats, but this was never going to sustain a four part story and a very thin, sub-*Avengers* style sub-plot, involving a wicked industrialist, was introduced. As the time travellers are too small to take much of a part in these dull scenes anyway, the story is effectively two separate halves: one of which could be equally at home in any contemporary spy or conspiracy series and has naff all to do with *Doctor Who*. Inch high time travellers were technically almost impossible to realise anyway with the special effects available at the time: a few shots could be achieved by inlay, which was a black and white version of green screen, but that was about it. There are some good scenes of the Doctor and Susan trying to avoid being flushed down the plughole (where the script and concept could also have usefully been dispatched) and some remarkably good moments where the TARDIS crew interact with a giant ant and a moving fly, both of them specially made props. In an unprecedented move, Verity Lambert ordered that the serial should be cut down from four episodes to three, and the third and fourth episodes were edited together.

---

[1] Louis Marks later wrote the well-received serials "Day of the Daleks" (1972), "Planet of Evil" (1975) and "The Masque of Mandragora" (1976).

There was a gap of four years between "Planet of Giants" and the next "sideways" in time adventure: this was the much better story "The Mind Robber" (1968), a Troughton tale which takes place in the fantasy void of the Land of Fiction. *Doctor Who* largely avoided such "sideways" adventures in the future, although Sylvester McCoy's Doctor mentions that there are universes "sideways" in time in "Battlefield" (1989). Wisely, he does not go to them.

## The Daleks are the Masters of the Earth!

Season two's second story is remarkable for establishing the template for the next six decades, and certainly for Pertwee's first three seasons, which he spends in exile as UNIT's scientific adviser on contemporary Earth. "The Dalek Invasion of Earth" (1964) is the first alien invasion story. Nominally set two hundred years in the future in 2164, the level of human technology and fashion is very much of the 1960s, as noted by a *Radio Times* reviewer of the Peter Cushing film version, which followed suit: "Fashion pundits please note – in 2150, we'll all be wearing sixties casuals." The story draws heavily on the Daleks' origins as symbols of the Nazis in depicting Britain (and specifically England) smashed by heavy bombardment. Some humans cower in cellars and plot resistance while others are carted off to a concentration camp in Bedfordshire. In short, this is Britain as it would have been if a Nazi invasion had been successful. Terry Nation draws heavily on the heroism of resistance fighters in occupied Europe: the poorly armed resistance attacks the vastly superior Dalek force aboard their spaceship and are repulsed with heavy losses; the crippled scientist Dortmun (an image Nation would return to in the similarly wheelchair bound Davros) launches a suicide attack against a squad of Daleks, determined to take a few with him so that Barbara and resistance fighter Jenny can escape. Verbal and visual imagery is from the Second World War, still very much in living memory, and is sometimes disturbing. The humans in the Daleks' camp are called "slave workers" and are on starvation rations; the Dalek in charge of the concentration camp is referred to

71

as the "kommandant"; humans trade jewellery for food with a black marketeer who slips in and out of the camp unnoticed[1]; an old woman and her daughter mend clothes for the slave workers and betray Barbara and Jenny to the Daleks for the sake of a few tins of food and oranges; the Daleks raise their sucker arms in Nazi salutes; the punishment for not working hard enough is extermination; and so on. The Robomen are unthinking servants of the Daleks, human beings turned into machines who pitilessly enforce discipline with whips and truncheons in a clear reference to the SS and the Gestapo (and wear somewhat kinky black PVC suits in the film). In one sequence, the Doctor, Susan and Tyler (another resistance member) evade the Daleks in the London sewers but have themselves to evade the sewers' alligators, which escaped from the zoo when the city was bombed. This sequence was perhaps inspired by actual events: knowing that the zoo could be destroyed by bombing in 1940, the more dangerous animals in Regent's Park zoo were shot for fear that they would escape. The alligator that actually appears on screen appears to be a sweet little baby one and is about eight inches long, but the idea was dramatically good[2].

The Robomen appear to have lurched straight out of *Buck Rogers* type pulp films serials of the 1940s, which arguably had a considerable influence on early *Doctor Who*s[3]. Robot plus men equals Robomen, which is a daft B-movie name anyway. In creating them, Nation was responding to one of the problems of the Daleks which has dogged all of their appearances in the original series. Designed for only one story, the Daleks work beautifully in the

---

[1] Patrick O'Connell, the black marketeer in the original serial is adequate, but Philip Madoc as the equivalent character in the movie is terrific.

[2] Did it inspire the 1965 episode of *Thunderbirds*, the immortal tale "Attack of the Alligators!", in which Virgil and Alan Tracy endure an onslaught by small alligators in a model swamp?

[3] There's a thesis to be written about this idea, you know… It is also to be regretted that the original production team didn't find a part for Larry "Buster" Crabbe, the actor who played Flash Gordon and Buck Rogers in the film serials. They only had fourteen hours to save the Earth.

television studio[1]: in "The Daleks" (1963-4), they can't even leave the smooth floors of their city. Once they are taken out on location, problems begin. Designer Spencer Chapman disrupts the Daleks' smooth lines by plonking them on a larger base unit which can accommodate larger wheels – their original smaller bases are clearly visible – and gives them radio discs on their backs. This is handy for the Doctor, who defeats them by interfering with the signals that allow them to move and to communicate with each other. These new Daleks are bigger than their original counterparts but can now, like their big screen cousins, clearly contain an actor, when the originals were designed to conceal that they were operated by one.

Daleks in London can't climb stairs, so need someone to do it for them. Hence the need for the more mobile Robomen. The Daleks' lack of mobility led to endless jokes, exemplified in a Birkett cartoon of 1978: confronted with a flight of stairs, the leader of a group of Daleks says, "Well, this certainly buggers up our plans to conquer the universe." The cartoon was printed on the cover of scripts for "Destiny of the Daleks" (1979) issued to actors and crew and perhaps prompted Tom Baker's taunting of a Dalek as he escapes up a rope: "If you're supposed to be the superior race of the universe, why don't you try climbing after us?" Fans suspected the auto-referential line to be inserted by new script editor Douglas Adams, who was ever alive to the series' absurdities and was accused of sending the series up, and they disapproved of it as drawing attention to the Daleks' dramatic limitations and thus spoiling the suspension of disbelief. It is hard to see Nation writing the line and he disliked the production team's handling of his original script for "Destiny of the Daleks". Even back in the 1960s, production crews puzzled over the Daleks' technical limitations. Hover Daleks were suggested for "The Chase" (1965) but they were not technically possible.

Birkett's card is still widely available today but was redundant even before the end of the original series. The Colin Baker story

---

[1] K9 had the same problem thirteen years later in "The Invisible Enemy". He couldn't even fit through the TARDIS door.

"Revelation of the Daleks" (1985) has an understated moment where a Dalek hovers (a shot realised using a commercially available model Dalek produced by Sevans Models) but this was soon forgotten by viewers. The end of episode one of Sylvester McCoy's "Remembrance of the Daleks" (1988) has the Doctor run up some cellar stairs to escape an Imperial Dalek. It then follows him. This was considered enough of a dramatic surprise – confounding those cynical viewers who shouted, "Run up the stairs!" to the Doctor – that it merited an episode ending on its own. The shot was achieved by putting a full-sized Dalek on a stairlift; the latter was then hidden by a red glow slapped on by video effects. The sequence was reprised in the revived series episode "Dalek" (2005) when Rose and Adam evade the Dalek by running up a flight of stairs. "Great big alien death machine," smarms Adam, "defeated by a flight of stairs." "Elevate," grates the Dalek, and follows him. Fans cheered across the U.K., not least because Adam was so annoying and merited total extermination.

In "Day of the Daleks", the Robomen are replaced by the ape-like Ogrons as more mobile servants. Ogrons might have been a feature of Louis Marks's original scripts for that story, which didn't feature the Daleks. Still, the human guerrillas are opposed by the Daleks' gorillas[1]. Production teams in the later 1970s also felt that the Daleks' dialogue was terribly slow and dull and slowed down the story telling: hence the perceived need to bring back Davros in "Destiny of the Daleks" (1979) and every subsequent Dalek story in the original series. Davros, with his more human speech patterns, could handle the dialogue better than the Daleks, although an irritating effect of his continuous inclusion was that the Daleks took a back seat in 1980s Dalek stories.

The Dalek operators themselves in "The Dalek Invasion of Earth" lamented the Daleks' limitations in different terms. Once inside their props, other actors tended to forget about them, and Dalek actors

---

[1] If you think this pun is bad, fans called the pig men who featured as the Daleks' servant in "The Daleks Take Manhattan"/"Evolution of the Daleks" (2007), Hogrons.

were left without refreshments when their fellows went to have their tea breaks. Comfort breaks were a similar problem. On location, the operators solved it by trundling their Daleks over drains at the side of the road, where they could blissfully relieve themselves in peace. One actor recalled setting the trend and a line of Daleks formed behind him, all queuing for the loo.

Sydney Newman may have loved "The Dalek Invasion of Earth" but sadly it has not really stood the test of time. The DVD draws attention to floor managers saying "Cue!" before a line of slave workers leaves the Dalek spaceship; Daleks zoom down its ramp, apparently – judging from a bang – to crash into something off-screen. The Dalek voices were produced by actors speaking into a ring modulator (an effect originally created for a robot voice in a pre-*Who* radio play), but the crew never remembered to write down the modulator's settings. Thus Dalek voices throughout the original series differ from story to story in their pitch and level of distortion: something that Nicholas Briggs, an actor and fan who has provided the Dalek voices since 2005, would never dream of doing. The Dalek voices in their invasion serial pipe and squeal and are barely distorted: they sound like a bad imitation of a Dalek voice by someone in a pub or playground. Furthermore, David Graham's Dalek voices are pre-recorded and played in live on set: they frequently overlap Peter Hawkins' live voices, and the result is chaos. (These actors are best known for providing, respectively, the voices of Parker in *Thunderbirds* and Captain Pugwash in the eponymous cartoon.) Some effects make fans wince. Ian and the Doctor watch the arrival of the Dalek saucer in episode one: on the DVD, viewers can choose between a *TV21* / revived series flying saucer thundering over the London streets, or opt for the original, a silver pie dish suspended from wires which is every bit as good as those in Ed Wood's film *Plan 9 From Outer Space* (1959).

**The Daleks Are Masters of the Big Screen!**

Before the advent of home video, fans' folk memories of this story were partly based on plot summaries and impressive photos published in such vehicles as the *Doctor Who Tenth Anniversary Special* (BBC, 1973). Some of course had actually seen and remembered its first broadcast. However, much of the affection for and excitement generated by mention of this serial arguably arises from its transmutation into the cinema film, *Daleks: Invasion Earth 2150 A.D.* (1966). This was Peter Cushing's second outing as Dr Who (sic) and was regularly shown on BBC television in the 1970s. Its imagery was repeated in some of the scenes of the Dalek invasion of Cardiff in *The Stolen Earth* (2008) and the cover art for the 1976 novelisation *Doctor Who and the Dalek Invasion of Earth* by Terrance Dicks. Here, the Roboman and Dalek on the cover were based on the film's versions, with illustrator Christos Achilleos adding a gas mask, goggles and a machine gun to the Roboman for added dehumanising horror (the Robomen in the television production apparently wear adapted lamp shades or waste paper baskets and speak like *Monty Python*'s Gumbies). The flying saucers raking London with fire are also from the movie version.

This second *Doctor Who* film was an attempt to cash in on Dalekmania, now on the wane[1], and to build on the box office success of the first film, *Dr Who and the Daleks*, released a year earlier. Such was the success of the Daleks that the Doctor doesn't even feature in the film's title and cinema trailers concentrated on the Daleks themselves, only mentioning in passing that Dr Who is played by Peter Cushing. It is a much better, less childish and more exciting outing than the first film. Producers Subotsky and Vegoda had listened to audience feedback from children who had seen *Dr Who and the Daleks* and were apparently disappointed that the Daleks only exterminated one person. There are effective extermination scenes a-plenty in the second film. Stuntman Eddie Powell, who doubled for Christopher Lee in the contemporaneous *Dracula* films for Hammer, and would go on to work as the eponymous *Alien* in Ridley Scott's 1979 film, runs to escape from

---

[1] And to be succeeded by Batmania, after the tv series with Adam West and Burt Ward began its screening in the UK.

the Dalek saucer over wrecked shop roofs and is brought down by Dalek firepower. Powell actually caught and injured his foot in the shop awning as he went down – something visible if you freeze frame the DVD. He is surrounded by Daleks, who exterminate him. There is a mass extermination of Philip Madoc, who plays the sneering black marketeer Brockley, later in the film. The Daleks' guns in both films were realised by shooting carbon dioxide fire extinguishers through their hollow exterminators. This was arguably a much more effective visual effect than the television equivalent: for all the 1960s Dalek stories, the extermination effect is achieved by turning the picture negative (an image which survived through the 1970s and 1980s to the present day, when Dalek extermination rays reveal an x-ray of the people they are blasting: an extrapolation of a negative). One problem with the film Daleks' firepower is that, although it is now clear which Dalek is firing, their range is limited by the range of the fire extinguisher (about eight feet). An American film critic erroneously assumed that the Daleks fired nerve gas. This is quite wrong as nerve gas does not cause buildings to blow up. Tsk.

The film benefited from a greater adherence to the original television version than *Dr Who and the Daleks*. Original story editor David Whitaker rewrote much of the dialogue and the tone is grittier and more serious, although the Nazi imagery was considerably toned down from the television original. The Daleks themselves sport the new vertical solar panels introduced into the 1965 television serial "The Chase" as an explanation for the Daleks' new power source outside their city. The budget was bigger than the first film – and many times larger than the television series' – allowing for impressive visuals of the Daleks' saucer and massed Daleks on location. The acting is of a higher quality: accomplished actor Ray Brooks plays David, whose television romance with Susan is cut as the film's Susan is much younger than Carole Ann Ford's; Bernard Cribbins (who was to play companion Wilfred Mott against David Tennant's Doctor from 2007-2010) replaces Roy Castle as comic relief Tom Campbell and Barbara is inexplicably replaced by Louise

(Jill Curzon), the Doctor's niece (huh?). We still don't get to meet Mrs Who, who perhaps died of despair at her husband's tinkering with his dimensionally transcendental police box in the garden. Andrew Kier provides Scottish gravitas as resistance fighter Wyler[1], who befriends Susan: Kier who went on to play the screen Quatermass in Nigel Kneale's approved Hammer film of *Quatermass and the Pit* (1967). Peter Cushing was ill for some of the shoot and the schedule had to be rearranged around his absence; some have argued that his illness affects his performance and that he is not quite the sprightly Doctor of *Dr Who and the Daleks*.

Better thought the second film was, it was released when interest in the Daleks was waning and it barely broke even at the box office. Subotsky and Rosenberg had the rights to make a third film, but this was shelved. In a 1980s interview, Subotsky said that this was to have been called *Dr Who's Greatest Adventure* and would have featured two Doctors (Patrick Troughton was playing the part on television when the third film would have been released). Subotsky went on to make *At The Earth's Core* (1976), featuring Doug McClure and a burrowing machine akin to the Mole from *Thunderbirds*. Peter Cushing plays scientist Dr Abner Perry and gives a performance that is virtually identical to his Doctor, thus suggesting that he could have continued as the screen Doctor with great success. Who might have played the other Doctor in *Dr Who's Greatest Adventure* remains a mystery, and how a human Dr Who might have regenerated is anyone's guess.

Aimed at children and intended to make money, the two 1960s Dalek films are fondly remembered parts of *Who* history. They also started a repeated, if not endless, series of attempts to bring the Doctor to the big screen; rumours of films have been rumbling since the 1970s and pre-production has started on actual films. In 2010, Steven Moffat quelled excitement over reports that a film was actually in pre-production by stating emphatically that any new film would have to include the television cast and would have to tie in

---

[1] The character was renamed Wyler from the TV series' Tyler. Why? Perhaps someone hit the wrong key on the typewriter.

with present programme continuity. As the television cast are heavily involved in making the ongoing series – as were William Hartnell and the other regulars when the two Dalek films were made – it seems highly unlikely that a film will materialise for the time being. This may be a blessing if we bear in mind such gems as the original script for the TV movie (1996). This featured the Doctor's escape from Gallifrey in search of his father, the great explorer Ulysses, and the Master as the Doctor's brother and President of the Time Lords. It was almost made and Paul McGann's auditions as the Doctor used extracts from the script: McGann is great – the script, if the extracts are anything to go by, is appalling.

## New companions

Susan leaves the TARDIS at the end of "The Dalek Invasion of Earth" to marry freedom fighter David Campbell. Carole Ann Ford, who played her, had become unhappy with what she saw as the lack of development of Susan's character. David Whitaker, now working under new story editor Dennis Spooner, wrote a two part story originally entitled "Dr Who and Tanni", to introduce Susan's replacement. This became "The Rescue" (1964), Tanni was renamed Vicki and Maureen O'Brien was contracted to play her. The actress was at the beginning of her career and unprepared for the high public profile brought her by playing Vicki. She recalled people recognising her on the London underground and nudging each other and for many years was uncomfortable with her association with the series, unwilling to give interviews and sometimes vehemently wishing that fanzine editors would leave her alone. In recent years, Maureen O'Brien has been a valued guest at conventions and has contributed much to our understanding of *Doctor Who*'s early years.

"The Rescue" is one of the series' neglected gems; beautifully written by David Whitaker and well-acted by a small cast, it centres on a crashed spaceship in the far future. Vicki is one of the survivors and so is Bennett, crippled by the crash. Vicki lives in terror of the alien Koquillion, who stalks around the ship, intimidating its occupants. The Doctor discovers that Koquillion is Bennett in disguise; Bennett had originally murdered the crew, including Vicki's father, but is himself killed by the aliens native to the planet. Now completely alone, Vicki gratefully accepts the Doctor's invitation to accompany him on his travels. "In that old box?" she asks. "We can go anywhere and everywhere in that old box," the Doctor chuckles. Ian and Barbara are keen that the Doctor should invite Vicki aboard, partly because they like her very much themselves, and partly because they believe she can help to fill the gap that Susan has left[1]. *The Rescue*'s theme of grief, loss and the healing power of compassion is touching and we are immediately drawn to Vicki, beautifully played by Maureen O'Brien. The actress prepared carefully for the shoot by "becoming" her character according to the Method school of acting, much, she recalls, to the amusement of the three established regulars.

Vicki was, to all intents and purposes, Susan with another name. She was human, granted, rather than a member of the Doctor's own race, but came from the far future and was bewildered by Ian and Barbara's lack of technical knowledge: she had no idea what aspirin was and was surprised on hearing the Beatles in "The Chase" (1965): "I'd no idea they played classical music." Like Susan, she was young, inexperienced and needed protecting; like Susan, the Doctor enjoyed a grandfatherly relationship with her and took him under his wing. Hartnell's Doctor often put his arm around her protectively, especially when danger threatened, as at the end of one of the episodes of "The Web Planet" when the Animus immobilises the Doctor and Vicki with a sticky spray of web. Like Susan, she leaves the TARDIS to be married off (often the fate of female companions of the first four Doctors): unlike Susan, she knows that her choice of husband will entail her own death, for her name is changed to Cressida, her husband is Troilus and the Trojan War is

---

[1] Speaking on the BBC Radio Four *Today* programme on Boxing Day 2017, Carole Ann Ford said that the Doctor took companions because he was lonely: he missed his granddaughter, Susan. Ford appeared on *Today* as part of a not very enlightening discussion of Jodie Whittaker's first appearance as the Doctor.

coming to its end ("The Myth Makers", 1965).

Vicki's similarity to Susan was a blessing to the story editors. Some script writers hadn't grasped that Susan was leaving and they could easily replace her name with Vicki's without causing any material damage to the story. Peter Purves was later to complain that the original script for "Galaxy Four" (1965) had been written for Ian and Barbara and he had been given Barbara's lines. The actor was singularly fed up at having to be afraid of the Drahvins, the race of female villains, whom he described as "singularly un-Amazonian". Confusion over companions was a consequence of hurried writing, itself attributable to the production of more than forty episodes a year. The issue grew to a head in Patrick Troughton's time, when unsuitable scripts were rushed into production because there was no replacement available[1], and was one of the reasons that the number of episodes was cut from about forty a year to twenty-five or so in 1970, when the series moved into colour and Jon Pertwee became the Doctor.

Companions come and go with a somewhat bewildering rapidity in Hartnell's time. Discovering that the Daleks' time machine can return them to Earth – albeit in 1965 rather than 1963 – Ian and Barbara opt to leave the Doctor at the end of "The Chase" (1965). Ian offers too little money for his bus fare and the incredulous conductor asks, "Where have you been, the moon?" "No, but you're close," Ian quips. The teachers are replaced by Steven Taylor (Peter Purves), an astronaut imprisoned by the Mechonoids in "The Chase". Peter Purves, best known in the 1970s as one of the regular presenters on the BBC children's magazine show *Blue Peter*, originally appeared in episode two of "The Chase" as hillbilly tourist Morton Dill, who encounters the Daleks at the top of the

---

[1] Script editor Terrence Dicks recalled that he had worked with new script writer Robert Holmes on "The Krotons" in 1968. This could be used as a last-minute replacement for one of the dreadful scripts the production team had to film because there was nothing else available. David Maloney was scheduled to direct "The Prison in Space" but said the script was awful and could he have something else? Dicks handed him the script for "The Krotons".

Empire State Building. Purves's performance impressed the production team who offered him a regular role as Steven: Purves, who was newly married and needed the money, accepted with relief.

Vicki is replaced first by Trojan handmaid Katarina, who was swiftly dispatched out of a spaceship's airlock when new story editor Donald Tosh realised her limitations: coming from that period of history, she wouldn't understand a lock, let alone a spaceship. Her replacement is space security agent Sara Kingdom, played by Jean Marsh, who had once been married to Jon Pertwee. Sara only featured in one story, the twelve episode epic "The Daleks' Masterplan" (1965-6), in which she shoots her brother Bret Vyon, believing him to be a traitor. Vyon was played by Nicholas Courtney, who went on to play the British commander of the United Nations Intelligence Taskforce, Brigadier Alistair Gordon Lethbridge Stewart, one of the show's best loved characters (and longest lived: Courtney created the role in "The Web of Fear" in 1968 and was still playing him in *The Sarah Jane Adventures* forty years later). Sara, like Katarina, is killed off, aged to death by the Daleks' time destructor in another sequence that had people of a nervous disposition bristling with concern at the effect of such horror on their children. They were the last companions to die until "Earthshock" in 1982, fondly remembered for the death of Adric.

Yet another companion joined the TARDIS at the end of "The Massacre", Dodo Chaplet (Jackie Lane), who only lasted five stories. The production team allowed Jackie Lane to use her own regional accent in filming for her first full story, "The Ark" (1966), but higher powers let it be known that principal characters should speak BBC English: thus Dodo alternates between received pronunciation and a regional accent in alternate film or studio sequences. The Doctor's fondness for Dodo in "The Ark" is not especially believable, considering that they had only just met, and one suspects some hasty scriptwriting for a generic companion figure. Dodo slips away from the series in "The War Machines" (1966), where she isn't even granted a farewell scene: yet another set of replacements are Londoners from the swinging sixties, seen by script editor Gerry Davis as necessary to bring the show up to date. These are the middle class Polly (Anneke Wills), notable for her long legs, miniskirts and enthusiasm, and the cockney sparrow Able Seaman Ben Jackson (Michael Craze), cor blimey guv'nor. There was intended to be some good-natured ribbing on the theme of class between Ben and Polly: Ben nicknames her "Duchess" and delivers many of his lines with a face and tone of angry incredulity. Polly, however, is terrific. They returned briefly in "Twice Upon A Time" (2017), now played by Lily Travers and Jared Garfield.

This bewildering parade of companions through apparently revolving TARDIS doors can be partly accounted for by changes in the production team and partly by actors' desires to move on from unrewarding roles. Verity Lambert left, to be replaced by John

*The author at Bedford Who Charity Con 3 in 2017 with (left to right): Peter Purves (Steven); Anneke Wills (Polly); FD; Maureen O'Brien (Vicky); Geoffrey Beevers (the Master).*

Wiles and then Innes Lloyd as producer; Dennis Spooner moved on, to be replaced by Donald Tosh and then Gerry Davis as script editor. Each production team had different ideas about who would be suitable as a companion, and each didn't always think much of the previous team's choices. William Hartnell was especially unhappy about the departure of the original companions. He got on well with Peter Purves and instructed him in the art of acting for television, suggesting that Purves made hand gestures near his face so that they could be picked up in close up: this presumably explains the first Doctor's habit of gripping his lapels. Steven Taylor at least stayed for some eighteen months and provided some continuity while female companions came and went, although Peter Purves himself wasn't entirely happy in the role. Interviewed in the late 1970s, he said he didn't think he was always very good and there was a tendency to overact when surrounded by peril and monsters. He also got tired of uttering "such earth-shattering lines as, 'What's happening Doctor?' and 'Doctor, look out!' and the inevitable, 'Where are we, Doctor?'" Not being a fan of the Daleks, he said he wished he'd never signed on the dotted line when he learnt they were to feature in twelve consecutive episodes (actually eleven, as they are absent from the Christmas Day episode, "The Feast of Stephen" (1965)). In the same interview, Purves explained that he stayed on because he needed a regular income; he also liked Bill Hartnell and they got on well together. Hartnell was upset when Purves said he wanted to move on and couldn't understand why the younger actor would turn his back on regular money in an ongoing part when he had a young family to feed. Indeed, Purves went from *Doctor Who* to unemployment and a job delivering cars while he looked for other acting jobs.

Terrence Dicks has argued that an actor can play the Doctor for five or so years without reaching the limits of the part[1], but the role of the companion is much more limited: two years is about as much as anyone can stand. Dicks said that this was in the nature of the companion's role, especially female companions, who are there to

---

[1] This appears to be about three years in the revived series, post-2005.

look pretty, ask questions, scream, get captured and have the Doctor rescue them. This is a not unfair summary of the companion's function in the black and white stories, until the advent of women's liberation, as feminism was sometimes known in the 1970s, led to the creation of more capable companions like Dr Liz Shaw and Sarah Jane Smith. The Patrick Troughton story "The Moonbase" (1967), contains the following exchange:

> Polly: You found something?
>
> Doctor: Oh Polly, I only wish I had. Why not make some coffee to keep them all happy while I think of something?
>
> Polly: All right.

Polly sympathetically squeezes the Doctor on the shoulder as she accepts that her role, like the good 1960s secretary she is, is to make the coffee while the clever men think of solutions. In the 1983 special "The Five Doctors", Janet Fielding (playing Tegan) objected to a scene in which the first Doctor (now played by Richard Hurndall) tells her to make tea for the recovering fifth Doctor (Peter Davison). A rewrite was hurriedly inserted to placate both Tegan and Janet Fielding as the fifth Doctor asks Tegan to humour the first Doctor; he was much more old fashioned when he was younger.

If such was the role of the female companion, it wasn't surprising that actresses didn't always want to play them for long. Some didn't want to get involved at all. Offered a recurring role as the Doctor's companion in the series, Pauline Collins, who played Samantha in "The Faceless Ones" (1967) turned Innes Lloyd down. She returned to play Queen Victoria in the 2006 story "Tooth and Claw". Carey Mulligan was asked if she wanted to stay on as Sally Sparrow after "Blink" (2007) but she turned the offer down and her career has been in a nosedive ever since.

## Gender politics and the series

Although Dicks' description of the companion's function is slightly tongue in cheek, and Barbara and Susan were much more resourceful than it suggests, it is true that the relationship between the Doctor and the women was formed by the gender politics of the time. Christopher Eccleston dismissively remarked upon the "patrician know-all and underwritten female companion" of the original series (his Doctor's relationship with Rose being so much more modern – Rose is in love with him which is very interesting indeed). *Doctor Who* has arguably struggled to escape its roots in sixties gender politics throughout its history, at least until 2017, when Jodie Whittaker was cast as the thirteenth Doctor.

Whittaker's casting could obviously be read as a radical attempt to realign a very old series with the gender politics of 2017. It has been seen as not before time – a female Doctor was mooted as long ago as 1981, although not particularly seriously – but it was controversial. Some viewers who would be quite happy to watch, say, Buffy kick vampire ass in *Buffy the Vampire Slayer* (1997-2003), were profoundly unhappy to have a female Doctor. (Were such viewers predominantly male?) The unhappiness could sometimes manifest itself as simple sexism, as in the *Daily Mail*'s review of the 2017 Christmas special[1], but was often profound uneasiness about such a wrenching of the series' format. Plenty of other fans were delighted. Jodie Whittaker pleaded with fans not to be put off by her gender. It should also be noted that, whenever a new Doctor is cast, there are fans who declare it is the end of civilisation as we know it and they will not watch a single frame of the new series. Peter Davison's casting was hailed in 1981 as the beginning of the end of the show.

Back in the original series, as long as there was an older Doctor

---

[1]    www.dailymail.co.uk/tvshowbiz/article-5212005/Christopher-Stevens-reviews-Doctor-Christmas-TV.html   26.12.17

and younger female companions, there was something paternalistic and arguably sexist about the relationship, even as late as 1987-9 with the seventh Doctor and the much younger Ace. As a younger and physically attractive Doctor, Peter Davison was told not to put his arm around Tegan, Nyssa or Peri, to negate any charges of hanky panky taking place willy nilly in the TARDIS. He was, however, allowed to put his arm around the male Adric or Turlough: apparently viewers, alive to a heterosexual subtext, wouldn't see a homosexual one. Tegan and Nyssa were even given their own shared bedroom in the TARDIS, a clearly feminine space with no signs of intrusion from the Doctor. Russell T Davies changed the dynamic of the companion and Doctor altogether by bringing sexuality and romance to the fore: both Rose and Martha are in love with the Doctor in the revived series. Thus Davies moved to liberate the series from 1960s gender politics and irritated some fans who preferred adventure to "soap opera romance", and some gay fans, who had felt at home with the Doctor's inclusive asexuality.

**"This old body of mine is wearing a bit thin."**

By the third season, William Hartnell had become increasingly unhappy about the endless changes in the show. He was also unwell, suffering from undiagnosed arteriosclerosis which made it hard for him to remember his lines. There have been many stories about how crotchety and difficult Hartnell could be on the set, but Maureen O'Brien and Peter Purves[1] have spoken warmly about him and have recalled how generous he had been. Maureen O'Brien said Hartnell lost his temper about three times a day but would quieten down quickly; Hartnell, she explained, only lost his temper if something wasn't going well or if a director or crew member hadn't done his job properly. "It wasn't so much that he got angry as that he got upset," she explained at Bedford Who Charity Con 3 in 2017; more specifically, he became upset and angry with himself, especially when he forgot his lines. O'Brien said she saw it as her role to look

---

[1] Speaking at Bedford Who Charity Con 3 in 2017.

after Hartnell and to calm him down, and they were very fond of each other. Peter Purves similarly spoke of Hartnell's generosity: Hartnell would take him out to an Italian restaurant once a week and would always produce a hamper of food and a bottle of champagne on the day of recording. This would, Maureen O'Brien recalled, be a day when the cast would be tense and say, "good luck, good luck" to each other before the cameras rolled. O'Brien couldn't see what all the fuss was about, as she was a theatre actress, this was television and there was nobody *there* as an audience. She admitted to being very nervous before a performance in the theatre.

O'Brien and Purves's memories have been confirmed by a 1980s interview with script editor Gerry Davis[1], who said that Hartnell had cared very, very deeply about the programme. He would frequently dry up and forget his lines or utter malapropisms: in "The Daleks", he mentions that the Thals have left "gloves" outside the TARDIS and quickly corrects the word to "drugs". Carole Ann Ford recalled that Hartnell told her character to "Check the fornicator" rather than "the fault locator" in a camera rehearsal for "The Brink of Disaster" (1964)[2]. Such mistakes survive in the finished episodes. In its early days, *Doctor Who* episodes were recorded in sequence with cameras moving from one set to another and scenes played in order, in real time, as though the actors were in a play. There might be one or, at the most two, recording breaks in an episode – for example, for a costume change, special effect or to move into the TARDIS set in "An Unearthly Child" – but that was all[3]. Video tape in the early 1960s was incredibly expensive and editing it almost unheard of; once programmes had been recorded, film copies were made of them for overseas sales (and occasional repeats) and the video tape

---

[1] In an edition of the *Doctor Who* Appreciation Society fanzine, TARDIS.

[2] This scene is included in Mark Gatiss's play, "An Adventure in Space and Time" (2013).

[3] These recording conditions determined that there should be several companions in the TARDIS: if there were more than, say, two principals, there were more possibilities for the cameras to pick up their ongoing stories on several different sets; the Doctor could only have one companion when the conditions of recording changed with the advent of colour in 1970.

itself was recorded over for taping another programme. It thus wasn't possible to retake fluffed lines and fluffed scenes unless something went badly wrong, and Hartnell's fumbled lines become more apparent on screen as his time as the Doctor went on and, sadly, his illness worsened. Verity Lambert was furious when a preoccupied Hartnell completely forgot his lines and necessitated a very expensive retake on an early episode. The twenty eight year old producer berated him for his "inexcusable" lack of professionalism and Hartnell, to his credit, accepted the rebuke and apologised. In a late Hartnell story, "The War Machines" (1966), the actor gives an excellent performance in the filmed sequences, presumably because film cameras made retakes and short takes possible; he is sometimes quite incoherent in its videotaped studio scenes.

Innes Lloyd, the new producer, realised that the punishing schedule of the show was taking its toll on Hartnell. The decision was made to continue with the series for a fourth season but to change the leading actor. Vere Lorrimer, who worked on "The Celestial Toymaker" (1966), recalled that one possibility was to have the Doctor change his form as a result of the Toymaker's interference. The Toymaker had rendered him invisible: could he look like a different person when he reappeared? In the end, the production team reasoned that the Doctor, because he was an alien, should have the power to change his form as part of his life cycle. At the end of "The Tenth Planet" (1966), Hartnell announces that his old body is getting a bit thin and collapses on the floor of the TARDIS. Before the astonished gaze of Ben and Polly, his face is suffused with a blazing light, which subsides to reveal the features of the second Doctor, Patrick Troughton.

# 4
# Cosmic Hobo

A central part of the ritual of following *Doctor Who* since, say, 1984 has been the casting of a new Doctor and the accompanying media circus. Hartnell had done three years and 126 episodes; Troughton three years and 127 episodes, Pertwee five years and 128 episodes and Tom Baker a mammoth seven years and 172 episodes[1], making him the longest serving Doctor to date. In the eyes of many Whovians, this writer included, Baker was the Doctor who towered over all the others. Tom Baker, in short, is and was Doctor Who, an opinion that appears to be shared by the actor himself.[2] Since 1984, the average length of service for a Doctor has been about three years and today's viewers are more than used to the Doctor changing his form, even if they don't always like it and predict that the every casting of every new actor will be the Beginning of the End of the show.

The arrival of the second Doctor in 1966 was, by contrast, almost a complete surprise to contemporary viewers. There had been some short articles in the newspapers explaining that Hartnell was leaving, usually taking up about three inches of column space, and mentioning that Mr Patrick Troughton, the well-known character actor, was to assume the role. Changes of Doctor usually occur as the climax to a season (or a Christmas special: a New Year, a new Doctor, renewal all round) and at the end of an exhausting and epic battle. The transformation from Hartnell to Troughton wasn't even at the end of the season. Troughton's first episode, part one of "The Power of the Daleks" (1966), went out on Guy Fawkes Night – a

---

[1] This figure excludes the six episode "Shada", which was to have rounded off the 1979-1980 season; it was never completed and was not broadcast.

[2] Baker has been playing the Doctor for some 44 years, reprising his role in Big Finish and BBC audio adventures and, most recently, in the DVD completion of "Shada", the story from 1979 whose production was halted by strike action at the BBC.

time when many of its target audiences would be more interested in getting burnt fingers from hot sausages and baked potatoes, and watching a fireworks display than watching television. The production team didn't consider that a change of Doctor would be sufficient to bring viewers in from the cold: the Daleks were the draw and it was hoped that the new Doctor could be sneaked in and accepted without too many people noticing. Commenting in 1993[1], the actor and rock star Toyah Wilcox said she had been appalled to see the first Doctor "dying"; she refused to accept the new Doctor but quickly fell in love with him which, Wilcox explained, just showed you how fickle children were.

"I've been renewed," the new Doctor explained in his first episode. "Part of me, part of the TARDIS. Without it I couldn't survive." This was a transformation, not a regeneration; indeed, the word "regeneration" wasn't used until "Planet of the Spiders" in 1974. Some of the production team in 1966 apparently assumed that this transformation was a *rejuvenation*: in other words, Patrick Troughton's Doctor was William Hartnell's Doctor when younger. "Dr Who is a modern phoenix," proclaimed that year's *Dr Who Annual* of the new Doctor. As the mythical phoenix could rise from its ashes to be reborn at the moment of its death, so the Doctor could rise again.

"I've been renewed. Part of me, part of the TARDIS. Without it I couldn't survive." The second Doctor offers the intriguing suggestion that the TARDIS is a necessary part of the transformation process. More than just a vehicle, it is a life support machine. Continuity in the original series was notoriously patchy and contradictory, but it could be that Troughton's first words were remembered and might account for the number of regenerations that have taken place inside the TARDIS: Hartnell/Troughton; Davison/Colin Baker; Colin Baker/McCoy. Post 2005, the show was written and produced by fans who knew continuity backwards and

---

[1] In the BBC special *Thirty Years in the TARDIS* (1993), a documentary released to celebrate the show's thirtieth anniversary without having to make any new episodes. *Doctor Who* itself had ended in 1989 and was in production limbo.

every single regeneration has been in the TARDIS: Eccleston / Tennant; Tennant / Smith; Smith / Capaldi; Capaldi / Whittaker. Presumably, the TARDIS is where the Doctor chooses to change his form, knowing that his machine will aid his passing – and renew itself once the regeneration energy has blasted it to bits because the production team fancy a new console room. All this builds on the fifth Doctor's debut story "Castrovalva" (1982), in which writer Christopher Bidmead gave the TARDIS a "zero room": a zone of tranquillity and healing in which a Time Lord could recover from his regeneration trauma. Apparently they were common on Gallifrey.

## Patrick Troughton

Patrick Troughton was a distinguished and highly experienced character actor when he was cast as the Doctor. He had been shortlisted for Johnny Ringo in "The Gunfighters" (1966). Troughton was initially reluctant to accept the role of the Doctor. He had apparently watched the show with his children and loved William Hartnell's performance[1], but also believed that *Doctor Who* had been "done to death and wouldn't last" an observation which perhaps arose from falling viewing figures and the feelings of many in the BBC that the show, like its leading man, was getting tired. Troughton was asked several times if he would like the part and kept turning it down until, apparently, the BBC offered him a fee that, with a large family, he couldn't refuse.

Troughton was a chameleon of an actor and able to play practically anything; he may have felt constrained by committing to a lead role in such a long running series and he both missed the challenge of other roles and feared typecasting. Barry Letts (producer 1970-1974) observed that he shouldn't have been worried, as he walked out of *Doctor Who* into the BBC's prestige drama series *The Six Wives of Henry VIII* (1970), starring Keith Michell

---

[1] *The Making of* Doctor Who, Malcolm Hulke and Terrance Dicks, London, 1972, p.37.

as the King and Troughton as the Duke of Norfolk. Troughton, like Hartnell, found the demands of producing forty episodes a year exhausting and often longed to return to the freedom of being a "jobbing" actor. He was tempted to resign when Deborah Watling left as Victoria in 1967 and showed his weariness when he was filming "The War Games" in 1969. The Doctor was to be next to an explosion and Troughton asked a visual effects man to demonstrate how big an explosion it would actually be. The visual effects man assured him it would be fine, but Troughton insisted, and the explosion was tested: it was so big that it would have easily caught him in its blast. "Now you know why I wanted you to test it," he explained to the explosives expert. Such incidents wore Troughton down and he thought, very firmly, after three years that enough was enough. When he and Peter Davison were shooting "The Five Doctors" in 1983, Davison confessed that he was unsure how long he should continue as the Doctor. He had done two complete years and was itching to return to other roles and other shows, which he had longingly observed being rehearsed next to *Doctor Who* in the BBC's rehearsal facilities. Troughton advised him to do three years, the same number he had done. They had made more than forty episodes a year in Troughton's time and around twenty six annually in Davison's, but Davison took the advice gratefully.

For years after leaving the show, Troughton said that he was "wearied" by reminders of his association with it. It didn't annoy him, he said, it just wearied him. He was reluctant, as he had been when he was the Doctor, to give interviews about playing the part. In the early 1980s, he wrote to decline an invitation to appear at a *Doctor Who* Appreciation Society convention. In his letter, Troughton recalled Dickens's novel *The Old Curiosity Shop* (1841), when Little Nell's asks her grandfather if she could look behind the Punch and Judy stall; the grandfather refuses, telling Nell that it would spoil the illusion[1]. Troughton argued that spilling the beans on the production process would be the same. He said that he wished

---

[1] Troughton had played the villain Quilp in a BBC classic serial of *The Old Curiosity Shop*, broadcast 1962-3.

the society well and was sorry to disappoint people, but that was how he felt.

Troughton needed similar persuasion to appear in the 1973 tenth anniversary story, "The Three Doctors". He eventually agreed to do it because he had left the programme three years ago, was no longer solely associated with it, and it would be his first appearance in colour. Pertwee and others recalled that there were some clashes between the Doctors on the set, but that's another story[1]. It was in fact Jon Pertwee who persuaded Troughton to accept some invitations to conventions because they were great fun. Pertwee recalled how they had chased each other up the aisles of an American convention hall having a water pistol fight, to the delight of the fans. Having had a change of heart, Troughton enjoyed reprising the role (for the second time) so much in the twentieth anniversary special, "The Five Doctors" (1983), that he asked producer John Nathan-Turner if he could do another one. He did return in the much less well regarded 1985 story "The Two Doctors", this time with Colin Baker as the resident Doctor, and Frazer Hines as Jamie. Troughton had allegedly wanted to appear with Zoe and Jamie, his last two companions, in "The Three Doctors" twelve years earlier, so having Jamie in 1985 belatedly fulfilled half his wish. Janet Fielding, who played companion Tegan, asked Troughton if he still hankered after stage work: "Oh darling, I don't want to do all that shouting in the evenings," he replied. Happy to be associated with *Doctor Who* in the 1980s, and getting lots of fun from it, Troughton tragically from a heart attack while attending a convention in Georgia in 1987. He was 67.

Troughton's slight ambivalence towards the programme as its star in 1966-1969 can be partly explained as the sense of frustration which a first class actor can feel when tied down to a particular part. Fans, who assume the leading actor loves the programme as much as

---

[1] In his autobiography *Who and Me* (King's Lynn, 2009), producer Barry Letts wrote that Pertwee loved to embellish and even to invent stories about his career. Pertwee cannot always, therefore, be considered a reliable sauce and his anecdotes must be treated with a pinch of anti-matter from Zeta Minor.

they do, sometimes find this hard to understand. Troughton certainly enjoyed many aspects of the show. Barry Letts, who directed him in "The Enemy of the World" (1967-8), recalled that he was always enthusiastic and always had inventive, good ideas. One sequence in David Whitaker's script said that the Doctor should paddle in the sea: Troughton thought this was a bit dull, and suggested he should wear a 1920s bathing costume and go for a swim, which was duly filmed. In some stories, Troughton had opportunities to show his chameleon acting skills by having the Doctor disguise himself as, variously, a washer woman and a German officer in the First World War; in "The Enemy of the World", he relished playing Salamander, the Doctor's double, as a Mexican-accented world dictator. Troughton got on well with his co-stars and particularly with Frazer Hines as Jamie, with whom he remained friends for life. Wendy Padbury, Hines and Deborah Watling, who played the second Doctor's companions, all speak warmly about Troughton and fondly of their memories of working with him. He was something of a practical joker, too. In "The Abominable Snowmen" (1967), Victoria (Deborah Watling) is hypnotised and the Doctor makes a loud noise to try and break her trance. She doesn't even flinch. In rehearsal, Frazer Hines and Troughton picked up a heavy chest that was part of the set dressing, lifted it high and let it smash to the ground: Watling, nicknamed "leather lungs" by the crew for her powerful screaming, never came down off the ceiling. In "Fury from the Deep" (1967), Watling's last story, the TARDIS crew come across mounds of foam on the beach, left behind by the intelligent seaweed monster that menaces the humans. The foam was produced in industrial quantities by a new foam machine, which the production team used to the full. Frazer Hines said that, by this point, he and Patrick Troughton had been working together for so long that they only had to look at each other to see what the other was thinking. He and Troughton ran up behind Deborah Watling, grabbed her, picked her up, and dunked her in the foam.

Patrick Troughton is one of the finest Doctors and arguably the only Doctor in the original series who always turns in a consistently excellent performance. When he was cast as the eleventh Doctor, Matt Smith watched some DVDs of his predecessors to bring him up to speed on the programme, and said that he was most impressed by Troughton's classic story "The Tomb of the Cybermen" (1967). Smith's wonderful performance as the Doctor could be said to be influenced by Troughton's. One of the original producers of the show argued that Patrick Troughton was the first "real" Doctor: Hartnell had created the part and had made it his own, but his was not a template that could be followed. Troughton had perhaps the hardest job in forging a new identity for the Doctor which viewers could accept. He was gentle, clever, kind, funny and eccentric but was also capable of showing steel and was unswerving in his moral outrage and disgust at evil and exploitation. In one novelisation, Terrance Dicks writes that the Doctor plays the fool to give himself time to think, and this is very apposite for Troughton's Doctor. People wouldn't always take him seriously and would under-estimate him: then he would surprise or defeat them. In "The Moonbase" (1967), the Doctor potters about and gets under everybody's feet. The very people who shout at him that he's an idiot and should get out of the way are surprised when they discover he has been quietly gathering evidence of the Cybermen's infiltration of the base, which he eventually exploits to defeat them. In "The Tomb of the Cybermen", the Doctor asks Victoria, who has been torn away from Victorian England, if she is happy with them and if she still grieves for her father (the Daleks exterminated him). He gently explains that he can remember his own family when he wants to, and encourages her to think that their lives are different from everybody else's: nobody else in the Universe can travel in time and space. From showing such compassion and thoughtfulness in one scene, he immediately pretends to agree with megalomaniac Eric Klieg's aims in reviving the Cybermen: they will give him total power, even over the thoughts of others. Klieg is pleased that the Doctor accepts his brilliance: the Doctor replies, "Well, now I know you're mad. I was just trying to make sure." The Second Doctor is always brave, as when he confronts the armed and dangerous Klieg, or demands to know the Cybercontroller's plans when the others shrink away in terror. The Third Doctor can't believe his ears when he hears his predecessor lambast the mad, renegade Time Lord Omega about being plucked away while he was minding his own business by a "horrible great jelly". "What are you trying to do?" Pertwee hisses. "Testing the limits of his self control. They're not very good, are they?" Troughton replies. The Pertwee Doctor relaxes: "No. No, they're not." The Doctors' methods are different, but their aims – to assess the threat that Omega poses – is the same, and the Second Doctor rightly earns his successor's respect.

It took Troughton some time to arrive at the performance which is now so admired. When he was cast, he admitted that he wasn't sure how to play it at all. He had a make-up and costume test in which he blacked up as a pirate. Sydney Newman, the show's creator who was still involved in some of the show's major creative decisions, said that Troughton should play the Doctor as "a cosmic hobo" (American slang for a tramp). The image stuck. Troughton wore a version of William Hartnell's costume, but with much less elegance. The trousers were baggier, he dispensed with the waistcoat, and favoured a rumpled shirt and a ragged bow tie (the bow tie was resurrected by Matt Smith as particularly "Doctor-ish", again suggesting Troughton's influence on his portrayal). Clothes in his first and third incarnation are rather important to him: now, it seemed as though he couldn't care less. Newman's choice of a "cosmic hobo" for the second Doctor was an apt, small piece of genius which exactly fitted the magpie wanderer in time and space, and is still influential in the current Doctors.

William Hartnell always had confidence in Troughton, describing him as "the *only* actor" who could take over as the Doctor. Troughton himself was much less sure about how to play the part and some of his early stories are uneven in tone and characterisation as he and the writers come to grips with the problem. There is a lot of dressing up and disguise and Troughton doesn't always seem at ease with Ben and Polly, the companions he had inherited from Hartnell; they were retained to help viewers accept that this new

Doctor was still *the* Doctor, as Sarah Jane Smith was retained for the Pertwee/Baker transformation in 1974-5 (and Rose and Clara were similarly retained in the revived series). Troughton seems much more at his ease when Ben and Polly leave, Jamie, his first companion, takes centre stage and is joined by Victoria (Deborah Watling) and, later, Zoe (Wendy Padbury).

## Reduce, re-use, recycle, burn!

Having said all this, the second Doctor is the hardest to write about because so few of his stories still exist in their entirety. The BBC not only recorded over original videotapes: they also junked episodes of television programmes which they considered no longer useful. It is mind bogglingly hard to imagine such a mindset today, but the BBC archives decided in the 1970s that it simply didn't have enough shelf space for all the programmes the corporation had produced, and that programmes which it couldn't fit on its shelves should be destroyed. The radical solution of building more shelves didn't occur to them. In the 1960s and 1970s, programmes were rarely repeated and the actors' union Equity demanded punishingly high repeat fees for old shows. The actors were understandably driven by worries that, if the BBC kept showing repeats, they would stop making new programmes and actors would be out of work. Current practice demonstrates that they needn't have worried, and actresses like Wendy Padbury have said what an agreeable surprise it is to have a cheque for a video release of a programme made forty or so years ago: it isn't a lot, but it pays for the week's supermarket shop.

Furthermore, the BBC in the 1970s had a policy of not repeating programmes that didn't feature the current Doctor. This policy was only overturned in 1981 when producer John Nathan-Turner promoted a series of repeats from the first four Doctors, under the umbrella title, "The Five Faces of Doctor Who", as a way of reminding people that there had been other Doctors before the seven year reign of Tom Baker, and with the aim of thus helping them to accept the new fifth Doctor, Peter Davison[1]. The BBC even applied this restriction on using any image of the Doctor other than the current one to the range of novelisations of the stories then released by Target books (which, in total, sold eight million copies and contributed considerably to children's literacy). In Tom Baker's time, Target was instructed only to use Baker's face on the cover; stories from different Doctors were not to include the lead actor's face.

But in the 1960s and 1970s, there was no cable or satellite television, no VHS or DVD and the only usefulness of old shows, as far as BBC Enterprises (the BBC's commercial arm) was concerned was to sell them to overseas broadcasters. Once overseas stations no longer wanted them, the shows were junked. Thousands of programmes were literally burned. The Pertwee stories had been made in colour but BBC Enterprises had produced black and white film copies to export to countries which didn't have colour television. Some colour Pertwee episodes were exported to the United States, but when this market dried up, Enterprises took the extraordinary decision to destroy the colour originals and keep the black and white film copies.

Ian Levine, a fan and consultant on the show in the 1980s, went to BBC Enterprises to buy some old *Doctor Who* film prints. He discovered the first Dalek story on the desk, marked "for destruction". Incredulous, Levine asked what it was doing there. "No-one wants them," was the reply. "They're just old black and white films." Levine wanted them, and told the BBC Enterprises person that he wanted to buy "The Daleks" (1963) right there. It is thanks to him and others like him that we can still enjoy so many of the 1960s episodes.

Patrick Troughton's Doctor suffered particularly from BBC Enterprise's purges. While most of Hartnell's stories were retained,

---

[1] "The Five Faces of Doctor Who" repeat season consisted of: "An Unearthly Child" (Hartnell); "The Krotons" (Troughton – pretty grim viewing but one of the only Troughton stories then complete in the archives); "The Three Doctors" and "Carnival of Monsters" (Pertwee); "Logopolis" (Tom Baker).

Troughton's output was butchered. A few single episodes were retained as historical examples of the sort of thing television had produced in the 1960s, of interest to researchers: many were junked, including both, highly regarded, Troughton Dalek stories. A few complete stories were retained from Troughton's final years as the Doctor.

With the advent of VHS and satellite television in the 1980s, and a change of heart by Equity – who perhaps accepted that the maw of multi-channel television had to be fed with something, and why not repeats if they could negotiate acceptable fees for their members? – the BBC stopped junking old shows and turned its energy, ironically, to recovering those it had destroyed. "The Tomb of the Cybermen" was returned from Hong Kong television in 1992 and went straight to the top of the video charts: perhaps partly because the show was no longer being made and British viewers snapped up any "new" *Who* that was offered. New video technology made it possible to combine the colour picture from American domestic video recordings of *Doctor Who* – which were not of broadcast quality – with the black and white film prints retained by the BBC, and "The Daemons" was the first recoloured story to be released on VHS in 1993. Technology is now so advanced that colour can sometimes be restored from the black and white film alone, which is how a colour episode of "Planet of the Daleks" (1973) episode three, came to be released on DVD in 2009; apparently the black and white film had traces of the original colour, which could be enhanced by computer. (Here, my level of technological understanding peaks; I am Jo Grant to the restoration team's Doctor.)

In spite of occasional discovery of old episodes[1], half of Troughton's output has been lost. It is thus very difficult to write about his time as the Doctor. Some argue that we can do so, as audio recordings of all his stories exist and have been commercially

---

[1] "Galaxy Four": "Air Lock" (1965) and "The Underwater Menace" episode 2 were returned in 2011. Two (almost) complete stories were found in 2013: "The Web of Fear" (minus episode 3) and "The Enemy of the World".

released with linking narration. There are also telesnaps of lost episodes: these are off-screen stills taken at the time of the original broadcast, retained by directors and others as a record of the programme before the days of domestic video recorders. We can reconstruct the experience of watching Troughton by listening to the audio, looking at the telesnaps and using our imaginations to fill in the gaps. However, this does not appeal to everyone, and perhaps not the casual, non-fan viewer of the show, as an agreeable activity. It doesn't replace the experience of watching the programme on the television, where it belongs, and it doesn't make for reliable judgements of those programmes which no longer exist in their entirety. Nor, grumblers might argue, can one make valid judgements of stories only completed by adding newly animated episodes to the existing television soundtrack: "The Moonbase" (1967) and "The Invasion" (1968) were completed thus for DVD, and "The Power of the Daleks" (1966) was released in an entirely animated version in 2016. It is particularly hard to make a critical judgement about those stories of which only one or two episodes remain. *Doctor Who* stories in the 1960s were told over four, six, seven or even ten weeks; the action unfolded slowly and single episodes from longer stories are unrepresentative of the experience of watching the whole. They can seem painfully slow: the Doctor, Jamie and Zoe barely feature in the surviving episode of "The Space Pirates" (1969) and seem to spend most of their time accepting their inability to escape from a pod drifting in space. The impression we have of Troughton's excellence as the Doctor is largely created by the complete, or very nearly complete, stories that do exist.

## Cybermen, Daleks, Monsters and Bases Under Siege

Although so few of Troughton's episodes remain, his era as the Doctor gave the programme some of its enduring tropes. One was an emphasis on monsters; another was the development of the story type known by fans as the "Base Under Siege": humans in a base are attacked from monsters without and infiltrators within, who want to destroy, convert or do other unspeakable things to the poorly equipped human beings. Of course, the Hartnell era had given the programme monsters too – and without the appeal of the Daleks in the second story (what if the production team had opted for "The Masters of Luxor" instead?) the programme would probably never have survived beyond its initial thirteen weeks.

Both aspects – the monsters and the base under siege – were trialled in Hartnell's final story, "The Tenth Planet" (1966), which introduced the Cybermen. Several planets came into conjunction to create this highly regarded story. The first was new story editor Gerry Davis's decision to beef up the scientific content of the programme by hiring a scientific adviser (he was anticipating UNIT's decision to hire the third Doctor in a similar capacity, perhaps). This was Dr Christopher (Kit) Pedlar, a surgeon and academic. Davis explained in an interview that, in his search for a scientific adviser, he invited several people into his office and asked them: if you wanted to take over the world using the newly finished Post Office Tower[1], how would you go about it? Pedlar gave a considered and thoughtful reply. In the best traditions of intelligent science fiction, he extrapolated fiction from established scientific fact and theory. He speculated that a computer in the Post Office Tower could connect itself to all other computers in the world via telephone lines, and presciently anticipated the internet. Perhaps these computers could further exert control over human beings by sending a hypnotic signal over the same phone lines? Pedlar's ideas linked into the perennial fear expressed in science fiction and continually returned to in *Doctor Who*: that, instead of machines serving human beings, human beings would come to serve the machines or – even worse – become machines themselves. This fear saw its full expression in the Cybermen and, to a lesser extent, the Daleks. The latter were also symbols of dehumanisation, which human beings have always feared, but by fascism and Nazism more than mechanisation. Davis was impressed by Pedlar's ideas, hired him, and the conversation in the office became the basis for "The

---

[1] Now the BT Tower, privatised by the Conservative government in the 1980s.

War Machines" (1966). Pedlar's lack of experience in writing for television necessitated another writer, Ian Stuart Black, translating his ideas into a workable script. In Troughton's period as the Doctor, Pedlar would co-write the scripts with Gerry Davis. Eventually they created *Doomwatch* (1969), a highly regarded science fiction series which warned of environmental dangers to the planet.

The friendship and collaboration between Pedlar and Davis led to their co-creation of the Cybermen, "cyber" here meaning mechanical rather than in the modern sense. These were half human, half machine. Pedlar had been involved in early research into heart replacement surgery and had become concerned about the possibilities of spare part surgery: human beings replacing parts of their bodies – perhaps perfectly good parts – with mechanical alternatives. What if they eventually replaced their irrational brains with computers, which were more efficient? What if the computers caused human beings to lose their empathy and emotions? What if they substituted such things with logic and – since it is logical that superior beings should rule the inferior – a desire for power?

## Daleks invade America. Or not.

The final planet in the conjunction was the more prosaic need to find a monster to replace the Daleks. Davis and producer Innes Lloyd could see the writing on the wall as far as the Daleks were concerned. They knew that Terry Nation had moved onto other projects with independent television (he eventually became script editor on the Tara King episodes of *The Avengers*); they also realised that the Daleks were money spinners and Nation would demand greater editorial control over their use. The culmination was Nation's decision to take the Daleks out of *Doctor Who* and launch them in their own series, designed for American television. There were, however, two Troughton Dalek stories, but both were written by David Whitaker; Nation apparently didn't like them but received a credit and a fee for the Daleks' use. The production team duly killed the Daleks off in a civil war in "The Evil of the Daleks"

(1967). Watching their city in flames, the Doctor murmurs that this is "the final end…"

Terry Nation sketched out some ideas for his Dalek television series in *The Dalek Outer Space Book* (1966), one of the 1960s Dalek annuals which didn't feature the Doctor. He resurrected the character of Sara Kingdom from "The Daleks' Masterplan" (1965), gave her the strength of ten men and the Space Security Service as military back-up to fight the Daleks. A pilot script was written. The new series was to be filmed in colour when *Doctor Who* was still shot on video and telecine in black and white. Studios were booked, pre-production began… and immediately ran into trouble. Nation turned to the BBC for financial help and for the loan of its Daleks. His company tried to place the new show on BBC 2, the only BBC channel to be broadcasting in colour. Its controller, David Attenborough, read the script, pronounced it "very exciting", a good adventure yarn in the *Doctor Who* tradition, and declined to show or invest in it as it was unsuitable for his channel. Nation eventually admitted defeat and his attempt to give the Daleks their own American series ran into the sands of Aridius. He did consider using the Daleks independently of the Doctor at the climax of series two of *Blake's Seven* when Blake and the evil Federation join forces to repel evil alien invaders. Why not the Daleks? Eventually, Nation opted for some rather dull shapeshifters who conveniently appeared most often as humanoids. The Daleks returned to *Doctor Who* after a gap of five years in "Day of the Daleks" (1972). Again, Nation didn't write the script but received a fee for the use of his creations. Dalek designer Raymond Cusick got bugger all as usual.

## Cyber designs and voices

The Cybermen featured in no fewer than four Patrick Troughton stories, some better than others. "The Moonbase" (1967), their second outing, was essentially a retread of their first appearance in Hartnell's last story "The Tenth Planet" (1966): the Cybermen attempt to infiltrate an Arctic base/moonbase in order to convert the humans within into Cybermen. It didn't especially help the Cybermen that their voices and appearance changed considerably for almost every story. The original Cybermen have been described as "rather absurd creatures" and looked as though they were the result of someone rooting around in the kitchen cupboards: they have silver bodies and chest units like reversed rucksacks, with a scaffolding-like head arrangement (not unlike the Robomen's) to hold up a massive torch. In fact, the design was an attempt to visualise Pedlar and Davis's intention that the Cybermen should be a parody of a human being. Human hands were visible – these were the only Cybermen whose actors didn't wear gloves – and the stocking masks over the actor's heads suggested the human features beneath. These Cybermen opened their mouths into a wide, static O shape to speak: the voices themselves were provided throughout the 1960s by actors elsewhere in the studio, and the combination of the static mouth and the weird, sing-song voice was both strange and disturbing. Pedlar's horror at humankind's dehumanisation as Cybermen was thus well realised[1].

Recognising that her first attempt wasn't entirely successful, Sandra Reid redesigned the creatures for their next appearance, giving them a more robotic look that was basically followed in all subsequent designs to the present. The scaffolding helmet was reduced in size to become the familiar "jug handles" shape; the cloth face became metal and the mouth was now a pillar box slit. However, Reid retained the eeriness of the Cybermen's speech: a panel behind the mouth, operated by the actor, slid down when the Cyberman began speaking and slid up only when it had finished, an effect which terrified the young Sophie Aldred, who was to play the seventh Doctor's companion Ace in the late 1980s. This new design

---

[1] These Mondasian Cybermen – Cybermen from Mondas – return in the 2017 story "World Enough and Time" and "The Doctor Falls". Steven Moffat admitted that the original Cybermen were the least effective design but they are brilliantly realised in these Peter Capaldi episodes. A plausible and logical end for the Doctor's companions is that they get consumed or killed by the horrors they encounter; companion Bill Potts succumbs to such a fate by being converted into a Cyberman.

lasted all of two stories (although the Cybermen seen in "The Tomb of the Cybermen" had a few ribbons added), before they were changed yet again for "The Wheel in Space" (1968), which introduced Zoe as the Doctor's companion. This story's Cybermen were so delicate that the pipes on the costumes kept breaking: the Cybermen become increasingly static as the six parter progresses as a consequence of the director's fear that even more of the costume would fall to bits. There was yet another redesign for "The Invasion" (1968), which added the ear muffs to the jug handles and became the basis for the Cybermen design used in "Revenge of the Cybermen" (1975) and the radical redesign for the 1980s stories from "Earthshock" (1982) onwards.

Unlike the Daleks, the Cybermen's voices changed from story to story. The original sing song chant was replaced by a buzzing voice created by the voice artistes putting a small buzzing disc – of the type slipped into the mouth by Punch and Judy men to produce Mr Punch's voice – and articulating the lines in virtual silence: the microphones picked up the rest. Voices were provided chiefly by Roy Skelton – who provided Dalek voices until the series' demise in 1989 and also voiced Bungle and Zippy in the children's series *Rainbow* – and Peter Hawkins, who also did Daleks and the eponymous hero of the cartoon *Captain Pugwash*. The Cybermen's 1960s voices, like so much of 1960s *Who*, were simple, strange and disturbing. When Russell T. Davies brought the Cybermen back for the second season of the revived *Doctor Who* in 2006 (*Rise of the Cybermen/The Age of Steel*), the regenerated show looked, as it did in so many ways, back to the 1960s for inspiration. Davies insisted that the new Cybermen should have the Pierrot teardrop added for "The Wheel in Space" and "The Invasion" as a sign that they were sad at what had happened to them: indeed, the newly converted Cyberman Yvonne Hartman weeps a tear of oil at her conversion in "Doomsday" (2006). The new Cybermen voices provided by Nicholas Briggs (who, like Peter Hawkins and Roy Skelton, also did Daleks, though not Zippy or Captain Pugwash) recalled the Troughton era voices. When a Cyberman begins to speak, an electric blue light (apparently Russell T Davies's favourite colour) snaps on behind the mouth and snaps off when he ceases, again recalling the effect in "The Moonbase" and "The Tomb of the Cybermen" that so terrified Sophie Aldred. Nicholas Briggs sent Davies an audio of about twenty slightly different Cybermen voices to choose from, all created – as was his Dalek voice – on his own ring modulator. Davies couldn't hear much difference between many of them and felt somewhat disorientated after listening to so many. By contrast, the actors who played Cybermen in "Revenge of the Cybermen" (1975) and the 1980s Cybermen stories provided their own voices, not always successfully. The Cyberleader in the former story, played by RSC actor Christopher Robbie, struts around with his hands on his hips and barks out his lines in a distinctly American accent. Graeme Harper, who directed "Rise of the Cybermen" (2006), said he thought the 1980s voices sounded like a bad Hollywood actor – a fair description of the plummy tones of David Banks, who played Cyberleaders in all of the 1980s stories.

Other monsters came and went as the production team, like their predecessors in the Hartnell era, wistfully tried to come up with a monster that would rival the Daleks in popularity. There were the Quarks – "Deadly, robot servants of the cruel Dominators" – who looked rather unfortunately like walking fridges. They were played by child actors, which accounted for their diminutive height, and piped their threats in feminine voices. The production team presumably thought highly of them as they are among the aliens the Doctor shows the Time Lords in a "thought channel" at his trial ("The War Games", 1969) as examples of the evil in the Universe that must be fought. *T.V. Comic* thought highly of them too and used them frequently, and without their humanoid Dominator masters (a rather dull race of humanoid conquerers), as the enemy in their dreadful *Dr Who* (sic) strip, which bore even less relation to the television series than the Peter Cushing movies. The comic used the Quarks without the permission of their creators, Mervyn Haisman and Henry Lincoln, who were understandably displeased. *TV Comic*'s editor had assumed that the rights to carry a *Doctor*

*Who* comic strip entitled him to use the programme's other intellectual property, which was of course copyright to individual, self-employed writers. Haisman and Lincoln's displeasure at the purloining of the Quarks eventually led them to part company with the *Doctor Who* production office.

## The Ice Warriors

More successful and enduring than the Quarks were the Ice Warriors. Rather quaintly, and in the traditions of H.G.Wells (whose novel *The Time Machine* had had more than a glancing influence in the show's genesis), these were inhabitants of the planet Mars and made their eponymous appearance in a 1967 serial. Martians in science fiction were passé even in 1967; if H.G.Wells's contemporaries had thought that the markings on the surface of the red planet were canals constructed by the Martians, even children knew better in 1967 and were aware that Mars was a lifeless rock. Scriptwriter Brian Hayles took this into account in "The Ice Warriors". In their first story, the Martians' spaceship landed on Earth many centuries ago, when there might conceivably have been life on Mars, and gets itself buried in a glacier. It is the Doctor's companion Jamie who names the Martians, Ice Warriors; the name apparently stuck with the humans and the production team, as they are invariably called Ice Warriors on screen in all their stories, perhaps to escape from the naivety of the name "Martians". The Ice Warriors are frozen in suspended animation and awoken by a process of ionisation in the twenty second century. This is an attempt by the humans to limit the impact of a new Ice Age – which occasionally replaced nuclear war in the 1960s and 1970s as the favourite feared apocalypse of popular imagination – by controlling the path of an advancing glacier: as it melts, it reveals the Ice Warriors' spaceship. The scientists' leader Clent has one of the ship's inhabitants, still trapped in a block of ice, brought back to the scientists' base for study (always a bad move in *Doctor Who*)[1]; the scientists speculate that he might be a Viking chieftain from examination of his mighty helmet. Of course, the creature thaws out and is revealed at the end of episode one to be still alive. Watching the episodes back to back, which was not possible when originally broadcast, it is obvious that the Ice Warrior's helmet and make up changes completely between episodes one and two.

Bernard Bresslaw, an actor best known for his appearances in the *Carry On* films, plays this Ice Warrior leader, Varga. He had just finished playing amorous berk Ken Biddle in *Carry On Doctor* before rehearsing "The Ice Warriors". Bresslaw was six feet seven inches tall, and is an impressive sight in his costume, towering menacingly over his captive, the Doctor's companion Victoria. He took the role seriously and considered the creature's design as inspiration for his performance: the reptilian Ice Warrior appears to have a soft skin, visible in its mouth and jaw parts, underneath an armoured exoskeleton (apparently inspired by a crocodile's back). Bresslaw used the creature's reptilian design to create its hissing, whispering voice, which recalled lizards and snakes for him. It was a simple and brilliantly effective decision and, like so much else in *Doctor Who*, immediately appealed to children who could copy both the voice and the Ice Warriors' lumbering gait. Here was something they could imitate in the playground while the Daleks were absent from the series. The Ice Warriors were frightening, strong and menacing, but fortunately so slow that the nimbler humans could run away from them: often a feature of *Who* monsters. Bresslaw also devised the Ice Warriors pulling their heads into their necks,

---

[1] Mark Gatiss repeats the scene in his 2013 story, "Cold War". Russian sailors on a nuclear-powered submarine are curious about a creature that appears to be embedded in a block of ice, so they bring it on board to thaw it out (oh dear…). They obviously hadn't watched "The Ice Warriors", a consequence of the fact that Soviet Russia didn't show *Doctor Who*, although Putin's Russia does. The entombed Ice Warrior escapes, of course. It is a sign of the much faster pace of the revived series' episodes that an incident which takes 25 minutes to tell in episode one of "The Ice Warriors" in 1967, is told in a three minute pre-credits teaser in 2013.

tortoise like, especially when they were disappointed or upset. Again, he appears to have been inspired by the design, which was reminiscent of a tortoise in the contrast between hard shell and soft inner parts. Uniquely in the four Ice Warrior stories, Bresslaw's Varga also has a wheezy giggle, which he utters as he puts the Doctor to death by withdrawing air from the ship's airlock.

Innes Lloyd, the producer, managed to secure the services of the famous actor Peter Barkworth to play Clent. BBC executive colleagues were impressed: first Marius Goring (as corrupt scientist Maxtible in "The Evil of the Daleks" (1967)), now Peter Barkworth. "When are you going to get Laurence Olivier in *Doctor Who*, Innes?" he was asked. Eighteen years later, producer John Nathan-Turner heard rumours that Olivier was interested in appearing in the programme. He thought of offering him the part of the mutant in "Revelation of the Daleks" (1985); perhaps Lord Olivier, by now frail and elderly, didn't fancy a winter shoot near an icy pond in hideous make up and the part was taken by someone else. It seems a shame that Nathan-Turner didn't think of Olivier for Rassilon's cameo in "The Five Doctors" (1983).

## Saving money

The Ice Warriors returned in the following year's story "The Seeds of Death" (1969) a story heavily rewritten by script editor Terrance Dicks from Hayles's original script. Dicks apologised profusely to Hayles for the necessity of the rewrites and recalls that Hayles, after letting him explain at length, asked him if he was a Catholic. Dicks replied that he wasn't, and Hayles, who was, said his lengthy breast-beating had suggested a Catholic sensibility and he wasn't to worry as he, Hayles, didn't mind at all. "The Seeds of Death" was a money-saving exercise: reusing the expensive Ice Warrior suits would save the team from having to design and build a new set of aliens, although there was enough money in the pot to create a new type of Ice Warrior. This was the Ice Lord, an aristocratic Martian in charge of the others, whose helmet only covered part of his face and lacked the plebeian warriors' jaw piece. He was played by Alan Bennion, who returned as Ice Lords for the two Jon Pertwee Ice Warrior tales.

After "The Ice Warriors", "The Seeds of Death" is something of a disappointment. Set on yet another moonbase, it recalls the events of "The Moonbase" a few years earlier, with the Ice Warriors replacing the Cybermen. It is yet another Base Under Siege story and the Ice Warriors could really be swapped for any monster. Gerry Davis, who had introduced this sub-genre with "The Tenth Planet" in 1966, argued that one of its advantages was making the best use of the show's limited budget. Instead of building lots of small sets, most of the money went on one large, showcase set: the gravitron control room in "The Moonbase", the Ioniser control room in "The Ice Warriors" or the T-Mat control room in "The Seeds of Death". While these large sets are impressive for television science fiction in the 1960s – and similar in function and spectacle, although on a much smaller scale, to the massive villains' lairs of contemporary James Bond films – they did take up much of the available studio space.

One consequence of the major sets, Davis noted, was that they took up room which might have been available for the large TARDIS interior set: thus many of the 1960s stories stay out of the TARDIS's interior as much as possible or, when they do feature it, limit it to a couple of roundelled flats and the control console. Similarly, in the show's final season of its initial run in 1989, the TARDIS interior is only briefly shown in one story, "Battlefield". By this point, the set was so bashed about that it only comprised one flat and the console; low level lighting was employed to hide the flaws. The revived, post-2005 series avoided the problem entirely by having the TARDIS interior as a standing set (and saved money by featuring it all the time, especially in extra scenes shot for *Children in Need* and DVD specials). The new TARDIS set seen in "The Snowmen" (2012) was built in the series' new studio home in Roach Loch, Cardiff Bay, the BBC "Drama Village". It hadn't been possible to move Matt Smith's first TARDIS set from the previous studio at Upper Boat, so the opportunity was taken to redesign the set and return to the machine look of the 1970s serials, thus moving away from the idea that the TARDIS was organic and, in the tenth Doctor's words, "Grown, not built" ("The Satan Pit", 2006). This was the only TARDIS set to have been built in 360 degrees: all the others had been missing the "fourth wall" to allow the cameras to film, but the Smith/Capaldi set was self-contained. The TARDIS interior blew up again at the end of "Twice Upon A Time" (2017) and the BBC released a time lapse video of the set being dismantled.

## Yeti

The other highly regarded Troughton monsters were the Yeti, who featured in "The Abominable Snowmen" (1967) and returned, slightly redesigned, in "The Web of Fear" the following year. Only one episode of "The Abominable Snowmen" survived the vandals' sledgehammer frenzy of destruction of the BBC archives[1]. The Yeti are robot servants of the disembodied Great Intelligence, an amorphous alien body which seeks physical manifestation: first, in a Tibetan monastery in the 1930s and, second, in the London Underground in the 1960s. Both stories featured Jack Watling as Mr, later Professor, Travers, a professor of anthropology who leads an expedition to search for the Yeti in the 1930s and returns to battle their robot counterparts in contemporary London. Watling was the father of Deborah Watling, who played Victoria, and said it was very strange to run down a Welsh mountain away from the Yeti, to be confronted by her dad at the bottom[2]. "The Abominable Snowmen" featured one of the programme's first extensive shoots in Wales, where the actors froze and envied the Yeti in their lovely fur costumes. Local children, who had come along to watch the shoot, were far from being frightened of the Yeti: Troughton recalled that they thought they were lovely and kept patting their fur. He counted

---

[1] David Troughton reads the novelisations of both Yeti stories on BBC audio and download, and his realisation of his father's voice is a flawless delight.
[2] See the *Radio Times* Doctor Who *Tenth Anniversary Special* (1973)

them as his favourite monster. One of the Yeti was played by extra John Levene, who also played Cybermen in the 1960s. He was eventually promoted to the role of Corporal Benton in "The Invasion" (1968), who became a regular UNIT character – Sergeant, then Warrant Officer, Benton – in the 1970s. Director Douglas Camfield praised his hard work, unfailing co-operation, and the fact that he, unlike other extras, didn't keep asking for a pay rise; hence he sanctioned his promotion out of the monster suit, into the human character.

The popularity of the Yeti ensured their quick return in "The Web of Fear" (1968). The Great Intelligence has now re-established its link with the Earth via a Yeti that is reactivated in a museum. This is achieved by the placing of its control unit, a small sphere, in the Yeti's chest: an image which terrified the young Paul McGann, who became the eighth Doctor, and who confused the Yeti control sphere with the image of Jesus revealing his sacred heart which he saw every Sunday in his Catholic church. The Yeti wreak havoc in the London Underground and cause the evacuation of the capital while the army tries to deal with the menace.

This scenario recalled the late Hartnell story "The War Machines" and set the template for Jon Pertwee's first three seasons, as well as providing story elements that are with us today. One of the regular army officers fighting the Yeti was a certain Colonel Lethbridge-Stewart, a talented soldier who is initially suspicious of the Doctor and even suspects him of being behind the menace. He was originally to be played by *Upstairs, Downstairs* actor David Langton, but Langton dropped out and Nicholas Courtney, who had been cast as Captain Knight, was promoted into the part. He was still playing Lethbridge-Stewart forty three years later[1].

Director Douglas Camfield sought London Underground's permission to shoot in the tube's tunnels, perhaps in the early hours

---

[1] Although "The Web of Fear" was returned to the archives in 2013, it lacked episode three, which introduced Lethbridge Stewart. As Gloucester says in *King Lear* : "As flies to wanton boys are we to the gods:/ They taunt us for their sport". (*King Lear* IV, I – adapted).

of the morning when the trains weren't running. London Transport either refused, or demanded an outrageous fee (accounts vary), so the BBC built the tunnels themselves. These were so realistic that, after the story had been broadcast, the BBC received a letter from an angry London Transport threatening to sue them for filming in their tunnels after all.

It might be suggested that, if running up and down corridors is a standard *Doctor Who* technique to fill up the running time of flagging scripts, then fleeing down tube tunnels from the Yeti is an example of filling six episodes by running up and down *extremely long* corridors. Having said that, the Yeti in the Underground is one of the programme's enduring and iconic images. It is recalled by the general viewer of the original series in the same breath as the Daleks gliding over Westminster Bridge; the Cybermen marching down the steps of St Paul's Cathedral; the Sea Devils rising from the waters, and the giant maggots rearing out of the green slime. The former captain of the English cricket team Mike Gatting[1], a *Doctor Who* fan as a child and an adult, said that he had just got used to travelling on the tube on his own; his mother would give him the fare and tell him to sit close to the guards' compartment, for security. At this point, he watched "The Web of Fear" on television, and his new-found confidence deserted him.

"The Web of Fear" was well received by the press and the public. A third Yeti serial was planned, and Jack Watling's Professor Travers character was scheduled to appear in the next alien invasion of the home counties story, "The Invasion" (1968). Watling was unavailable, however, and a replacement professor was shoehorned into the script. At this point, the Yeti's creators, Mervyn Haisman and Henry Lincoln, fell out with the BBC over copyright issues. Although their next story "The Dominators", which introduced the Quarks, was filmed, they refused to give permission for their names to be used as writers, and the serial went out under the pseudonym of Norman Ashby. The Great Intelligence returned in the 2012 Christmas special "The Snowmen" in its first encounter with the

---

[1] Speaking on the BBC documentary *Thirty Years in the TARDIS* (1993).

Doctor and his third encounter with it. It returned again in "The Name of the Doctor" (2013), again played by one Richard E. Grant.

## No more adventures in space and time...?

The production team noted the success of "The Web of Fear". Plans were afoot to reshape *Doctor Who*. The team was feeling the strain of making so many episodes every year and the small budget was heavily overstretched with the need to come up with different alien environments every four or six weeks. Script editor Terrance Dicks recalled that Derrick Sherwin, the new producer, kept commissioning stories and then rejecting them, even if they had been rewritten several times. Poor scripts, or scripts which were not ready, sometimes had to go into production. When director David Maloney was handed the script for a humorous serial about a prison in space, he protested, saying the script was terrible. Couldn't he make something else instead? The crafty Dicks had kept a script from new writer (and former policeman) Robert Holmes up his sleeve as a fall back. This was "The Krotons", originally submitted to the BBC as a science fiction play that had no connection with *Doctor Who*. Dicks, only too aware, and exasperated by, the problems of finding workable scripts, had worked on "The Krotons" with Holmes as a possible stop-gap, rewriting it for *Doctor Who*. It was eventually broadcast over the new year of 1968-9. This intelligent science fiction script is sadly buried by grotesque over-acting and the ludicrous design of the Krotons themselves, which Dicks described as possibly the worst ever *Doctor Who* monster. Crystalline in origin, the Krotons on screen look like supermarket cartons decorated with egg boxes, topped off with a revolving lampshade. The only redeeming feature is their splendid voices, provided again by Roy Skelton, who based it on a South African sergeant major. The command that rings through the humanoids' learning hall at the episode one – "Stop! This is a warning. Leave the learning hall. All Gonds leave the learning hall now!" – is arresting, hilarious and eminently imitable. The South African accent was also an astute choice, linked as it now was then with the oppression of apartheid and appropriate for a villainous alien race. The show returned to apartheid imagery in the Jon Pertwee story "The Mutants" (1972), where the Mutts and the Overlords were subject to a policy of separate development. In a remarkable twist of fate, the human Overlords, who had colonised the planet, got the best of everything and left the indigenous Mutts in poverty. Writers Bob Baker and Dave Martin, who hated apartheid, had wanted to call the aliens Munts, a racist nickname for black people originating in Rhodesia (now Zimbabwe). Someone at the BBC got cold feet about this and insisted they changed the name to Mutts. This was an aberration of a decision as the BBC was usually quite happy to offend the racist Apartheid regime in South Africa. A 1970s episode of the hugely popular comedy *The Goodies*[1] (1970-1982) featured Philip Madoc as a ludicrously racist South African colonel, who played the piano: the black keys were all at one end, and the white keys all at the other. The South African Embassy protested at this insult to its government, as it always did when anyone made a satirical joke about apartheid, and the BBC had to explain patiently, for the umpteenth time, that we had free speech in Britain (which translates, roughly, as "get stuffed"). Perhaps whoever it was at the BBC who insisted Baker and Martin turned down the satire had thought satire unsuitable in what was, as everybody knew, a children's programme. This was a daft decision, given that satires has always been a staple genre mined by the show, and one that betrayed Sydney Newman's desire that *Doctor Who* should educate as well as entertain. Parents explaining to their children that the new *Doctor Who* story was actually about oppression in South Africa would have been fantastic for children's political education, but the middle classes in the 1970s thought that it was not nice to talk about

---

[1] *The Goodies* is much less well remembered now than *Monty Python's Flying Circus*, but it was as inventive and funny in its way and regularly garnered more viewers. It was also on BBC 1: *Python* was on the minority interest channel, BBC 2, probably because it was considered too weird to suit the mass audience.

politics as it was a private matter between the adult and the ballot box.

Back in 1968, the *Doctor Who* production team felt oppressed by the need to find suitable scripts and the smallness of the budget. They were unhappy with the unconvincing realisation of alien worlds. If *Doctor Who* was to survive into the 1970s, they reasoned, it needed to be reshaped. The success of "The Web of Fear" led to the decision to ground the Doctor on Earth, where the home counties could double as the home counties rather than other planets, and money could be saved on sets. Derrick Sherwin had enjoyed Nicholas Courtney's performance as the Colonel: would he consider returning as a regular character? Courtney, wise like any actor to the advantages of regular work, agreed. Lethbridge-Stewart, now promoted to Brigadier, returned in "The Invasion" in 1968 as the head of the British section of the United Nations Intelligence Taskforce or UNIT, an international army dealing with the alien, "the odd, the unexplained". The army, with the Doctor, foil an attempted invasion of contemporary Earth by the Cybermen ("The Invasion", 1968); Kevin Stoney, who had played galactic super villain Mavic Chen in "The Daleks' Master Plan" (1965-6), returned to give a splendid performance as treacherous industrialist Tobias Vaughn, who aids and betrays the Cybermen in a double-crossing attempt to rule the world himself.

By 1969, viewing figures were sagging dangerously around the three million mark and serious consideration was given by the BBC to cancelling the series: after all, it had been on for six years, which was a good run for a television show, and the star wanted to leave. Wiser counsels prevailed and *Doctor Who* was renewed for another season. The number of episodes would be cut from around forty to about twenty-five a year, thus ending Sydney Newman's conception of a continuing, year-round serial of adventures in space and time. All of this, it was hoped, with the new Earth-bound setting, would save money. It didn't.

Strangely enough, *Doctor Who* wasn't under the most severe threat of cancellation at the end of its sixth season, Patrick

Troughton's last, but at the end of Jon Pertwee's successful first season, and the series' seventh, when the viewing figures had picked up healthily and Pertwee had been acclaimed in the role. Script editor Terrance Dicks and new producer Barry Letts were instructed by the BBC to come up with a Saturday evening replacement serial in 1970. One of their ideas was for a *Crocodile Dundee*-like serial featuring a bush Australian in modern London. This was a similar concept to the BBC's *Adam Adamant Lives!* (1966-1967) which Verity Lambert had produced on leaving *Doctor Who*, featuring a revived Victorian adventurer loose in contemporary, swinging London. It was intended to have been a rival fantasy show to ITV's *The Avengers*, but suffered from being made on video when *The Avengers* enjoyed the greater flexibility and enhanced look of film; it was also considered by many as frankly odd and was cancelled after only one season. Dicks and Letts also thought about remaking Nigel Kneale's *Quatermass* series of the 1950s and arranged a viewing in the BBC's internal cinemas. They considered the original productions to be ludicrously dated, a strange perspective from today's point of view, when Kneale's series are highly regarded and repeated exposure to early television on VHS and DVD has taught us to be tolerant of vintage production values. Perhaps, however, Dicks and Letts' viewing of the old *Quatermass* serials bore some fruit, as the new team's plots ruthlessly plundered *Quatermass* in 1970s *Doctor Who*s, much to Nigel Kneale's irritation. The 1988 story "Remembrance of the Daleks" also makes a reference to Quatermass, this time as a character in the *Doctor Who* universe. Contemplating a Dalek infiltration of London in 1963 and bewildered about how to find an appropriate response, one character says to another: "I wish Bernard was here." "The British Rocket Group's got its own problems," she replies. Bernard is Quatermass's first name and the British Rocket Group is his creation.

Eventually, Dicks and Letts reported their inability to find a good concept to replace *Who* and the show was renewed for an eighth season. It went on from strength to strength as a mainstay of Saturday tea time viewing for the rest of the 1970s, and was not seriously threatened with cancellation until the arrival of Michael Grade (aka He Who Must Not Be Named) at the BBC in the mid-1980s (see chapter eleven).

## "The War Games"

The Doctor would have become UNIT's scientific adviser even if Troughton had continued in the role. As it was, he was ready to leave after three years. Terrance Dicks and Malcolm Hulke were tasked with writing a replacement script for a four part and a six part story which had, as was common at the time, fallen through. They very quickly came up with the epic adventure "The War Games" (1969), an example of how tight deadlines and necessity can focus creativity, here to create one of the series' best stories.

"The War Games" starts with the TARDIS landing in No Man's Land in the First World War. The Doctor, Jamie and Zoe are initially welcomed by friendly British soldiers, but the mysterious General Smythe hypnotises his officers into believing that they are deserters and German spies. The Doctor is apparently shot by firing squad at the end of episode one. Smythe is in fact a member of the War Lords, a race of aliens who have been abducting soldiers from different wars in Earth's history, transplanting them to an unnamed planet and leaving them to fight out their wars to the death. The War Lords' devilish plot is to bring together the survivors into one huge army and use it to conquer the galaxy. This potty scheme doesn't bear much scrutiny – won't the survivors be injured or exhausted? – so the story cracks along at a brisk pace to distract the viewer from the daft central premise. The TARDIS crew pass through one time zone to the next, encountering Roman soldiers and Confederates and Yankees from the American Civil War. Some of the soldiers have resisted the War Lords' conditioning and are able to pass through the time zones, recruiting similar veterans into a resistance to fight the War Lords.

In one excellent idea among so many, the War Lords are helped by the War Chief, played by Edward Brayshaw, who was to find fame

119

as Mr Meaker in the BBC children's series *Rentaghost* (1976-1984), where he would sport a similarly alarming gringo moustache. The War Chief is a member of the Doctor's own race, who provides the War Lords with the space/time machines (apparently called SIDRATs, though not named as such on screen) required to ship the soldiers from Earth. Brought face to face with the Doctor, he proclaims: "You may have changed your appearance, but I know who you are." The Doctor is unmoved and unafraid: "Oh, do you?" The principle that members of the Doctor's race can recognise each other whatever their outward appearance is thus established: in "Terror of the Autons" (1971), the Master has no trouble recognising the Doctor, although he presumably has not previously encountered his third incarnation; in "The Deadly Assassin" (1976), Runciple the Fatuous recognises the Fourth Doctor and asks him if he's had a facelift.

Eventually, the War Lords are defeated by the resistance. Unable to send all the soldiers back to their own time on his own, the Doctor calls for help to his own people, the Time Lords. This is the first time they are named and the question implied by the programme's title – Doctor *Who*? – is answered after six years. The Doctor explains to Jamie that the Time Lords have immense powers: they have the secret of time and space travel, "we can live for ever, barring accidents", and that he ran away from them because he was bored. With all their great power, all the Time Lords ever do is observe; this wasn't enough for the Doctor, with a whole universe to explore, countless times, places and people to visit. He stole a TARDIS and fled.

It is suggested by the narrative of "The War Games" that the Time Lords were conceived in opposition to the War Lords; if the latter are the lords of war, the former are the lords of time. The Doctor has broken two of their laws: first, he stole a TARDIS (which was broken and in for repairs, which explains its unreliable steering and stuck chameleon circuit, and why the Doctor was able to get his hands on it in the first place[1]); second, that he broke the most important law of the Time Lords by interfering in the affairs of other races. The Doctor is well aware that he risks sacrificing his freedom: by calling for the Time Lords' aid at the end of episode nine, he also gives away his own location in time and space and spends much of the rest of the story trying to escape from the Time Lords' grasp. In episode ten, the War Lord – an icy study of evil from the wonderful Philip Madoc – is tried by the Time Lords, who find his scheme diabolical, dematerialise him and place a force field around his planet so that it can no longer be a threat. They then turn their attention to the Doctor, who is put on trial.

In one of the series' best scenes, the Doctor mounts a defence of his actions and the programme's support of the just war theory: it is sometimes necessary to use violence to defeat evil. "True, I am guilty of interference, just as you are guilty of failing to use your great powers to help those in need." The Time Lords accept his defence and agree that there is evil in the universe that must be fought. The Doctor is hopeful: "You mean you're going to let me go?" Not entirely: the court's sentence is that the Doctor is to be sent to the planet Earth in the twentieth century, a world more vulnerable than the others, in exile, for as long as the Time Lords think fit. For that time, the secret of the TARDIS will be taken from him. The Doctor protests that he is known on Earth and it will be very embarrassing for him: the Time Lords reply that his appearance will change again as part of the sentence. When shown a succession of faces to choose from – thus establishing that Time Lords can have some choice in their appearance and partly excusing the dreadful regeneration scene in "Destiny of the Daleks" (1979) – the Doctor makes trouble and rejects the lot. Patrick Troughton's last moments as the Doctor have him spinning in a void, protesting, as the Time Lords choose his new body for him and send him into exile. There

---

[1] The moment when he actually nicks the TARDIS is shown in "The Name of the Doctor" (2013). One of the Clara Oswalds directs the first Doctor (realised here by incorporating original footage of Hartnell in the part) to a TARDIS which will be much better than the one he was going to pick at first.

is no transformation scene of Troughton morphing into Pertwee, which is a little odd as Pertwee had been cast by this point: perhaps the budget hadn't run to paying his fee for a cameo appearance. We get our first glimpse of the third Doctor in 1970 in episode one of "Spearhead from Space": the TARDIS lands in a wood, the doors open, Pertwee stumbles out and promptly collapses. The series was now in colour, for those privileged viewers who could afford to rent or buy colour television (it is a sign of the Master's villainous extravagance that he insists on a *colour* television for his cell in 1972's *The Sea Devils*).

Meanwhile, there was the summer break to get through while science fiction audiences had to endure Saturday evenings without *Doctor Who*. The BBC filled the gap in the schedule with a new science fiction series, imported from the United States.

I wonder if you have heard of it? It was called *Star Trek*.

# 5
# Exiled to Earth – in Colour!

The Doctor bitterly resented his exile to Earth: the new production team wasn't too happy about it either. In the end, it lasted for the seventh and eighth seasons. Terrance Dicks, continuing as script editor from the Troughton era, explained the show's new remit to his friend Malcolm Hulke. He had boarded with Hulke in the 1960s while learning his craft as a writer and the older Hulke had acted as something of a mentor. They wrote some scripts for *The Avengers* together and collaborated on "The War Games" in 1969. Hulke, who went on to write some of the best Pertwee scripts, considered Dicks's description of the new structure for *Doctor Who*, sucked on his pipe and concluded: "Right, that basically leaves you with two plots: invasion from outer space or mad scientist." In fact, writers in the early seventies brilliantly undermined the series' self-imposed limitations. Hulke himself broke the mould in the second Pertwee story "Doctor Who and the Silurians" (1970), where the monsters were not alien invaders but had always been here, dormant and buried beneath the Earth. The Silurians were reptilian bipeds from the age of the dinosaurs, frozen for millions of years and awakened as a side effect of human technology (shades of Varga in "The Ice Warriors").

When interviewed, Jon Pertwee often told the story of how he contacted his agent when he heard that Patrick Troughton was going to leave the programme[1]. He wanted to put his own name forward; his agent wasn't sure this was the right career move, but phoned the BBC anyway and asked if they had considered his client, Jon Pertwee. There was silence from the other end. "Don't worry," Pertwee's agent said, "it's probably not a very good idea". "No, it's just that we're staggered," came the reply. "He's one of the two at the top of our list." The first choice was Ron Moody, fresh from his

---

[1] For example, in his one man show *An Evening with Jon Pertwee* (1996).

success as Fagin in the film of *Oliver!* One version of the story is that Moody was offered the part and turned it down. Much later in his career, he is said to have told Tom Baker he wished he'd accepted it. Jon's son, the actor Sean Pertwee, said that his father was simultaneously offered the role of the Doctor and Captain Mainwaring in *Dad's Army*; his father, he said, had been glad to have taken the former as playing Mainwaring would have deprived the world of Arthur Lowe's wonderful performance[1].

In 1969, Pertwee was identified as a comic actor who provided a range of voices to the long-running BBC radio series *The Navy Lark*, inspired in part by his experience in the navy in the Second World War. He had featured in three *Carry On* films[2] and in West Ends hits like *A Funny Thing Happened on the Way to the Forum*. Given the slant of his career, it seems possible that producer Derrick Sherwin was looking to replace Troughton with a like-for-like replacement, inflected towards comedy. If this was the plan, Pertwee's reading of the part was quite different and he tended to play the Doctor deadly straight. The third Doctor has been bracketed with action heroes like James Bond – both loved gadgets and raced around in motor boats and motorbikes, thought the BBC's budget would hardly run to the hardware employed by Bond in the movies. The social commentator Bidisha has affectionately referred to Pertwee's Doctor as "a chap" – a decent, upright Englishman you could reply on – and Paul Cornell once referred to him disparagingly as "a Tory", presumably a reference to the Doctor's name-dropping references to London gentlemen's clubs and his love of good cheese and wine[3]. Sartorially, the third Doctor's flamboyance was of a piece with Jason King in *Department S* or even Adam Adamant from Verity Lambert's old show. Publicity photos of Pertwee's Doctor

---

[1] Sean Pertwee speaking on *This Morning*, ITV 6th May 2016. *Dad's Army* ran on BBC 1 from 1968 to 1977, so Lowe played Mainwaring for even longer than Pertwee played the Doctor. As he was cast as the Doctor in 1969, Pertwee's anecdote conflates the timing to a degree.

[2] *Carry On Cleo* (1964), *Carry on Cowboy* (1965) and *Carry On Screaming* (1966).

[3] See, for example, the television story "Day of the Daleks" (1972) and the novelisation *Doctor Who and the Day of the Daleks* (1974).

tended to show him with hands on his hips, handsome face set in a quizzical expression with a jutting chin, flowing cape and ruffled shirt billowing in the wind. Colin Baker once identified the third Doctor as the least humorous of all the Doctors, but Pertwee's had a dry wit and sometimes relaxed into comic business. In "Spearhead from Space", his first story, the Doctor sings tunelessly in the hospital shower before nicking other people's clothes to dress himself [1]. Once the third Doctor had been firmly established as a serious fellow in the viewers' eyes, he could have some fun. Pertwee's penchant for funny voices is exploited in "The Green Death" (1973), in which he disguises himself as an elderly Welsh milkman in order to infiltrate the murderous Global Chemicals: shades here of Troughton's early use of disguises, but here employed at the end of the Doctor's career rather than the beginning and demonstrating confidence in Pertwee rather than, as with Troughton, early uncertainty about how the part should be played. Tom Baker said that, in considering how to play an alien with secrets and unutterable strangeness, he had decided to play it as Tom Baker; Pertwee similarly said, "I am Doctor Who and he is me." By contrast, Barry Letts explained that Patrick Troughton had given a performance as the Doctor, and that it was nothing like Troughton as a person.

Although Dicks and Letts were unenthusiastic about the Earth-bound setting, Pertwee embraced it enthusiastically, at least in public. "There's nothing more alarming than coming home to find a Yeti sitting on your loo in Tooting Bec" (a rather run down area of south London), he said in early interviews. This pointed to the contrast between the alien and the everyday that the 1970s stories exploited so successfully, following the template established in "The War Machines" (1966), "The Web of Fear" (1968) and "The Invasion" (1968). Chris Chibnall presumably remembered Pertwee's remark when he came to write the "red button" mini-episode "Pond Life" – featuring the home life of the eleventh Doctor's companions

---

[1] A sequence reprised for the eighth Doctor in the 1976 TV movie and for the eleventh Doctor in "The Eleventh Hour" (2010).

Amy and Rory – to accompany the 2012 season. Opening his bathroom door early in the morning, Rory does a double-take when he sees an Ood sitting on the loo, blinking at him piteously.

The seventh season surrounded the Doctor with an ensemble cast of UNIT personnel who would carry the story with him. The Brigadier returned, initially with a different Captain for every story, including Paul Darrow in "Doctor Who and the Silurians": Darrow would eventually find fame as the second, and then first, lead in *Blake's Seven*. Sergeants came and went too, although Corporal Benton, who had featured in a small way in "Invasion" (1968), reappeared in "The Ambassadors of Death" and "Inferno" (both 1970). The regulars settled down in the eighth season and Captain Mike Yates was introduced as a possible love interest for Jo Grant. Ian Marter auditioned for the part, was seriously considered and was eventually cast by Barry Letts three years later as the fourth Doctor's companion Harry Sullivan. Richard Franklin played Captain Yates and Sergeant Benton became the regular, resident sergeant.

## "I'm your new assistant!"

Responding in a small way to the growth of feminism (or Women's Liberation as it was sometimes known back then), Pertwee's first companion was a very clever and capable scientist, Dr Liz Shaw. Sensibly clad in a suit for her first story, Liz was a far cry from some of the 1960s companions, whose primary purpose sometimes appeared to be to be attractive, get captured and get rescued. In "Spearhead from Space" (1970), Brigadier Alistair Gordon Lethbridge-Stewart approaches Liz to be UNIT's scientific adviser when he is unable to locate the Doctor, his first choice. She is immediately intrigued by the landing of two showers of meteorites in the same wood in Essex, knowing that the odds against such a thing are scientifically unacceptable. She takes little nonsense from the Brigadier and stands up to the Doctor as an equal, at least in the first story: she becomes more of an assistant for the rest of the season and the Brigadier later tells the Doctor[1] she sees her role as "holding your test tubes and telling you how brilliant you are." Caroline John played the role beautifully as a scientist as near the Doctor's intellectual equal as it is possible to be. Presumably in an attempt to be as glamorous as the assistants of old, she affects mini-skirts and a huge hat in "The Ambassadors of Death" (1970). However, Barry Letts considered that her role in the series was limited: as she was clever, the Doctor had no need to explain things to her, and as she was capable of looking after herself, the opportunities for her to get captured and to need rescuing were limited.

Not much of this could be said for the new companion Jo Grant (Katy Manning), who joined the Doctor in "Terror of the Autons" (1971), the first story of season eight, and was capable of falling over when running through a perfectly flat field in "The Daemons" at the end of her first season. Liz was unceremoniously written out in the gap between seasons: perhaps her lack of a proper farewell was explained by the production team's uncertainty about whether there actually would be an eighth season, as *Doctor Who* came under its most serious threat of cancellation at the end of Pertwee's first year. In fact, Caroline John was expecting her first child when her final stories were shot and might have had to leave the series anyway, at least temporarily[2].

Jo Grant was deliberately conceived as the antithesis of Liz. On her first meeting with the Doctor, she ruins the experiment he's working on, putting out his welding of the TARDIS's dematerialisation circuit with a fire extinguisher. The Doctor is horrified and tells the Brigadier that she's got to go. In fact, she stayed for three seasons. In a witty piece of scripting, Jo similarly ruins the experiment of Professor Clifford Jones when she encounters him in her last story, "The Green Death" (1973). He is trying to find a cure for the disease caused by the giant maggots and

---

[1] In "Terror of the Autons" (1971).
[2] Her husband, Geoffrey Beevers, played a UNIT corporal in "The Ambassadors of Death", and appeared as the Master in "The Keeper of Traken" (1981).

has prepared microscope slides of their slime; Jo knocks a jar of his nutritious fungus all over them and he is furious. As it was with the Doctor, Jo's ruining of a scientific experiment is clearly part of an unconscious courtship ritual. She eventually marries Professor Jones, describing him to the Doctor as "like a younger you." The Doctor bids her farewell and silently leaves her engagement party early; he climbs into Bessie and drives off into the sunset. In the novelisation of this story, Malcolm Hulke articulated that which had been implied for the three years Jo had been part of the series: that in their time together, the Doctor had come to love her very much. Yet the love is not mentioned – it never needs to be – and is a far cry from Rose and Martha's noisy pining after the Doctor in the revived series. Similarly, his silent exit at the end of "The Green Death" is much more touching than the endless farewells of "Doomsday" (2006) and "The End of Time" part two (2010). Some fans found the companions' later love for the Doctor tiresome and considered it got in the way of telling the story. The implied love between the Doctor and Jo, and later the Doctor and Sarah, might be preferred as it never pushed the adventure to one side.

Jo is apparently about nineteen years old when we first encounter her. She tells the Doctor that she took General Science at A level (a contrast to the degrees taken by Liz); she later tells him "I didn't say I passed." The production team was delighted with Katy Manning's performance and she was a great favourite and friend of Pertwee's. Indeed, the whole cast apparently got on very well together and there was much fun and larking about on the set, sometimes to the irritation of the people who were trying to get the show in the can. The warmth between the regulars can perhaps be seen in the performances each gives in the UNIT stories. There seems to be little rivalry between the actors and they graciously give space for each other's performances: something that wasn't always so in a show that was so obviously a star vehicle as *Doctor Who*. We might again contrast *Star Trek*, where William Shatner – Captain Kirk – allegedly insisted on hogging the close ups and the best lines, much to the alleged rage of his co-stars[1]. Jo was a popular companion with children, who immediately identified with her gentleness and quietly expressed love for the Doctor. The relationship between them was that of a father and daughter, or perhaps an affectionate uncle and neice, and the Doctor, in the tall, handsome and protective form of Jon Pertwee, became a father figure for millions of children in a way that his two predecessors had, arguably, not managed. I remember talking in the playground at the end of my primary school years about Elisabeth Sladen's departure as Sarah in 1976: many of my friends had much preferred Jo to the sometimes spiky Sarah and several of them remembered how they had cried when she left in 1973. "I cheered when Sarah went," said one ingrate.

Popular as Jo was with children, her inclusion in the series did move its trajectory more firmly towards the younger audience. This is a problem for some fans, who are keen for the programme to be seen as a serious piece of science fiction: it wasn't a problem for the children watching at the time. I remember finding Liz a bit too serious: as a small child, watching her and Pertwee together was another example of watching the bewildering rituals and antics of grown-ups which were before me every day. Jo was a helping hand back into the series for younger children. She was no intellectual, so the Doctor could explain the story to her; although she was resourceful and bright, she also got captured and got into trouble, so the Doctor had to come and rescue her. She is easily hypnotised by the Master in "Terror of the Autons" (1971) and nearly succeeds in bombing the Doctor's lab; she leads a raid on the IMC spaceship in "Colony in Space" (1971) and is captured by their captain and cruel security chief.

**Now on the small screen – in Colour! (If you could afford it.)**

Much has been written about the excitement of season seven being the first season of *Doctor Who* to be made in colour, but this had less impact than might be expected on British viewers when it was

---

[1] See William Shatner, *Star Trek Memories*, Harper, 2009

first broadcast. Most people still watched television in black and white. Only about half the broadcast programmes were actually made in colour in 1970, sets were prohibitively expensive to buy and a colour television licence cost much more than a black and white one. Renting a colour set was a more popular alternative than buying one, but still beyond the budgets of many Britons on average and below average incomes. Colour brought the advantage of Colour Separation Overlay (CSO or chromakey) to the production team. CSO was the BBC in-house name for what is now universally called green screen, although the favoured keying-in colour was usually blue at the BBC. Indeed, it could be said that 1970s *Doctor Who* over-relied on this effect, which was much cheaper than Inlay (the black and white equivalent) and much easier to realise in the studio. There are some gloriously psychedelic and seriously trippy moments in early Pertwee stories, achieved through CSO: the caves of Sondergaard in "The Mutants" will blow your mind, man.

All this said, colour television for many viewers was a far from daily treat. My family didn't get its first colour set until 1980. I vividly remember walking into the living room and thinking that there was something wrong with the new television, which was showing the cricket, although I couldn't work out what it was: it was, in fact, that the pictures were now in colour. Episode one of "The Leisure Hive" (1980) was the first *Doctor Who* I was able to watch at home, in colour. From "Frontier in Space" (1973) onwards, a kind family friend had invited my twin brother and me to watch *Doctor Who* at her house, in colour. She also provided coke and crisps, and the pairing of these with Jon Pertwee episodes constituted no better earthly happiness when you were eight years old. It is probably impossible to convey the extraordinary experience of seeing programmes in colour to people not brought up to take it for granted. Why, I nearly exploded with excitement when I saw that the crew of the Starship Enterprise wore different coloured jumpers.

**Stateside sales**

It might be suggested that *Doctor Who* was shot in colour, as were later series of *The Avengers*, to make it easier to export the show overseas and particularly to the largest world market for television programmes: the United States. Unlike *The Avengers*, however, *Doctor Who* was never sold to an American network (broadcasting nationally rather than locally), not least because it was made on video and the Americans, having a different video system from the British, tended to dismiss British shows made on video as cheap and tedious to convert. *The Avengers*, for example, only secured its place on an American network when it abandoned video and adopted (black and white) film for Diana Rigg's first season in 1965; the Honor Blackman and Ian Hendry episodes, made on video, never reached the US networks and American viewers considered season four of *The Avengers* to be a new show. Pertwee *Doctor Who*s were shown overseas, but often in commonwealth countries which had compatible video technology (like Australia and New Zealand) or television stations that only broadcast in black and white, like Nigeria. As with the Hartnell and Troughton episodes, film copies of all the Pertwee stories were made by pointing a film camera at a monitor. These films were in black and white and, when BBC Enterprises merrily slashed and burned the original colour videotapes, were often the only copies of Pertwee episodes to survive. There was some limited take-up of Pertwee episodes in the United States in the early 1970s, but by local stations rather than networks[1]: 1972 advertising from the BBC's agents,

---

[1] Time-Life television exported Pertwee's first three seasons to the United States in 1972, converted from PAL video (British, 625 lines) to NTSC video (American, 525 lines). "Spearhead from Space" didn't feature as part of the package, no doubt because it was a regeneration story. As that story also contained much of the background to the Doctor's time with UNIT, American viewers might have been baffled by the show's continuity. Not only that, but local PBS stations apparently didn't realise that *Doctor Who* was an ongoing serial and showed the stories in any old order. Furthermore, American viewers in the early 1970s had no access to the black and white episodes. No wonder the series didn't make much impact Stateside

Time-Life television proclaimed, "Twenty half hours with Dr Who and you're cured! Part Whodini. Part Whodunnit. Every inch a hero."

By the time Pertwee rounded off his time as the Doctor with "Planet of the Spiders" in 1974, colour television had more widely colonised British television, both in terms of the proportion of programmes broadcast and made in colour and in the number of British homes renting or owning a colour set. This increased penetration of colour television was, by 1974, a worldwide phenomenon and would have been a wizard wheeze for the Nestenes, who distributed desirable and apparently harmless products to consumers[1] before activating them as deadly weapons. In the real world (whatever that is) of 1974, BBC Enterprises decreed there was no need to make black and white telerecordings of *Doctor Who*, and Tom Baker's stories were exported on video, in colour, to overseas broadcasters. They arrived on American PBS (public service broadcasting: local, not national, stations) in 1978, to audiences who had, in the main, not seen the Pertwee episodes. American enthusiasm for the show began in earnest with endless reruns of Tom Baker stories from "Robot" (1974) to "The Invasion of Time" (1978). The episodes were heavily edited: clips from each episode formed a pre-credits teaser with voice over by American actor Howard da Silva (sample: "On a distant planet, a giant sandminer combs the desert for minerals. Inside it is fully manned by robots, with a skeleton human crew. But when the Doctor arrives with Leela, his new travelling companion, he seems to bring

---

until Time Life television took firmer control of syndicating Tom Baker's episodes from 1978. (Domestic video recordings of the Pertwee stories were used by the BBC to re-colour black and white telerecordings of episodes when the colour master tapes had been wiped. The BBC could then re-sell these serials on VHS and abroad, and the newly colourised "The Daemons" got a repeat showing on BBC 2 in 1992.)

[1] The Nestenes and Autons appeared in two Pertwee stories, "Spearhead from Space" (1970) and "Terror of the Autons" (1971). Both returned in the first episode of the revival, "Rose" (2005).

catastrophe…"[1]) and the cliffhanger was immediately followed by a trailer for the next episode (sample: "But if the huntress cannot defend herself…who can?"[2]). Chunks of the episode proper were snipped to make way for the narration, much to American fans' annoyance. This first package of Tom Baker *Doctor Who* episodes was also marketed as television movies, with credits and reprises of cliffhangers cut. PBS stations often considered *Doctor Who* as frightening and adult fare, thus demonstrating that there was no American equivalent to the British prejudice that science fiction was both childish and for children. In 1980, a voiceover on one PSB station in Oklahoma intoned: "Weeknights at ten, *Doctor Who* presents adventures that will quell the bravest spirit."[3]

## The BBC decides not to activate the Doomsday Weapon: the show is renewed for season eight

When the eighth season was confirmed after the BBC abandoned its flirtation with cancellation, producer Barry Letts partially restored the Doctor's power of movement. The Time Lords periodically activated the TARDIS by remote control to send the Doctor to fix a problem for them, sometimes without telling him: they were thus revealed as a sneaky and devious lot who undermined their own official policy of non-interference in the affairs of other races. (We might compare *Star Trek*'s United Federation of Planets, which has a similar doctrine of non-interference unless its will needs to be stamped on an upstart civilisation: not a bad metaphor for 1960s US foreign policy.) The Doctor and Jo are sent to the planet Uxarieus in the twenty fifth century ("Colony in Space", 1971) to stop the Master getting his hands on the Doomsday Weapon, which would threaten the Time Lords' domination of the cosmos.

After the seventh season, when they had been handed a template

---

[1] Voice over for "The Robots of Death" (1977) episode one.
[2] Voice over for "The Robots of Death" (1977) episode two.
[3] I know all this because kind American pen pals sent audio cassettes of Tom Baker stories to my brother and me, in the days before VHS.

and cast largely tooled by the previous production team, Dicks and Letts set about reshaping the series into a more family-friendly and cosy mould for season eight. The futuristic Afrika-Korps-like UNIT uniforms were replaced by more regular army wear; in spite of Nicholas Courtney's plaintive lament in a 1973 interview that "I don't want the Brig to look a twit", the Brigadier becomes funnier. He is shown to be ridiculously squeamish, wincing as the Doctor dissects a solid rubber doll – used to murder Mr Farrell – in "Terror of the Autons" (1971). He hurriedly cuts short the revelation of his love life by "Professor" Clegg in "Planet of the Spiders" (1974): Mr Clegg reveals his powers of extra-sensory perception by examining the Brigadier's watch, given to him by the sea ("Brighton, was it?") by "a young lady called...Doris...she said it was to express her gratitude for—" "All true, absolutely spot on," huffs the Brigadier, snatching the watch back. In "The Three Doctors" (1973), Courtney plays the part for laughs. Unable to transport the TARDIS and the second Doctor to his rocky realm inside a black hole, the renegade Time Lord Omega transports the whole of UNIT HQ instead. Opening the door onto a barren landscape, the Brigadier opines that they have arrived in "Norfolk or somewhere like that"; he goes out to do a recce and muses, "I'm fairly sure that's Cromer."

Softening the show extended to the costumes. The Doctor's black tail coats were replaced by soft velvet jackets in a variety of colours. (Seeing them change from purple to green to red week by week was one of the great joys of colour television.) Even the Doctor's hair was fluffier. Jo, the new companion was a seventies archetype of male conceptions of femininity: if the 1970 series had responded positively to feminism, the 1971 series took a step backwards. The pairing of Jo and the Doctor was perhaps what Christopher Eccleston had in mind when he spoke disparagingly of "the patrician know-all and the underwritten female companion" of earlier years. Yet the viewing figures held up and even improved, *Doctor Who* continued to be a success, the show was renewed for season after season and all talk of cancellation was silenced for the rest of the decade. So much for political correctness.

In spite of a renewed slanting towards children in the eighth season, Jon Pertwee's time as the Doctor included some of the series' most intelligent and thoughtful scripts. In the best traditions of literary science fiction, the show was used as a vehicle to explore issues in the real world, as perhaps had not been the case since the introduction of the Cybermen and the Daleks in Hartnell's time. This renewed interest in real world issues was partly attributable to the pairing of script editor Dicks with the producer Barry Letts. Letts, a Buddhist, exemplified that faith's belief in the capacity of human beings to ruin themselves and the world through following the wrong path: this played well with Dicks's leaning, expressed in his work, towards liberal and left-of-centre politics. Two others joined the quartet of socially minded writers and had a considerable influence on the series' trajectory for the next five years. One of these was Robert Sloman, who wrote several scripts with Barry Letts; the other was Malcolm Hulke.

## Environmentalist themes: a left-leaning show?

A recurring theme in Pertwee's era as the Doctor is the danger of uncontrolled, untested technology. In "Doctor Who and the Silurians" (1970), the cyclotron research establishment is created as an attempt to produce cheap, plentiful energy. Similarly, the Inferno project attempts to tap the power of the Earth's molten core to supply the planet's energy needs ("Inferno", 1970). Both projects appear to mirror contemporary British, and world, fascination with nuclear power; the "white heat of technology", in the words of British prime minister Harold Wilson (1964-1970, 1974-6) which, the public was told, would be so wonderful that the energy created would be limitless and, therefore, virtually free. Excited by its potential, not enough attention was paid to the by-products of nuclear power: nuclear waste that couldn't be disposed of, irradiation around the nuclear reprocessing plant at Sellafield and a higher than usual level of leukaemia in children who lived nearby, not to mention the horrors of Chernobyl and Fukushima that were to follow. In *Doctor Who*, the scientists behind the energy projects are not evil, but narrow minded and obsessed with their pet projects. Dr Lawrence resists all attempts to close down the cyclotron, eventually to the point of hysteria; Professor Stahlman arrogantly dismisses all the Doctor's objections to project Inferno. In both stories, the by-products of using technology before it has been properly thought through and tested are, in fictional terms, as horrifying as the by-products of nuclear power. Lawrence's project awakens the Silurians from their deep sleep; after murdering his older leader, the aggressive young Silurian flatly refuses to share the planet with upstart apes and initiates two projects to exterminate them. The first is a plague, originally used in his time to wipe out the apes which raided the Silurians' crops. It is hideously effective on human beings, but the Doctor and Liz find the cure. The second is to destroy the Van Allen Belt, which protects the Earth from the more harmful rays of the sun: without it, Liz explains, we would die of sunburn on a cloudy day. 1970 *Doctor Who* showed itself to be way ahead of its time, concerned about global warming long before it had become a mainstream concern. The awakening of the Silurians is an indirect effect of the use of technology and a warning that actions have consequences; it also highlights the impatience, even greed, of human beings who, hungry for solutions to real problems like the energy crisis, cling to pet schemes and close their ears to any objections that the technology is unreliable. There are echoes here of the current British government's enthusiasm for fracking, which will provide us with further reserves of gas: objections that fracking poisons the water supply are brushed aside and we can confidently predict that serious exploitation of the project will release a race of Homo Reptilia to take over the world.

In "Inferno" (1970), the link between over-ambitious, untested technology and disaster is made even more apparent. Stahlman's project releases a slime that turns human beings into slavering, primitive monsters called Primords. Although unconvincingly realised on screen as hairy, fang toothed brutes who looked as though they had stepped out of an early movie of *Dr Jekyll and Mr*

*Hyde* (aged four, I remember my brothers shouting "Hippy!" at them in 1970), the Primords are an effective metaphor for the greed and arrogance that motivates Stahlman. Human beings who forgot their capacity to reason and follow their baser passions – here, of greed and arrogance – become animals. This is literally realised in the Primords of "Inferno" but is an idea that goes back as far as Shakespeare and the Elizabethans; it has a good pedigree long before science fiction or *Doctor Who*. If the Primords were not enough, the Doctor's tampering with the TARDIS's console transports him to a fascist, parallel Earth where Project Inferno does break through to the Earth's core: the resulting volcanic explosions destroy the planet. Returning to our Earth with this terrible warning, the Doctor discovers that all is not lost: Stahlman has become a Primord and the project is shut down. His experience leads the Doctor to muse that free will is not an illusion: it is Stahlman's choice whether he continues with the experiment of not; the Earth's destruction is not inevitable or pre-ordained but a result of human beings' choices. This is an environmental message that the Pertwee stories often repeat, and chimes with the emergence of the green movement in the Ecology Party (later the Green Party) and Friends of the Earth, both products of the early seventies. (The parallel universe scenes were added to save money and to pad the story out to seven long episodes: a case of serendipity, as they are some of the most dramatic scene of "Inferno".)

The link between technology and its terrifying by-products is articulated most clearly in "The Green Death". This 1973 story is one of the series' most fondly remembered episodes, not least because it is "the one with the maggots" and provides some of the iconic imagery of *Doctor Who*: giant maggots sneaking up on people and attacking them. Written by Robert Sloman and an uncredited Barry Letts, "The Green Death" is one of the series' most uncompromising attacks on capitalism and greed, and is one reason why writers like Dominic Sandbrook and Michael Hogan[1] have

---

[1] See, for example: Michael Hogan, "Why is a female Doctor so hard for men to accept?", *The Daily Telegraph*, 18th July, 2017.

identified *Doctor Who* as a programme on the left of the political spectrum. Global Chemicals has pioneered a chemical process that increases the energy yield of petroleum by more than 30%. Unfortunately, the by-product of the process is a filthy green slime which cannot be broken down by any chemical process. The company blithely flushes it down a disused coal mine and then denies all knowledge of it. (This could never happen in the real world.) The slime infects and eventually kills anyone who touches it – the green death – and causes a mutation of giant maggots which spread the infection. There is no cure.

Opposed to the irresponsibility of Global Chemicals is the Wholeweal Community led by Professor Cliff Jones, who eventually marries Jo Grant. The name Wholeweal puns on "weal" for "welfare" as well as "wholemeal" as in bread, thus affectionately suggesting that the environmentalist do-gooders both want to promote the welfare of the whole world and are the sandal-wearing, muesli-and-wholemeal-bread-eating, environmentalists lampooned in mid-1970s comedy. Wholeweal protests against Global Chemicals ("More muck! More devastation! More death!") and seeks alternative, peaceful lifestyles. To prevent Wholeweal from becoming too twee and earnest, Sloman shows that it is not popular in the local community, who dub it "the Nuthatch" and, in the novelisation, daub their cottage with graffiti: "Nutters go back to Cardiff". The villagers lost their jobs when the mine closed and are interested in the promise of jobs in Global Chemicals: Professor Jones is shouted down as a middle-class do-gooder who doesn't understand their problems. Again, the show connects with the real world: middle class intellectuals earnestly want to help the working classes, who, in their turn, want these environmentalist middle classes – who patronise them and plead that they really, really understand them – to bugger off.

Nevertheless, while Global Chemicals seeks a solution to the fuel crisis that is devastating the British economy, Wholeweal seeks a solution to world starvation. Professor Jones is trying to exploit the possibilities of a high protein fungus which, of course, is discovered serendipitously to cure the green death itself: a maggot eats half of the fungus cake and dies. This is an obvious metaphor: the cure for the problems of rampant capitalism is environmentalism.

Much of the radicalism of Pertwee *Who* came from the writer Malcolm Hulke, who had, at one time, been a member of the Communist Party. Hulke's scripts are often attacks on capitalist greed. In "Colony in Space" (1971), the efforts of a group of colonists to found a farming community on a new planet are almost ruined by the rapacity of the Interplanetary Mining Corporation. IMC finds that the planet is rich in duralinium and is determined to strip-mine the colonists' home: it tries to scare them away by murdering two of their number and blaming it on savage native lizards, and then resorts to open murder and intimidation. Again, there is an environmentalist theme. One of the terrors of the 1970s was over-population: in "Colony in Space", almost every square inch of Earth has been built on and human beings live cramped together in tiny, duralinium-based, apartments. Hence IMC's interest in Uxarieus: the planet's duralinium will provide over two million living units on Earth, and maximise the company's profits. The planet's name is a pun on "usurious": the practice of usury or relating to usury, that is, the lending of money at exorbitant sums and, more broadly, the centring of one's life on money that is Malcolm Hulke's critique of capitalism. The Doctor favours the colonists' alternative: human beings need space to live on and land to farm, rather than living like a lot of battery hens.

Having satirised ruthless multinationals and rapacious capitalism, Hulke also ties an environmental theme into the serial which he had previously used in "Doctor Who and the Silurians". The colonists' crops will not grow: even their cover crop withered and died. The planet's infertility is a by-product of the Doomsday Weapon built by its previous inhabitants: the Crab Nebula was created when the weapon was tested. Once the super race had designed and built the weapon as a pinnacle of its technological achievement, it went into decline and degenerated into various primitive species (shades of the

Primords) who worship and fear the weapon. The Doomsday Weapon is maintained by a tiny, puppet like guardian (realised as a small puppet with a face like a cabbage) who needs its radiation to survive. The Master explains to the guardian that he intends to use the weapon to rule the cosmos; the guardian, horrified, agrees with the Doctor that such power must never be used. It commits suicide, the weapon is destroyed, the radiation disappears and the crops grow again. Some critics have criticised the scientific implausibility of the radiation immediately dispersing, but the narrative suggests that, once harmful technology is removed, nature and human beings will flourish. The Doomsday Weapon is *Doctor* Who's satirical take on nuclear weapons: they are too powerful to possess, too terrible to use and owning them impoverishes the nation that has them, which could better spend the money on improving the living conditions of its citizens; not to mention the dangers of radiation from such weapons. The happy ending of "Colony in Space" also recalls science fiction's roots in Romantic literature: after the crisis, there is plenitude and growth.

We might at this point ask what possessed Hulke and the production team to call Pertwee's second story "Doctor Who and the Silurians", since it had been established for seven years that "Doctor Who" was not the character's name. After all, scripts had been called "Doctor Who and the ..." before, such as "Doctor Who and Tanni" (which became "The Rescue" (1964)), before the mistake had been picked up by eagle-eyed script editors. Similarly, the Doctor sometimes referred to himself as "Doctor Who" in scripts before they were edited. "Doctor Who and the Silurians" seems to have been a mistake that slipped through, or could be attributed to a new team that didn't fully grasp the series' vocabulary. After all, the story introduced the Doctor's Victorian roadster Bessie, which had the number plate Who 1, again implying that "Who" is the Doctor's name and causing earnest fans to turn cartwheels in their attempts to write the number plate into series continuity. It seems simplest to suggest that production teams make mistakes. Even Homer nods. One of the technical crew on the Radio Four *Doctor Who* play "The

Paradise of Death" (1993), also by Barry Letts and starring Jon Pertwee, told me that the script continually referred to the Doctor's ship as "TARDIS" rather than "*the* TARDIS": it was only the presence of a fan in the recording studio which saved the mistake from being broadcast in the finished programme. In the revival, Steven Moffat has both Matt Smith and Peter Capaldi's Doctors indicate that "Doctor Who" is actually the character's name, even if it is an adopted name. In a 2017 episode, Missy explains to Bill: "He says, 'I'm the Doctor' and they say, 'Doctor who?'… His real name is Doctor Who. He chose it himself, you know, trying to sound mysterious. And he dropped the 'Who' when he realised it was a tiny bit on the nose."[1]

Before left-wingers could become too smug with the series' new political credentials, Hulke's final script for the series squarely targeted over-zealous environmentalists for its satire. In "Invasion of the Dinosaurs" (1974), London has been evacuated because of the appearance of terrifying prehistoric monsters. These provide the monster of the week that the Pertwee stories excelled at, but the real monsters are, as so often in the show, human beings themselves. The dinosaurs have been transported by a machine called the Timescoop, created and operated by Professor Whitaker (another dry performance from Peter Miles, who played Dr Lawrence in "Doctor Who and the Silurians" and thus cornered the market in fanatical scientists). Whitaker believes that human beings have ruined their planet with pollution, wickedness and war, and that the only solution is to roll back time to an earlier, greener state: a golden age, when human beings lived a simple agrarian existence and were in harmony with nature. Working with him are traitor Captain Mike Yates, who sabotages the Doctor's counter-moves at every turn, and Sir Charles Grover, a member of the Cabinet who wrote the acclaimed book *Last Chance for Man*. The Doctor applauds Grover's book and approves of the man, but Grover's environmentalism has led him to despair of solving the world's environmental problems: the only solution is to start again and avoid

---

[1] From "World Enough and Time"

the mistakes which led human beings to despoil their planet. Grover's smiling conviction is horribly plausible[1] . Once the Doctor learns of the plan, he tells Mike that the Golden Age is an illusion and it never existed. Here, he is in good literary company: Shakespeare similarly harps back to the golden age in *As You Like It*, but the characters' attempts to capture it in the Forest of Arden are hardly successful and Arden is often shown in productions to be a bit grotty.

New assistant Sarah-Jane Smith (Elisabeth Sladen) is kidnapped by Grover and wakes up on a spaceship travelling away from Earth. On board are kindly environmentalists, who firmly believe that they are going to a new world not unlike Earth, peopled by simple humanoids whom they will guide and help ("The WholeWeal in Space", perhaps? No? Oh well, please yourselves). Sarah realises the whole thing is a trick: the spaceship is a mock-up in a nuclear shelter under London; the planet they are travelling to is Earth in the past, when time has been rolled back and people in the present have ceased to exist. In response to Sarah's objections, Grover insists that this isn't murder as the people thus erased would never have existed. When she explains her findings to the idealists on the "spaceship", one of their leaders, Ruth, tells her that she mustn't say such things. Ruth then rapidly moves from wondering if Sarah will be happy with them to suggesting that she might have to be destroyed as a disruptive influence, for the good of the community, of course. Commenting on the story in the DVD extras, Terrance Dicks said that Hulke would have based Ruth on the sort of do-gooding leftie he would have known from his time in the Communist Party: Ruth, he said, is the sort of person who knows what's best for you and what you should think, and, if you disagree, will, most reluctantly, insist that you have to be sacrificed for the good of all. The idea is terrifying and all too true.

---

[1] On the BBC audio of the novelisation, Martin Jarvis makes Grover sound awfully like Peter Mandelson, Tony Blair's right hand man (dubbed "The Prince of Darkness" by right-wingers for his success in the black arts of spin doctoring).

Eventually, the duped environmentalists insist that Operation Golden Age is evil and they will have no part in genocide. Whitaker and Grover activate the Timescoop and time starts going backwards. The Doctor, unaffected because he is a Time Lord, is able to reverse the process: time goes forward again but Whitaker and Grover, caught in the field of the Timescoop, have vanished. Where? "Back to their Golden Age," the Doctor says. "I hope they like it."

## Problems with dinosaurs

Excellent though the script is, there were huge production problems with "Invasion of the Dinosaurs". Producer Barry Letts was keen on dinosaurs in London because he believed they were now technically possible. He had been impressed by the Drashigs in "Carnival of Monsters" (1973) – and they are splendid, standing up well even for today's viewers – and wanted the BBC visual effects designers responsible for them to produce the dinosaurs for the new story. Unfortunately, the designers weren't available and the dinosaurs were farmed out to an external effects company who assured Letts that they could do the job convincingly. When the dinosaurs were delivered to the studio, Elisabeth Sladen said she could have cried[1]. Letts was furious. The tyrannosaurus model was operated by a crank in its tail which allowed it to writhe and that was about it; all the dinosaurs shuffled along with rods in their legs and the larger tyrannosaurus head, used for close ups, doesn't match the smaller model. The dinosaurs were shot in the studio on video. Director Paddy Russell (one of *Who*'s few female directors) recalled that the only way Sarah could be seen in shot with a tyrannosaurus was to stand Elisabeth Sladen against a blue screen, put the dinosaur model on another camera, and zoom out on Sarah until she was about the right size relative to the dinosaur. As the dinosaurs were on video, they didn't match properly with the filmed exterior sequences and appear to be floating above the ground. There are, of course, no

---

[1] Elisabeth Sladen, *The Autobiography*, London, 2011, p.117. Sladen writes that the dinosaurs were "awful, just so amateur looking".

shadows. One or two shots are passable: there is a good glove puppet pterodactyl that smashes the window of the Doctor's jeep and attacks him; Sarah is locked in an aircraft hangar with a tyrannosaurus and, as a child, I remember being terrified as it woke up and tried to get at her, even as I realised that the visual effects weren't that good.

The series was originally entitled "Timescoop" but was changed to "Invasion of the Dinosaurs" by the production team, ever on the lookout for a catchy title. Hulke accepted the change but fell out with Dicks over a last minute decision to retitle episode one as simply "Invasion", to keep the inclusion of the dinosaurs as a surprise. The *Radio Times*, which Letts said was a law unto itself, revealed in the listings for episode one that the monsters were dinosaurs anyway, so the surprise was blown in any case. Hulke was angry because he feared that the dull retitling would lose the story viewers and affect his reputation as a writer. Letts apologised and Hulke and Dicks made their peace, but Hulke said he had had enough of his work being interfered with and was glad that he was leaving television to concentrate exclusively on writing prose.

## Novelisations

Malcolm Hulke was among the first writers to be contracted by Target Books in 1974 to write new *Doctor Who* adaptations, called "novelisations" to indicate they were adaptations of scripts in novel form and, presumably, to distinguish them from original novels. Three *Doctor Who* novelisations had been published in the 1960s: *Doctor Who* – with the tagline, *"In An Exciting Adventure with the Daleks"* (1964[1]); *Doctor Who and the Crusaders* (1964), both by David Whitaker, and *Doctor Who and the Zarbi* (1964) by Bill Strutton, an adaptation of his own scripts for "The Web Planet" (1964). These books were reissued with new covers by Target in the 1970s and immediately sold so well that their editors asked the production team for more *Doctor Who* novels. Terrance Dicks,

---

[1] Reissued by Target in 1974 as *Doctor Who and the Daleks*

knowing that he was soon to move on from the series, offered to do some in spite of never having written a novel before. His first effort was the excellent *Doctor Who and the Auton Invasion*, based on Robert Holmes's script for "Spearhead from Space" (1970). Target had a habit of jazzing up the titles when it thought the original story title was too dull to catch the attention of children, although it insisted that cover illustrations were faithful to the televised story. This was a disappointment to illustrator Christos (Chris) Achilleos, who had been enthusiastically looking forward to drawing giant ants for *Doctor Who and the Zarbi*, Target told him to go back to the television designs instead[1].

Malcolm Hulke wrote six of the new novelisations: *Doctor Who and the Cave Monsters* (an adaptation of "Doctor Who and the Silurians", 1970); *Doctor Who and the Sea Devils* (working title, *Doctor Who and the Sea Monsters* – an attempt to tie in with the first Silurian tale); *Doctor Who and the Doomsday Weapon* (from 1970's "Colony in Space" and a far better title than the original serial); *Doctor Who and the Space War* (adapted from the equally dully titled "Frontier in Space", 1973); *Doctor Who and the Green Death* and *Doctor Who and the Dinosaur Invasion*. Originally written for children, Hulke's novelisations are especially well regarded and stand up well as fine versions of the original stories. His prose is sometimes a little shaky – he tends to repeat the same noun two or three times in three lines – but Hulke effectively takes advantage of the medium of the novel to expand intelligently on the original television scripts. On television, the Silurians were simply referred to as "Old Silurian" and "Young Silurian": in the novel, they have names and personalities.　　When he brought back the

---

[1] Chris Achilleos's cover designs and illustrations for the 1970s novelisations are masterpieces of sci-fi art. Highly valued by fans, they were eventually issued as limited edition prints. BBC Books secured Achilleos's services again to draw covers for re-issues of *Doctor Who – Vengeance on Varos* and *Doctor Who – Battlefield* in 2015 and Achilleos has always been happy about his association with the programme.

ドクター・フー・シリーズ

時空大血闘！／関口幸男訳

デイヴィッド・ホイティカー

POLICE
TELEPHONE

IGOR et GRICHKA
BOGDANOFF
présentent

DOCTEUR
WHO
LES DALEKS

MALCOLM HULKE

TOHTORI KUKA
JA LUOLAHIRVIÖT

WEILIN + GÖÖS

*Overseas editions of the
Target novelisations:*

*Top:* Doctor Who [In An
Exciting Adventure with
the Daleks] *in Japanese
and French.*

*Left:* Doctor Who and the
Cave-Monsters *in
Finnish.*

Silurians in 2010, Stephen Moffat sent writer Chris Chibnall away
to read *Doctor Who and the Cave Monsters* as source material for

his scripts, and we can see Hulke's influence in the individualised Silurians of "The Hungry Earth" (2010): rather than being a race of indistinguishable, generic monsters like the Ice Warriors, these Silurians are individuals with their own conflicting agendas.

Hulke sometimes writes from the monster's point of view. In *Doctor Who and the Cave Monsters*, a Silurian that has wandered out on the moor tries to make sense of the humans, who all look alike to him: he refers to the moustached Brigadier as "fur under nose" to distinguish him from the other apes. In *Doctor Who and the Green Death*, episode five's cliff hanger is rendered from the maggot's point of view: as it edges up to the tasty treat of Jo's exposed thigh, it wriggles with happiness at the prospect of so much meat and blood just waiting to be sampled. (In the same novel, Jo also offers to go topless for Professor Jones to distract him from his experiments, but his mind is on his work: not a line that could be played in the television version.) The tyrannosaurus that menaces Sarah in the aircraft hanger (in *Doctor Who and the Dinosaur Invasion*) remarks to itself upon her screaming and remembers that many of its meals make similar noises before it eats them. It moves its head towards her and finds it very puzzling when its nose bumps into something invisible: this is the glass of the office which stands between it and Sarah.

In adapting Robert Sloman's scripts for "The Green Death", Hulke emphasises the story's anti-capitalism even more than the televised version. When told that Professor Jones has a Nobel Prize, Dr Stephens, the Head of Global Chemicals, is impressed; but, we are told, Dr Stephens was always impressed by success because he was a snob. Stephens gives the Brigadier a whisky made as a bi-product of Global's chemical process; he reminds the computer BOSS that their whisky is actually poisonous and BOSS chuckles because it will make money for Global Chemicals. Stephens remembers, as a small boy, listening to the radio to hear Adolf Hitler screaming, *"Ein Reich, ein Volk, ein Fuhrer!"*: when BOSS's plans for world domination make him remember that broadcast, he turns against it.

## Christianity and Christianophobia

Christianity also appears to be have been important to Hulke. His novels are laced with Christian references which are not found in the televised stories. In prison on Earth for his crimes against humanity, the Master says goodbye to Jo and asks that God will go with her. The prison governor, Trenchard, in the Master's thrall, tells him that he sometimes thinks the Master is the Devil (the goatee beard helps here). In *Doctor Who and the Doomsday Weapon*, Ashe, the colonists' leader, is fascinated by a book from antiquity he has brought with him from Earth which seems to be largely about somebody called God. In the book, there are four versions of a story about a man who sacrifices himself for others, which puzzles Ashe: why should anyone allow himself to die for others? Yet Ashe follows Christ's example. IMC insists that all the colonists pack themselves off into their spaceship and leave the planet, knowing that it is quite likely the ship will explode at take off. The colonists escape from the ship under cover of darkness and Ashe takes off alone, sacrificing himself when the ship blows up to save his colleagues. In a particularly touching scene in the same novel, the Doctor teaches the colonists how to hold a funeral. Winton says they must dig "holes" for their dead, and the Doctor quietly corrects him to say "graves"; he encourages Winton to say good things about those who are lost, arguing that it's what the mourners expect, even though they don't know that they expect it. The Doctor is reconnecting human beings with the spirituality they have lost in their sterile, overcrowded, existence back on Earth. In *Doctor Who and the Green Death*, Yates tells Stephens that he has no right to turn humanity into the company's slaves, arguing that God gave man the right of free will. Stephens concedes the point, but says that free will makes people unhappy. Under the rule of BOSS, people will sing happy songs and have an untroubled existence as contended slaves.

On television, the original run of *Doctor Who* (1963-1989) wisely avoided established religion and had never offered an opinion on its truthfulness or otherwise. Some critics argue that, when religion does appear in the series, it's usually as a primitive cult and that therefore the series embraces atheism but the argument doesn't hold water: the existence of false religions does not negate the possibility that there is a true one. With their smaller circulation, the novelisations are perhaps the place for Christian reference, rather than a television series watched by millions which has a stronger potential to offend. We might contrast Hulke's light touch in the novels with Russell T Davies's occasional references to Christianity in the revived series. Christians were pleased when the tenth Doctor tells Astrid that he "got the last room" in the Inn at Christ's nativity and was present at the first Christmas ("Voyage of the Damned" (2007)). They were less pleased when he hints that the Resurrection never happened in the 2009 Easter special "Planet of the Dead", when the Doctor starts to say, "Although, what really happened was –" and is interrupted. Davies went further in the spin-off series *Torchwood*: in episode one, a character is brought back to life and splutters that there is nothing after death, thus denying the after-life in the *Doctor Who* universe. These references could be seen as of a piece with Davies's other modernising agendas in promoting gay characters and lifestyles, and casting regardless of the actor's colour: all things which most Christians are comfortable with. However, Davies, an atheist who told the BBC's Mark Lawson that Christianity is "just nonsense", unfortunately joins the contemporary Christianophobic zeitgeist. Richard Dawkins, anti-theist and husband of Lalla Ward, appeared in "The Stolen Earth" (2008) to explain that the planet has moved. As Dawkins' subject is biology rather than astronomy, there was no need for him to appear as an astronomical expert, although one might suggest he knows as much about astronomy as he does about theology[1]. Russell T Davies enthused about Dawkins's cameo in the series: Dawkins repaid the

---

[1] Reviewing Dawkins' book *The God Delusion*, the Marxist and atheist critic Terry Eagleton wrote that reading Dawkins on theology was like reading a work on genetics written by someone who had once read *The Collins Book of English Birds*.

favour by telling *Doctor Who* Magazine he didn't like *Doctor Who* and that religious believers were "faith heads", thus equating them with "crack heads" as addicted to a mind-altering drug. Christianophobia insists that knocking Christianity is fair game and upsetting Christians doesn't matter. Under showrunner Stephen Moffat, himself an atheist, such potentially offensive and controversial religious references have been notably and thankfully silenced.

In spite of the showrunner's atheism, the Doctor himself was sometimes presented as a Christ substitute by Davies: millions of people all reverently murmur "Doctor!" at the same time in "Last of the Time Lords" (2008) and the Doctor is resurrected as a glowing super being who offers the Master forgiveness. The Master (John Simm) is incredulous and wonders that he can be defeated by the power of prayer. So are the viewers: the sequence makes no sense.

## Leaning back towards the Establishment?

Having argued in favour of the liberal, pro-environmentalist and leftist leaning of the Pertwee *Doctor Who*, all were sometimes undermined or contradicted by various factors. Pertwee's Doctor claims he is a member of establishment clubs and is on good terms with senior civil servants; he is an expert on good food and wine. Verity Lambert, the show's original producer, considered the Doctor a fundamentally anti-establishment character and was profoundly unhappy about this period of the series when he works for the military and, therefore, the establishment. Whereas American audiences are broadly supportive of, and comfortable with, the military – there were no complaints about the military set-up of the starship Enterprise and Star Fleet, for example – a large proportion of the British audience viewed the military with some suspicion. However, perhaps to counterbalance these views, the UNIT characters are treated with sensitivity and portrayed as human beings and individuals. The Brigadier is intelligent and reasonable, at least in his first season: he accepts it is his duty to follow his orders in supporting Dr Lawrence (in "Doctor Who and the Silurians") and Professor Stahlman (in "Inferno"), but opposes them when they become dangerously fanatical about their respective projects. Captain Mike Yates is shown to be an idealist who supports Operation Golden Age ("Invasion of the Dinosaurs", 1974) and turns his back on UNIT for what he sees as the good of humanity. The Brigadier allows him to leave UNIT quietly after extended sick leave rather than having him court-marshalled: a compassionate decision which acknowledges Mike's previous service. Mike then embroils himself in more trouble as he seeks peace of mind in a Buddhist meditation centre, only to discover it is being used to open a channel to malevolent alien forces ("Planet of the Spiders", 1974). These are soldiers who are flawed human beings, not the military blimps of popular prejudice. There is no contradiction between the sympathetic portrayal of the military and the show's occasional left-wing leanings: socialists and social democrats in Britain have largely acknowledged the necessity of defending the nation and prominent figures in the Labour Party served with distinction in the Second World War. Denis Healey, Secretary of State for Defence until 1970 and Chancellor of the Exchequer from 1974-9, commanded a beach regiment in the landings on the Italian coast in Anzio.

We might argue that Verity Lambert didn't perhaps watch the Pertwee series closely enough. The Doctor remains an anti-establishment figure and is as irritated by UNIT as he is resentful of the Time Lords. He chafes against his exile; working for UNIT, at least in Pertwee's first season, is something of a marriage of convenience. He makes it clear in "Spearhead from Space" (1970), his first story, that he will work for the Brigadier in return for a place to live, to sleep and to try and get the TARDIS working again. Frequently, his obsession with doing so is his primary motivation in a story: in "Inferno" (1970), his main interest in Stahlman's project – to tap the Earth's core for its limitless source of free energy – is to use the energy thus released to power the TARDIS. In other stories, he is irritated by the Brigadier's problems as a distraction from his real work of resuming his travels in time and space. The Doctor often disagrees with the Brigadier's solutions and acidly remarks that "military intelligence" is "a contradiction in terms". He is horrified when Lethbridge-Stewart destroys the Silurians' base after the Doctor has sought a peaceful solution. The Doctor wants humans and Silurians to share the planet; the Brigadier thinks this is impossible and kills them. Again, the situation is complex and neither the Brigadier nor the Doctor is shown to be entirely right. The narrative suggests the Doctor is naïve to think that the Silurians would peacefully share the planet with the humans: they did, after all, release a disease to exterminate humanity. As the Doctor's negotiations with the Silurians fail, is the Brigadier right to exterminate them before they exterminate us? Or is the Brigadier's action racist genocide of ugly non-humans who probably deserve it anyway?

The tenth Doctor is at the centre of a similar moral dilemma at the end of his first story, "The Christmas Invasion" (2005). Again, the revival shows its debt of gratitude to the original series in revisiting its themes. The Doctor sees off the departing Sycorax spaceship with the warning that the planet is defended: if they return, there will be consequences. This is sufficient for him, but not for Prime Minister Harriet Jones. As the ship pulls away from Earth, she orders Torchwood to open fire and it is destroyed. The Doctor is incandescent with rage at this unnecessary barbarity; Harriet Jones insists that she is right – the Doctor comes and goes, but she has to defend Earth when he isn't around. She couldn't risk the Sycorax returning and does not trust them. Again, neither character is shown to be entirely right, but the tenth Doctor, unlike the third, takes his revenge on the establishment figure: he starts a rumour that brings down her government ("Don't you think she looks tired?"). He is a more dangerous figure than his frilly-shirted predecessor. In destroying the Sycorax ship, writer Russell T Davies makes an historical reference to Prime Minister Margaret Thatcher's order to sink the Argentinian aircraft carrier *General Belgrano*, even while it sailed away from the Falkland Islands and the British government's "total exclusion zone". More than five hundred Argentinian sailors were killed, the action was condemned at the time and the full truth about Mrs Thatcher's decision is only now emerging as papers are released under the Thirty Year Rule. Davies, who is no Conservative, may be making a wistful reference in "The Christmas Invasion": Harriet Jones' shooting down the Sycorax ship leads to the end of her premiership: Margaret Thatcher's hold on power in became almost unassailable as a result of the Falklands War. Is Harriet Jones's fate a sly statement of the appropriate fate for Mrs Thatcher after the sinking of the Belgrano?

*Doctor Who*, a fantasy and science fiction show, has a profound connection with the world around us and debates complex moral and political issues. It is its thoughtfulness, rather than any perceived childishness, which partly accounts for its popularity with children in its refusal to patronise its audience.

# 6

# I am usually referred to as the MASTER!

Back in 1970, it wasn't at all clear that Jon Pertwee would be asked to do a second season as the Doctor and the BBC asked producer Barry Letts and script editor Terrance Dicks to consider ideas for a replacement show. *Doctor Who* was under threat of cancellation. That the dogs were called off seems to have been because no-one was particularly enthused by the ideas for a replacement series. Richard Marson has written[1] that the programme similarly continued to survive into the 1980s not because of any great love for it among the higher powers at the BBC, but because they couldn't work up much enthusiasm for a replacement. Marson quotes Jonathan Powell, controller of BBC 1 in 1984, who said that *Doctor Who* "was looked at as part of the furniture" and provided twelve hours or so of television a year. Far from jumping up and down with excitement at the prospect of a new season, as fans might imagine, BBC executives languidly appear annually to have said, "Um, I suppose we continue with *Doctor Who*?"

At the same time as wondering whether they could resurrect *Quatermass*, Dicks and Letts started to consider ideas for the eighth season. When it eventually aired, it was such a ratings and critical success that the dogs of cancellation were kennelled for a few years.

The first move for season eight was to throw off the restraints imposed by the Troughton production team who, by exiling the Doctor to Earth, had hugely limited the range of stories that could be told. Letts had also been unhappy with season seven's concentration on purely science fiction stories: he wanted to restore some of the freedom of fantasy, thereby recalling the original 1963 to writers of

---

[1] Richard Marson, *JN-T: The Life and Scandalous Times of John Nathan-Turner*, Tadworth, 2013

the show: *Doctor Who* was to be neither straight science fiction nor historical drama nor fantasy; writers were free to explore any genre which they felt best suited the story they wanted to tell. This flexibility is, of course, one reason why the programme has lasted so long: it has the most flexible format ever devised for any drama programme on television.

Dicks and Letts chatted in 1970 about the similarities between *Doctor Who* and Sherlock Holmes, with the straightforward, prosaically minded Brigadier playing Watson to the Doctor's Sherlock. (An equivalence between the two heroes were highlighted again in 2010, when Mark Gatiss and Steven Moffat, writer and show runner of the revived series, came together to devise *Sherlock*.) So, if the Doctor was Sherlock, he needed a Moriarty, an arch-enemy of equal talent. The story goes that Dicks went home, mused overnight, and came back into the office the next day to announce, "I've thought of a name for him and it's the Master." Letts thought this was brilliant. Master, like Doctor, is an academic title. Master can also signify academic superiority to a Doctor (e.g. a PhD – Doctor of Philosophy) as it is a common title for the head of a college at Oxford or Cambridge. The word can conversely signify inferiority, as a Master of Arts or Science (MA, MSc) is an inferior degree to a PhD, which might account for the Master's raging sense of jealousy at the third Doctor's smooth command of all he surveys. This is demonstrated in "The Sea Devils" (1972) when the Master and the Doctor duel with rapiers: the Master's face is contorted with rage and effort while the Doctor eats a chicken sandwich and chats urbanely as he hold his enemy at bay. The point about Master and Doctor being academic titles never makes it to screen and was lost on the audience, which, as it encapsulates the truth about the Time Lords' relationship, is a pity.

Letts told Dicks knew exactly the right actor to play the Master: Roger Delgado, an actor with Spanish and sinister good looks who often played mysterious characters. In the same way that none of the subsequent Doctors could make the part their own after the seven year domination of Tom Baker in the role (at least, in the original series), so it might be argued that none of the other subsequent Masters could touch Delgado's suave original – at least, perhaps, until John Simm and Michelle Gomez came along in the post-2005 revival. The Master is the Doctor's antithesis. Like the Doctor, he (later she) is a Time Lord who has escaped from Gallifrey in a stolen TARDIS; like the Doctor, he (she) is brilliant, resourceful, charming and charismatic. Like the Doctor, he (she…) is a powerful hypnotist: while the Doctor uses his hypnotism to heal (for example, by releasing Victoria from the control of the Great Intelligence in "The Abominable Snowmen" (1967)), the Master uses it to dominate: his catchphrase, in his Delgado incarnation, is "I am the Master: you will obey me." Unlike the Doctor, he has no wish to explore the Universe: as his only goal is power, he wants to dominate it instead. The Doctor is dedicated to good and champions the weak against the strong: the Master is dedicated to evil and takes delight in crushing the weak beneath his heel. The Master is vicious, ruthless and sadistic, using his talents for his own amusement and gratification in his search for power. In casting Delgado, Barry Letts hit upon an actor who could be a match on screen for the dynamic Pertwee. Like Pertwee, Delgado was middle aged, good looking and had a beautiful speaking voice; like Pertwee's Doctor, Delgado's master was charming – he always scrupulously addresses Jo as "Miss Grant" or even, "My dear Miss Grant" – and likeable. He demands the best: the Master's TARDIS is a gleaming mark two, much to the Doctor's annoyance as he is unable to use its dematerialisation circuit, which he steals, in his own mark one; while the Doctor drives the sprightly Bessie, the Master has a chauffeur driven limousine in "The Mind of Evil" (1971) and, for that story only smokes large cigars – the classic prop for super-villains in popular 1970s entertainment. Re-crafting the Master for the twenty first century, Russell T Davies's approach recalled the original Pertwee-Delgado dynamic: the Master (as played by John Simm) is a fine match for David Tennant's tenth Doctor. This new Master is apparently the same age as the Doctor, similarly good looking and similarly funny. There is a wonderful scene in "The Sound of

Drums" (2008) when the American President can barely contain his rage at the Master who, responding to the President's request that he shut up, mimes zipping his lips and nods solemnly at everything the latter says.

Dicks and Letts always insisted that each new season had a strong opening episode, hoping that this would hook a large audience which would stay with the show for the rest of the season: a strategy which worked as well as could be expected. In 1971, the good first night was the first appearance of the Master; in 1972, it was the reappearance of the Daleks for the first time in five years ("Day of the Daleks"); in 1973, it was "The Three Doctors" for the programme's tenth anniversary later that year; in season eleven, it was a new companion in Sarah Jane Smith and a new monster in the Sontaran, Lynx; for their final story, the first story of season twelve, it was the arrival of the new Doctor, Tom Baker. There were *Radio Times* covers to herald all but the last of these debuts (Tom Baker's Doctor never got a *Radio Times* cover). In 1970, the *Radio Times* contracted comics artist Frank Bellamy to draw some arresting, comic strip style covers. Their style immediately recalled the popular and well-drawn *Doctor Who* comic strip then running in *Countdown/TV Action*. Aged six, I remember being particularly thrilled by Frank Bellamy's cover for the first *Radio Times* of 1972, whose headline announced, "The Daleks are Back!": the Doctor, grim faced, is set against a red planetary background streaked with jagged lightning and menaced by two Daleks chanting, "You are the Doctor... You are the enemy of the Daleks... You will be exterminated..."

The Master makes his first appearance in "Terror of the Autons" (1971). This story is a re-tread of the previous year's "Spearhead from Space", in the same way that "The Sea Devils" (1972) would be a virtual re-write of 1970's "Doctor Who and the Silurians", with the addition of the Master to the plots of the Nestenes and Silurians/Sea Devils respectively. While assisting the Nestenes and Autons with their second invasion attempt, the Master has a lot of fun trying to kill the Doctor in various ingenious and nasty ways.

He leaves a grenade as a calling card, hypnotises Jo into delivering a bomb to the Doctor's lab, and takes advantage of the Nestene's ability to animate any kind of plastic by having the Doctor's phone cord come to life and nearly strangle him. The Nestenes become as irritated as unemotional life forms can be by the Master's feud with the Doctor and warn him that he will be eliminated if the feud continues to interfere with their great plan.

The Master and the Doctor eventually meet in episode three and reveal a mutual liking and respect for each other. The Master says that the Doctor is his intellectual equal – "Almost" – and that he will kill him "but not without considerable regret". Later stories reveal that the Master and the Doctor were once friends on Gallifrey and went to the Time Lord Academy together. Jon Pertwee went so far as to say that Nick Courtney had suggested the Master and the Doctor were brothers, and that this idea had been enthusiastically picked up by the production team until Roger Delgado's untimely death prevented its use. When this was put to him in an interview in the late 1970s, Courtney was amazed and had no memory of the suggestion at all[1]. The idea fizzled on for years until Russell T Davies eventually scotched it in "The Sound of Drums" (2007): Martha asks the tenth Doctor if he and the Master are brothers; the Doctor rolls his eyes and says that she has been watching too much television. Nevertheless, the mutual respect and affection between the two Time Lords – although they despise each other's values absolutely – is apparent throughout Pertwee's tenure as the Doctor. "Terror of the Autons" was originally to have ended with the Doctor saying he would continue to fight the Master "until I destroy him or he destroys me". This was considered too downbeat and, to reflect the chemistry between the actors and the characters, was rewritten. The Doctor says he thinks the Master will turn up again. Jo expresses surprise that he doesn't seem too worried about the prospect; the Doctor smiles and replies, "I'm not. As a matter of

---

[1] The interview was conducted in the Connaught Theatre, Worthing, by Simon and Frank Danes, and published in their fanzine *Fendahl* in 1980, in their days of youth and promise.

fact, I'm rather looking forward to it."

Lest the Master be too attractive a character, Robert Holmes' script for "Terror of the Autons" shows him also to be a spiteful sadist. In episode one, he unnecessarily and viciously throws a scientist to his death from the steps of a radio telescope, simply because he is in the Master's way. Later, he delights in the humiliation of Professor Phillips, whom he has hypnotised and disguised as a clown in Rossini's circus. He invents a plastic armchair that swallows and suffocates anyone who sits in it. We are introduced to the Master's favoured method of murder: a matter concentration gun that shrinks his victims to the size of dolls. The Doctor discovers one of the radio telescope's scientists propped up in his own lunch box: a very effective special effect achieved by overlaying the actor into the lunch box using blue screen. Later stories – such as "The Deadly Assassin" (1977) and "Logopolis" (1981) – would instead opt for prop dolls or Action Men dressed in miniature costumes, to risible effect. In the revived series, Russell T Davies re-imagined the Master as a psychopathic mass murderer. He orders the Toclafane to remove one tenth of the Earth's population in "The Sound of Drums" (2008), accelerates the Doctor to extreme old age, has him live in a tent on his space station and leaves out a drinking bowl for him labelled Dog. Spite in Delgado's portrayal transforms into psychological obscenity in Simm's. When the Master returns in a female regeneration as Missy ("Short for Mistress – well, I couldn't very well go on calling myself the Master, now could I?"), she is apparently less vicious, until Clara asks if she has become good. This is Missy's cue for shooting a security man and noting that he was a father as there was some baby posset on his jacket. "No," Missy concludes, "I'm not good." John Simm's Master returns in "World Enough and Time"/"The Doctor Falls" (2017), not quite the sadistic lunatic he was under Davies and now sporting a goatie beard (fans cheered) to link him with Ainley and Delgado's portrayals. The scenes with the Master and Missy together are a joy, Moffat clearly relishing the possibilities of having the two together in one time zone. Furious with the idea that her destiny has led to assuming a role as the Doctor's ally in fighting the Cybermen, Missy stabs the Master – metaphorically and literally – in the back, and he repays the favour by shooting her. If the Pertwee and Troughton Doctors squabble when they meet in "The Three Doctors" (1973), the two Masters take delight in actually murdering each other. Asked if the Doctor could ever be played by a woman, Moffat pointed to Missy and asked, what more of a precedent do you need? Jodie Whittaker's casting as the thirteenth Doctor was announced in 2017. Michelle Gomez announced that she would not return as Missy after Peter Capaldi had left, but fans, accustomed to being fed half-truths by mischievous production teams, hope that a female stand off between the two Time Lords is on the cards.

Back in Jon Pertwee's time, the Master appeared as the major villain in every story of the 1971 season. Sometimes his appearance is delayed – his entrance as the Administrator in "Colony in Space" comes half way through the story – but there is an inevitability about it which becomes wearisome for some viewers; Letts and Dicks themselves admitted it was a mistake to use him in every story of season eight. In "The Daemons", the Master memorably appears as the new vicar, the Reverend Mr Magister (Latin for "Master"): a good persona which the script doesn't fully exploit. After failing to persuade the Daemon Azal to pass on his planet-destroying powers to himself, the Master is finally captured by UNIT. This sequence was shot in a Wiltshire village. In 1972, Malcolm Hulke wrote that director Christopher Barry asked the village children to boo the Master as he was taken into custody but, in a sign of how much they liked the character, they cheered him instead[1].

The Master appeared occasionally for the next two seasons, in "The Sea Devils" (1972), "The Time Monster" (1972) and "Frontier

---

[1] See p.31 *The Making of* Doctor Who, London, 1972. I'm not sure if this story can be true: wasn't "The Daemons" made before the Master had been established as a character on screen? How then could the children have such an affection for a character they didn't know? Truth or embellishment, the story does illustrate how much children loved Delgado's Master at the time: next to the Doctor, I remember him being the most popular character to assume when playing *Doctor Who* in the playground.

in Space" (1973). One effect of the occasional use of his character was to dry up the offers of work Roger Delgado received after his first season. Casting directors hadn't woken up to the fact that he wasn't in every *Doctor Who* story and he was sometimes out of work. Delgado spoke about this to Barry Letts and said he thought he must leave as the Master; Letts was sympathetic and asked if he wanted to be written out quietly or to go out in a big bang. "Oh, let it be a big bang!" Delgado said enthusiastically. The then production team didn't consider regenerating and hence recasting the character and it would have been hard to replace the much-loved Delgado with anyone else; this might be one reason why the Master didn't appear again until "The Deadly Assassin", three years later in 1976. He was now a decaying, skeletal corpse and *Doctor Who* had become a gothic horror show rather than the family-friendly adventure series it was under Pertwee.

Back in 1973, some early story ideas were drawn up with the Master helping the Doctor against a threat that menaced them both, and there have been some suggestions that the Master was pencilled in for the role that eventually became Lupton's in "Planet of the Spiders" (1974), Pertwee's swan song. Tragically, Roger Delgado was killed in a car accident while filming in Turkey. The news shook the tight-knit cast and was instrumental in persuading Katy Manning, and then Jon Pertwee, to leave. The Master's final appearance in his Delgado incarnation is in "Frontier in Space" (1973). Here, the Master joins up with the Daleks in an attempt to start a war between the rival empires of the Draconians and the humans; after their mutual destruction, the Daleks will mop up the survivors and dominate the galaxy. No doubt the Master intended to ditch them at some point along the way. He is last seen surrounded by Ogrons, desperately scrabbling for his gun to get a shot in at the departing Doctor.

Robert Holmes, who wrote the Master's debut story "Terror of the Autons" (1971), reintroduced him in "The Deadly Assassin" (1976): one of the best *Doctor Who* stories ever made, it riffs on the film *The Manchurian Candidate* (1962) in having the Master frame the

Doctor for the assassination of the Time Lord President. Although the Master looks quite different, and is played with wonderful, vicious menace by Peter Pratt, his dialogue could have been written with Delgado in mind. He taunts the Doctor by explaining why it had to be him the Master chose to frame for the assassination: "Who else but you? So despicably good, so insufferably compassionate!" Producer Philip Hinchcliffe had stressed that the Master should be between regenerations so that a new actor could be eased into the part if a future production team wanted to bring the character back. At the end of "The Deadly Assassin", the Master's face is superimposed on his departing TARDIS (now in the form of a grandfather clock) and appears to be regenerating. This image was forgotten when he reappeared in "The Keeper of Traken" (1981), now played by Geoffrey Beevers but still maintaining his skeletal form. Beevers apparently used the same mask as Pratt but with the bulging eyes removed, as producer John Nathan-Turner insisted that an actor's eyes were hugely important to his performance. In fact, Beevers appears to be wearing make-up rather than the mask as the Master's skull teeth appear to be painted on his lips. His appearance is altogether less effective than the horror movie image of Peter Pratt in "The Deadly Assassin", but that story had been a watershed in terms of complains about the series' horror and violence, most frequently levelled by the indefatigable Mrs Mary Whitehouse, she of the "Clean Up TV campaign" and one of the most implacable of the Doctor's adversaries. Mrs Whitehouse's campaign led to BBC executives' demand in 1976 that *Doctor* Who's horror content should be diluted, arguably to the show's detriment; Tom Baker's final four seasons as the Doctor were much less well regarded by children who were at school with me, than his first three years of glorious gothic horror. Perhaps the whole saga of the Whitehouse campaign was recalled with a shudder by the team on "The Keeper of Traken", and the Master's make up was made duly unfrightening.

## A new body – at last!

The Doctor and the Master meet in the final episode of "The Keeper of Traken". At the end of his twelfth regeneration, the Master attempts to steal the Doctor's body, but instead opts for that of Tremas (Anthony Ainley), the father of new companion Nyssa. In a show-stopping climax to the final episode, the Master's ravaged face merges with Tremas's and the new Master is born. With his goatee beard and swept back, black hair, he looks very like Roger Delgado, and fans throughout the land exhaled in ecstasy.

Anthony Ainley played the Master for the rest of the original series' run and provided some continuity in the face of rapidly changing Doctors. He appeared opposite Tom Baker, Peter Davison, Colin Baker, and Sylvester McCoy in the original show's final episode, "Survival" (1989). Sadly, Ainley's performance is not well regarded and he comes across as a silky, Machiavellian, even pantomime villain. Ainley seems to grit his teeth and grin throughout his portrayal, and continually gives a "heh-heh-heh" chuckle as he contemplates his dastardly machinations. This is, of course, partly the fault of the producer and the directors, who dress him in black velvet to emphasise his villainy – subtle, that – and give him some very silly schemes. In "The King's Demons" (1983), the Master attempts to stop the signing of Magna Carta for no very good reason; even the Doctor notes that this is small time villainy by his standards. Former script editor Douglas Adams observed that bringing the Master back wasn't a good idea, and that the new production team apparently considered having a black beard was sufficient explanation for his evil; there was no need for other motivation. Adams clearly made a gibe at his former show at the end of an episode of *The Hitch-Hiker's Guide to the Galaxy* (season two, Radio 4): the Book asks if the peril to be faced by our heroes will be "something exciting, or will it just be a monster trying to take over the universe for no very good reason?"

The Master's continual inclusion in the original series also meant that he, like the Daleks, suffered from the law of diminishing returns. Every scheme of his is thwarted by the Doctor and he ends up looking rather like Sylvester Sneekly/The Hooded Claw from the Hanna-Barbera cartoon *The Perils of Penelope Pitstop* (1969-1970) who, however badly his scheme to mash Penelope has gone in the previous episode, returns each week with a fiendish new plan which is at once thwarted by the resources of the Ant Hill Mob. Chris Howarth and Steve Lyons wrote that the Master is "nutty as squirrel shit"[1], and this pithy phrase encapsulates the point nicely. He, like the series itself in 1989, needed a long rest. When the Master returned, it was in the Paul McGann TV movie of 1996, played with camp charisma by American actor Eric Roberts. The Master's inclusion in the TV movie was probably determined by rights issues. As he had been created by BBC staffers Barry Letts and Terrance Dicks, he was copyright to the BBC, and could be easily included in any rights package for another production company which wanted to make *Doctor Who*.

## *Doctor Who* violence condemned

The Master's first story, "Terror of the Autons" (1971) prompted the first serious wave of concern about horror and violence in the programme. One of the Nestene's weapons was a devil doll, which, when animated by heat, strangled its victims. Barry Letts recalled there were reports of children throwing away their teddy bears for fear of suffering a similar fate. The Doctor and Jo are rescued by policemen in a patrol car. Suspicious because they won't speak to him, the Doctor pulls away a policemen's face to reveal the Auton beneath. The Autons then proceed to blast away at them in a quarry. Letts received letters from the police force, asking him never again to make policemen frightening for children. He conceded the point, although android policemen appear in "Resurrection of the Daleks" (1984, produced by John Nathan-Turner) and shoot the Daleks' enemies with high velocity rifles. Questions were asked in

---

[1] Chris Howarth and Steve Lyons, Doctor Who *The Completely Useless Encylclopedia*, London, 1996.

Parliament in the early 1970s about the level of violence in what was still considered a children's programme (because it was science fiction and science fiction is childish – QED) and the newspapers weighed in. A *Daily Telegraph* article, published just after "Terror of the Autons" had aired, protested that the forms taken by the Autons were from a child's domestic sphere and were therefore more frightening than such fantasy creatures as the Daleks and Cybermen. The writer perhaps had a point: suffocation by plastic chair and strangulation by telephone cable are not the usual fare of early evening family viewing. Letts reined in some of the programme's violence after, he thought, going a little too far with the second Auton story, and tried to confine it to the realms of ray guns and the Doctor's own brand of the martial arts, Venusian aikido. This consisted of Pertwee crying "Haiii!" and flipping a stunt man over his shoulder.

Either the production team took its eye of the ball or relaxed its restrictions when the fuss had died down, as there was some real violence in later Pertwee stories: characters are graphically shot down with arrows in "Death to the Daleks" (1974), for example. The programme came to the attention of Mrs Mary Whitehouse again with "Planet of the Spiders", Pertwee's final story in 1974. Mrs Whitehouse criticised the story for playing on children's arachnophobia and suggested the programme should be put on after 6.30 p.m., or that the BBC should commission an analysis of its special effects on the under fives. It might be argued that the quality of the spider effects mitigated against any horror. Although the spiders are very effective in some sequences, there is an awful lot of ropey blue (actually yellow) screen; some of the spiders are virtually static and obviously puppets; some just bob up and down on a visible wire. Indeed, visual effects designer Ian Scoones had made a huge, horror-movie type spider as a prototype for the story, which was vetoed by the production team as too terrifying. Aged nine, I watched this serial on its first broadcast and, as so often with 1970s *Doctor Who*, was quite aware that the effects weren't terribly good. This at once took the edge off my fear while it in no way interfered with my enjoyment of the story: ropey special effects was something you accepted at the time, put to one side, and then got engrossed in the plot. Anyway, the spiders scared me much less than the materialisation of the false Ageddor in the same season's "The Monster of Peladon" (1974): my twin brother and I delighted in terrifying each other as we climbed up to darkened stairs by imitating the noise of the monster's materialisation.

The BBC's research in the early 1970s confirmed that 60% of *Doctor Who*'s audience were adults; although it was perceived as a children's programme, only 40% of the audience actually were children. At the same time, an internal report by the corporation into violence on television revealed that the pre-watershed *Doctor Who* was the most violent of its dramatic fiction series, with an average of four violent incidents per twenty five minute episode. The first Doctor, William Hartnell, claimed around this time that he had left the programme in 1966 because it was no longer made for children and that too much evil had entered into the spirit of the things. This may have been a case of rationalising after the event; Hartnell had been ill and exhausted after three years in such a demanding role. Jon Pertwee said he was sometimes approached by parents who complained to him that *Doctor Who* was much too frightening for their children. "Well, it's very simple," he replied to them, "You reach out for the button on your television and turn it to the 'off' position."

## "A complete adventure in one programme"

Regular repeats of Pertwee adventures were one splendid innovation of his time as the Doctor. The black and white episodes had been very seldom repeated, presumably because of the hassle of negotiating repeat fees with the actors' union, Equity. There had in fact been only two repeats in the 1960s: "An Unearthly Child" was reshown before the second episode for the benefit of those who had been distracted by President Kennedy's assassination a week before and "The Evil of the Daleks" (1967) was repeated to fill the gap between the fifth and sixth seasons over the summer break. In Pertwee's time, repeats took the form of (heavily cut) episodes edited together to make a feature film, and fans' hearts leapt when they read the words "A complete adventure in one programme" in the *Radio Times*. The BBC presumably thought that people wouldn't have the patience to sit through unedited episodes; having seen them once already, would people really want to sit through all those title sequences and cliffhangers again? The same thinking prevailed when *Doctor Who* was first released on VHS in 1984 with the story "Revenge of the Cybermen" (1975), which had its opening titles and cliffhangers lopped off. Such editing wasn't confined to *Doctor Who* video releases: even the first commercial videos of *Fawlty Towers* cut most of the title sequence because it was thought viewers wouldn't have the patience to sit through them. Video tape buyers protested that they didn't want their programmes cut, and BBC Enterprises graciously conceded the point; as a happy service to consumers, they released the programmes on video again, uncut, to a public that was thrilled to pay for them twice over.

Back in the 1970s, however, the repackaging of episodes into feature film repeats was determined by the still-prevailing notion that television was trivia and ephemera; cutting it didn't really matter. The same notion dictated the wholesale burning of old episodes. The Pertwee stories weren't best served by cutting them: chunks of story disappeared, rendering the plotting as incoherent as some of the Sylvester McCoy episodes. Furthermore, the pacing no longer really worked. *Doctor Who* episodes were designed to build to a climax every twenty two (or so) minutes: it seemed very lame to have our heroes facing certain death one minute and perfectly safe the next. The same objections were raised by some viewers in the United States at the end of the 1970s, whose local public broadcasting stations opted to show episodes as TV movies with the opening and closing titles removed (although not as heavily cut as the BBC in-house compilation repeats). Similarly, script editor Eric Saward and other writers said how difficult it was to write forty five minute episodes for Colin Baker's first season, arguing that *Doctor*

*Who* lent itself best to short, twenty five minute, bite-sized instalments.

In spite of all these objections, the repeats were a huge treat for young fans who were desperate to see old stories again. These were the days before Target books made it possible to relive old adventures through the novelisations (indeed, some have argued that one reason people consider Pertwee adventures so good is because the novels are so good: returning to the original programme, viewers are disappointed); only those with expensive cassette recorders could tape the soundtrack and there was, of course, no home video. "The Sea Devils", "The Green Death" and "Planet of the Spiders" were repeated as TV movies. The BBC started to screen the Peter Cushing Dalek movies on a regular basis, sometimes as replacements for rained-off test cricket; it even showed the compilation of "The Sea Devils" as a cricket substitute. Much to my rage, I missed it. A few of the Tom Baker stories were repeated as edited movies: "The Ark in Space" (1975) was cut together; "Genesis of the Daleks" (1975) was first repeated over the Christmas holidays. "The Sontaran Experiment" (1975) was shown as one programme, but as it was only two episodes long, it didn't need to be cut. In Tom Baker's time as the Doctor, the BBC realised that tastes had changed and viewers would accept unedited repeats. A pattern emerged of a couple of stories being repeated every year over the summer holidays on BBC 1, often with one episode being screened every evening. These were eagerly awaited by fans and the viewing figures held up well for the time of the year.

**"I will give the process a little push and the cells will regenerate – he will become a new man."** [1]

With four seasons under his belt, Pertwee felt that the team around him was breaking up. Katy Manning had announced her intention to leave at the end of the tenth season; Barry Letts and Terrance Dicks also intended to move on to new projects. The death of Roger

---

[1] Cho-Je, actually K'Anpo Rinpoche, in "Planet of the Spiders" episode six (1974)

Delgado had affected Pertwee and the whole cast; with so many others departing, he felt the time was right to move on as well. In his one man show "An Evening with Jon Pertwee", which successfully toured British theatres in the 1990s, Pertwee repeated the story that he had been prepared to stay for the twelfth season but had asked for more money. The BBC declined and Pertwee moved on. Years later, Barry Letts questioned the story's veracity. If Pertwee had wanted to stay and has asked for a rise in his fee, he would have approached Letts who would, in turn, have asked for a bigger budget from Shaun Sutton, the Head of Drama, to cover the star's pay rise. This was the normal procedure in BBC television. Letts said no such approach was made. It is also suggested that Pertwee was actually offered a sixth season as the Doctor, but turned it down. He would leave at the end of season eleven.

Season eleven introduced Sarah Jane Smith as the new companion. Elisabeth Sladen, who played her, recalled that Pertwee missed Katy Manning very much during the filming of his final season and became more withdrawn as the season went on; he would sit aside and answer his fan mail instead of chatting with the other actors between scenes. Pertwee was mentally preparing himself to break from the series. When he filmed the regeneration scene with Tom Baker, the two actors barely spoke to one another. It was an understandably difficult time for man who had starred in the show for five years. Another factor which had perhaps upset the equilibrium in the final season was the fact that Sladen wasn't the first actress who had been tried for Sarah Jane. Rehearsals had begun with another actress, April Walker, who did not work out. Elisabeth Sladen was cast and almost immediately bussed down to the location filming for "The Time Warrior" (1974), the first story of the new season. Sladen hadn't been to a rehearsal or read through; these had been completed with Walker and the show had to stay on schedule.

Some critics have argued that Pertwee became bored with the series in his final season, and his boredom is sometimes reflected in his performance. He certainly admitted to impatience with the scripts, and not just in his final season. Interviewed in the 1970s, he stated that some of the scripts he did were absolutely dreadful, all of them six episodes. He did, however, like Robert Sloman's stories, and hardly altered a line of them; others, he altered a very great deal. Terrance Dicks recalled that Pertwee particularly disliked what *Star Trek* fans call "technobabble" – pseudo-scientific gobbledegook uttered to explain away an unlikely event or to move the plot forward. Pertwee did, however, once tell Dicks that he liked a line saying he was to "reverse the polarity of the neutron flow": easy to remember and it tripped off the tongue. Pertwee used variations of the line in several of his stories and it became something of a catchphrase. At conventions in the 1980s he apparently sang about the Doctor's early days to a tune from Gilbert and Sullivan's comic opera *HMS Pinafore*: "When I was a lad I served a term, As office boy to a Gallifreyan firm, When they shouted 'Jump!' I had to go And reverse the polarity of the neutron flow... I reversed that flow so easily, That I vowed I'd do it twice before episode three." Dicks gave Pertwee the line in the twentieth anniversary special "The Five Doctors" (1983), and he smiles as he says it, perhaps relishing its repetition. He said it again in the run of the 1988 stage play *Doctor Who – The Ultimate Adventure*, again by Dicks. When Colin Baker replaced Pertwee later in the show's run, the line was changed as it was considered only suitable for the third Doctor.

Bored or not, Pertwee was given a run for his money in his final season. He loved gadgetry and often drew the production team's attention to new vehicles: he found the balloon-wheeled, powered tricycles that the Doctor and Jo escape on in "Day of the Daleks" (1972). In fact, the tricycles didn't go very fast, so the Ogrons chasing them had to move *very slowly*. Pertwee had a futuristic car called "the Alien" designed and built for him. It resembled a small silver hovercraft with wings sweeping towards its tail; the police banned him from driving it in traffic as other drivers, watching it with amazement, took their eyes off the road. It appeared in "Invasion of the Dinosaurs" and "Planet of the Spiders" as the Whomobile (never named as such on screen), where, in a very unconvincing blue (actually yellow) screen sequence, it is seen to fly. Being Pertwee's own property, the Whomobile vanished from the series when Tom Baker took over and the fourth Doctor had to make do with Bessie. Part two of "Planet of the Spiders", Pertwee's swan song, is a very long chase between the Doctor and Lupton, who has stolen the blue crystal from Metebelis III that is vital to the plans of universal domination for various arachnid factions. The Doctor pursues Lupton in a one man helicopter, the Whomobile, Bessie and a hovercraft. The sequence was exciting on first viewing but entirely superfluous to the story: its one advantage was that it could be neatly pruned out of the compilation repeat.

### "Planet of the Spiders" and Buddhism

"Planet of the Spiders" is a splendid, Buddhist-influenced tale by Barry Letts and Robert Sloman (although only Sloman is credited). It refers back to events in "The Green Death" a year before. A running joke in the series had been the Doctor's wish to take Jo to Metebelis III, the fabulous blue planet of the Actaeon galaxy. He eventually manages this in episode one, and is attacked by giant eagles and tentacle plant life for his pains. He does, however, manage to get hold of one of the blue Metebelis crystals, which he brings back to Earth. These have strange properties: they can clear the mind and amplify its powers; Mike Yates has been programmed by BOSS to murder him, and the Doctor uses the crystal to free him from the possession. In "Planet of the Spiders", a mentally handicapped worker in the community called Tommy is "cured" by the crystal and goes from reading Ladybird early readers for children, to William Blake in the same evening.

In episode one of "Planet of the Spiders", Mike Yates and Sarah are investigating strange goings on in a meditation centre in "darkest Mummerset" (Sarah's words). They discover that the guests' meditations have formed a link with the giant spiders in the far future of Metebelis III. One of the guests, Lupton, allows a spider (they are about fifteen inches in diameter) to jump on his back and share his mind. Lupton is a convincing study of a small-minded, embittered, twisted man and is brilliantly played by John Dearth. Once sales manager of his firm, Lupton was broken and dismissed by bullying managers; he now seeks to use the spiders' power to take his revenge by dominating the whole Earth. The other members of the meditation community are similar unfortunates suffering from stress: one of their number, Barnes, says that he came to the community in search of peace of mind. They are broken enough to be dominated by Lupton and the spiders.

The monastery is led by Cho-Je, a Tibetan monk, and the mysterious abbot K'Anpo Rinpoche, whom no-one ever sees. Cho-Je warns his western disciples against the demons and divinities which they may encounter in the course of their meditations; he later identifies the spiders as such, thus confirming their symbolic function as representations of their human carriers' repressed greed, desire and rage. The Doctor and Sarah eventually meet the Abbot in episode five. The Doctor asks if they have met before and, in one of the Pertwee era's most effective scenes, remembers K'anpo as the old hermit who lived behind his house on Gallifrey. K'anpo is a Time Lord and the Doctor's guru (a reference to the Eastern religions in which Westerners were becoming increasingly interested at the time of the story's broadcast). He tells the Doctor that he must return the Metebelis crystal to the Great One, a spider the size of a cathedral that thirsts and aches for it, which will give her power over all of time and space and turn her into God. She taunts the Doctor that he is afraid of her ("You are not accustomed to feeling frightened, are you, Doctor? You are very wise to be afraid of me!") and K'anpo tells him that he must face his worst fear. As the smaller spiders represent the lesser humans' repressed darkness, so the Great One represents the Doctor's greed: he explains this to Sarah as his greed for knowledge, for information. If he hadn't gone to fetch the crystal in "The Green Death" (1973), none of these events would have happened. The Doctor accepts that all the story's horrors are basically his own fault: to make amends and to atone, he must give the crystal to the Great One even though

172

the radiation in its cave will destroy him. The Doctor does so; the power from the Great One's completed web is too great and destroys her; the Doctor is lost in the time vortex until the TARDIS brings him home, to UNIT headquarters. Before the eyes of the Brigadier and Sarah, he regenerates.

Much of "Planet of the Spiders" is excellent. John Dearth, who had voiced BOSS in "The Green Death", steals the show as the scruffy, villainous Lupton; the actresses who provide the spiders' voices – including Kismet Delgado, Roger's widow – are wonderful in their hysteria and absolute conviction. The story prepares for the new Doctor by using the term "regeneration" for the first time in the series; K'anpo is attacked by the possessed humans, collapses and regenerates into Cho-Je. Cho-Je is, of course, a projection of K'anpo's own self and doesn't really exist: this puzzles the Doctor and indicates K'anpo's highly developed mental powers as a very senior Time Lord. The scenes set on Metebelis III aren't nearly as dreadful as sometimes claimed: there is some ropey acting from the human natives but at least we get to see Gareth Hunt in his pre-*New Avengers* days sporting a gringo moustache as Arak, the leader of the two legs. (The spiders dislike being called "spiders" and, in a piece of intelligent verbal coinage, insist on being called "the eight legs"; the word "spider" is forbidden and insulting. Humans are dismissively termed "two legs", thus building on Orwell's slogan in *Animal Farm*: eight legs good, two legs bad.) Robert Sloman said he was unhappy about the treatment of Tommy and argued that such a piece of scripting wouldn't be considered now: who are we, he asked, to sit in judgement over the unfortunate? For a child watching at the time, however, Tommy was an attractive and sympathetic character whom they immediately liked: my nine year old self was horrified to see him mistreated by Barnes and Lupton, who make him cry. John Kane, who plays Tommy, was a veteran of the Royal Shakespeare Company and gives a beautiful and rounded performance. We might object now to the word "cured" to describe the change that has come over him, but it is still touching to see that he is not affected by the rays of energy with which the spiders' servants blast down their victims; nor is Mike Yates. "His compassion protected him," K'anpo explains to Sarah, "just as Tommy's innocence was his shield." This is a powerful metaphor for the qualities which evil can never overcome. Equally poignant is an exchange between Tommy and Sarah: noticing his change, Sarah exclaims, "But you're different! You're just like everybody else!" Glancing at the murderers, sinners and misfits around him, Tommy replies, "I sincerely hope not."

## Racism

There is some critical objection to the supposedly Tibetan K'anpo and Cho-Je being played by a white British and a white Australian actor respectively (George Cormack and Kevin Lindsay: the latter had played Lynx the Sontaran at the beginning of the season). In the highly-regarded Tom Baker story "The Talons of Weng-Chiang" (1977), the leading Chinese character was played by the white Englishman John Bennett, under heavy make-up. Smaller Chinese parts were played by Chinese actors. The serial is considered racist by some, not just because of its casting, but because of the treatment of the Chinese: they are relegated to the position of fanatical cult followers of Weng-Chiang. The characters played by Chinese characters are minor characters who have no space for development: they are stock characters, rather than (racist) stereotypes... but they do speak poor English ("Bag gone, Lord!") which might be realistic but could be ridiculed by those with a racist streak. All this makes a modern viewer uneasy and the script would be very different if made today: although we should note that the only explicit racism is that of the white imperialist British characters, who spout the prejudices of their time. If only the BBC had cast a Chinese actor as Li H'Sen Chang, half the problems would have been solved. In 1980, TV Ontario refused to show the serial on the grounds that it was racist.

Racial politics in the entertainment business was certainly crude in the 1970s and parts went routinely to white actors: seeing a non-

Caucasian face was unusual in 1960s and 1970s *Doctor Who*. It was not until the end of the decade that (white) directors started to listen seriously, for example, to black actors' objections to Othello being played by a white actor in make-up. The part is never now played by a white actor (except for one production starring Patrick Stewart – Captain Jean Luc Picard in *Star Trek: the Next Generation* – in which Othello was white and all the other characters were black). There were distant echoes of the row over "The Talons of Weng-Chiang" in objections to "Dalek" (2005), twenty nine years later. Some American fans argued that the serial was anti-American because a) Van Statten is the villain and b) Van Statten is American. By this reasoning, we could argue that "The Seeds of Doom" (1976) – is anti-British because a) the villain, Harrison Chase, is British and b) he is a baddie. Nevertheless, the revived, post-2005 series is much more inclusive in casting non-Caucasian actors in lead roles and cannot be accused, unlike the original series, of unintentional racism.

# 7
# Fourth Time Lucky

With shooting on 1973's season eleven well underway, it fell to Barry Letts to find a new Doctor. Many actors were considered and invited to meet Letts at the BBC. He usually greeted them with the formula that he wasn't offering them the part, but if it were to be offered to them, would they be interested? Several people were under serious consideration. One was Michael Bentine, an actor and comedian who had worked on *The Goons*, the long-running BBC radio comedy by Spike Milligan featuring Milligan, Peter Sellars and Harry Secombe. Bentine said he was interested but insisted that he would have to have considerable input into rewriting the scripts: this was how he had always worked and he expected to have the same latitude on *Doctor Who*. This wasn't the way *Doctor Who* worked, however, and Letts moved on.

Another actor who was interviewed was Richard Hearne, who had played the popular children's character Mr Pastry. Letts recalled that Hearne didn't seem to understand what he was being offered: he said that he liked *Doctor Who* but that he didn't think that Mr Pastry was right for the character and they weren't the same at all[1]. Jim Dale, a lead in many of the *Carry On* films, was considered: he was flattered and interested, although the discussions ultimately came to nothing. Letts talked to Graham Crowden, who said he would enjoy playing the Doctor but might want to leave after one year if there was a lovely part going at the National Theatre. One year wasn't enough (although it was for Christopher Eccleston), and Crowden had talked out himself out of the running[2]. Letts considered Fulton Mackay, who later became famous as the disciplinarian prison office

---

[1] In "Twice Upon A Time" (2018), the twelfth Doctor calls the first, "Mr Pastry" – a reference to the Hearne character.

[2] Crowden later appeared as Soldeed, the major villain of "The Horns of Nimon" (1979) – enough said.

Mr Mackay in *Porridge* (BBC 1974-1977). Mackay had played Dr Quinn to perfection in "Doctor Who and the Silurians" (1970); Letts considered him a fine actor who, like Troughton and unlike Pertwee, would give a performance that was quite unlike his private self. Again, this discussion came to nothing.

Time was getting on. The new actor would have to be cast soon if he were to rehearse the shows for the new season. Bill Slater, the Head of Serials at the BBC, asked Letts if he had considered an actor called Tom Baker. Baker was a National Theatre player and had been the lead in Slater's BBC production of *The Millionairess* by George Bernard Shaw, which co-starred Maggie Smith. Letts and Dicks interviewed Tom Baker in their BBC office and were immediately enthusiastic. Letts told Baker that he seemed ideal, but the problem was that he had never seen him act. Tom Baker replied that he had played the villain in the feature film *The Golden Voyage of Sinbad*, then showing in London, and Letts and Dicks could see him in that, if they liked. Producer and script editor took an afternoon off to see the film, loved Baker's performance as the evil magician, and cast him as the Doctor.

The BBC had let it be known that Jon Pertwee would leave the programme at the end of the season and that the search was on for the new Doctor Who (sic). Baker's casting was announced while "The Monster of Peladon" was airing on television. He appeared in the papers aside Elisabeth Sladen and a Cyberman from "The Invasion" (1968) (with regular *Who* extra Pat Gorman in the costume). As a child, I was horrified to see him in my father's *Guardian* newspaper. How could this man be the Doctor? I only had vague memories of Patrick Troughton and, aside from the Peter Cushing films, only knew Jon Pertwee as the Doctor. Certainly, Tom Baker was virtually unknown among the public at the time, yet he became arguably the most successful of the Doctors, playing the role for longer than anyone: seven seasons to Pertwee's five, Tennant's three and a bit, Matt Smith's and Peter Capaldi's three. He dominated viewers' conception of what the Doctor should be for the rest of the original show's run, and, for viewers who had grown up with the classic series, for the revival too. Colin Baker said people who recognised him as the Doctor kept asking, "Where's your scarf?", which had been Tom Baker's distinguishing item of dress. Just weeks before the series returned in 2005, *The Observer* expressed a hope that Christopher Eccleston would be wearing the "loop the loop" scarf. It was Tom Baker who appeared as the Curator (a future incarnation of the Doctor – we think) in the fiftieth anniversary special, "The Day of the Doctor" (2013). The actors who had played the other Doctors in the classic series had come to understand that they wouldn't be in the special, and Colin Baker expressed understandable unhappiness that, of all of them, Tom Baker would be appearing after all and they wouldn't.

## Doctor Who and The Daleks in Seven Keys to Doomsday

Baker came into the studio to record the transformation scene for "Planet of the Spiders" in 1974. He changed into Jon Pertwee's costume and the regeneration was achieved by a simple cross-fade between the actors: unlike the revived series, this regeneration did not cause the whole room to blow up.

The regeneration scene was completed and broadcast on 8th June 1974, just as alternative fourth Doctor was preparing at the Adelphi Theatre in London for the Christmas 1974 debut of *Doctor Who and the Daleks in Seven Keys to Doomsday* by Terrance Dicks. Never since the film *Daleks: Invasion Earth 2150 AD* (1966) had there been such a clumsily titled mouthful of a title, but the play's producers presumably thought that "*Doctor Who* **and** the Daleks" was a bigger pull than *Doctor Who* alone. Indeed, some viewers who had only a glancing acquaintance with the series thought it was called "*Doctor Who and the Daleks*" anyway; various friends in the primary school playground had sometimes tried to convince me that the show's original monsters had always been the Daleks and other creatures had only arrived much, much later. They were presumably repeating their parents' imperfect memories of the Hartnell era, when, granted, there *were* lots of Dalek episodes, but I knew better and wasn't having any of it.

This was the second commercial *Doctor Who* play after *Curse of the Daleks* by David Whitaker in the early 1960s[1]. *Seven Keys to Doomsday* begins with a projected film sequence of Jon Pertwee collapsing. On stage, the Doctor gets up in the form of Trevor Martin, an actor who had played a Time Lord in "The War Games" (1969). Two youngsters rush onto the stage from the front row of the audience: these were to be the Doctor's companions for his adventure and one of them, Jenny, was played by Wendy Padbury (Zoe in Troughton's final season). The plot rattles along cheerfully: in an echo of "The Keys of Marinus" (1964) and anticipating the Key to Time season (1978-9), the Doctor must collect seven keys from Karn in order to thwart the Daleks' schemes. He is opposed by the Master of Karn, played by Simon Jones (who was to become the original Arthur Dent in *The Hitchhiker's Guide to the Galaxy*), and crocodile-like humanoids called Clawrantulas.

The play's run was curtailed by fears of an IRA bombing campaign in the capital: they had already bombed pubs in Guildford, only a few miles from London, and in Birmingham. Television advertisements for the play were put out in the ITV London region in an attempt to drum up punters. These consisted of a caption of the poster with a Dalek voice announcing "*Doctor Who* and the Daleks at the Adelphi Theatre in London" and were about ten seconds long, but they failed to entice a scared public into the West End and *Seven Keys to Doomsday* closed early. A kindly family friend had tickets to take my brother and me to the play but the performance was cancelled. The kindly family friend asked if we would like to see *The Sound of Music* (or some such thing) instead, an offer that we rejected with the utmost scorn. Terrance Dicks re-used some of the plot elements of the play in "The Brain of Morbius" (1976), including the name Karn for the planet, but the show was never revived until it was issued as an audio play in 2008 by the company Big Finish, who had released many original *Doctor Who* dramas and

---

[1] Dicks would also write the play *Doctor Who – The Ultimate Adventure* (1989), which starred Jon Pertwee and, later, Colin Baker. See chapter 14, Limbo.

were the keepers of the sacred flame while the show was taken off air by the malignant forces at the BBC between 1989 and 2005[1]. Trevor Martin reprised his role as the Doctor.

## One novelisation a month

Like Malcolm Hulke before him, Dicks concentrated as a freelance prose writer after leaving the show, writing the bulk of the *Doctor Who* novelisations. He adapted his own stories and, if the script writer didn't want to write the book, would make him a reasonable offer: I do the work and you get half the money. Robert Holmes was quite happy for Dicks to write up his stories, saying that he found writing prose fiction about as much fun as digging trenches. By the end of the seventies, Target Books was publishing a new *Doctor Who* title every month and Terrance Dicks was writing about nine of them a year. Dicks explained that he had to write so many of them he didn't have time to rethink how to describe established characters, monsters or artefacts like the TARDIS, for every new book. Instead, he established a shorthand for descriptions which were endlessly re-used. These became affectionately regarded, and occasionally parodied, by fans: the fourth Doctor was "a tall man in a collection of vaguely bohemian looking garments... a broad brimmed hat jammed onto a mop of curly hair"; the TARDIS's materialisation and dematerialisation noise[2] was "a wheezing, groaning sound". Fans laughed at the endless repetition of this image, so Dicks amended it in a much later novel to, "a *defiant* wheezing, groaning sound."[3] The books sold a total of eight million copies, contributed enormously to children's literacy in the United Kingdom and were in constant demand in school libraries. Some

---

[1] Not including repeats and the hiccup of the 1996 TV Movie.
[2] Originally created by recording and distorting the noise of a key running down the strings of a grand piano.
[3] The *Doctor Who* strips in *Doctor Who Weekly/Monthly/Magazine* (1979-present) opted for "Vworp! Vworp!", which became almost as famous as an alternative to "a wheezing groaning sound". Malcolm Hulke preferred "the trumpeting of a thousand mad elephants" in *Doctor Who and the Doomsday Weapon* (p.18, London, 1974).

people came to *Doctor Who* through the novelisations rather than the televisions series. Novelist Eion Colfer spent his childhood reading them and only caught the tv series later. It was Hartnell who most clearly matched the Doctor of his imagination and Colfer duly used Hartnell's Doctor in his e-book *A Big Hand for the Doctor* in January 2013. South African radio wrote to the BBC in the late 1970s asking if they could adapt these novels about the adventures of Doctor Who into a radio series. The letter landed on producer Graham Williams' desk and his reply explained gently that the novels were actually themselves adaptations of an exisiting television show.

The *Doctor Who* novelisations were celebrated by Mark Gatiss in a BBC Radio Four documentary in 2008; a correspondent to *The Times Educational Supplement* lamented the lack of novels based on the revived series, arguing that some children needed to have had visual images (here, memories of a television programme) to support their reading[1]. The BBC was producing original *Doctor Who* novels from 2005. BBC Books believed there was a limit to the number of types of *Doctor Who* books that shops would take; also, the revived series was endlessly repeated on BBC 3 and freely available on DVD. A major reason for the success of the original novels was that they allowed people to revisit adventures which usually only screened once. Nevertheless, the BBC did reprint some of the old Target novelisations, five in 2011 and another five in 2012, with new introductions by *Who* luminaries and notes on the text's puzzling contemporary references to, for example, feet and inches, rather than centimetres. 2018 saw the launch of new novelisations of "Rose" by Russell T Davies; "The Christmas Invasion" by Jenny Colgan; "The Day of the Doctor" by Stephen Moffat and "Twice Upon a Time" by Paul Cornell[2]. This warm bath of nostalgia, vividly recalling skipping down the high street to the newsagent to buy the new book *Doctor Who and the Revenge of the*

---

[1] Frank Danes, Letters, *The Times Educational Supplement*, 17th July 2009
[2] http://www.radiotimes.com/news/tv/2017-11-15/doctor-who-books-steven-moffat-russell-t-davies/

*Cybermen* (ludicrously placed next to *Doctor Strange* by our local shopkeeper) in 1975, is one into which older fans cannot wait to plunge and which, it is to be feared, might be an excitement altogether too strong for them. I have already written my will.

## "Robot"

Tom Baker's first story, "Robot" (1974-5) was the last to be produced by Barry Letts. Terrance Dicks wrote it as a freelancer, having handed script editing duties over to Robert Holmes. Dicks had persuaded the BBC that it was always a *Doctor Who* tradition that the outgoing script editor wrote the first story of the new season; the BBC bought the idea, which Dicks had just then made up.

"Robot" is essentially a Pertwee story with a new Doctor: the Brigadier, Sergeant (now Warrant Officer) Benton and Sarah Jane are all present and the Doctor continues to work for UNIT. It was made back-to-back with "Planet of the Spiders" and Elisabeth Sladen (Sarah) had to use her rest days from that serial to go and shoot its location sequences. Dicks wrote the new Doctor as an essentially generic Doctor[1]: he is eccentric, manic, excitable, brilliant and very funny, true to the warning K'Anpo gives at the end of "Planet of the Spiders": "[The regeneration] will shake up the brain cells a little. You may find his behaviour somewhat – erratic." I remember one of my brothers remarking on the first episode, in the politically incorrect language of the time, "Well, Patrick Troughton was a clown but this new Doctor is a loony." Dicks admitted that he

---

[1] Does writing for a new Doctor entail finding a new speech style for him? Steven Moffat was asked if there was a difference in writing for each of the new series Doctors up to Capaldi and replied that the Doctor was essentially the same character, so the answer was no or, not really. The actor's performance creates the difference. Contrastingly, Russell T Davies did point out to Matthew Graham, the writer of "Fear Her" (2006), that his first drafts made Tennant sound like Jon Pertwee. Did the Doctor then tell Rose – "my dear" – to keep quiet, leave things to him and to go and make the tea?

had written the part as very eccentric but said that future script editors could tone the Doctor down if they wanted to.

In "Robot", the Doctor regenerates under the eyes of Sarah and the Brigadier. Dicks felt the dramatic crux of whether the new Doctor is who he says he is had been dealt with before[1] and repeating it would get in the way of telling the story. The new Doctor is provided with a new assistant. This is Lieutenant Surgeon Harry Sullivan, on secondment to UNIT from the Royal Navy, played by the square jawed, good looking Ian Marter. Barry Letts had cast him before casting the Doctor; it was felt that Harry, a young action hero, could handle the rough stuff if an older actor as the Doctor could not (shades of Ian, Steven and Ben to Hartnell's Doctor, hmm my boy, yes). As Tom Baker was in his early forties, the Doctor was quite capable of looking after himself in a fight, and this function of Harry's character quickly became redundant. Nevertheless, he was an engaging and entertaining companion, British to the core and liable to call Sarah "old thing" or "old girl", and exclaim "I say!" at the sight of a new wonder. When he disguises himself as a man from the Ministry in order to infiltrate the sinister Think Tank organisation, he sports a bowler hat and looks just like John Steed from *The Avengers*. Sarah confirms his status as a hallmarked English hero by telling him that his undercover work gives him the chance "to be a real James Bond".

Tom Baker liked the script of "Robot" and gave a splendid performance as the Doctor. He was clearly working very hard, in his first few stories, to give a performance; he relaxed more into the role by the end of the season and thereafter apparently played the part effortlessly. Tom Baker admitted that the best way to play a benevolent alien with secrets was to play it as Tom Baker; unlike Troughton, but like Pertwee, he played the Doctor as himself.

In the first episode, the Doctor vanishes into the TARDIS to find a new outfit: he appears, with astonishing rapidity, as a Viking and a Pierrot. The Brigadier objects, reminding him that UNIT is a secret organisation: "Do you think I might attract attention?" asks the

---

[1] In "The Power of the Daleks" (1966) and "Spearhead from Space" (1970)

Doctor, wide eyed under a huge Viking helm; "It's just possible," the Brigadier replies, stony faced. The Doctor's final outfit is the familiar Bohemian collection of red corduroy jacket, golfing jumper, tie, floppy hat and enormously long scarf, a much more anarchic assembly that Pertwee's velvet smoking jackets. The costume was designed by James Acheson (who later designed the film *The Last Emperor* (1987)) and inspired by Henri de Toulouse Lautrec's poster for the nightclub star Aristide Bruant: Bruant's heroic, striding pose in the poster is exactly right for the new Doctor.

A lady called Begonia Pope was asked to knit the scarf; nobody told her how long it should be and she used all the wool she was given. The finished article was about fourteen feet long and was immediately adopted into the new Doctor's costume and repertoire. By the end of part two of "Robot", he is stretching it between two pillars in an attempt to trip the Robot up, and Tom Baker devised business with the scarf throughout his seven year run. The scarf did for him on location filming for his third story "The Sontaran Experiment" (1975): Baker tripped over it on location in Dartmoor, broke his collar bone and was as rushed to hospital as you could be when filming in such a craggy region. Without the Doctor, the production team hurriedly decided to carry on filming with Baker's stuntman Terry Walsh playing the Doctor in long shot, Walsh imitating Tom Baker's loping stride. When he returned from hospital, a somewhat immobile Tom Baker shot all the close ups, the scarf concealing his neck brace.

"Robot" is a good, straightforward story designed to introduce the new Doctor. The plans and parts for a new disintegrator gun are stolen; several people are killed in the robberies and one involves a tunnel into a subterranean vault. Benton observes that it has no pit props and whoever was in it wouldn't have been able to breathe; the Doctor replies darkly that whoever was in it wouldn't have needed to breathe. The culprit is experimental Robot K1, designed by the environmentalist Professor Kettlewell; made of living metal, with the capacity to grow, it can think and has been imprinted with the Professor's own principles. Unfortunately, the Robot has become a weapon in the hands of the Scientific Reform Society (SRS), a crackpot organisation led by Miss Hilda Winters that wants to reorganise the world along "scientific" (i.e. totalitarian) lines. Forced to go against Kettlewell's prime directive ("I must serve humanity and never harm it") it goes mad. The SRS gets hold of the launch codes for the world's nuclear weapons (as you do), which the governments of the world handed over to a responsible power. This power would publish them if international tension looked likely to develop into nuclear war; faced with other governments accessing and perhaps using their own nuclear missiles, prime ministers and presidents would back down. "Naturally enough," states the Brigadier, "the only country that could be trusted with them was Great Britain." "Well naturally," replies the Doctor, "I mean, all the rest were foreigners." The disintegrator gun is built and assembled, the SRS retreats into a nuclear bunker to blackmail the world, and the Brigadier attempts to dispose of the Robot using the disintegrator gun. Unfortunately, the energy released causes the Robot to grow to giant size: the Doctor eventually destroys it with a virus which attacks Kettlewell's living metal.

### Environmentalist satire

Terrance Dicks admitted that the story was heavily influenced by the movie *King Kong* (1933). Sarah strikes up a friendship with the Robot, as Fay Wray had with Kong, and Sarah is similarly saved by the beast when the giant Robot goes on the rampage. This borrowing was perhaps inspired by a maxim of Malcolm Hulke's, often quoted by Terrance Dicks: "What *Doctor Who* needs is good, original ideas. They do not, however, have to be your good, original ideas." The new producer, Philip Hinchcliffe, who took over after "Robot", and his script editor Robert Holmes shamelessly raided the movies and stories of popular culture for the three years of their tenure. The SRS is the sort of tin-pot fascist organisation that sprang up in Germany in the 1920s. Its origins can be seen by removing its middle letter, and one of its nerdy members, who tells Sarah her trouser suit would forbidden in the new order, is described as a "Himmler type" in the script. The story is a last gasp for the Pertwee-era environmentalist satires. Kettlewell is a committed environmentalist who has developed new solar batteries which would provide a source of free, endless and clean energy. Naturally, the authorities aren't interested. Exasperated and upset, Kettlewell teams up with SRS to make world governments stop ruining the planet by blackmailing them: stop, or there will be a nuclear war. The Doctor reminds Kettlewell of the series' central premise, that

186

the end never justifies the means. Kettlewell is horrified when he realises that Miss Winters intends to launch the missiles – "You want a better world, don't you?" she sneers – and has no intention of giving up when the governments call their bluff. The story wrestles with the problem of the nuclear deterrent: is it a bluff and would we actually use the missiles if our bluff were called? Such engagement with the world of reality had earned the praise of Shaun Sutton, the Head of Drama at the BBC in 1972: "I think the reason for the success of the show is that it's got a quality of moral indignation. Beneath the entertainment there is a concern for real issues."[1] When Hinchcliffe and Holmes took over, *Doctor Who* often dropped satire in favour of gothic adventure and horror narratives: the narratives were of elemental battles between good and evil, not always specifically tied to a satirical point. (An obvious exception here is "Genesis of the Daleks" in Baker's first season, which had been commissioned by Letts.)

## Feminism

Sarah, who refused to be patronised by the Doctor in her first season, had been introduced as a response to the feminism which was now coming into mainstream popular consciousness. In the early 1970s, news magazine programmes like the BBC's *Nationwide* had invited feminist thinkers to appear so that they could be chortled at by middle aged, male presenters for suggesting we should use such ludicrous terms as "chairperson" or "house husband". Dicks decided on a female villain for "Robot" as a response to contemporary feminism. This was a sympathetic attempt to create a strong female role for an actress, but Miss Winters herself could be criticised as conforming to the stereotype of a feminist. She wears glasses, is apparently uninterested in men[2], shouts, and is

---

[1] Hulke and Dicks, *The Making of* Doctor Who, London, 1972, p.8
[2] Although an avowedly lesbian character wouldn't join the show until 2017 in the person of Bill. This was twelve years after the gay / bisexual / ominisexual Captain Jack Harkness was introduced in "The Empty Child" (2005).

aggressive. On the other hand, and following the fascist origins of the SRS, such women had crewed the concentration camps; the horror felt by the Allies at finding some of the most vicious SS guards were female had quickly killed off the patronising nineteenth century assumption that women were, by their nature, the gentler sex. Miss Winters was, in any case, one of the more successful and believable of *Doctor Who*'s few female villains. A previous villainess had been vetoed. Michael Briant had cast Susan Jameson as the IMC's vicious security chief Morgan in "Colony in Space" (1971), but reports of a female sadist wearing PVC and shooting colonists had caused cluckings of alarm in the top floor of the BBC, who demanded that Morgan's gender should be changed. This was no doubt to pre-empt crowing headlines in the tabloids ("Kinky klad killer wields whip in saucy new Dr Who!"). Susan Jameson was paid off and the part went instead to Tony Caunter.

In "Robot", the Brigadier pulls a gun on Miss Winters and orders her to cancel the destructor codes; she taunts him by saying, "You won't shoot, Brigadier," which is of course true: the Brigadier could *never* shoot a lady. Sarah, however, has no such qualms, and trains the gun on Miss Winters, who backs down.

"Robot" was directed by Christopher Barry, a veteran *Doctor Who* director. He was perhaps chosen because of his experience in introducing a new Doctor to the public: he had previously directed "The Power of the Daleks" (1966), Troughton's first serial. Mindful of the problem of mixing film and video which had marred so much of the previous season's "Invasion of the Dinosaurs", Letts and Barry opted to shoot all location sequences on video. Previous stories had always shot location sequences on film, not least because film cameras were portable while video cameras were lumbering monsters. However, the BBC had recently invested in new, lightweight video cameras designed for outside broadcasts: these had been successfully used to shoot an episode of *Z Cars*, the BBC's long-running police drama, and "Robot" was the second BBC production to use them. Rodney Bennett employed them again to shoot "The Sontaran Experiment", which was entirely made on location. With studio and location footage on video, the sequences with the Robot at giant size were combined with a degree of success: the sequences are certainly much more effective than the risible dinosaurs. The Robot strode around a blue screen set (in fact, with yellow used as the keying-in colour), smashing down model telegraph poles and stomping on miniature wooden huts. Viewing the rushes, it was found that the Robot's silver costume reflected the yellow screen; when the location footage was added, his legs kept disappearing. A reshoot was ordered. There are still some transparent robotic legs in the final programme, but the money had run out, as it had for the tank ordered up by the Brigadier to take care of K1. The production team opted to use an Action Man toy tank against blue screen, in a sequence which vies with the giant rat in "The Talons of Weng-Chiang" (1977) as the worst effect ever to appear in colour, original series *Doctor Who.* Fans cringed with embarrassment and their enemies rubbed their hands gleefully, ready to tease them about the dreadful shot when schools resumed after Christmas. The sequence added nothing to the final programme and could have easily been cut.

Much of the production's effectiveness comes from James Acheson's wonderful design of the Robot. Dicks had wanted it to be massive and terrifying, yet human and appealing as well. Acheson's design succeeded on all counts, not least because its fan-shaped head grille suggests eyebrows raised in puzzlement at the terrifying orders it is given. The Robot was played by Michael Kilgarriff, who had been an Ogron in "Frontier in Space" (1973) and the Cybercontroller in "The Tomb of the Cybermen" (1967) (and, later, in "Attack of the Cybermen" (1985)). His Robot costume was so heavy that he wore a lightweight, foil and balsa version for rehearsals. In an interview, he recalled that he couldn't get up when he fell over but lay there like an upturned beetle; he also lacerated his legs from the sharp edges of the aluminium. The Robot costume still exists and was for many years displayed in the window of the Museum of the Moving Image on London's South Bank; Terrance Dicks said he liked to wander over to it when passing, "to have a look at my Robot".

## Holmes and Hinchcliffe take over

Terrance Dicks and Barry Letts moved on after "Robot", although both were to return to the show. Dicks wrote several more stories and Letts directed "The Android Invasion" (1975) before returning as executive producer for Tom Baker's final season, mentoring the inexperienced producer John Nathan-Turner. Back in 1974, Robert Holmes continued as script editor and Philip Hinchcliffe took up the reins of producer. They faced a similar situation to their predecessors in 1970 in that a previous production team had set the shape of the new season, commissioning stories which neither much liked. Bob Baker and Dave Martin had provided another Sontaran tale; the Cybermen were to return after an absence of seven years; John Lucarotti had submitted an unfilmable science fiction story and Terry Nation had turned in the third Dalek story in as many years. Lucarotti had written three historical stories for Hartnell's Doctor: the well regarded "Marco Polo" (1964, the fourth story of the first season), "The Aztecs" (1964) and the curiosity "The Massacre" (1966), concerning the slaughter of Huguenots on St Bartholemew's Eve by Catholics in Paris in 1572. The latter tale hadn't been well regarded by the then production team, who thought its subject matter too obscure for popular television; the then story editor Donald Tosh rewrote the scripts, to Lucarotti's dissatisfaction. What became "The Ark in Space" (1975) was Lucarotti's first science fiction script for *Doctor Who*: it was uneven in pacing and required special effects that were way beyond the series' budget, including, apparently, the Doctor standing on the hull of the space station and using a golf club to dispatch the aliens into space. Robert Holmes completely rewrote the scripts and received the sole on-screen credit for the new story. In doing so, Holmes extended a practice which would last throughout his time as script editor and anticipate the way of working of the revived series' show runners: the script editor would rework scripts into the new house style, undertaking root and branch

190

re-workings of stories, and even rewriting scripts from experienced *Doctor Who* writers. It seems likely that Holmes wrote some of "Genesis of the Daleks" (1975); he certainly completely rewrote the twelfth season's final story, "Revenge of the Cybermen" (1975). This was to be made back-to-back with "The Ark in Space", using the same impressive sets of the Ark as a cost-saving measure.

Gerry Davis, who had created the Cybermen with Kit Pedlar, produced his first script for the programme in eight years. As "Return of the Cybermen", he confined the Cybermen to the Ark and included both the Doctor's five hundred year diary (a Troughton hallmark) and the destruction of the Cybermen by something called an X-ray laser. Philip Hinchcliffe took immediately exception to the latter as too childish. He wrote to Davis to explain that the proportion of adults in the show's audience now far outnumbered the proportion of children, and that the audience demographic was thus radically changed from the mid-sixties, when Davis had been story-editor. Some in the audience who were very conversant with science and had BSc's, wouldn't put up with nonsense like an "X-ray laser"[1]. Holmes rewrote the script, introducing the Vogans and their planet of gold. Gerry Davis later said Holmes had done so because the BBC suddenly discovered it had more money than it thought, and that he didn't like what appeared on screen at all.

To be fair to Davis, "Revenge of the Cybermen" is one of the weakest of the early Tom Baker stories. There are only three Cybermen, their costumes slightly redressed versions from "The Invasion"; they want to destroy Voga because it supplied the gold ammunition which did for the Cybermen in the last Cyberwar. This nutty new piece of Cybermen lore is only really sold to us by the absolute conviction with which Tom Baker delivers a line about the Cybermen being defeated by the advent of the "glitter gun". The Cyberleader is as camp as Christmas and the Cybermen clump

---

[1] Christopher H Bidmead made the same point when he was script editor for Tom Baker's final season. In his guide to writers, he stressed that any science in the programme should be credible and, at the very least, the writers should consult the relevant page of an encyclopaedia.

around the planet of gold for three episodes taking pot shots at the Vogans. Kevin Stoney, who played the villain Tobias Vaughn so marvellously in "The Invasion" (1968), turned up as Tyrum, leader of the Vogans, but he is wasted as a goodie and invisible under all the high forehead, heavy eye-lidded Vogan make up.

The Vogan sequences were shot in Wookie Hole in Somerset, a cave system supposed to be haunted; Elisabeth Sladen fell into a swift-flowing underwater river and was nearly killed. She was saved by a stuntman just before she was swept away. Director Michael E. Briant thought the script dull and just an excuse to "bring back a boring monster"; he was wary of directing "The Robots of Death" in 1977, fearing that he would have to make yet more expressionless robot creatures exciting. Even the Doctor seems irritated by the Cybermen:

> You've no home planet, no influence, nothing. You're just a pathetic bunch of tin soldiers skulking around the galaxy in an ancient spaceship.

## Horror

Hinchcliffe and Holmes' intention was to direct the programme towards the upper age range of the family audience. In doing so, more overt horror was allowed than had been the case in the Pertwee seasons and Hinchcliffe and Holmes were responsible for the three seasons that are among the most highly regarded of the programme's fifty-plus years. The fourth Doctor is less of a reassuring, fatherly figure than the third and voyaging with him is not the comforting experience it had been for his companions. There is no longer the same sense that everything will be all right and they need only run to the Doctor for him to protect them: this new Doctor is apparently younger, more vulnerable, more liable to physical pain than his predecessor. In "Genesis of the Daleks", the Doctor is punched and beaten by Kaled soldiers. He appears quite as hurt as a human being would be, when Pertwee would have cried

"Haiii!" and whisked them over his shoulder in no time. The new Doctor is also more alien, given to moods of distant abstraction when he stands, eyes wide and unblinking, gazing into the middle distance while the Morestrans strut about in "Planet of Evil" (1975) or Sarah tries to cheer him up in the first TARDIS scene of "Pyramids of Mars" (1975)[1]. The Doctor's universe is similarly a more frightening place as Hinchcliffe and Holmes immediately increased the horror content on Letts' departure: Styre the Sontaran tortures humans to death in experiments designed to test their weakness to invasion and to gratify his sadism; Noah, the commander of the Ark in Space, slowly transforms into an insectoid Wirrn, the hideous new form burning into his flesh.

Hinchcliffe also thought the UNIT set up was childish and silly, disliking what he referred to as all these soldiers running around shooting at things, and got rid of it. The familiar characters of the Brigadier and Sergeant Benton were phased out after "Terror of the Zygons" (the first story of season thirteen) and Nicholas Courtney didn't return as the Brigadier until "Mawdryn Undead" in 1983. He had been was written into "The Android Invasion" (1975) and "The Seeds of Doom" (1976), but Courtney, seeing that his days as a regular were over, was unavailable and had returned to the theatre. The Brigadier's lines were given to two military types, Colonel Faraday in "The Android Invasion" (Patrick Newell, who had played Mother in *The Avengers)* and Major Beresford (John Acheson) in "The Seeds of Doom". There was a sharp rise in the number of viewer complaints that the programme was now much too frightening. Holmes responded by saying that it should no longer be watched by small children. Nevertheless, all but one of the episodes in Tom Baker's first two seasons went out before the 6.00

---

[1] Mark Gatiss picked up on the Doctor's alien nature in his script for "The Unquiet Dead" (2005). The script has Christopher Eccleston's Doctor "at his most alien" (stage direction) when he tells Rose that the Gelth's request for human cadavers as vehicles for their disembodied bodies is perfectly reasonable: she can get used to it, or go home.

p.m. watershed and so were foolishly scheduled as suitable for all[1]. The BBC belatedly rescheduled Tom Baker's third season (mostly) after six o'clock, but concerns about its horrific content had by then become too entrenched to save Philip Hinchcliffe (see chapter eight, "Gothic Horror").

## "Genesis of the Daleks" – the best *Who* story of all time and space?

Unhappy with the Cybermen, the new production team was similarly unenthusiastic about the presence of a Dalek story in their first season. To the disappointment of younger viewers, both Daleks and Cybermen were unceremoniously dropped from the new two seasons in favour of new monsters. In a significant shift, single villainous figures like Davros, Sutekh, Morbius, Harrison Chase, Heironymous, Eldrad and Magnus Greel came to replace the uniform races of monsters favoured in the Pertwee years. James Chapman has rightly pointed out that these megalomaniacs and psychopaths are all too recognisable as science fiction versions of "the Hitlers, Stalins, Amins and Pol Pots of the *Doctor Who* universe"[2]; as such, they are arguably much more terrifying and plausible than, say, an undifferentiated cohort of Cybermen. They were also popular with actors. Michael Spice, who voiced Morbius and played Magnus Greel in "The Talons of Weng-Chiang" (1977), said that acting was usually about restraining emotions, suggesting moods with small changes in facial expressions and tone: thus he loved playing Morbius and Greel because he could really let rip ("Let the talons of Weng-Chiang shred your Fleeeeeeesssh!"). Yet,

---

[1] Programmes scheduled between 6.00 and 9.00 p.m. were classified as suitable for families with adult guidance and, after 9.00 p.m., as for adults only. *Star Trek* regularly went out in the early 1970s at 7.10 p.m.. I know this because my bedtime was 7.30 p.m.. My father, who thought *Star Trek* was rubbish (although he loved *Doctor Who* and, aged ninety, still does) wouldn't let me stay up to see the whole programme and my brother and I used to make up the ending. These tended not to involve the original *Star Trek* series' cop out of Kirk and Co being saved by god-like aliens who give the baddie a smack and send him packing.

[2] James Chapman, *Inside the TARDIS*, London, 2006, p.117

in spite of Holmes and Hinchcliffe's unhappiness with the Daleks, "Genesis of the Daleks" (1975) is one of the most intelligent, most well-acted and best written of all the *Doctor Who* stories. It regularly won the "best ever story" award from readers of *Doctor Who* magazine, until it was eventually knocked off its perch by "The Caves of Androzani" (1984), "Blink" (2008) and "The Day of the Doctor" (2013) in subsequent polls. Yet "Genesis" always made it to the top five.

Around 1974, Terry Nation buttonholed Robert Holmes, who was shadowing Dicks as script editor, at a social event for *Who* writers. Nation told him he thought there should be a Dalek story every year. Holmes, who had come up with the title "Death to the Daleks" (1974) as an expression of his disdain, replied, "Do you, Terry?" and wandered off. He was somewhat surprised to receive a letter from Nation's agent saying that he had agreed to commission a Dalek story annually from his client.[1]

Letts commissioned Terry Nation to write him a third Dalek story in 1974. When the scripts came in, Letts spoke to Nation, saying, "It's a very good story, Terry, but you've sold it to us four times already." Nation, amused, asked what he meant and Letts detailed the list of plot elements he had used before. It is something of an axiom among fans that Nation's scripts are always the same: in "Planet of the Daleks" (1973), for example, Rebec hides inside a Dalek which the other Daleks blow up just after she has nipped out of it, as Ian had done in "The Daleks" (1964); the deadly Spiridon jungle is much the same as the deadly Kembel jungle in "Mission to the Unknown" (1965), killer plants and all. Letts said to Nation that he had never told us where the Daleks came from and asked him to

---

[1] Speaking as showrunner, Steven Moffat said that it made sense to have a Dalek story every year as a year was a long time for a child: two years would be too long to wait if you were a child and the Daleks didn't appear in one season. Peter Davison also said he didn't feel as though he really was Doctor Who until he was matched up against the Daleks (he had to wait until his final season in 1985). Perhaps some doubters will finally accept that Jodie Whittaker is the Doctor when she fights the Daleks.

write their origin story. Enthused, Terry Nation wrote the scripts for "Genesis of the Daleks".

Presumably rewritten to some degree by Robert Holmes, "Genesis of the Daleks" (1975) is a fine piece of science fiction that debates the ethics of eugenics, genetic engineering and philosophy in the context of a strong adventure story. Anyone who thinks that *Doctor Who* is a children's programme should watch it and it will shut their lying mouths for good. Forseeing a time when the Daleks will have dominated all other life forms, the Time Lords send the Doctor back to Skaro just before their creation. They give him three options: to avert their creation; to alter their genetic development, so that they evolve into less aggressive creatures, or to destroy them utterly[1]. After a thousand years of war, Skaro is a hideous, barren wasteland peopled by mutations. The warring sides, the Thals and the Kaleds, have retreated to their respective cities under protective domes. The war is a virtual stalemate and resources are almost exhausted: Harry and Sarah observe that one of the dead soldiers wears both animal skins and synthetic fibres, and carries both a single shot rifle and a large ray gun[2]. General Ravon, the very young general who interrogates Harry and the Doctor, informs his men that ammunition must be conserved: thus the time travellers will be hanged rather than taken out and shot, as in the past, as a happy piece of economy.

The Thals first appeared in the original Dalek story and returned in "Planet of the Daleks" (1973): the Kaleds are new to the series. Black haired while the Thals are blond, they are dominated by an elite scientific group which operates from its own bunker. This Elite is now so powerful it can demand anything it wants, much to the regular army's resentment. Their leader is Davros, a crippled scientist confined to his wheelchair. The Elite's original intention was to produce weapons capable of ending the war; they soon realise this is futile and direct their efforts towards the survival of

---

[1] Fan historians in 2005 argued that these are the first moves in the Time War which led to the annihilation of the Daleks and the Time Lords by the Doctor. Sort of. Until time was rewritten in "The Day of the Doctor" (2013). I think.

[2] A prop reused from "Galaxy Four" (1965).

their race. Davros has experimented on Kaled flesh, treated it with chemicals and finally discovered its ultimate evolutionary form: a shrivelled and malevolent green bundle of tissue. As it cannot survive without artificial intervention, this creature will clearly need a mobile machine as a life support unit. The mutation and the life support machine combine to become the Dalek: an anagram of the origin race, Kaled.

Davros, however, has become obsessed with the development of the Daleks: they are to be creatures made in his own megalomaniacal image, without morals and without pity, and eventually become his shock troops and bodyguard. Others among the Kaled scientists are alarmed: Ronson helps the Doctor and Harry escape, charging them to report Davros's experiments to the few members of the Kaled government who still have the power to stop him. Councillor Mogran orders an investigation, which Davros welcomes with great interest, agreeing to stop work on the Dalek project. He immediately betrays the Kaleds to the Thals, giving them the necessary chemical formula to allow their rocket to destroy the Kaled city; he has Ronson exterminated as the traitor responsible. The Doctor is recaptured and forced to tell Davros the reason for every Dalek defeat in the future: they will be programmed with this knowledge and there will be no defeats. Davros explains that the Doctor will tell him because, "You are afflicted with a conscience": if he does not co-operate, and in a scene which exemplifies the fearless approach to violence of the new production team, Harry and Sarah will be tortured to death in front of him.

In a quiet conversation after this session, Davros plays the kindly host and offers to talk to the Doctor "as men of science". Davros argues that the Daleks are not a power of evil, but of good: when all other life forms are suppressed, then there will be peace. Nation here emphasises that Davros is evil because he believes, as did the Nazis on whom he is modelled, that the end justified the means: the Doctor is a hero, and is good, because he never believes that, and is filled with outrage at the treatment of human or other intelligent beings as means, not ends: as less than themselves in any scheme, however well intentioned. In "Robot" (1975), the Doctor tells Professor Kettlewell that he cannot stop the nations polluting the world by threatening them with a nuclear war. In a much-praised sequence, the Doctor asks Davros if he would allow the use of a virus which would destroy all other forms of life. Davros is fascinated and says he would indeed allow it: such power would set him up above the gods, "and through the Daleks I shall have that power!" The Doctor thus proves him to be a megalomaniac and a madman, and no philanthropist. Later in the story, the Doctor agonises over the ethics of means and ends. With no option left but genocide, he questions his right to destroy the Daleks: some things might be better with them, future worlds will stop warring against each other and combine together, just because of their fear of the Daleks. If he commits genocide, wiping out an intelligent race, he is no better than they are. He asks Sarah if someone who knew the future pointed out to her a child who would grow up to be a ruthless dictator who would destroy millions of lives, could she then kill that child? Sarah dismisses the argument: matters for simpler for her, the Daleks are the most evil creatures ever invented and they must be destroyed[1]. The Doctor is saved from making the decision by the apparent success of a coup against Davros.

Both of these sequences show Tom Baker at the height of his powers as the Doctor, absolutely convincing in his anguish and in his careful argument about the virus that traps Davros into revealing his true nature as a megalomaniac. It has been pointed out that it would be hard to see Pertwee playing the same scenes with such intensity and success.

Other characters in the story debate the ethics of science. Gharman applauds the intention to allow his race to survive in the new travel machine, but insists that the creature must have a conscience, a judgment of right and wrong, "all the qualities that we

---

[1] The dilemma returns to haunt him when the twelfth Doctor encounters a child in a minefield ("The Magician's Apprentice", 2015): the child is the young Davros. Does the Doctor save him, or leave him to die so that the universe might be saved?

consider essential in ourselves"; it must do good things and evil ones, "but it cannot be allowed to become a heartless machine". He and the other scientists who oppose Davros are exterminated for their pains, but then, inevitably, the Daleks discover their true nature and start operating independently of their creator. The remaining Elite, still loyal to Davros, are to be exterminated. Davros pleads for their lives, urging the Dalek leader to have pity: "Pi-ty?" it grates. "I have no understanding of the word. It is not registered in my vocabulary banks." The last Kaled alive in the bunker, Davros implores the Daleks to obey him as he is their creator; but they are the creatures he has made them, and the Dalek leader states that they are the superior beings. Davros, an inferior, must be exterminated. Finally realising the horror he has created, Davros speeds his chair towards the bunker's self-destruct switch but is gunned down before he can activate it. The Doctor belatedly blows up the Dalek creatures' incubator room but says he has only delayed them for a short time – perhaps a thousand years.

The success of "Genesis of the Daleks" is attributable to a number of factors other than its excellent script, not least the design and lighting. The bunker is convincingly realised as functional, metallic corridors; the lighting designer intelligently lit the artists, rather than the set, so there are menacing shadows everywhere. Davros's mask is a wonderfully convincing sculpture by John Friedlander, who also created the Ogrons and Draconians; it was based on the Mekon from the *Dan Dare* comic strips of *The Eagle*, enjoyed by the young Philip Hinchcliffe. The Daleks are also well realised. Mindful of the problems experienced by taking them to quarry locations in the previous two Dalek stories, director David Maloney confined them to the studio. Painted a gun metal grey, they are convincing weapons of war and the paint job and low lighting successfully hid the flaws in what were now ageing props. (They are practically falling apart by the time of their reappearance in 1979's "Destiny of the Daleks".) The original script called for the Daleks to be different from the Daleks we now know, simpler, less finished. This accounts for the Doctor's line in episode two, "A Dalek...very primitive, but undeniably a Dalek" when the Mark III travel machine is first exhibited to the Elite by Davros. Given that it looks the same as ever, the line is slightly puzzling to viewers. Presumably the budget wouldn't run to refurbishing the Dalek props. Some fans objected to the rewriting of Dalek history: the original Dalek story back in 1964 had called the Daleks' ancestors the Dals, not the Kaleds, and some of the Dalek annuals and comic strips (considered by some fans as canonical) had posited a different history of the Daleks as created by a scientist called Yarvelling. Back in 1975, however, and with memories of the original Dalek story dimmed to extinction by its single screening, no-one cared about such things (and perhaps they shouldn't now). The novelisation *Doctor Who (In An Exciting Adventure with the Daleks)* doesn't mention the Dals and nor does the movie *Dr Who and the Daleks*.

Michael Wisher's performance as Davros is superb and he dominates every scene; he is by turns ranting, demented, wheedling, reasonable and soothing. His Davros is a perfect match for Tom Baker's towering performance as the Doctor. Wisher was a *Doctor Who* regular, having appeared as Wakefield in "The Ambassadors of Death" (1970); Rex Farrell in "Terror of the Autons" (1971) and Kalik in "Carnival of Monsters" (1973). He provided Dalek voices for "Death to the Daleks" (1974) and went on to play Magrik in "Revenge of the Cybermen" (1975) and Morelli in "Planet of Evil" (1976), both of them minor roles. Wisher reasoned that, as his face and eyes would be hidden beneath the mask, his performance would have to rely almost wholly on his voice. He therefore elected to rehearse the part with a paper bag over his head, which sent Tom Baker into hysterics, as he did his first sight of Frederick Jaeger's anti-man-beast make up for "Planet of Evil" (1975). Jaeger looked like an ape-like Mr Hyde.

The Nazi origins of the Daleks were emphasised by the production. The Kaleds wear SS-style uniforms and give each other Nazi salutes. Davros's henchman Nyder (another wonderful performance by Peter Miles) wears Himmler-like wire framed glasses and, for the first studio session, an Iron Cross, which he was asked to remove for subsequent recordings. These elements follow the clear lead of the scripts, with its reference to the Bunker as the leader's last refuge and the expulsion of the mutations – Mutos – into the wasteland with Nyder's explanation, "We must keep the Kaled race pure. Imperfects are rejected." Miles commented[1] on the plausibility of Davros's rise to power: when society is at rock-bottom, the man who says he has all the solutions is the one who is trusted.

Nation had originally intended Davros to be in an ordinary wheelchair, but David Maloney elected to make it look like the lower half of a Dalek. This made explicit the link between Davros and his creations, and the Doctor's point that Davros is trying to perpetuate himself in the Daleks; it also led to a mistake common among viewers who watched the show *very* casually, that Davros was what a Dalek looked like when you took its top off. Mike Tucker[2] examined the original design drawing of Davros's wheelchair, which refers the designers to a page in "Dr Who book". This was, Tucker realised, the 1973 Radio Times *Doctor Who* Special, with its ludicrously inaccurate plans to build you own full sized Dalek. The job was given to visual effects assistant Tony Harding (who designed K9 two years later), and explains why Davros's chair doesn't quite match a Dalek's "body".

Nation's decision to have Davros attempt to destroy his creations was absolutely right, thematically and dramatically. It fitted completely into the philosophical logic of the story: an aggressive creature programmed to survive and to consider itself superior to all other beings would destroy those it considered inferior. Having said this, it seems a contradiction that Nation immediately blurred the boundaries by insisting in the script that we were not to see Davros actually exterminated on screen, in case he, Nation, or a future production team, should want to bring him back. Here, Nation explained that he was trying to learn from his errors in the first Dalek story: at the end, the Daleks were so thoroughly and utterly

---

[1] See the DVD extras on "Genesis of the Daleks", BBC Worldwide DVD 2006.
[2] Speaking at Bedford Who Charity Con 3 in 2017.

destroyed that he had to puzzle over how he could resurrect them for "The Dalek Invasion of Earth" (1964). The solution was to set the second story before the events of the first. This wasn't entirely satisfactory as the Daleks who invaded Earth were much more advanced than the Daleks of the original story, supposedly set in the future, who couldn't even leave their city and apparently had no space travel.

## Davros returns

That Davros was resurrected, and appeared another four times in the original series, was to contradict his determination to destroy his creations and therefore dramatic nonsense. When he returns in "Destiny of the Daleks" (1979), all his qualms have been forgotten and he is keen to lead the Daleks again. He is also a much less interesting character and his resurrection is not helped by David Gooderson's lacklustre performance. To add insult to injury, the budget in inflation-wracked 1979 couldn't stretch to a new mask. Michael Wisher's original mask was returned to the BBC after being displayed at the long running *Doctor Who* exhibitions at Longleat House in Wiltshire and on Blackpool's Golden Mile. It didn't fit Gooderson, visibly wobbles on screen, and didn't meld with the new actor's mouth: what looks like melted chocolate appears to be applied to his face to hide the join.

Davros returned again in "Resurrection of the Daleks" (1984) to menace Peter Davison's Doctor. In his ninety year imprisonment on board an Earth ship he has learnt all about regeneration and was now played by Terry Molloy, best known as milkman Mike Tucker in the BBC Radio 4 soap opera *The Archers*.[1] Michael Wisher had been signed up to reprise Davros for this story, but production dates were shifted when it was moved from the twentieth to the twenty first season because of industrial action. Molloy was apparently cast because of his abilities to imitate the original: his Davros sounds

---

[1] Mike Tucker is not to be confused with Mike Tucker, the special effects designer and writer, who does not deliver milk in Ambridge. As far as we know.

quite like Wisher's but he is now much more of a ranting lunatic, which is character development of a sort. Molloy is certainly better than David Gooderson. The BBC had even found enough money to make him a new mask. Much bigger than the original, as Molloy was a much bigger actor physically than the slight Michael Wisher, the mask is yellow tinged and impressed Russell T Davies as zombie-like and very frightening. Molloy gives a fine performance in the Colin Baker story "Revelation of the Daleks" (1985), in which Davros, now apparently a decapitated head in a transparent tank, calls himself The Great Healer and heads a death care facility called Tranquil Repose. Here, the rich can deposit their loved ones at the moment of death, to be kept in suspended animation until a cure can be found for the diseases that killed them. Davros then cheerfully harvests the corpses to create a new breed of Daleks, before he is carted off by a race of Skarosian Daleks to stand trial for his crimes. He finally appears inside the Emperor Dalek in Sylvester McCoy's "Remembrance of the Daleks" (1988) at the head of the Imperial Daleks, thus revealing a capacity to escape from certain death that rivals the Master's.

Russell T Davies resurrected Davros in "The Stolen Earth"/"Journey's End" (2008), paying more attention than previous writers to Davros's character and origins in "Genesis of the Daleks". Perhaps because he had tried to destroy them in his first story, Davros's relationship with the Daleks is now ambivalent and uneasy. They appear to have accepted him, perhaps because they acknowledge his past achievements: he did try to help them win the war against the robot Movellans in "Destiny of the Daleks", after all. Certainly, there is no more talk of putting him on trial or pitched battles between his Daleks and the "official" Daleks. However, Davros is confined to a vault on the giant spaceship The Crucible, where he is attended by only a few Daleks as servants and his role is merely to advise. The tenth Doctor asks him what exactly his relationship is with the Daleks: Davros replies, uneasily, "We have…an arrangement." The Doctor taunts him by putting his finger on its exact nature: he is the Daleks' "pet".

Julian Bleach plays Davros in this story and his nuanced performance, clearly modelled on Wisher's original, is hugely effective. He is quietly menacing and acidly intelligent, noting that the Doctor prides himself as the man who abhors violence and never carries a gun because he takes ordinary people and turns them into weapons: a fair comment on the bomb-wielding Jack Harkness and gun-toting Rose and Jackie Tyler. The Doctor is silenced by the argument. Davros recognises Sarah Jane, now among the tenth Doctor's companions, as having been there at the beginning on Skaro. Bleach saves his energy for occasional demented outbursts which out-Wisher Wisher: he screams at the Dalek Supreme to "Detonate the reality bomb!" which will destroy everything in every Universe that is not Dalek. Davros is left in the burning Crucible as the Doctor's human clone (don't ask) destroys all the Daleks on board; Davros ignores the Doctor's offer of rescue and shrieks, "I name you forever, the Destroyer of Worlds!" The ship collapses around him and he is apparently helpless; he has, of course, escaped to fight another day, and reappears in the Capaldi story "The Magician's Apprentice"/"The Witch's Familiar" (2015), in which Missy (the Master) is miffed to learn that the Doctor considers Davros, and not her, as his arch-enemy.

# 8
# Gothic Horror

Viewing figures for Tom Baker's first season stayed strong: ten million for "Robot", eleven million for "The Ark in Space" and never falling much below nine million for the rest of the season (even for the lacklustre "Revenge of the Cybermen"). Tom Baker was a success, but the season was cut to a mere twenty episodes: the shortest in the programme's history so far. This was owing to a decision to change the running slot for *Doctor Who* from December (or January) to June, to a September start with the season running through the winter and into spring. The BBC felt *Doctor Who* would beef up its autumn season in the ratings war with ITV, which was to begin scheduling glossy American shows – such as Gerry Anderson's *Space: 1999* – against it. When the revived series debuted in 2005, the BBC and ITV sometimes came to a gentlemen's agreement not to compete against each other when scheduling the same genre of programme: thus, a truce was arranged not to screen the BBC's *Strictly Come Dancing* against ITV's *The X Factor*. In the 1970s, it was war. Before the days of home video, science fiction fans who wanted to watch science fiction on Saturdays had to choose between *Space: 1999* (1975-1977) – quickly followed by *Buck Rogers in the Twenty Fifth Century* (1979-1981) – or *Doctor Who*. As a choice, this wasn't too much of a dilemma of choice as the former was a bit dull and the latter was rubbish, but we didn't know that as the time. Both new shows ate into the BBC viewing figures.

Nevertheless, the autumn to spring run was popular amongst viewers. Newspapers warbled about the pleasures of taking your children to see the football match, to arrive home in the dark and cold to be refreshed with tea, crumpets and *Doctor Who*. Steven Moffat appealed to this spirit when he justified the shifting of Matt Smith's third season to an autumn 2012 start, saying that the programme worked better against dark winter evenings than sunny summer days. As the first batch of season thirty three episodes was screened in a September of glorious sunshine, this appeal fell a bit flat and we had to wait a year for the second half of the season: the BBC, presumably, saving money again.

The change of scheduling meant that the cast and crew worked continuously on *Doctor Who* from season twelve to season thirteen: there was no summer holiday after shooting wrapped on "Genesis of the Daleks", the final season twelve story to be made. A six episode version of "Terror of the Zygons" had been planned to end the season but it was held over to start season thirteen and cut down to four episodes by Robert Holmes, who rewrote it extensively.

Season thirteen, like season eight for the previous production team, was the first season under the exclusive control of Philip Hinchcliffe and Robert Holmes. Their vision of *Doctor Who* ran riot for the next two years, with even more of an emphasis on horror than season twelve. Both producer and script editor raided the back catalogue of literature and films that they enjoyed, writing shameless pastiches to rework them into the *Doctor Who* world. Cosy old monsters and enemies were dropped in favour of new and terrifying ones. The only adversary to return was the Master in "The Deadly Assassin", and he had been given a Hinchcliffe/Holmes horror make-over in his new guise as a decaying corpse.

After a slow start of seven and a half million for "Terror of the Zygons", viewing figures for 1976 and 1977 went through the roof, averaging ten million per episode and peaking at nearly twelve million for "The Android Invasion" (why?) and "The Deadly Assassin" before reaching almost thirteen million for "The Robots of Death". The series was at a height of popularity that it hadn't achieved since Hartnell's days, loved by the public and the fans. The three years of Hinchcliffe and Holmes' tenure are regarded as among the best episodes ever made. I remember general disappointment among my comprehensive school friends at the new episodes produced by Graham Williams from 1977: still starring Tom Baker, they were held generally to be not as good as the Hinchcliffe stories and the critical prognosis at morning break was that the series was past its best.

Yet in spite of its popularity, the show again attracted unwelcome, or even welcome, attention in the form of renewed criticism of its violent and horrific content. Eventually, these unseated Hinchcliffe as producer and took *Doctor Who* in yet another new direction.

There is much less political and social commentary in the Tom Baker stories than there had been in Pertwee's time, not least because the trio of Dicks-Letts-Hulke had moved on; aside from isolated stories like "The Sun Makers" (1977), the show now avoided such social engagement. Tom Baker's first three seasons were instead rollicking science fiction/horror adventures, but always with the strong moral driving force of good fighting evil, and the moral message that good can triumph against apparently overwhelming odds if it asserts itself. In "Pyramids of Mars" (1975), the Doctor is captured by Sutekh, a member of the Osiran super-race, now imprisoned beneath a pyramid in Egypt and powerless to move. The Osirans were hailed as gods by the ancient Egyptians and Sutekh is still possessed of awesome powers. He is also a moral relativist: the Doctor tells him fearlessly that he is evil, and he replies, "Evil? Your evil is my good. I am Sutekh the Destroyer. Where I tread I leave nothing but dust and darkness. I find that good." The Doctor curses him as a "twisted abhorrence" and is blasted into agony for his pains: before Sutekh he is a "grovelling insect" whom Sutekh might "keep...alive for centuries wracked by the most excruciating pain … an amusing diversion". Yet the Doctor heroically defies him, pitting his puny goodness against Sutekh's mighty evil. Eventually, of course, Sutekh is destroyed.

The dialogue of "Pyramids of Mars" is delicious in its richness and melodrama, both hallmarks of Robert Holmes, who is rightly regarded as one of the programme's best writers. Holmes delights in language and his scripts, and scripts rewritten by him as script editor, are jammed with wonderful and quotable lines. Like Dickens, he delights in giving each character an individual idiom. In "The Talons of Weng-Chiang" (1977), Leela and the Doctor journey back to London in the 1880s; a toothless old crone, who has stepped

207

straight out of the pages of Dickens' *Our Mutual Friend*, spies a corpse floating in the Thames. "It's a floater, ain't it guv?" she gabbles to the policeman fishing out the body with a boathook. When they see the corpse is mutilated (by a giant rat), the crone is subdued: "Oh my eye! You wouldn't want that served with onions. Never seen anyfing like it in all me puff." Arrested with a Chinese tong member, Leela demands of the corpulent police sergeant, "Put our prisoner to the torture!" "Well, if that don't take the biscuit," the sergeant chuckles. "This ain't the Dark Ages, you know, miss."

"Pyramids of Mars" is also notable for including a thoughtful scene on the paradoxes of time travel which would become the staple fare of Steven Moffat's scripts in the revival. If Sutekh is freed, he will destroy the world. Sarah protests that they know the world didn't end in 1911: "Do we?" asks the Doctor, and takes her and Lawrence Scarman, an Edwardian gentleman, forward to 1980, Sarah's time, in the TARDIS. They look out on a landscape of hell, winds roaring around desolate rocks and shattered buildings. This is how Sutekh would leave Earth, the Doctor explains: a dying planet circling a dead sun. "Fascinating," Lawrence Scarman interjects. "Do you mean the future can be chosen, Doctor?" "Not chosen. Shaped. It takes a being of Sutekh's almost limitless power to destroy the future." The trip forward in time silences the objections of Sarah and the viewers, who might have been wondering what all the fuss was about. Sarah realises that they have to go back to 1911. This was one of the first scenes since "Day of the Daleks" (1972) to suggest the existence of what became named as alternative time lines. Russell T Davies was so impressed by it that he suggested repeating the scene in Christopher Eccleston's season in 2005; in fact, it doesn't appear.

"Pyramids of Mars" is, of course, a pastiche of horror films with mummies and Egyptologists awakening ancient curses with their meddling. The original script was by Lewis Griefer, who had written for Patrick McGoohan's cult series *The Prisoner* (1967-8), but couldn't adapt to the requirements of *Doctor Who*. Robert Holmes said Griefer's script largely took place in the British museum and the mummies were given as much prominence as the Doctor. He wrote to Griefer, explaining that for the show's audience, Egyptology meant ancient curses and mummies lumbering out of the fog. Griefer was eventually paid off and the story was completely written by Holmes, but it went out under the pseudonym of Stephen Harris. The horror was given a science fiction makeover and the mummies were lumbering robots, servants of Sutekh who sought to free him from his ancient bonds.

Most of the other stories of seasons thirteen and fourteen were pastiches of literature and film. "Planet of Evil" (1975) was inspired by *Doctor Jekyll and Mr Hyde*. A Morestran expedition led by Professor Sorenson lands on Zeta Minor at the edge of the known universe. The planet is on the boundaries between the universes of matter and anti-matter and Sorenson raids its ore, rich in the power needed to refuel the dying Morestran sun. This is a glance at the perennial energy crisis of the 1970s but, unlike the Pertwee stories, a potentially satirical reference to the real world is quickly buried under horror and adventure. The anti-matter creature of Zeta Minor silently registers its displeasure at its planet's despoliation by killing off the Morestrans, sucking all life from their bodies and leaving them as withered, skeletal husks. Author Louis Marks extrapolates intelligently from *Dr Jekyll and Mr Hyde* in the transformation of the planet by day and night: by daytime, it is relatively harmless; at night, the anti-matter creature stalks its prey. Sorenson is infected by the anti-matter and becomes anti-man, who shambles around the Morestran ship and murders its crew: his make up is directly influenced by Hollywood's Mr Hydes in numerous horror films.

As a child, I found "Planet of Evil" the most frightening thing I had ever seen. I had seriously to consider not watching the summer repeat or reading the novelisation: my first exposure to it had led me to sleep with the light on for about a fortnight.

### "The Brain of Morbius"

Having raided Stevenson, the production team turned their attention to that other Hollywood staple and earliest of Gothic novels, Mary Shelley's *Frankenstein*. This became "The Brain of Morbius" (1976), a splendid tale which turned the dial of horror and violence up full. On the storm-lashed planet of Karn, the obsessed scientist Dr Mehendri Solon (Philip Madoc at his best) lurks in his castle, guarded by his deformed servant Condo, and protecting the terrible secret he keeps hidden in his crypt. (How many Gothic motifs have you ticked off so far?) He has preserved the brain of the renegade Time Lord Morbius, executed by the Time Lords for his crimes and run to ground on Karn, where he had promised his followers the elixir of eternal life, venerated by the Sisterhood of the Flame. Solon has made a body for Morbius's brain, using bits of corpses from the crews of spaceships which regularly crash on Karn. He needs only a head, and the head of the Doctor would do so well (another Time Lord, he chuckles to Morbius: "The crowning irony"). The Doctor is unwilling to lend his head to the project, so Solon opts for an artificial brain case – looking like a goldfish bowl – to contain the brain, and Morbius lives again. The story concludes with the Doctor and Morbius locked in a contest of mind-bending: Time Lord wrestling in which one opponent thinks the other back through his life to his beginnings. "It's usually a game but it can end in death lock," the Doctor tells Sarah. Morbius loses, becomes a ravening animal and is herded off a cliff by the Sisterhood of the Flame: as he went over, stuntman Stuart Fell, playing the Morbius monster, caught the camera with his brain case and there is a visible shake on screen.

"The Brain of Morbius" is highly regarded but had a troubled production history. Hinchcliffe asked Terrance Dicks to provide a story about a robot and in the original, it is the robot which preserves Morbius's brain. Having delivered his draft, Dicks went on holiday and couldn't be contacted when Hinchcliffe decided he'd gone off the idea of the robot idea; in Dicks's absence, Robert Holmes rewrote the script and introduced Solon. He was very apologetic about the changes when Dicks returned, but the latter objected vigorously. There are certainly some plot holes, which

Dicks remedied in his novelisation: why doesn't Solon use Condo's head or Sarah's for the Morbius creature? (The novel explains both are too small, which doesn't quite fit Condo's hulking appearance.) Why does Solon need to build a body at all, when he could just use Condo's?

Dicks also protested against the mind-bending match. The Doctor and Morbius are each connected by a head set to a tubular metal lash-up topped by a screen. As he begins to lose, the Doctor's previous incarnations appear on this screen – photos of Pertwee, Troughton and Hartnell – and Morbius shrieks, "Your puny mind is powerless against the strength of Morbius! Back to your beginnings!" and yet more faces appear. These, is seems, are the Doctor's previous selves: in fact, they are photographs of the production team, including Hinchcliffe, Holmes and regular director Douglas Camfield. The scene is a continuity howler as it goes against the established idea that the Hartnell Doctor was the first. In his novelisation, Dicks writes that there was a confused flurry of faces on the screen and continuity hounds later suggested the pre-Hartnell faces were Morbius's, which doesn't fit the dialogue. Dicks told Holmes he wanted his name taken off the script. What name should go on it? Holmes asked. "I don't care," Dicks said, "just put it out under some bland pseudonym," and banged the phone down. He was amused when he saw the listing in the *Radio Times* a few weeks later: the story credited to one Robin Bland.

## Pastiche

Other stories followed the lines of pastiche. *The Android Invasion* (1975) was a doppelganger story and Terry Nation's first script without the Daleks since *The Keys of Marinus* in 1964: was it commissioned to placate Nation and his agent, who had said Robert Holmes had promised a Dalek story ever year? Perhaps not: the production team were just using a good, established writer. Much as they wanted to encourage new writers, both the Hinchcliffe and Williams production teams found that new writers often didn't understand what they were supposed to produce for the show; their scripts had to be heavily rewritten or abandoned. Commissioning established writers saved time, work and money.

*The Seeds of Doom* (1976) relied heavily on *The Day of the Triffids* for its central premise, plant life dominating animal life; "The Deadly Assassin" was inspired by the film *The Manchurian Candidate*; "The Robots of Death" was a science fiction version of such Agatha Christie tales as *Ten Little Indians* and "The Talons of Weng-Chiang" was a heady, eclectic mix of borrowing. Corpses in the river came from Dickens's *Our Mutual Friend*; Magnus Greel lurking under the music hall came from *The Phantom of the Opera* (which Holmes was again to mine as a source for "The Caves of Androzani" (1984)); the Doctor investigating the crimes which baffle Scotland Yard is pure Sherlock Holmes, and, to reinforce the point, Tom Baker substituted a deerstalker and cape for his usual hat and scarf; there are murderous Chinese gangs, a murderous ventriloquist's dummy (actually the Peking Homonculous, a cyborg with a pig's cerebral cortex which has a murderous hatred of humanity), giant rats in the sewers, girls disappearing off the streets to have their life forces fed into Weng-Chiang: a character speculates that "Jolly Jack" is up to his tricks again. The only prostitute ever to appear in *Doctor Who* turns up in episode three, to be hypnotised and abducted by Greel's acolyte Li H'Sen Chang. In the novelisation, Terrance Dicks writes that this woman was quite accustomed to being approached by men at strange hours of the night. Did anyone still think *Doctor Who* was a children's programme?

"The Talons of Weng-Chiang", like "Genesis of the Daleks", is another frequent winner of the Best Ever Story poll in *Doctor Who Magazine*. It is a wonderful pot pourri of imagery and borrowing, bound together with a strong story, excellent acting, first class dialogue and characterisation. The Doctor is assisted by Henry Gordon Jago, a colourful owner and manager of the music hall, modelled perhaps on Vincent Crummles from Dickens's *Nicholas*

*Nickleby*[1]. Holmes gives him some wonderful lines. When the Doctor suspects Jago has been recently hypnotised, he hypnotises Jago with a pocket watch. Jago is scornful and protests, "I am a man of determination and character, sir. The Rock of Gibraltar could be more easily... more easily..." and duly falls under the influence. Leela and the Doctor also team up with Professor Litefoot, "England's premiere pathologist," according to Jago. Litefoot (Trevor Baxter) is impressed with the Doctor's diagnosis in the autopsy of the murdered cab driver – the chisel-like teeth marks must be the work of a giant rat – and invites him and Leela to supper. This cold collation has been laid out by Litefoot's housekeeper Mrs Hudson, named after the housekeeper in ITV's *Upstairs, Downstairs* (1971-1975)[2]. Leela seizes the joints of beef in her hands and tears the meat off the bone; as a Victorian gentleman, it is part of Litefoot's code never to make a guest feel uncomfortable, so he puts down his knife, fork and plate and eats with his hands. Jago and Litefoot eventually team up against Weng-Chiang in the final two episodes. Weng-Chiang – actually a fifty third century war criminal called Magnus Greel ("The Butcher of Brisbane!") – snarls that they will die slowly, to give entertainment to his wolves. "You filthy bounder," Litefoot observes with dignity. The line is hilarious and absolutely just: to a Victorian gentleman, Greel has trespassed over the bounds of what is acceptable, thus he is a bounder.

"The Talons of Weng-Chiang" was originally written by Robert Banks Stewart, who had turned in strong scripts for the previous season's "Terror of the Zygons" and "The Seeds of Doom". Holmes rewrote it extensively and received the sole on-screen credit. He

---

[1] Christopher Benjamin, who played Jago, went on to play Crummles in the RSC's nine hour epic production of *Nicholas Nickleby* in the early 1980s: on the DVD commentary, he notes the similarities between the characters.

[2] Enormously popular throughout the world, *Upstairs Downstairs* was created by Jean Marsh, Jon Pertwee's first wife. She had played the Hartnell companion Sara Kingdom; the witch Morgaine in "Battlefield" (1989) and had a cameo with Anneke Wills in the fiftieth anniversary play *An Adventure in Space and Time* (2013).

originally toyed with including the Master as the phantom beneath the theatre, crippled by his failed regeneration and using the life force of abducted young women in an attempt to renew himself. Holmes replaced the Master with Magnus Greel, a war criminal whose experiments in time travel led mankind up a technological cul-de-sac. Greel arrived in his time cabinet in nineteenth century China, where he was hailed as the god Weng-Chiang by Li H'sen Chang (John Bennett), who gives him shelter and protection. The time cabinet is claimed as booty by British soldiers, who take it to England, where it ends up in the home of Professor Litefoot. Greel and Chang follow the time cabinet to London and search for it feverishly. Greel's experiments in time travel have made him ill to the point of death; only recovering the time cabinet will make him whole. He holes up beneath Jago's theatre, guarded by rats he has enlarged to the size of lions. The Doctor protests that activating the zygma beam of the time cabinet will destroy London, but Greel goes ahead anyway, only to be killed by the Peking Homonculous who has grown bored and is indulging its hatred of mankind in a killing spree. The production is only let down by the notorious giant rat, a cuddly and shapeless costume which bumbles down the sewer sets to seize Leela by the leg. Louise Jameson (Leela) screams valiantly but the sequence makes fans squirm and their enemies guffaw.

**Revenge of the Children of Light**

The diet of horror and violence that *Doctor Who* served up under Hinchcliffe once more drew the programme to the attention of Mrs Mary Whitehouse. This lady's rather extraordinary interpretation of the Christian faith determined her to campaign against sex and violence on radio and television, and particularly on the BBC, that bastion of socialism, liberalism, loose morals and enemy of all right thinking (and Right thinking) people. God called her to form the National Viewers' and Listeners' Association in the late 1960s and Mrs Whitehouse gathered together fellow-minded citizens to protest about the malign influence of television on our youth, positing a connection between what one saw on screen and what one enacted in one's own life. If one saw people having sex on television, for example, one might want to have sex. If one saw people engaged in violent acts, one might copy them. Mrs Whitehouse's thesis, such as it was, was not proven by her own life: forced exposure to televisual filth did not transform her into a chainsaw-wielding sex-crazed psychopath. Nor was it proven by research, which suggested that screen violence *might* prompt some people to imitation, but only if they were seriously disturbed and deranged before they watched the film or programme in question. But zealots ignore evidence and Britain, as Michael Gove has so rightly said, has had enough of experts. Mrs Whitehouse's mindset might be identified by her use of the words "dirty" and "dirtiness" to describe sexual scenes on television. Nigel Kneale's prescient satire on what would now be called reality television, *The Year of the Sex Olympics* (1968), was termed one of the dirtiest plays Mrs Whitehouse had ever seen; she entirely missed the point of the satire, which was that television viewers will eventually laugh at reality shows whose climax is the participants' death.[1]

Sir Hugh Greene, Director General of the BBC from 1960-1969, cheerfully admitted that he viewed Mrs Whitehouse as a "persona non-grata and persona non-exista" and ignored her. Greene had been a journalist in pre-war Nazi Germany and had listened to news conferences in which Goering had triumphantly crowed about the regime's latest invasions of sovereign territory ("Well boys, I know you love a story and have I got a story for you," Greene recorded Goering, who spoke English, as saying). Greene perhaps could tell the difference between real evil and its fictional representation, which appeared to confuse Mrs Whitehouse. Yet her views were

---

[1] Ben Thompson (*Ban This Filth!*, London 2012) argues that Mrs Whitehouse believed that the BBC was a communist organisation which wanted to bring about the revolution and the fall of all that was bright, bold and true. Softening up the moral fibre of the nation by a daily assault of sex and violence was all part of the BBC's pre-revolutionary plan. Mrs Whitehouse might have loathed *Doctor Who*, but her preposterous conspiracy theory outdid even the most outlandishly satirical plots of the show.

finding increased public support in the mid-1970s, perhaps as a consequence of fears of an increasingly violent society: the Troubles in Northern Ireland, for example, had claimed many lives. A woman of similar Christian faith, politics and lack of imagination who agreed with Mrs Whitehouse was the new leader of the Opposition and the Conservative Party, a Mrs Margaret Thatcher: the two ladies were to meet in 1986 to discuss the banning of sex toys under an extension of "[liability] to deprave and corrupt" provisions of the Obscene Publications Act 1959, perhaps forgetting the Lady Chatterley trial of 1961 which had booted the act into irrelevance. Was Mrs Thatcher's visceral dislike of the BBC – warmly embraced by her neoliberal Conservative followers to this day – partly engendered by memories of Mrs Whitehouse's fully justified attacks on the morally bankrupt corporation which screened such depraved and dirty material? In this new political climate, the BBC began to take Mrs Whitehouse seriously. Letters to the *Radio Times* complained that children would be able to see little difference between the opening sequence of "Genesis of the Daleks" and events in the Falls Road area of Belfast. These sequences included soldiers in gas masks being gunned down in slow motion; the Doctor, Sarah and Harry wrenching respirators from corpses to avoid suffocation and worse in a gas attack on the Kaled trenches. Mrs Whitehouse pronounced the story "tea time brutality for tots". I was nine when I first watched "Genesis" and remember being sorry for the dead, propped up to make the trench look fully manned, and fully understood the necessity of the Doctor and his companions robbing them of their gas masks to escape the poisoned gas; otherwise, they would have been killed. I now see that I was quite wrong and that my exposure to fifty plus years of *Doctor Who* has turned me into the slavering psychopath that writes this book in crayon, which is quite hard when you're wearing a straightjacket.

Tom Baker's second season was criticised by Mrs Whitehouse for its depictions of strangulation by "obscene vegetable matter" (the Krynoid in "The Seeds of Doom") and "by claw" in "The Brain of Morbius", when the Morbius monster strangles one of the sisterhood of Khan (my ten year old self was unconvinced by this sequence on first broadcast as I noticed that the claw didn't move when it was around the woman's neck). *Doctor Who* was lumped together with such adult fare as *I, Claudius* by Mrs Whitehouse and deemed similarly harmful to the nation's health: "and just for a little variety, show the children how to make a Molotov cocktail"[1]. Michael Grade once noted that Mrs Whitehouse never saw the context in which the particular moment she singled out for criticism was placed: the Doctor asks Scorby to prepare and throw a Molotov cocktail at the Krynoid so that he can make his escape and develop a plan to save humanity, but Mrs Whitehouse was more concerned with exercising her moral indignation.

Hinchcliffe and script editor Robert Holmes continued full steam ahead on this sea of sin for Baker's third season but hit trouble in the third story, "The Deadly Assassin" (1976). At the end of episode three, in a filthy river blazing with ignited marsh gas, the Doctor and Chancellor Goth (the Master's agent) battle in the dreamscape of the Matrix, apparently intent on beating each other to death. In a sequence famous among fans as a turning point in *Doctor Who*'s history, Goth holds the Doctor's head under the water and splutters, "Finished, Doctor! You're finished." The end theme crashes in over a three second close-up of Tom Baker's face underwater.

Hinchcliffe was not a cavalier producer and took his responsibilities seriously. He had already edited out a shot from the previous season's "The Seeds of Doom", of a character slowly mutating into a Krynoid, as being too disturbing for children. Viewing the ending of episode three of "The Deadly Assassin", Hinchcliffe decided to let the "drowning" shot go through. He argued that the audience knew that it wasn't really the Doctor underwater: the whole episode has established, and reinforced through cutaway shots, that the Doctor himself was actually lying on a couch in the Time Lords' archive room: only his mind was in the Matrix, so he couldn't actually be drowned. Again, Mrs Whitehouse

---

[1] Quoted in Tracey and Morrison, *Whitehouse*, London & Basingstoke, Macmillan, 1979

ignored the context: one wonders if she would have condemned the blinding of Gloucester in *King Lear* as an encouragement to theatre goers to gouge out each other's eyes, ignoring the context in which Shakespeare put the scene: it presents the depravity of human beings at their worst and appals all the characters who are not completely depraved. "The Deadly Assassin" episode three was transmitted uncut and Mrs Whitehouse pounced. Interviewed in the 1990s, she said she "[could] see until this day, the final shot of Doctor Who drowning." The BBC took the complaint seriously: this marked the final U-turn in its attitude to Mrs Whitehouse. Sir Charles Curran, the BBC's Director General, apologised to her for drowning the Doctor and cut the sequence from the repeat of the story in the summer of 1976. In fact, it was cut from the master tape and was only restored to the later VHS and DVD release from an American, uncut, copy: the consequent fall-out in picture quality on both is very obvious.

This was the beginning of the end for Hinchcliffe. He and Holmes were planning a fourth season for Tom Baker and had started work on a new breed of monsters who they promised would be terrifying. As production of the final stories of the 1976-7 season got underway, Hinchcliffe found a young man called Graham Williams trailing him at planning meetings. This was his first inkling that Williams was to be the new producer and that he, Hinchcliffe, was to move on; in fact, to develop a new post-watershed police series called *Target*, created by Graham Williams, with 1970s heart throb Patrick Mower. Here, Hinchcliffe would continue to do damage to the nation's psyche with a series full of unbridled violence and sex. In practice, he and Williams exchanged jobs. Musing on Mrs Whitehouse in 2004, Hinchcliffe said: "I always felt that Mary Whitehouse thought of *Doctor Who* as a children's programme, for little children, and it wasn't... so she was really coming at the show from the wrong starting-point."[1]

---

[1] DVD extra on "Pyramids of Mars", BBC Worldwide, 2004

## Less violence.  Less money.

Graham Williams took over *Doctor Who* with a brief from the Head of Series and Serials to reduce the violence and to make it more suitable as family-friendly viewing. The obvious thing to replace the violence with was humour, something very much in tune with Tom Baker's inclinations for the show. Williams was also concerned about the "improbability" of the Doctor arriving on a planet in peril at the start of every story owing to a malfunctioning TARDIS: perhaps an odd thing to worry about, given that it had served the programme well for fourteen years. He proposed an umbrella theme for the new season. The Doctor was to be given the task of assembling the six segments of the Key to Time: an awesomely powerful MacGuffin which would restore the balance (of what, exactly, was never made clear) of the Universe. One segment would be found in each story and the quest was to be directed by the White Guardian: an awesomely powerful being opposed by the equally awesomely powerful and equally opposite Black Guardian. These demi-gods partly owed their creation to Williams's feeling that the Time Lords had lost their god-like status in the series. Certainly, "The Deadly Assassin" had portrayed them as a squabbling, decadent and politically corrupt race: rather like the human beings whose outward appearance they shared.

Production time was pressing, however, and Williams was unable to get the Key to Time arc up and running for the fifteenth season: it was held over to the following year (1978-9). Williams' first season was an uneasy hotch-potch of tone, quality and style, overshadowed by the departure of Robert Holmes as script editor after three and a half years, and of Louise Jameson as Leela. *Who* veteran Terrance Dicks had penned the first tale, a Gothic piece luridly entitled "The Vampire Mutations". This almost immediately ran into trouble as it clashed with the BBC's consanguineous production of *Dracula* with Frank Finlay and Louis Jordan: perhaps unsurprisingly, the producers of that serious television movie were not keen to have their project "undermined" by a *Doctor Who* story that could be seen as a spoof. "The Vampire Mutations" was pulled from the fifteenth season (it would eventually resurface as the eighteenth season story "State of Decay") and Terrance Dicks hurriedly wrote a four part replacement, "The Horror of Fang Rock". Set on a nineteenth century lighthouse, the story belongs to the pseudo-historical vein of *Who* in which the historical setting is enlivened by the inclusion of an alien and science fiction elements.[1] Robert Holmes instructed Dicks to research the historical background of lighthouses thoroughly, perhaps as a revenge for a similar request Dicks had made of him when Holmes wrote the 1974 medieval tale "The Time Warrior". "The Horror of Fang Rock" has much to recommend it: strongly drawn, well-acted characters, excellent lighting, a building menace (and a menaced building) as the lighthouse's inhabitants are murdered one by one by the marauding Rutan. On the debit side, the Rutan resembles a luminous football and the story is too slow to act as an effective season opener. Episode one ends with the dullest cliff-hanger in years as a hideously unconvincing balsa-wood model yacht crashes into the island. The story, uniquely in the programme's history, was shot in Pebble Mill at Birmingham; Paddy Russell, the director, praised the innovation and dedication of the technical team but the lack of resources away from London is all too obvious on screen. "Horror of Fang Rock" also suffered from its juxtaposition with the final story of the previous season, the much loved "Talons of Weng-Chiang", also set in Victorian times.

### K9 and two space operas

From Fang Rock, the TARDIS careered wildly into the world of space opera for the second story, "The Invisible Enemy". Space opera was always difficult on *Doctor Who*'s limited budget, as demonstrated by 1973's "Frontier in Space", whose Earth ship was

---

[1] The purely historical stories had been abandoned by producer Innes Lloyd after "The Highlanders" in 1966, deemed insufficiently exciting compared with the programme's science fiction yarns.

piloted by actors sitting on office chairs jacked up on wooden pallets. Ian Scoones, who had previously worked on *Thunderbirds*, provided some ambitious spaceship miniatures which still couldn't compete with the Eagle transporters and Moonbase Alpha to be seen on ITV at the same time. Long term script writers Bob Baker and Dave Martin borrowed heavily from *Fantastic Voyage* (1966) for scenes where miniaturised clones of the Doctor and Leela clamber around in the Doctor's brain, hunting for the nucleus of the virus which wants to take over the galaxy. "What was that?" Leela asks as a light zaps by them. "Just a passing thought," the Doctor cries. The nucleus itself is eventually manifested as a giant prawn which is so immovable it is mounted on castors and pushed around by its minions, who pretend that that isn't what they are doing at all. Tom Baker quipped that "a large deep fat fryer would have put paid to his schemes".

Entertaining mess that it was, "The Invisible Enemy" was most notable for introducing K9, who remained a feature of the programme up to 2013. Russell T Davies seriously considered having K9 accompany the ninth Doctor, Christopher Eccleston, in season twenty seven (season one); in the end, he turned up in "School Reunion" (2006) with Sarah Jane Smith and went off with her into the children's spin-off *The Sarah Jane Adventures* (2007-2011). K9 was a robot computer dog owned by Professor Marius (Frederick Jaegar) who was not permitted to bring his real dog to the Bi-Al Medical Foundation. Missing him, Marius had K9 made up. Ian Scoones did the initial design for K9, imagining him as a metal Doberman which could contain an actor. The effects work for "The Invisible Enemy" was so heavy that it was eventually divided between Scoones, who worked on the miniatures, and Tony Harding, who handled the studio effects and designed the small, radio-controlled K9 which is so familiar today. Voiced by John Leeson, scripted as sarcastic and engaging, K9 was an immediate hit with younger viewers and filled the tonal gap created by the exclusion of gothic horror. Robert Holmes phoned Baker and Martin to say, "Well, I think it's a knockout, this dog," and asked for their permission to keep him in the series. Graham Williams hedged his bets and two story endings were filmed: one, for K9 staying with Professor Marius, and another for him going with the Doctor.

In fact, K9's inclusion in the regular line up caused enormous problems. Scoones' original design for K9 as an actor in a prop might have been better technically than the final radio controlled version. Harding lamented that K9's frequency was the same as the cameras', which often scrambled his radio control and sent him crashing into the scenery. K9's motor was so noisy that he almost obliterated dialogue until the arrival of the second K9 in "The Ribos Operation" (1978), which didn't sound quite so much like a liquidiser on the highest setting. Like the Daleks, K9 had only been designed for one story. He could cope with the studio floors but not grass – he had to run rather obviously over wooden boards in "The Stones of Blood" (1978) – and certainly not on Brighton beach in "The Leisure Hive" (1980)[1]: in spite of an expensive refit, he eventually had to be pulled over the shingle on a fishing line. He was too big to get through the door of the TARDIS and there was usually a very obvious cutaway shot when he needed to disembark. John Nathan-Turner solved this by opening both doors on a new police box prop from "The Leisure Hive" onwards.

Terry Nation thought that K9 would upstage the Daleks and refused to allow him to appear in "Destiny of the Daleks" (1979): Douglas Adams, the new script editor, wrote him out with an attack of laryngitis, a cop-out lame enough for the Doctor to ask why a machine would catch such a virus anyway. K9 sometimes stayed in the TARDIS for whole stories: he couldn't have coped with the marshy Norfolk locations of "The Power of Kroll" (1979) and "Image of the Fendahl" (1977), the story after "The Invisible Enemy", couldn't accommodate him because it was already well advanced in production. Tom Baker loathed K9 as "insufferable" –

---

[1] The 1964 production crew had similar difficulties with the Daleks on location in London for "The Dalek Invasion of Earth". The props were plonked on top of larger fenders which contained bigger wheels; otherwise, as Raymond Cusick remarked, they would have rattled along like biscuit tins.

he always had to kneel down in a two shot with him – and was alleged to have booted the prop round the set. A surviving outtake has the Doctor ask K9 how deep they are; K9 says the data is unavailable and Tom Baker snarls, "Yes, you never know the fucking answer when it's important." Baker was only reconciled to K9's inclusion in the series by his friendship with John Leeson. Both were devotees of *The Times* crossword; there is a story of Tom Baker sitting next to the prop K9 and working on the crossword with him. In fact, Leeson was supplying the answers via a fold-back speaker, but the sight of the Doctor and K9 working out crossword together startled and amused the onlookers.

Older fans, ever-sensitive to taunts that *Doctor Who* was a children's programme, lamented K9's introduction into the series as another lurch into childishness. Children, on the other hand, loved him: like the Daleks, he was easy to draw and had a voice that could be imitated. In 2005, Russell T Davies realised the simplicity and the importance of this aspect of K9's appeal and insisted that the aliens, like Cassandra, could be drawn by children. As with the Daleks again, the BBC made vast sums from merchandise: a Talking K9 appeared almost immediately, with a smaller plastic figure joining Denys Fisher's *Doctor Who* toy range. Designers Raymond Cusick and Tony Harding didn't make a penny from their designs as they were salaried employees: the profits were shared between the BBC and the writers Bob Baker and Dave Martin, who owned the copyright.

The third story of the fifteenth season, "Image of the Fendahl", was a Gothic horror throwback. It was also the last *Who* story from Chris Boucher, who had written both "The Face of Evil" and "The Robots of Death" the previous year: the latter regularly featured in the top ten best story polls in *Doctor Who Magazine*. Boucher moved on to script edit the new SF new series *Blake's Seven* (1978-1981). Created by Terry Nation and produced by David Maloney, *Blake's Seven* was billed as being altogether more mature than *Doctor Who* and was squarely aimed at adults in a post-watershed slot. It had an even smaller budget than *Doctor Who* but bravely attempted the space opera at which *Star Wars* (1977) was the example par excellence. Mat Irvine gleefully recalled that the visual effects budget for *Blake's Seven* was fifty quid per episode. Nevertheless, the series endured and employed many writers who had previously worked on *Who*. When John Nathan-Turner let it be known that Robert Holmes's services as writer would no longer be required, Boucher repaid the favour that Holmes had paid him: Holmes had commissioned three stories from Boucher for *Who* and Boucher commissioned several episodes of *Blake's Seven* from Holmes. Gareth Thomas (Blake) wanted to include a scene where Blake walks down a corridor to find the Doctor going in the opposite direction: one says, "Morning Doctor", the other, "Morning Blake", and they go off to save their respective universes. Michael Keating, who played Vila, recalled that Tom Baker had asked him if he know what the difference was between *Doctor Who* and *Blake's Seven*. "No, Tom," said Keating, "what is the difference between *Doctor Who* and *Blake's Seven*?" "I'm not in *Blake's Seven*," Baker replied.

## "The Sun Makers"

Before the fifteenth season fell apart completely, Robert Holmes wrote one of the series' best loved stories, "The Sun Makers". Set on Pluto in the far future, Holmes presented a humanity cowed by an oppressive regime run by the Collector, a Usurian who keeps his work units docile by working them to death and taxing the life out of them. "The Sun Makers" had its roots in Holmes's annoyance with the then Labour government's high taxation policies and the story's biting satire, and arresting design based on Fritz Lang's 1927 film *Metropolis*, delighted viewers. The Collector sported bushy eyebrows as a reference to Chancellor of the Exchequer Denis Healey (who also had them) and his pin striped robe alluded to Middle Eastern oil potentates, then frequently blamed for high oil prices that were driving the country into recession. There was some criticism from right-wing viewers of the Doctor behaving like Fidel

Castro and starting a revolution among the work units (a superbly rousing speech delivered by Baker with absolute conviction: "Remind them that they're human beings, and human beings always have to fight for their freedom!") but this criticism could be offset by the equally beastly treatment of James Callaghan's Labour government by the story. "The Sun Makers" was notable too for the Usurian's use of a gas pumped into the city to keep the populace docile and frightened at all times: this was lifted by Holmes from a story pitched to the production team by a new writer bursting with innovative science fiction ideas, one Douglas Adams.

As the season continued, it became clearer and clearer that the money was running out. *Doctor Who*, like the United Kingdom, was becoming a victim of high inflation. Some of the scenes in "The Sun Makers" appeared to be performed against magnolia-painted flats or black drapes: Williams later lamented the need to find story reasons to perform scenes against those black studio drapes as an economising measure. "Underworld", the fifth story of the season, starts strongly on impressively designed spaceship around which a whole planet begins to form. Having spent all the budget on episode one, the production team found they had nothing left to finance three episodes set in a cave system. Location filming, or building studio sets, were non-starters. They eventually opted for shooting the episodes against blue screens, keying in model caves using blue screen. The results are questionable to say the least: either dreadful or, if one feels like being kind, an interesting case of the first virtual set in science fiction. "Underworld" also suffered from including, as the Doctor said, "another machine with megalomania" (after the previous season's Xoanon in "The Face of Evil"), poor acting (often a problem in the series' original run 1963-1979) and aliens wearing what appeared to be waste paper baskets on their heads with chocolate buttons for eyes and nose.

If "Underworld" was full of problems, the season finale, "The Invasion of Time", was a work of desperation. Pennant Roberts had submitted a script set on Gallifrey which featured the planet's other, previously unheard-of, inhabitants, a race of intelligent cat people.

The story ("The Killer Cats of Geng Singh") called for an arena filled with thousands of the things. Although some designs were completed, including an impressive cat person, Williams cancelled the story when it became clear it was far beyond the programme's means. He had recently been disheartened by the release of *Star Wars* in 1977; returning to the production office after seeing the film, he lamented that there was no way they could match its production values and special effects. (In-house effects designer Mat Irvine recalled that he had been asked if the BBC Visual Effects Department could do effects "like *Star Wars*" and he had replied, "Sure, if you give us the money.") Williams and Antony Read, the new script editor, wrote "The Invasion of Time" quickly, keeping the Gallifrey setting and following Robert Holmes's advice that a six parter should be written as a four parter followed by a linked two parter: a structure Holmes had used with great success in "The Talons of Weng-Chiang".

"The Invasion of Time" is a mess with little to recommend it. It requires the viewers to have seen, and to have remembered, the Gallifrey story "The Deadly Assassin" from the previous season: a tall order in the days before domestic video recorders were available to anyone save the very rich. As a twelve year old, I remember being confused and upset by the portrayal of an apparently evil Doctor who sides with the Vardans (tinkly aliens made, it seemed, of tin foil) and is only revealed to be good in later episodes, by which time some of the viewers had given up. Gallifrey is invaded and the Vardans manifest themselves as singularly unimpressive short humanoids dressed as East German traffic policemen. They bark orders and are promptly banished by the Doctor only to be replaced by the Sontarans in part four's cliff hanger: the story's single effective moment. The Sontarans then run around Gallifrey (or "rampage", as the *Radio Times* had it); the Doctor and his friends take refuge in the TARDIS's many rooms, but there was no money for sets so the scenes were shot in the brick corridors of a disused lunatic asylum (a metaphor for the story's tone and production history?). Leela is hurriedly written out, staying on Gallifrey with a drippy Time Lord called Andred at whom she has never previously looked but is now apparently in love with, K9 is left on Gallifrey only to be replaced by K9 mark II ... and mercifully the season came to an end. Steven Moffat was so haunted by the dreadful production values and the sight of the regulars pretending that the TARDIS had brick interior walls that he commissioned writer Stephen Thompson to set a story entirely inside the TARDIS for the 2013 season[1]. This became "Journey to the Centre of the TARDIS" and was made at a time when the show actually had enough money to build impressive interior sets for the ship.

Back in 1978, season fifteen's problems presumably contributed to a decline in viewing figures. Although they rarely dipped much below eight million and peaked at ten and a half million for "The Invasion of Time", this was some way off the eleven million who watched "The Hand of Fear" (1976) and "The Face of Evil" (1977), let alone the twelve million who watched "The Deadly Assassin" (1976) and the whopping twelve and a half million who tuned in to "The Robots of Death" (1977). The figures seem huge by today's standards, where producers, in a multi-channel age, would bath in champagne if their shows garnered an audience of eight million (something regularly achieved by the re-tooled, post-2005 *Doctor Who*), but there were only three channels in 1977 and *Doctor Who*, although by no means a worrying failure, appeared to be in decline.[2]

Determined to get a grip on the series, producer Graham Williams finally managed to launch his Key to Time arc the following season. Under Antony Read's stewardship as script editor, the sixteenth season's stories were better written and better made than season fifteen's. Ratings held up but didn't greatly improve. Tom Baker was proving harder to control and his "antics" – Williams' word – often left the producer exhausted. Philip Hinchcliffe had said managing Baker was like riding a huge and powerful horse, but one

---

[1] *Doctor Who* Magazine 454, November 2012

[2] By way of comparison, average viewing figures in the UK for Peter Capaldi's seasons were around 6.4 million ("Public Image", *Doctor Who Magazine* no. 522, March 2018.)

that was pointing in roughly the right direction. Under Graham Williams, the horse appeared to have thrown off its rider and galloped off alone.

Another development was the acceptance of a story by a new writer. Nothing very new in that, except that this writer was simultaneously at work on *The Hitch Hiker's Guide to the Galaxy* for Radio 4, and his name was Douglas Adams.

# 9

# The Key to Time
# and the Talking Cabbage

There were some good stories in the Key to Time season, which ran from September 1978 to February 1979. It was the series' fifteenth season, which saw it notch up its five hundredth episode and one hundredth story, "The Stones of Blood" (1978). Producer Graham Williams had asked Elisabeth Sladen to return as Sarah Jane Smith, but she turned him down: asked about this offer at an American convention, she said she had thought, "How lovely – but no." Much as she had enjoyed *Doctor Who*, Sladen had found there was only so much you could do with the part of a companion and playing second fiddle to two Doctors had sometimes had limited charms. John Nathan-Turner later asked Louise Jameson to return as Leela, perhaps for another story set on Gallifrey, but she also declined.

## Romana

Williams thus had to devise another companion character. He came up with Romanadvoratrelunder, a young, female Time Lord assigned to the Doctor by the White Guardian to help him in the search for the Key to Time. She is only one hundred and forty years old (though she says she is one hundred and twenty five in "City of Death" the following year) and had graduated from the Academy with a brilliant degree (far better than the Doctor's). Script editor Anthony Read said that, like most brilliant young graduates, she thought she knew everything but lacked experience. Travelling with the Doctor would teach her what the Universe outside Gallifrey was really like. By the end of episode one of "The Ribos Operation", the first story, Romanadvoratrelunder is trapped under a descending stone door and screaming as an awakening Shrivenzale, a local crocodile-like monster, advances on her. "I never imagined...!" she exclaims after escaping. "Are there many creatures like that in other worlds?" "Millions! Millions!" the Doctor snaps back. The Doctor's role in teaching Romanadvoratrelunder recalled Philip Hinchcliffe's initial idea for Leela as an Eliza Doolittle character to the Doctor's Professor Higgins[1]: Leela, an alien savage descended from the crew of a crashed Earth ship, would be introduced to civilised behaviour by encountering other humans. The premise appears in "The Talons of Weng-Chiang" (1977), when the Doctor takes her to see her nineteenth century ancestors, and in numerous stories like "Image of the Fendahl" (1977) where he tries to teach her that violence isn't the answer. Leela wants to attack a security guard and his guard dog at Fetch Priory:

> Leela: There is a guard. I shall kill him.
> Doctor: No!
> Leela: Why not?
> Doctor: You'll frighten the dog.

Relations between the Doctor and Romanadvoratrelunder are initially frosty and the Doctor resents being given an assistant: perhaps a reflection of Tom Baker's insistence that he could manage without one and could carry the show on his own. The Doctor tells Romanadvoratrelunder that her name is far too long, and by the time he had called, "Look out, Romanad–" something awful would have happened to her.

> Doctor: I'll call you Romana.
> Romana: I don't like Romana.
> Doctor: It's either Romana or Fred.
> Romana: All right, call me Fred.
> Doctor: Good. Come on, Romana.

Graham Williams was somewhat more dismissive of Romana's

---

[1] From Bernard Shaw's 1914 play *Pygmalion*.

character genesis than Anthony Read, saying that now they had done the primitive savage it was time to do the ice maiden, and this was going from one stereotype to another. We might compare the comments of script editor Eric Saward, who lamented that the character outline for Tom Baker's final companion Tegan was "an Australian", and for Peter Davison's final companion Peri, "an American": both nationalities were chosen to boost the appeal of the series further in these respective countries, where it was doing well.

Mary Tamm was cast as Romana and her first costume – making her look like illustrations of the White Witch in *The Lion, the Witch and the Wardrobe* – emphasised her ice maiden character: white furs, suitable to the icy world of Ribos. Mary Tamm was best known for her role as Sigi in the 1974 film *The Odessa File*, based on the novel by Frederick Forsyth, and was hesitant about taking on the role in *Doctor Who*. This hesitancy might explain her somewhat uncertain performance in some episodes. Romana's introduction wasn't helped by poor management of the press releases, which said she was a "new time lady companion" for the Doctor. "Time Lady" apparently meant female Time Lord (Lord/Lady – see?) but this wasn't a term the show had ever used before and was ambiguous for many, not least my twelve year old self. I assumed that "time lady" just meant "lady who travelled in time", and since almost all of the Doctor's female companions had done that, I couldn't understand why being a "time lady" made Romana special. As a character, Romana suffered from the same problem as Dr Liz Shaw, Jon Pertwee's first companion: she was simply too clever and there was no need for the Doctor to explain things to her. Douglas Adams tried to get round the problem in "The Pirate Planet" by having her and the Doctor explain things together to the simple natives – much to the Doctor's irritation, who thinks that explanations are his job – but the writers soon fell back on the expedient of the Doctor telling her things which, as a Time Lord, she should already know. John Nathan-Turner thought Romana didn't work and wondered why she and the Doctor didn't just wink at each other and say, "It's solution number 93". She was written out in Tom Baker's final season.

## Technological advancement: K9 and the VCR

With Romana came K9 mark II, apparently made by the Doctor after the original had been left on Gallifrey. In the real world, a technological innovation was the domestic video recorder, now becoming more widely available now that VHS had replaced the cumbersome, expensive and unreliable u-Matic system. VHS recorders had begun to appear in British homes in 1977 and some fans had taped the fifteenth season off air. The machines were still hideously expensive, as were the tapes, but renting expensive electrical equipment was a more common option in the 1970s and 1980s than it is now, and came with the advantage of free servicing and upgrades when the models were superseded. My brother and I bought our first VHS video recorder – a Ferguson Videostar, no less – in time to tape the repeat season "The Five Faces of *Doctor Who*" in September 1981. It cost £400 (perhaps £800 in today's money) and a three hour tape was £10: hugely expensive for sixth form students like us on a tight budget when we also had to buy beer. You could fit seven episodes on a tape; there was only standard play, not long play and the Ferguson Videostar was mechanical: you had to jam down its mighty play and record buttons together (like a contemporary cassette player) to make it record and there was no remote control. How I kicked myself when the Ferguson Electronic Videostar came out a few months later, with a remote control and long play, doubling the number of episodes you could get on a tape! At least we didn't get a Betamax, the rival system to VHS which died a death in the mid-1980s. Nevertheless, with video fans could watch the show as many times as they wanted and not reply on summer repeats to see it again. We could notice, for example, that "The Power of Kroll" (1978) used the same shot of the native Swampies running towards the camera twice in different episodes, and that the Mute who menaces the Doctor on the space station, outside the TARDIS, in "The Armageddon Factor" (1978) kicks up the set's carpet as he comes into shot. We didn't know it at the time, but home video would revolutionise the way we watched television and greatly influence the way television was made. Fans would be able to sneer when John Nathan-Turner denied that the programme had been better in the past when speaking on air about "The Trial of a Time Lord" (1986): we had the tapes and could see that he was wrong. Some critics could even justify incoherent story telling on Sylvester McCoy's stories by saying that they made perfect sense if you watched them fifteen times (note: they still didn't).

The sixteenth season began strongly with Robert Holmes's "The Ribos Operation" (1978), featuring Iain Cuthbertson as con-man Garron who is trying to sell Ribos to the fanatical warlord, the Graff Vynda-K[1]. The Doctor is given the task of finding the six segments of the Key to Time (sometimes referred to on screen as the Key *of* Time as the scriptwriters or actors slip up) by the White Guardian (Cyril Luckham), a civilised cove in a 1920s linen suit, chatting about the end of order in the Universe as he sips a green brandy. The Doctor is reluctant to go on a quest and asks what will happen to him if he refuses. "Nothing," says the White Guardian, pleasantly. "Nothing? You mean, nothing will happen to me?" the Doctor asks hopefully. "Nothing at all," the White Guardian repeats. And then quietly adds: "Ever."

## Douglas Adams and "The Pirate Planet"

The first segment recovered, the Doctor and Romana travel to Calufrax to find the second in "The Pirate Planet". Their first attempt at landing is aborted: something appears to be trying to materialise in the same space as the TARDIS. With Romana at the helm, showing off, their second attempt is successful. Checking the readings, the Doctor congratulates her on arriving at precisely the right point in space and precisely the right point in time. But on the

---

[1] Played by Paul Seed, who later directed the BBC's *House of Cards* trilogy with Ian Richardson as silky Conservative Prime Minister and murderer, Francis Urquhart. The series was remade by Netflix in 2013.

wrong planet. "This planet," states the Doctor gravely, "wasn't here when I tried to land."

The Time Lords have arrived on Zanak: a hollow, space jumping planet built by the Captain (Bruce Purchase) under the direction of Queen Xanxia. Zanak materialises around other planets, sucks out its minerals and wealth and leaves it, and its inhabitants, for dead.

This was Douglas Adams' first commissioned story for *Doctor Who*. Adams had previously submitted some story ideas to Graham Williams for the fifteeenth season. He suggested a story about an aggressive planet where the people had been pacified by the Time Lords, who built an enormous statue that sucked all the aggression out of them; unfortunately, the Time Lord engineer who maintained the statue gets stuck inside it and absorbs all the aggression. Adams explained in an interview that the story was very complicated, even in its story break-down form, and that after he had read it to Graham Williams, Williams slid down in his chair and muttered that he now knew how Stanley Kubrick felt. The pacifying element was purloined by Robert Holmes for "The Sun Makers" as the Usurians' means of keeping the human workforce quiet and docile. Adams was invited to pitch for the series again and came up with "The Pirate Planet". He had simultaneously been commissioned to write six episodes of a science fiction comedy for BBC Radio 4. This was *The Hitch Hiker's Guide to the Galaxy*, which would make him famous and would eclipse his work on *Doctor Who*. Adams, however, had always loved *Doctor Who* and explained often that it, and *Dan Dare* in the *Eagle* comic, were huge influences on *Hitch Hiker's*. He was a graduate in English Literature from the University of Cambridge and interested in real science (he introduced his friend Richard Dawkins to Lalla Ward, who would become Dawkins' wife): both, and a spell writing for the Monty Python team, were hugely influential on his work for *Doctor Who*.

"The Pirate Planet" is a fine story with wonderfully inventive ideas, but suffers in its last episode from a huge information dump of technobabble to explain how the Doctor releases Calufrax from the jaws of Zanak. This explanation apparently makes scientific sense to science graduates, but was way beyond most viewers at the time. The story also suffers from some dreadful acting by two supporting artists: as is common with so much of *Doctor Who* in the 1970s, actors in minor roles can sometimes be embarrassingly bad. One *Doctor Who* director explained that directors sometimes owed someone a favour, or an agent a favour, and felt obliged to use "actors" in certain roles. It might also be argued that some actors have no idea how to approach science fiction: considering it nonsense, they therefore under- or over-act, or make no attempt to apply their training (assuming they have had any) in creating a character, or character background, for their part. Better actors realise that the way to play science fiction, like anything else, is with total conviction: however preposterous the situation, it must be played for real. In Shakespeare, this sells to an audience the idea that girls can dress up as boys and nobody notice; in *Doctor Who*, it sells to viewers the idea that you are an embittered cyborg space pirate engineer who has invented a space-jumping planet. Adams himself was unhappy with some of the acting in "The Pirate Planet". He approved of, and injected, much humour into *Doctor Who* but deplored what he saw as a tendency for some actors to see a joke and think it gave them licence to give their character a silly voice, or a funny walk, or to camp it up in general. This view is slightly at variance with Adams' account of writing "The Pirate Planet". He said he left a note in the script's margin saying, "It needs something silly in it, so how about a robot parrot?" He returned to the note, thought, "God, don't be stupid," and then thought, "Why not?" Adams also thought the robot parrot – the Polyphase Avatron – would be a specially designed enemy for K9 to fight, and the two square up in part three, the parrot apparently defaecating electronic globs onto K9 as he blasts it with his nose laser. At the fight's conclusion, K9 presents the destroyed Polyphase Avatron to the Doctor in the manner of a gun dog presenting its master with its game. Adams said the parrot originally had lines like "Pieces of silicate!" and "Pretty Polyphase Avatron!" but he thought them so awful that he cut them. Dick Mills, who designed the wonderful sound effects for the show for many years, said he thought the parrot was a good idea but the problem was it didn't look much like a parrot on screen. It couldn't be painted parrot colours of green, yellow or blue because these were the colours used for colour separation overlay or chromakey (now generally called "green screen"), so it had to be painted brown and therefore wasn't obviously recognisable as a parrot to all the viewers.

One actress who gave her all to the story was the uncredited elderly lady who played Queen Xanxia, held immobile in the last moments of her life by the Time Dams powered by Zanak's plundering of other planets' energy (a typically inventive Adams science fiction idea). If Graham Williams would increase her fee, this lady would remove her teeth to look more decrepit. Williams agreed and the actress complied.

**More segments**

The season's third story, "The Stones of Blood" (1978) was hailed by fans at the time as a classic and won the season poll in the *Doctor Who* Appreciation Society's magazine, *TARDIS*. It is actually quite a forgettable affair, with a cult worshipping an ancient goddess that appears to have stepped out of "The Daemons" (1973). An almost identical cult appears in the lamentable spin-off *K9 and Company* three years later (1981). The eponymous stones of blood monsters are giant lumps of rock on castors pushed into shot by stage hands. The fourth story, "The Androids of Tara" (1978), is a wonderful Ruritanian romp and a return to the sort of pastiche favoured by Philip Hinchcliffe and Robert Holmes. It is virtually a re-telling of Anthony Hope's novel *The Prisoner of Zenda* (1894) with Peter Jeffery as a splendid villain, Count Grendel (we can tell he is the villain because he has the same name as the monster in the Anglo-Saxon poem *Beowulf*). Grendel attempts to seize the Taran throne by various daft schemes involving android copies of the Princess Strella, engaged to marry the rightful heir, Prince Reynart. Romana is the spitting image of Strella and is blackmailed into assisting

Grendel; Grendel kidnaps the Prince to prevent the coronation but the Doctor, working for Reynart's party, provides an android copy of the Prince to be crowned in his stead. The story ends with a swordfight between Grendel and the Doctor on the castle ramparts: Grendel dives into the moat with the parting line, "Next time I shall not be so lenient!", setting himself up for a return match which sadly never materialised.

One interesting notion in "The Androids of Tara" is that the engineers and technicians are the peasants: Reynart and his court have no idea how a horse works, let alone an android, and the Doctor is treated with some disdain for his technical skills. This is presumably a satirical point about the useless, pampered aristocracy who are maintained by the toils of the peasants: an idea in science fiction that goes back to H.G.Wells' *The Time Machine* (1895) where the workers evolve into the Morlocks who devour the skill-less and useless descendants of the aristocracy, the Eloi[1]. "The Androids of Tara" also contains some sexual references which are highly unusual in the original series. Grendel's android engineer, a woman called Madame Lamia, appears to have been his mistress: he tells Romana that she is attached to him "for certain favours I once showed her" and she hates Romana for having attracted Grendel's attention. Grendel also threatens Lamia that their past relationship will not preclude her punishment if she makes a mistake: "I shall have you flogged, and don't imagine that I won't."

Robert Holmes provided the script for the penultimate story "The Power of Kroll". It is one of the more disappointing of the stories he wrote for *Doctor Who* and was his last until "The Caves of Androzani" in 1984. Holmes was perhaps constrained by the brief from Anthony Read to include "the biggest monster ever seen in *Doctor Who*". This wasn't a great idea on the series' budget and Holmes wasn't keen: having said this, the story has many good

---

[1] *The Time Machine* appears to have been a source text for the first Dalek story back in 1963, with the Daleks as the Morlocks and the Eloi as the Thals; the imagery of the film version, *Dr Who and the Daleks*, in turn borrows heavily from the 1960 film of Wells' novel.

points and intelligent ideas. A methane refinery on the third moon of Delta Magna is sending the gas back to the main planet as an energy supply, energy crises being a perennial theme in 1970s *Doctor Who*. The planet's original inhabitants, termed "Swampies" by the racist humans, have been moved to reservations on the third moon in a manner analogous to the Native Americans in the nineteenth century. They are now in the way again and Thawn, the ruthless human leader, wants to wipe them out as his company establishes more refineries. The source of the methane is in fact Kroll, a giant squid hideously mutated and enlarged by the fifth segment of the Key to Time: once the Doctor has extracted the segment, the power source is removed, Kroll disintegrates into lots of little baby squids, and the humans have to find a new modus vivendi with the Swampies.

The story was shot in Norfolk. The boggy terrain was completely unsuitable for K9, who didn't appear. John Leeson, who provided K9's voice, played refinery member Dugeen instead. The actors playing the Swampies are green and their make-up had to be waterproof. This proved difficult to remove and the actors had to repair to a local RAF base and scrub themselves down with Swarfega, a heavy duty cleaner used by engineers to remove oil from the skin. Tony Harding, the story's visual effects designer, explained that the refinery model was about two feet across: on screen, it looks even smaller and Harding was very disappointed with the shots transmitted. Kroll was a much more effective model, four feet across, and operated as a puppet. The live action scenes shot in Norfolk were to be combined with the footage from the model studio of Kroll waving his tentacles around: visual effects decided on a soft edged wipe to achieve the combined shot. Unfortunately, Harding explained, the cameraman on location was very young and had been given the wrong information about how to achieve a soft edged wipe. On screen, the division between the two pictures is marked by a dirty great flickering black line which appears to cut off the marsh's reeds half way up. There was no possibility of returning to Norfolk to reshoot, and Harding was desperately disappointed with the imperfect shots transmitted[1].

## "An awesomely powerful Key" but what does it actually do?

The season's final story is "The Armageddon Factor" by *Doctor Who* stalwarts Bob Baker and Dave Martin. They had to conclude the Doctor's quest for the Key to Time: Williams had set it up but hadn't determined on a clear ending, although it was also claimed that the Doctor, having assembled the Key, would always have said, "Well, there it is – I'm going to chuck it away now." Baker and Martin opted for the bi-partite structure of a six part serial favoured by Robert Holmes (write it as a four parter followed by a two parter). The first three episodes are set on the planet Atrios, which is locked in a nuclear war with Zeos, its neighbour, and losing heavily. The possibility of a nuclear war and the accelerated arms race with the Soviet Union deeply alarmed sections of the British public at the time, as did the election of Ronald Reagan as President of the United States in 1980. Reagan's advisers had seriously considered the possibility of a pre-emptive nuclear strike against the USSR. Membership of the Campaign for Nuclear Disarmament soared. The Atrians are led by the Marshall, played by John Woodvine at his Churchillian best. In a clear echo of right wing alarm about the enemy within (as CND was perceived by some at the time), he accuses pacifists Surgeon Merak and Princess Astra of colluding with the enemy Zeons to bring about a swift end to the war.

The Marshall is under the influence of the Shadow, the Black Guardian's agent. While the Doctor has scoured the Universe for the first five segments, the Shadow has sensibly located the sixth segment and waited patiently for the Doctor to bring him the other five. He traps the Doctor in his lair, the planet of evil (actually a space station), where the Doctor wanders around for several episodes. The Shadow's lair was originally conceived as a fun fair or ghost train, with strange noises and sudden giggles heard from dark corners. Dick Mills revealed this was dropped when people

---

[1] Tony Harding interview, *Fendahl* fanzine, 1980 ed. Simon and Frank Danes

began asking why there should be people giggling in dark corners: altogether too suggestive for the time slot. The Doctor meets Drax, a Time Lord with a cockney accent in the Shadow's employ, who addresses the Doctor as Theta Sigma. This upset people at the time as the non-classically educated among us assumed "Theta Sigma" was the Doctor's name, now finally revealed on television. One fan reviewer transcribed it as "Feet Asigma". Theta and Sigma are of course two Greek letters, but comprehensive school educated boys like me didn't know this, or recognise that it was unlikely the Doctor was named after two Greek letters. Fans put it about that Theta Sigma was the code by which the Doctor had been known at the Time Lord academy, and Terrance Dicks explained it as such in his novelisation of the story.

Another minor continuity mistake is the Doctor's line "I've never seen him do that before" as K9 revolves on the spot before communicating with Mentalis, the Shadow's war computer. Dick Mills[1] noted that K9 *had* done it before in "The Pirate Planet", because he had provided the whirling sound effect for it. The point was made during the recording but time was pressing and the mistake went through.

In a clever piece of scripting, the sixth segment is revealed to be Princess Astra (Lalla Ward). She calmly accepts her destiny and is transformed into a component. Romana is appalled, as is the Doctor, who nevertheless insists they have to return the Key to the White Guardian. The Doctor is himself affected by the Key and Tom Baker has a speech of ranting megalomania in which he insists that he could become a god: the scene is played and scripted for laughs and we see the influence of Douglas Adams again, who had just taken over from Read as script editor. Presumably the Doctor's experience of the Key's effect on himself is one reason for his decision to dismantle it, as it is too powerful for any one being to possess, but the point again isn't made clear on screen. The Black Guardian arrives and poses as the White Guardian to persuade the Doctor to hand the Key over. As he now looks and sounds like Valentine

---

[1] Speaking at the Doctor Who Appreciation Society Panopticon convention, 1979

Dyall and not Cyril Luckham, the Doctor should have spotted the substitution. He eventually does so when he asks the Guardian about Astra's fate: the Black Guardian says it's regrettable that Astra has died but with the future of the Universe at stake one can't be too careful. Knowing that the White Guardian would never have such a callous disregard for human life, the Doctor activates the TARDIS's defences (we know this because the Black Guardian has the line, "Doctor! You have fully activated all the TARDIS's defences!"), dematerialises and scatters the Key again in time and space. This restores Princess Astra to her human form and to her drippy lover, Surgeon Merak: after Leela and Andred, this is the second time in two successive season finales that major female characters have been married off to male wet blankets. Probably the floppy seventies hair doesn't help[1].

The story's ending is hugely unsatisfactory and as full of holes as the original premise for the Key to Time. It is never clear what the Key is supposed to do: "restore the balance", yes, but of, or between, what? The Doctor says at the end of "The Armageddon Factor" that there should always be a struggle between good and evil: this is one reason why he hesitates about destroying the Daleks for ever in "Genesis of the Daleks". If the balance were restored between good and evil, would there then be no conflict, or would the sides just be evenly matched? Certainly if conflict would end then so would the series, but this is never made clear. "The Ribos Operation" suggests the Key is needed to balance much vaguer cosmic "forces" in the Universe, without which the Universe will fall apart. Is this some reference to the threat of entropy in "Logopolis" (1981), through which the Universe is disintegrating and is only held together by the block transfer computations of the Logopolitans? Dispersing the Key might thus mean the Universe is still under threat of collapse. As the Doctor has failed his mission for the White Guardian as well, won't he be looking for revenge as well

---

[1] Some seventies actors were extremely proud of their flowing locks and refused to cut them to appear in the BBC's Second World War drama, *Secret Army* (1977-1979). See Andy Priestner, *The Complete Secret Army*, Cambridge, 2008.

as the Black Guardian? Yet when the Fifth Doctor encounters both again in "Enlightenment" (1984), the White Guardian seems to have forgotten all about his threat of eternal nothingness as a punishment for the Doctor's lack of co-operation, and is as civil and avuncular as ever. Both Guardians are ludicrously costumed in this Peter Davison story, the Black Guardian wearing a vulture's head as a hat, and the White Guardian a dove: perhaps their choice of headgear indicates a weakening of their mental powers, which would explain why the White Guardian can't remember things.

## Randomising on screen and in the production office: season seventeen

With filming on the season nearly completed, Graham Williams concluded that the umbrella theme – what we would today call a story arc – had been a success but couldn't be repeated easily. It had, he thought, imposed too many constraints on the writers. Next season would see the Doctor resume his random travels in time and space and "The Armageddon Factor" ends with the Doctor fitting a new device to the TARDIS console. This is a randomiser, which, he explains, operates on the "very, very complex scientific principle of pot luck". "Now no-one knows where we're going," sighs Romana, "Not the Black Guardian. Not even us." "No," says the Doctor, and smiles hugely as the season ends. All this indicated that the Key to Time was so vague and unsatisfactory a plot device to motivate the Doctor's travels that Williams might as well have stuck with the 1963 original premise that the TARDIS is erratic and keeps landing in random locations. That Williams introduced the randomiser at the end of the season was a bit of an acknowledgement on his part that the random journey premise was, after all, best.

The chaos generated by the randomiser was mirrored by more chaos in the show's production. Mary Tamm was adamant that she would do one season only and not renew her contract. Graham Williams kept trying to persuade her to do one more year – "Mary will come back next year, won't you Mary?" he's said to have kept

242

saying – but she kept saying no. By the time Williams realised that she really wouldn't return, the final scenes of "The Armageddon Factor" had wrapped and Mary Tamm hadn't been written out. Tamm suggested to Lalla Ward, who had played Princess Astra, that she should put herself up for the role of the companion. Lalla, who had enjoyed a regular part as Lottie in *The Duchess of Duke Street* (BBC, 1976-77), was interested. She had found favour with the production team for her sensitive performance as Astra. Someone realised that, as Romana was a Time Lord, she could regenerate and Lalla Ward could play her, rather than another character.

The problem was that a regeneration scene hadn't been shot and Mary Tamm would not have agreed to return to shoot one. The Doctor's regeneration had always been carefully planned and built up to in the course of a story. How then could Romana regenerate at the beginning of the new season? The new script editor, Douglas Adams, solved the problem with his application of his customary humour, or, if you would rather, flippancy. In the opening scene of season seventeen's first story, "Destiny of the Daleks" (1979), Romana is seen trying on bodies as an Earth woman would try on clothes: one midget form, dressed in Zilda's garb from "The Robots of Death" (1977), says, "I quite like this one, but it's a bit short." "Well, lengthen it then, go on," the Doctor replies. Fans hated the scene for its flippant tone and the frivolity with which it dealt with the serious concept of regeneration: a Time Lord has twelve regenerations but Romana apparently wastes more than half of them trying on different forms. Viewers are also asked to swallow that Time Lords can wear copies of bodies and the Doctor tells Romana that she can't wear Princess Astra's body: "Why not?" says Romana, "I thought it looked very nice on the Princess." To be fair to Adams, he was making the best of a bad job and trying to write an impossible scene. However, this was a huge and indigestible change in tone from the previous season which, though often funny, had largely kept Tom Baker's performance, and the humour, under control and subordinate to the drama. Now it seemed that the series had become *The Hitch Hiker's Guide to the Galaxy*. Romana's rapid changes of form recalled the Hagunenons, the super evolving species from the original radio series, who would evolve a longer arm instantaneously if they needed to reach a cup of coffee from the other side of the room. In fact, this sequence was written by John Lloyd rather than Adams, who was busy with *Doctor Who*, but perhaps Adams recalled it anyway when faced with the problem of Romana's changing face.

Graham Williams had offered Adams the post of script editor partly because he felt that the combination of Adams's inventiveness and humour, and Tom Baker's sense of humour, would lead to an explosion of creativity. In fact, it radically changed the programme, inflecting it towards humour and auto-referentiality (where the fiction reminds its audience that it is a fiction) in a way that influenced it permanently. It has been argued that Russell T Davies was influenced by Adams' sense of the absurd in his treatment of the revived series after 2005 and Kim Newman has argued that Adams's arrival marked the moment when the show jumped the shark. In 1979, some fans rejoiced at the fresh inventiveness of the show; others lamented its lack of seriousness and "undergraduate" humour, and fandom was split down the middle. Adams allowed Romana and the Doctor to speculate about flying down from the top of the Eiffel Tower rather than taking the lift in "City of Death" (1979). This has been seen as a charming and amusing moment, or as irritating beyond words because it treats Time Lords as Superman-types with super powers, when it has never been established in the show that they are like this. Douglas Adams would not let continuity stand in the way of a joke, however good or bad it was. As script editor, he pitched several story ideas to Williams that the latter rejected as too silly for the show. One was to pitch the Doctor against a race called the Krikkitmen: Adams postulated that every planet had variations on a game called cricket, and the English game was related to the sinister variety played by the evil Krikkitmen. This was a variation on a *Hitch Hiker's* idea that every planet had a drink called gin and tonic or its homophonic equivalent. Williams said the Krikkitmen were too silly and Adams replied that this seemed a strange thing to say about a series which centred on an alien clad in a hat and scarf who travelled the Universe in a police box with a robot dog. He tried to turn the script into a film, *Doctor Who and the Krikkitmen*, but nothing came of it. Never one to discard old story ideas, Adams re-used the material in his third *Hitch Hiker's* novel. He similarly recycled Professor Chronotis from the abandoned story *Shada* (1979) into his novel *Dirk Gently's Holistic Detective Agency*. Adams also submitted a story in which the Doctor retires from saving the Universe, arguing he has done enough, before being drawn back into his heroic role by a new threat. Williams toyed with the idea and then turned it down, but it perhaps formed the basis for the eleventh Doctor's retirement in "The Snowmen" (2012). Distraught at the loss of his companions Rory and Amy, the Doctor goes into seclusion in Victorian England and ignores repeated attempts by Silurian Madame Vastra, her maid Jenny and Sontaran manservant Strax to re-engage him with combating evil. Adams's enduring influence on the series can perhaps be seen in the triumvirate of bizarre characters in the 2012 Christmas special, "The Snowmen". The Doctor (Matt Smith) of course has his interest reawakened by the enigmatic Clara (Jenna-Louise Coleman) and the animated snowmen, manifestations of the Great Intelligence…

**Daleks lurch about and try to destroy**

The seventeenth season also hit problems with the rampant inflation of the late 1970s. Former producer Philip Hinchcliffe submitted a story called "The Valley of the Lost", centering on a plane crash in a South American jungle. Adams turned it down on the grounds of cost, explaining in a letter to Hinchcliffe that they now made *Doctor Who* on about one third less of the money that had been available to the former producer. In a margin of the proposed script, Adams wrote, "*Close Encounters* of the extremely expensive kind…?" The production values of the seventeenth season were poor in comparison with the sixteenth, let alone the Hinchcliffe/Holmes serials. The Daleks looked reasonably good on location for "Destiny of the Daleks", but were bashed about considerably when they returned to the studio, allegedly after being hired out to *Blue Peter* and to private users. For a small fee at the time, you could hire a Dalek from the BBC for, say, a parish fete: Dick Mills lamented the need to provide a tape for hired Dalek voices. My brother Simon tried out a BBC Dalek in 1979 in its "Destiny" livery. It had been hired by a local picture framer who wanted to use it as a model for two Daleks he intended to build (and I think never did) for his youth club.

In the studio, the Daleks were decrepit: their paint was chipped, their wheels squeaked (apparently the budget didn't run to a can of oil) and one had a diamond panel banged onto its base section to hide its damage. The props were also so old that each was slightly different from the others, with different coloured dome lights and rings around the same and so on. This meant that it was therefore very obvious which Dalek prop was doubling as another Dalek once it had been exterminated.

There appeared to be almost no money at all for the final two stories, "Nightmare of Eden" and "Horns of Nimon". Some of the former's spacecraft scenes were shot against black drapes and the passenger extras were clad in head-to-toe cagoules, complete with hoods, and dark glasses: no doubt to save money on costumes. The Skonnon parliament in "The Horns of Nimon" contained about five members sitting on black rostra, doubtless indicating how far Skonnon democracy had declined under the despotism of Soldeed (Graham Crowden). It seemed that much of the money was spent on "Creature from the Pit", the first story to be shot, which had included expensive jungle sets and filming at Ealing Studios. "City of Death" was partly filmed in Paris, but apparently the location filming was no more expensive than shooting in this country, thanks to the canny budgeting of the production unit manager, John Nathan-Turner, who became producer for the eighteenth season. The team kept costs down by shooting on the hoof: they set up the camera without permission to shoot the Doctor, Duggan and

Romana in Paris and hurriedly decamped when the local gendarmerie started to take an interest. "Shada" would presumably have been an expensive finale but was abandoned because of industrial action at the BBC, with only one of its three studio sequences, plus its location filming, completed. John Nathan-Turner attempted to remount it in the following year but was unable to make it work. It was eventually released as a commercial VHS in 1992, with Tom Baker providing linking narration (in character as the Doctor) for unfilmed sequences. Big Finish remade it as an audio with Paul McGann as the Doctor and Lalla Ward reprising her role as Romana. It was available to stream on the BBC website, with limited animated visuals, was eventually published as a novel by Gareth Roberts in 2012, and was completed with animation for DVD release in 2017.

The seventeenth season was thus a chaotic one with a hotch-potch of stories of even more varying quality and tone than season fifteen. John Leeson had left as the voice of K9 and his replacement, David Brierley, had none of the original's charms. Adams attempted to explain K9's change of voice as an attack of laryngitis in "Destiny of the Daleks", but this hilarious explanation was undermined by the Doctor asking, "How can a machine get laryngitis? I mean, what do you need it for?" No answer was forthcoming. John Nathan-Turner persuaded John Leeson to return as K9 for Tom Baker's final season and Leeson has provided K9's voice ever since for *Doctor Who*, *The Sarah Jane Adventures* and Bob Baker's lamentable Australian children's series *K9* (2009-10).

Adding to the general sense of confusion was Tom Baker. He had now played the Doctor for five years and was embarking on his sixth, longer than any previous incumbent in the role. Tom Baker felt that he knew the part and understood the series better than anyone else. Asked to stay on for another season, Baker wrote a long letter to the Head of Series and Serials saying that he would only stay on if he had more control over the scripts. He suggested that his new companion should be so fat she couldn't keep up, or a talking cabbage who would sit on the Doctor's shoulder and offer opinions. Strangely, neither of these suggestions were taken up, although he did have more and more control over the scripts – which he and Lalla Ward would apparently rewrite in rehearsals – and over what appeared on screen. He appeared to enjoy Adams's sense of humour and ad-libbed constantly. There is one sequence in "Nightmare of Eden" when the Doctor is attacked by the Mandrels; Baker, off screen, ad-libs, "Oh, my fingers, my arms, my legs! My everything! OOO!" He then staggers towards the camera in a ragged coat, looking like a cartoon character who has experienced a terrible disaster: say, Tom from *Tom and Jerry* after a bomb has gone off. Other Baker interpolations followed. In "The Horns of Nimon", he gives K9 the kiss of life and draws attention to the woefully unfrightening Nimon costumes by asking, "Tell me, Nimon, are you terribly fierce?" Lalla Ward, perhaps trying to compensate, plays the whole story completely straight. Graham Crowden, apparently infected by all the hilarity, laughs his head off during his death scene; he was, it seems, unaware that this was a take, not a rehearsal. Graham Williams recalled that "we would be tearing our hair out in the gallery while Tom was going through his antics" on the studio floor. He and Baker clashed to the extent that they had a meeting with senior BBC executives Shaun Sutton and Graeme McDonald. Knowing the problems with Tom Baker not taking the material seriously enough – they had sent Williams notes expressing reservations about the level of humour in the new scripts – McDonald nevertheless told Williams that Tom Baker's Doctor delivered up to thirteen million viewers a week, and that, if a choice had to be made between them, Williams would go and Baker would stay. The pair agreed they could work together. In his autobiography, Baker rather decently expresses regret at his behaviour to Williams and realises that his suggestions exhausted his producer.

In spite of all the mayhem off screen, the viewing figures for season seventeen were exceptionally good. "Destiny of the Daleks" gained thirteen and a half million viewers, and "City of Death" fourteen and a half million: the programme's highest ever audience.

As Letts and Dicks had found when they opened the ninth season with "Day of the Daleks" (1972) – nine and a half million viewers and the season's biggest ratings winner – Daleks were a great hook for casual viewers in the opening episode. The exceptional figures for "Destiny" and "City" were partly explained by the lack of competition, as ITV was again blacked out by industrial action. This plagued all television production in the 1970s as show business unions, like others, ignored the pleas of the then Labour government and the Trades Union Congress to keep wage demands low and reasonable. In some cases, unions selfishly and recklessly did neither, demanding preposterous settlements and raising their own nemesis in the form of Mrs Thatcher's Conservative government, whose legislation castrated the union movement. The industrial craziness hit the BBC in a yearly dispute about which union was responsible for the clock on *Play School* (the BBC's main programme for under-fives). For *Doctor Who*, union silliness manifested itself as an endless dispute about who should operate and maintain the time rotor which rose and fell on the TARDIS console. Philip Hinchcliffe got so fed up with this that he wrote the time rotor out in the fourteenth season, which introduced a new, Jules Verne type control room whose console was based on a davenport and had no time rotor. Graham Williams, anxious to restore the show's science fiction look, reintroduced the gleaming white control room in "The Invisible Enemy" (1977), time rotor and all: based on the Hartnell set, it was basically used until the original series folded in 1989.

As is the case with most of the seasons, viewing figures drained away in the course of the season, falling to eight and three quarter million for "The Horns of Nimon" (1979-80). The decline was attributable in part to ITV broadcasting again. It might also be argued that the final Nimon story was so dreadful that it put viewers off *Doctor Who* for much of the next season. "The Leisure Hive" (1980) barely managed to scrape together five million viewers, and the eighteenth season averaged about six million, peaking at just over seven million for the excellent "Warriors' Gate" (1981).

Although hailed as a Saturday evening institution, people weren't watching *Doctor Who* much. The decline led new producer John Nathan-Turner to push for a change of scheduling and Peter Davison's three seasons as the Doctor transmitted twice weekly on weeknights. There was an immediate improvement in ratings: Davison's first story garnered nearly ten million viewers and the rest of his season averaged over nine million. Davison himself expressed some regret at the change in timeslot but acknowledged Nathan-Turner's reasoning for it.

## City, Creature and the Nightmare of the Horns of Nimon

There are some good stories in season seventeen. "City of Death" (1979) is often hailed as a classic and is packed with inventive science fiction ideas. Douglas Adams and Graham Williams, working under the in-house pen name of "David Agnew", which had been used as a credit for "The Invasion of Time" (1977), rewrote a script from David Fisher about art theft. This had featured a detective in the Bulldog Drummond mode who became the bumbling Duggan, engagingly played by Tom Chadbon. At the dawn of time, a Jagaroth spaceship explodes on take-off on prehistoric Earth, scattering its single survivor across different periods in Earth's history. Each of the separate selves tries to push forward mankind's development so that its twentieth century self, Count Scarlioni (Julian Glover) in Paris, will have sufficient technology to build a time machine, return to the past and stop his original self from launching the ship. The time experiments are financed by art thefts, including the theft of the Mona Lisa. The story is witty, well-acted and entertaining but arguably spoilt by Tom Baker's performance, now almost wholly inflected towards comedy and undermining the dramatic moments.

"Nightmare of Eden" (1979), Bob Baker's solo writing venture for the series, is also a good story. Coming out of hyperspace, the cruise liner *Empress* and the cargo ship *Hecate* half materialise around each other. The *Empress*'s mayday is answered by the Doctor and

Romana. In a nice touch of realism, the Doctor poses as an insurance agent trying to sort out the rival claims for damages from each of the captains. Also on board the *Empress* is zoologist Tryst, whose continual event transmuter has allowed him to store sectors of the planets he has visited on data crystal. He is financing his experiments with drug running: the monstrous Mandrels, reduced to ashes, form the basis of the drug vraxoin. The Doctor is appalled at the presence of vraxoin on the ship: he reinforces the story's anti-drug message repeatedly by reiterating the evil of drug running, which destroys whole planets while the merchants make fortunes. The original script called the drug "zip" but Lalla Ward was concerned that this sounded too attractive a name for children, so it was changed. At the story's end, Tryst appeals to the Doctor to understand, as a fellow scientist, that he never wanted to be a drug runner but had to finance his research. The Doctor, who never acknowledges that the end justifies the means (at least, until his Sylvester McCoy incarnation: a disgraceful distortion of the series' morality), disgustedly tells him to go away.

Good as these stories are, there are moments to make the viewer wince. Both feature a scientist with a cod Germanic accent: Kerensky in "City of Death" and Tryst in "Nightmare of Eden". Williams really should haff spotted zis und put a schtop to it. Colin Mapson was the visual effects designer on "Eden" and lamented Williams's decision to save money by shooting his beautiful and elaborate models in the television studio to save money. On the model stage, with high speed film cameras, effective filming of spaceships was possible; in the television studio, with lumbering electronic video cameras the size of a piano, it wasn't. Williams expressed himself very pleased with the time and the money saved: Mapson hated it. Colin Mapson also criticised the design of the Mandrels, which hugely resembled the larger muppets from *The Muppet Show*, then running on ITV, and provoked hysterics across the land when one lunges out at the Doctor and Captain Rigg at the end of episode one. As was common in *Doctor Who* for the period, the spaceship sets were over-lit, which exposed the cheapness of their construction. The public address system is very clearly a drain cover screwed into a flat. The story also collapsed behind the scenes. Alan Bromley, who had directed "The Time Warrior" (1973-4), walked out half way through following disputes with the cast and Graham Williams had to handle the final studio session.

The less said about "The Creature from the Pit" and "The Horns of Nimon", the better. Christopher Barry returned to direct the former and found a very different Tom Baker from the actor he had worked with in "Robot" and "The Brain of Morbius". He objected to Baker reworking scenes and would wait till he had finished improvising before trying to shoot the scene as he, Barry, wanted it. Much of the season's money appears to have been spent on an impressive jungle set at Ealing studios and the eponymous creature is a Kroll-sized disaster. Special effects designer Mat Irvine and his team created Erato – for that is the creature's name – from weather balloons and it bundled greenly along the studio floor with a huge penile probe extended when it wanted to communicate with people. There was a pause when it was unveiled in the studio, broken by one of the cameramen saying, "Who's a big boy, then?", followed by general hilarity. Christopher Barry was furious and modifications were made to the creature for the second studio session, where it looked less obscene. Barry, Williams and Irvine were involved in an internal BBC inquiry to discover who had sanctioned such a disaster. As usual, it was trying to deliver an ambitious effect with a lack of time, communication and money. The quality of "Creature from the Pit" was depressed even more by also a silly sub plot about some bandits whose leader sounds and looks like Fagin from various films of *Oliver Twist*: he even calls his henchmen, "my boys".

A similar effects disaster occurred five years later with the Myrka, the Silurians' dinosaur pet in "Warriors of the Deep" (1984). Released to destroy the humans on the sea base, the Myrka was operated by the two pantomime horse actors from *Rentaghost* and was about as realistic. It wasn't ready for the studio session and was still wet with paint; its verisimilitude wasn't assisted by guest star Ingrid Pitt, who decided she should launch herself at it with a karate kick, which doesn't seem a sensible way to deal with a dinosaur. The Myrka was in good company in this story. Working against the clock, the director screamed at the Sea Devils who had just fallen over and died – their costumes buckling at the back in the process, revealing the actor underneath – to get up and die again.

"The Horns of Nimon", the season's final story, is extraordinary. Anthony Read's script is actually pretty good and in the pastiche tradition of Hinchliffe and Holmes via "Underworld" (1978): the latter was a version of Jason and the Argonauts, "Nimon" is a version of the Minotaur legend, signposted by the virtual Nimon/minotaur anagram in case we can't work this out for ourselves. The Nimon are a plague of galactic locusts who land on a planet, promise its inhabitants great wealth, then strip it of all its riches and energy before moving on. This is called "The Great Journey of Life". One Nimon has promised Soldeed (Graham Crowden) such riches and technology but endlessly defers it while it accepts tribute from Aneth (i.e. Athens), defeated by Skonnos (Knossos) in war. The tribute takes the form of highly ineffectual young men and women whom the Nimon slaughters for no good reason. One was played by Janet Ellis, who went on to become a presenter on *Blue Peter* and looks and sounds like one in this story. The Nimon has high opinions of itself and lives in the Power Complex (geddit?). Romana and the Doctor defeat him and Soldeed and the season lurched to a premature end: the next story, "Shada", was abandoned because of industrial action.

"The Horns of Nimon" is perhaps the worst story of the 1970s. Tom Baker sends the whole thing up and sucks any dramatic tension out of every scene. In episode one, the Doctor is dismantling the TARDIS console to make it work more effectively: when he tests it, it emits a stock comedy sound effect of whoops and boings used in BBC shows like *The Goons* and *The Goodies*. This is an effective metaphor for what Tom Baker and Douglas Adams were doing to *Doctor Who* at this point: taking it to pieces and reassembling it as puerile comedy. Graham Crowden catches the general mood of hilarity and grotesquely overacts as Soldeed. Only Lalla Ward tries to keep things on an even keel by playing it straight and she is fighting a losing battle. The money has clearly run out by this point, too. The Nimon are played by dancers in black body stockings, clad in wispy golden loincloths and clumping around in the sort of platform shoes favoured by glam rockers. Their heads appear to be bull masks sculpted in plastic and are so unconvincing that original viewers thought they must be helmets to hide the real, hideous alien within. This was indeed the plan but there wasn't enough money to make real, hideous aliens, so the production team hoped the ridiculous helmets would suffice. They didn't. The co-pilot shot by the Nimon splits his costume and reveals his red underpants.

As a penultimate story before a six part epic, "The Horns of Nimon" might have been quietly forgotten as an embarrassment. As the final story of the season, it was a disaster and left many fans depressed and miserable about the show's prospects. It seems odd to think of now, when Tom Baker remains one of the most popular Doctors and is so loved, that many fans wanted him to go by the start of season seventeen, hating the way he sent the show up and fearful that the public wouldn't accept a new actor as the Doctor. Douglas Adams departed for other *Hitch Hiker's* related projects at the end of season seventeen and Graham Williams left the BBC altogether to run a hotel. BBC executives had continued to be concerned about Tom Baker not taking the show seriously for some years; Graeme McDonald had even asked Williams if he wanted to fire him, which Williams thought completely unnecessary. The new producer of *Doctor Who* was John Nathan-Turner and was given a firm brief from BBC executives to keep Tom Baker under control.

# 10
# All Change

John Nathan-Turner had been production unit manager on both *Doctor Who* and the BBC's long-running vet saga *All Creatures Great and Small* (1978-80; 1988-90), based on the autobiographies of James Herriot. He was thus the keeper of the purse strings and was adept both at bringing in his shows on budget and making that budget go a long way. As such, he was thought to be a safe pair of hands for *Doctor Who*. However, the BBC noted his inexperience as a producer and appointed Barry Letts as executive producer for the eighteenth season. Letts read and commented on all the scripts and mentored Nathan-Turner in the role of a producer.

John Nathan-Turner immediately set about "putting the money on the screen". Season eighteen's production values were far higher than season seventeen's although the budget was more or less the same. Nathan-Turner cut back on expensive location work and alien environments were convincingly realised in the television studio: "The Leisure Hive" had only one location sequence on Brighton beach; "Meglos", "Warriors' Gate" and "The Keeper of Traken" had no location filming at all.

## New producer, new music, new titles

A new title sequence was commissioned from graphic designer Sid Sutton. In place of the familiar time tunnel – which Nathan-Turner thought looked like racing down the tube of a vacuum cleaner – was a star field which forms the Doctor's face. The stars also formed the new logo: the shield, which had been used since Pertwee's last season and for seven years, was replaced by a tubular logo. Both title sequence and logo were disappointing. A shield suggested the Doctor's role as knight errant fighting evil; a tubular logo suggested inventive domestic lighting. The star field put the theme of space travel across convincingly enough but time travel was now absent.

Furthermore, the stars weren't particularly well realised: they appeared fully formed in the middle distance, rather than coming into shot gradually, and the star field was far less effective than that used in *Star Trek*'s opening titles which dated back to 1966. That they recalled *Star Trek* at all showed how old hat the new titles were. Nathan-Turner used a new portrait of Tom Baker for the titles, arguing that the original portrait had been used since 1974 and didn't match the actor's ageing. Baker's face would be replaced by Peter Davison's for the following season – which appeared from a venetian blind-like wipe, thus complementing the domestic interior design theme of the logo – and eventually by Colin Baker's, which broke into a huge and ghastly grin. The closing titles ended with a white star exploding onto the screen in a white out. Composer Peter Howell[1] recalled that Sutton had been advised not to use this image, as white outs always showed up the viewers' dirty television screens, but he used it anyway. The new theme was a more boppy, disco version of Ron Grainer's original, which began with the scream that had signalled the cliffhanger of previous years (something copied in the new theme for Christopher Eccleston and David Tennant's Doctors). The scream was repeated for the cliffhanger, but was too high pitched and short to generate excitement as had the deep base original of previous years. *Doctor Who* had entered the colourful eighties and the new theme was apparently played in British discos at the time to warn the staff that there was a fire. When the show returned in 2005, Russell T Davies's team looked to the original Baker sequence for inspiration, thus perhaps indicating the enduring worth of its star field replacement. The 2005 sequence copied the Tom Baker TARDIS hurtling through the time tunnel and the imagery within the programme itself showed the TARDIS travelling in the same tunnel when in flight (the original series had tended to use a space background for sequences when the TARDIS flew). This re-use of 1970s imagery confirmed the original Baker sequence as representing the time vortex, something that had never been made

---

[1] Speaking at the Doctor Who Appreciation Society convention Panopticon in 1981

explicit at the time. Davies and Moffat dispensed with the Doctor's face for all the title sequences until the 2012 Christmas special, "The Snowmen", where Matt Smith's face appears fleetingly against cosmic clouds.

Nathan-Turner was unhappy with the six part serials, believing that they sagged in the middle and were usually padded with running up and down corridors. He asked for an extra two episodes for Tom Baker's final season (the eighteenth) so that he could make seven four part stories rather than five four part stories and a six parter, the twenty six episode pattern that had been standard for the past five years. Nathan-Turner made the request with some trepidation, thinking that he might be asked to make two episodes fewer instead, but the BBC, in a sign of their confidence in him and their hope the show could be revitalised, agreed. Had they insisted on twenty four episodes we might have been spared the dreadful "Meglos", a tale not of a talking cabbage but a talking cactus, but that's another story. In the course of making season eighteen, Nathan-Turner apparently felt the strain of stretching the budget over twenty eight episodes and requested a twenty six episode run again for season nineteen, Peter Davison's first, concentrating the money saved into the twenty six episodes. Nathan-Turner avoided a sagging six episode tale in Davison's first season by making six four part stories and one two parter: the historical 1920s tale "Black Orchid" (1981) by Terence Dudley.

**Goodbye K9. Or not.**

Nathan-Turner intended to write out both Romana and K9, thinking both were far too clever and made it too easy for problems to be solved. Unfortunately, the announcement that K9 was to go led *The Sun* newspaper to run a "Save K9" campaign ("Save him! Save K9 from the beastly Beeb!") and Bill Cotton, the outgoing Controller of BBC 1, insisted that K9 should return to television within a year. This either meant including him again in *Doctor Who* or giving him his own show. Thus a pilot episode for a new series, *K9 and*

*Company* (1981), was made. Elisabeth Sladen returned as Sarah Jane Smith with John Leeson as the voice of K9. Elisabeth Sladen was horrified by the technical limitations of the K9 prop and not over-enamoured of the script, which concerned a cult of pagan goddess worshippers led by a greengrocer, played by Bill Fraser. This plot wasn't a good idea as it had been already done in "The Stones of Blood" eighteen months previously and such tales were arguably an ill fit with a science fiction show. Sarah Jane Smith's character had undergone some alterations: she was more acerbic than the Sarah we had last seen in "The Hand of Fear" (1976) and she had learnt to dispatch bad guys with high kicks. Had writer Terence Dudley confused her with Leela? It was nice to see Sarah's Aunt Lavinia make an appearance, played by the fine actress Mary Wimbush (Julia Pargetter in *The Archers* and Aunt Agatha in *Jeeves and Wooster*, both formidable ladies) but hard to see how the pilot could be stretched into a series. Apart from a coven of witches, what other evils could threaten the village of Moreton Harwood? *K9 and Company* remained a single-episode spin-off, but was assimilated back into the parent show and thus regarded as canonical when Sarah reappeared with K9 in the twentieth anniversary special "The Five Doctors" (1983) and in the revived series in "School Reunion" (2006).

New companions were introduced towards the end of the season. The first was Adric, a mathematical boy genius, described in the brief to writers as fifteen, small for his age, wiry and strong. Boy geniuses in science fiction shows are the sort of idea which production teams feel are excellent and viewers dislike intensely. Adric, like Wesley in *Star Trek: the Next Generation* (and probably Conor in *Angel* (1999-2004)) was conceived as a character for younger viewers to identify with but, as Sydney Newman noted when planning the series in 1963, such viewers tend to identify with the next generation up and find characters their own age irritating and patronising. While *Next Generation* fans were hoping that "that brat didn't save the ship again", *Doctor Who* fans squirmed in embarrassment at Adric. Adric might have worked if a good young actor been cast but Matthew Waterhouse's range is somewhat limited. In his first story, "Full Circle", he is upstaged by Richard Willis as his brother Varsh and some critics wondered why the casting was not reversed. Fans breathed a sigh of relief when Adric blew up with the Earth freighter on prehistoric Earth ("Earthshock", 1982). Some even considered he didn't quite merit the end titles rolling in silence over his smashed badge for mathematical excellence – a trick used for Charlie's death in *The Duchess of Duke Street* (season two, 1977) – or Nyssa and Tegan's grief in the following story, "Time Flight".

The second new companion was Nyssa (Sarah Sutton), introduced in "The Keeper of Traken" and retained as a companion at short notice after that story's conclusion. "Logopolis" had to be hastily rewritten to incorporate her; she was brought from Traken by the Watcher, the intermediate projection of the Doctor between his fourth and fifth incarnation. Completing the trio was Tegan (Janet Fielding), an Australian air hostess whose aunt is murdered by the Master in the first episode of "Logopolis". All three new characters were much younger than either version of Romana and presumably introduced to lower the show's demographic in an attempt to appeal to a younger audience. This created problems when a younger Doctor was added to the mix. Peter Davison was only twenty nine when he began playing the part and was strictly forbidden from putting his arm around either Nyssa or Tegan: Tom Baker could, but didn't, because that would have been fatherly, whereas if Davison had done it, that might suggest indulgence willy-nilly in hanky-panky in the TARDIS. He was, however, allowed to put his arm around Adric and, later, Turlough. Nathan-Turner thought that including more companions would allow each to have her or his own sub plot, thus increasing the dramatic possibilities available to the writers and reproducing the multiple plot structures of the Hartnell and Troughton stories.

## Tom Baker's final season

Arguably the biggest problem facing the new producer was the show's star. Nathan-Turner had firm ideas about how Tom Baker was to play the Doctor and cut back on the control the actor had had on the character in the Graham Williams seasons. Partly in an attempt to "tidy him up" in Nathan-Turner's words, the new producer introduced a new version of the Doctor's costume; the greatcoat, scarf and hat were retained but in a uniform burgundy. Thus Baker's choice over a simpler, more comfortable costume, often stripped of waistcoat, jumper, jacket and tie, was removed. John Nathan-Turner also instructed directors to insist that Baker stuck to the script and limited his ability to re-write, ad-lib and improvise. Baker gives a more subdued and intense performance as the Doctor in his final season; with the humour now under control, this is one of his most effective years as the Doctor. However, the new approach understandably led to friction between the producer and his star. Nathan-Turner apparently felt that the only way to establish proper control over the Doctor was to cast his own actor in the role. Tom Baker was offered another season, on the same conditions of performance as the eighteenth season, but he declined. In his autobiography, Baker explained that one reason for leaving was his unhappiness with the new companion characters (Adric, Nyssa and Tegan). His departure from the series was announced on the BBC *Nine O'Clock News* while "Meglos" was being broadcast and illustrated with a clip from that lacklustre serial. Now married to co-star Lalla Ward, Baker returned to the theatre, playing Oscar Wilde in *Feasting with Panthers* at the Chichester Festival Theatre (which I saw: he was excellent) and Frank in the original production of Willy Russell's *Educating Rita*, a twentieth century version of *Pygmalion* and a perennial favourite for GCSE English Literature. Willy Russell took advantage of Baker's casting to insert an in-joke into the play. Rita, who has decided to drop her Liverpudlian accent in favour of a posh one, alarms Frank into saying that "I am not giving a tutorial to a Dalek." Rita replies "I am not a Dalek" (a version of the oft quoted line "I am a Dalek" which, like "Beam me up, Scotty", was allegedly never said).[1] The line was understandably cut in the film with Michael Caine, as he had never played the Doctor and it was presumably felt that American cinema audiences wouldn't have got the reference; although, with the wide dissemination of Tom Baker serials on PBS stations, many of them probably would have done so. When Katy Manning played Rita in a production in Australia, the Dalek line was retained and *Doctor Who* fans in the audience laughed their heads off.

Nathan-Turner asked Christopher H. Bidmead to join the show as the new script editor. Bidmead wasn't keen. He was a scientist and writer who hated recent versions of the show and particularly deplored its reliance on "magic". He might have been thinking of the sequence in "City of Death" where the Doctor and Romana suggest that they fly down from the top of the Eiffel Tower. Nathan-Turner reassured him that the show was to be re-tooled with a harder science fiction edge, and Bidmead came on board. Like Holmes and Adams, he rewrote many of the serials presented to him. David Fisher's "The Leisure Hive" had been written for the previous production team and concerned an alien Mafia organisation muscling into the entertainment industry: it was full of humour, which Bidmead tamed, to Fisher's disappointment. The aliens were the Foamasi (an anagram of Mafiosi), trying to buy out the Argolin Leisure Hive. This was established by the Argolins as a multi-cultural meeting and learning place where different races can put aside their differences as a move of reconciliation after a hideous war with the Foamasi. In the serial's best lines, the Doctor asks the Argolin leader Mena how long the war lasted. "Twenty minutes," she replies. "As long as that?" the Doctor comments, surprised. Wry smiles all round from viewers thinking of nuclear holocaust with the election of Ronald Reagan and the renaissance of CND. Bidmead rewrote "Full Circle" by an eighteen year old fan, Andrew Smith, who had been submitting stories to the production office for some years. He also tried to rewrite "State of Decay" by *Doctor*

---

[1] In fact, a Dalek says it in "The Chase"(1965): just one of that story's great lines.

*Who* veteran Terrance Dicks. This had been originally submitted to the production office as the first story of season fifteen, entitled "The Vampire Mutations", and had been vetoed because it clashed with the BBC's new film of *Dracula*. High camp Gothic horror, however, was not easily rewritten into hard science fiction and in the end it was Dicks's version that was made. One wonders if the experienced Dicks might have had something to say about his work being heavily rewritten by a novice production team.

The fifth story was "Warriors' Gate". Steve Gallagher was a prose writer of science fiction and his submitted scripts and story ideas read like a novel. Bidmead agreed to rewrite them as a script, and the result is a superb science fiction serial. Slavers on Captain Rorvik's spaceship The Privateer trade in Tharils, time sensitive aliens who can navigate the time winds for vessels when plugged into its consoles. The slavers and the TARDIS arrive in a limbo between universes. Here, the Tharil empire once stood, the Tharils themselves enslavers of human beings who rose up against them, building the robot Gundan to drive them out. The story is wonderfully witty and beautifully shot. The actors are superimposed onto a pure white void for the scenes in limbo, or onto black and white photographs of a Welsh castle and garden for the scenes in the Tharils' empire, both achieved through green screen. Rorvik's crew are a bunch of bored, recalcitrant malcontents, with very funny performances from Kenneth Cope and David Kincaid as engineers and a wonderful Rorvik in Clifford Rose. Rose was famous as the SS Standartenführer Kessler in the BBC's *Secret Army* (1977-1979). Anxious not to make that character a stereotype, Rose developed a private life and a girlfriend for him. He brought the same level of research and seriousness to Rorvik. Interviewed on the DVD release, Clifford Rose said he found the scripts hard to understand (and they do contain some baffling science fiction concepts) but got a handle on Rorvik by seeing his similarity to Captain Mainwaring in the BBC's long running *Dad's Army*, another character of limited competence and authority who has to motivate even greater incompetence. Rose's performance as a man struggling to stay in command of his crew and of himself is a delight.

"Warriors' Gate", like "Nightmare of Eden" in the previous season, hit serious problems behind the screens. Paul Joyce, the director, was experienced in theatre and brought an innovative style to the show which grated with BBC routines. He elected to shoot off the set into the lighting gantry, which had been used as a double for machinery in 1973's "Carnival of Monsters": the technicians objected. The set design for the Privateer ship was a two level gantry supported by scaffolding: health and safety said it wouldn't take the weight of artistes or cameras, so Joyce opted to use a hand held camera when shooting on it. He borrowed a spaceship corridor from the BBC television version of *The Hitch Hiker's Guide to the Galaxy*, then shooting at the same time, to increase the sense of space on board the Privateer. Joyce apparently took ages setting up shots and the show became dangerously behind schedule; he was sacked and then apparently brought back when no-one else could figure out how to shoot the rest of the script. Nathan-Turner apologised to his superiors for employing Joyce and accepted full responsibility for his mistakes; he also congratulated Joyce on the finished product. On the DVD extras, Joyce recalled Nathan-Turner saying, "They're great shows, Paul" but admitting that he didn't understand them. This was a worrying presentiment for a new producer. It has often been alleged that Nathan-Turner brought in the show on budget, and it often looked good, but he left the story-telling to others. It has further been alleged that he took almost no interest in the story-telling at all and, by the end of his ten year run as producer, was as weary of the show as the BBC itself was[1].

Bidmead also reworked Johnny Byrne's script for "The Keeper of Traken", concerning the intrusion of the evil Melkur into the pastoral idyll of Traken. Nathan-Turner wanted to bring back the Master and Bidmead worked him into the script. The Melkur statue became the Master's TARDIS, which is odd since it walks around a

---

[1] See Richard Marson, *The Life and Scandalous Times of John Nathan-Turner*, Tadworth, 2013

lot and we'd never seen a TARDIS do that before, and the Master returns in his withered "Deadly Assassin" state. His regeneration cycle used up, he employs some of the powers acquired as the Keeper of Traken to steal the body of Tremas (another anagram, this time of Master), Nyssa's father, who becomes the new Master. Both Tremas and the Master were played by Anthony Ainley. "The Keeper of Traken" is a fine story and very much better than Johnny Byrne's next effort, the Gallifrey based "Arc of Infinity" (1983), known to some fans as "Arse of Inanity"; the difference in quality suggests that much of the good writing came from Bidmead, not Byrne.

Bidmead wrote the season's final story, "Logopolis", which rather belies his dislike of magic for its inclusion of two extraordinary ideas. In the first, the Master's TARDIS has appeared inside the Doctor's TARDIS console room. This leads to lots of excellent scenes of recursive occlusion, when the Doctor and Adric walk through the Master's TARDIS – also disguised as a police box – into another TARDIS control room, inside which is another police box, which they enter to find themselves in another TARDIS control room containing another police box, which they enter to find themselves in another TARDIS control room containing another police box, which they enter to find themselves in another TARDIS control room containing another police box ... and so on, to apparent infinity. The Doctor decides the best way to flush the Master out of the TARDIS is to land it under the Thames, open the doors and let the water do its work. He and Adric stay in the console room and viewers notice the obvious flaw: wouldn't he and Adric drown?

The second strangeness concerns the mathematical race of Logopolitans. The Universe has passed the point of its normal heat death according to the third law of thermodynamics – entropy increases. Here, the dialogue fulfils some of the series' original educational function from 1963 in getting some real physics across to its dullard viewers. The Universe is only prevented from collapsing by the block transfer computations of the Logopolitans.

This seems to involve them muttering or intoning numbers which mathematically map the universe and therefore keep it from collapse (eh?). "The Daemons", following Isaac Asimov, established that alien science advanced beyond our comprehension would be indistinguishable from magic, but, to the non-scientific viewer, block transfer computation looks awfully like magic. Barry Letts, the executive producer, thought it was a stunningly imaginative concept.

Also in "Logopolis", the Master broadcasts to the entire Universe from the Pharos Project on Earth, a Jodrell Bank-like radio telescope, demanding its complete obedience to his will or its annihilation. Quite what the Master would want with the whole Universe is never explained and former script editor Douglas Adams criticised his reappearance in the series. Adams argued that if you had someone with a black beard and an evil laugh, you didn't need to give him any plausible motivation.

**The fifth Doctor**

In looking for a new Doctor, John Nathan-Turner wanted someone as unlike Tom Baker as possible. He also wanted an actor who might be more biddable. In casting both the fifth and the sixth Doctors, Nathan-Turner had a clear idea of who he wanted and didn't hold auditions: Peter Davison and Colin Baker were his first choices. When it came to casting the seventh, auditions were held – with Janet Fielding reprising her role as Tegan – perhaps an indication of Nathan-Turner's weariness at still being in charge of the show after seven years and no longer having the enthusiasm to choose decisively. Richard Griffiths was apparently considered (later famous as the chef/detective in *Pie in the Sky*) and Ken Campbell was auditioned but the part went to Sylvester McCoy. The producer got on well with him and found a new lease of life for himself in the show's final three years.

Back in 1981, Nathan-Turner phoned Peter Davison and asked him if he would be interested in playing the Doctor. Davison was very surprised to be asked and had never considered himself as the Doctor, thinking he was far too young for the part. He took several days to consider, under strict instructions to tell no-one about the offer, apart from his immediate family. Still undecided after a week, Nathan-Turner took him out to lunch and finally persuaded him. Davison recalled that one reason he accepted was because he thought it was a marvellous opportunity, but also because he couldn't bear the thought of someone else playing the Doctor after he had turned it down. Furthermore, he would be sworn to secrecy about the offer after declining it. Davison was well-known for playing Tristan Farnon in *All Creatures Great and Small*, one of the three leads with Christopher Timothy and Robert Hardy. He wondered how he was to play the Doctor and sought advice from some younger *Doctor Who* fans, one of whom said he should be "like Tristan, but brave". Davison thought this was admirable advice and went through his first season with wide-eyed innocence, recapturing some of the wonder felt by the Doctor as he encounters new and extraordinary worlds and situations. He was still feeling his way into the part when shooting The Visitation (1982), filmed second but transmitted fourth. Davison recalled that the director, Peter Moffatt, assumed that he knew how to play the Doctor and allowed him to get on with it, affording him the customary respect as the star that had often been given to Tom Baker. Davison actually wanted some direction and asked Moffat for help in shaping the part, which Moffat was pleased to give him.

The nineteenth season, then, was shot out of sequence, as the changing length of Davison's hair between stories testifies. "Four to Doomsday" (transmitted second) was followed by "The Visitation" and "Kinda" (transmitted third) before work started on Davison's first story "Castrovalva" by Christopher Bidmead, a sequel to "Logopolis". Nathan-Turner had been forced into shooting the season out of sequence because of problems with the script for the first story, "Project Theta-Sigma", which had run into several drafts and eventually had to be abandoned. "Castrovalva" was a late replacement and the script wasn't ready for the first shooting session. Nathan-Turner made a virtue out of necessity by arguing that shooting the season out of order helped Davison get into the role. Certainly, his performance in "Castrovalva" is much more assured than in "The Visitation" and "Four to Doomsday", although his performance in "Kinda" (actually written for Tom Baker) is splendid. Some reviewers questioned whether it was quite such a good idea to make "Castrovalva" a sequel to a story that had been broadcast nine months previously, but the problem was smoothed over by a repeat of "Logopolis" in October 1981.

"Logopolis" was the Tom Baker/Peter Davison offering for a series of repeats on BBC 2 in the autumn of 1981 under the umbrella title of "The Five Faces of *Doctor Who*", commissioned by Nathan-Turner to remind viewers that there had been other Doctors before Tom Baker and to prepare them for Peter Davison. These were the first repeats on the BBC to include Doctors other than the present incumbent, and they were well received by the public, grateful fans and the press.[1] *The Guardian* hailed the in its listings guide with the rapturous, "O tempora!  O TARDIS!" (a play on Cicero's despairing comment on Roman times under Mark Antony: "O tempora!  O mores!" – "Oh the times!  Oh the manners!").  Hartnell was represented by the first story "An Unearthly Child", Troughton by "The Krotons", Pertwee by "The Three Doctors" and "Carnival of Monsters". The episodes were stripped across weekday evenings from Monday to Thursday. At the *Doctor Who* Appreciation Society convention in 1981, Frazer Hines despaired of the choice that represented his Doctor – "Oh, not the Krotons!" – and said that he, Troughton and Wendy Padbury had hated it and, while filming it, they had inevitably called the enemies "the croutons".

Nathan-Turner was so pleased with the reception of the repeats that he arranged for three more stories to be shown the following year (1982) under the title of "*Doctor Who* and the Monsters": "The Curse of Peladon" (Ice Warriors), a hacked four episodes edit of "Genesis of the Daleks" and "Earthshock" from Davison's first

---

[1] If we discount the repeat of "Planet of the Spiders", shown before "Robot" but after the regeneration into Tom Baker.

season, representing the Cybermen. The success of "The Five Faces of *Doctor Who*" apparently led Nathan-Turner erroneously to believe that, because so many people loved the old episodes, they would want to see elements of the old episodes – characters and enemies – in new stories. This led to the poorly-scripted and poorly received second Davison season, which contained a returning element from the series' past in every story. This twentieth season started *Doctor Who*'s slide from hugely popular family viewing to a cult show arguably made for, and watched by, fans, many of whom ironically didn't like what was being offered them anyway. Viewing figures thus slid from ten million in 1982 to under four million in 1989, when the axe finally fell.

Peter Davison was himself disappointed with the scripts for his second season. He was under contract to make a third season but had to decide if he wanted to stay for a fourth year during his second. He decided to move on, not least because of the quality of the scripts and because he wanted to do other things. Elisabeth Sladen recalled that she and Tom Baker would take time out of rehearsals to peep in at other shows being rehearsed simultaneously. While she and Baker thought they looked awfully dull, and Baker telling her they should go back to saving the Universe, Davison looked longingly at his fellow actors in rehearsals on exciting projects. There was some improvement in script quality in his third year as the Doctor and he did sometimes regret his impending departure, but the die was cast – and so was Colin Baker.

Season nineteen was rescheduled from Saturdays to a bi-weekly slot, retained for all three of Davison's seasons, apparently to test the water for a bi-weekly soap opera which eventually materialised as *EastEnders* in 1985. Episodes were transmitted at about 7.00 p.m. and the later timeslot anticipated and deflected complaints about horror or violence. Both, however, were on the wane in Davison's time – with one or two notable exceptions – and the heat had gone out of Mrs Whitehouse's campaign against *Doctor Who* anyway now that the BBC had assimilated her criticisms in shaping the programme. By this point, length of an episode was something of an anachronism. Soap operas were the only other dramas in 1982 which had half hour, or twenty five minute, episodes: forty-five minutes, or one hour, slots were preferred. One reason for showing two episodes a week was to satisfy the demands of viewers used to longer running times for their favourite shows. They might not get a single forty five minute episode of *Doctor Who* until "Resurrection of the Daleks" in 1984, but they did get fifty-odd minutes' worth if it was shown twice a week. Colin Baker's first season was broadcast as in forty five minute episodes (re-edited to two twenty five minute episodes for some overseas broadcasts), perhaps in an attempt to inherit the mantle of serious science fiction from *Blake's Seven*, which had been broadcast in the more adult-friendly length of forty five minutes and had now finished its run. After the cancellation crisis in 1985, Colin Baker's second season resumed as twenty five minute episodes: a format that looked increasingly ridiculous when compared with, for example, two hour filmed episodes of *Inspector Morse* on ITV. Now filmed exclusively on video, *Doctor Who* might as well have had a "condemned" sign slapped across its title sequence for its final four series from 1986-1989. It was deliberately packaged as an old show which no-one cared about, and so was ripe for the chop when Peter Cregeen finally axed it in 1989.

Nathan-Turner wasn't entirely happy with the twice weekly timeslot, or the inevitable consequence that the programme now ran for thirteen weeks a year, rather than the twenty six or so with previous Doctors. He tried to get the programme shifted back to an autumn timeslot, not least so that it would be on the air during the twentieth anniversary on 23$^{rd}$ November 1983. The controller of BBC 1, Alan Hart, turned him down. Starting the programme in the autumn would mean that Peter Davison wouldn't be available to shoot *Sink or Swim*, the BBC comedy in which he co-starred with Robert Glenister (Salateen in "The Caves of Androzani") and which ran for Davison's first two years as the Doctor. Hart wasn't prepared to tell comedy to move its production schedules just to accommodate *Doctor Who*. He did, however, agree to Nathan-Turner's plan B, which was for a special drama to be made and broadcast on or around the twentieth anniversary. Extra money was thus found for the ninety minute special, "The Five Doctors" (1983).

There are some very good stories in Davison's first season. There are also signs of the incomprehensible and garbled elements which would baffle the general public and lead to the programme's decline. "Castrovalva" is a good story based on the graphic works of M.C.Escher. Recovering from his regeneration, which he fears is failing, the Doctor seeks a dwelling of simplicity – known as Castrovalva – in which he might rest and heal. There are effective scenes of the Doctor and his companions running around Escher-esque architectural impossibilities: running away from a village square, they only run back to it and so on. One of Castrovalva's senior members is the Portreeve, a gentle soul who helps the Doctor recover. The Portreeve is in fact the Master in disguise: a genuine revelation for some viewers, thanks to Anthony Ainley's subtle and beautiful performance as the Portreeve. The *Radio Times* and end credits kept the surprise by listing the Portreeve's actor as "Neil Toynay", an anagram of "Tony Ainley". Castrovalva isn't real either: it's a block transfer computation conjured up by the Master and vanishes into the ether.

With only two stories under his belt, the new Master was already starting to become samey and irritating. As with his appearance in every story of season eight, his continued reappearance in Davison's and Colin Baker's time suffered from the law of diminishing returns and unfortunately, we didn't have Roger Delgado's wonderful performance to enjoy.

### "Kinda"

The third story, "Kinda" (1982), is one of the series' finest, beautifully acted, made and scripted as a heady draught of Buddhism, Christianity and a satire on colonialism. Humans have established a scientific observation dome on the paradise planet Deva Loka, inhabited by the mute, peaceful, humanoid Kinda. The military head of the expedition is Sanders, a suitably British colonial

270

name for a colonial administrator played, in a coup of casting, by British war movie veteran Richard Todd. He tells the Doctor the Kinda are ignorant savages, "But they smile a lot. Or at least they used to. Before we took the hostages." Sanders' deputy, Hindle (Simon Rouse) has a complete nervous breakdown and goes mad, threatening the Doctor and Adric with death and the surrounding rainforest with obliteration. The jungle, convincingly realised as a studio set, is an idyllic Eden, and in every Eden there is a snake. This is the Mara, a being from "the dark places of the inside", which possesses Tegan when she falls asleep in the place of the Dreaming. Several scenes are set in Tegan's mind, where she encounters figures from Buddhist teaching (which includes the Mara itself). Eventually, the Mara manifests itself as a giant snake (like Satan in Eden). The Doctor surrounds it with reflective panels from the dome, arguing that evil can never face the sight of itself. The Mara panics at its reflection and is banished back to the dark places of the inside.

The story is an intellectual tour de force. It also works well as exciting drama and the supporting cast is terrific. Nerys Hughes was cast as Todd, in an early example of Nathan-Turner's preference for casting actors principally known for light entertainment in *Doctor Who* (Nerys Hughes was one of the leads in *The Liver Birds* (1969-78)). Ever-concerned that it would provoke ridicule from the uninitiated, fans worried that this tendency undermined the seriousness of the drama, but Nerys Hughes gives a wonderful performance (she wasn't just capable of comedy, after all) and there is some erotic tension between her and the apparently younger Doctor, culminating in the parting will he/won't he kiss her goodbye. Mary Morris, who had excelled as one of Patrick McGoohan's tormenters, Number Two in *The Prisoner*, is superb as the wise seer Panna, who is apparently dispatched by her visions of the Mara. "Kinda" was written for Tom Baker's Doctor and writer Christopher Bailey considered him more suited to the Doctor's role as wise man in the story; he was somewhat concerned that Peter Davison wouldn't exert as much authority, but he needn't have worried. Bailey was less happy with some aspects of the production and disliked the appearance of the Kinda, beautiful Caucasian extras who looked as though they had just stepped out of a Timotei shampoo advertisement. His hopes for his story were somewhat at odds with those of the director, Peter Grimwade, who viewed the script with some impatience, thinking that Bailey wanted to write *Play of the Month* and was trying to shoehorn a religious allegory into the unreceptive vessel of *Doctor Who*. Bailey in turn grew weary of some of the rewrites he was asked to perform, especially those which required him to give more explanations or information. He believed that he was expected to explain absolutely everything, and memorably said that if *Doctor Who* had tackled "Little Red Riding Hood", he would have been obliged to fit a transmogriphication device on the wall of grandmama's cottage to explain why Little Red Riding Hood didn't spot that her grandmama was actually the wolf in disguise.

Some critics have said that the Doctor's statement that evil cannot stand its own reflection is optimistic at best. However, there is a story of Reinhard Heydrich, responsible for the so-called "final solution" and the Nazi extermination camps, catching sight of his own reflection in a full-length mirror and emptying his revolver into it. This incident has been variously interpreted as indicating Heydrich's self-loathing and disgust; it might be an historical example of evil loathing its own reflection.

### "Earthshock"

The Cybermen stomped back onto our screens in "Earthshock" (1982), hijacking an Earth space freighter which they intend to crash into an interplanetary peace conference. This is captained by the female Briggs, described in the script as a) tough and b) physically imposing but was played on screen by light comedy actress Beryl Reid, who was neither of these things. Reid's unfamiliarity with science fiction led her to quip, "We're going to Warp Drive. Is that near the Awkright Road?" during rehearsals. The Cybermen were redesigned but retained the basic features of their last appearance in "Revenge of the Cybermen" (1974). The basis of the costume was now a military pilot's uniform rather than a rubber wet suit and, in keeping with the eighties look, they wore silver sprayed moon boots rather than sprayed wellies. These new Cybermen lost the teardrop but gained a hang-dog look to their mouths which turn down at the corners; this feature was criticised at the time as being too like the stormtroopers from *Star Wars*. John Nathan-Turner asked for the chin piece to be transparent plastic so that the actor's jaw (inexplicably painted silver) should be visible: a reminder of the Cybermen's organic origins to viewers who might have thought they were robots. This detail was abandoned for subsequent appearances and replaced by a solid silver jaw. As with "Revenge of the Cybermen", the Cybermen were voiced by the actors who played them, rather than by another artist as in the sixties and post-2005 stories. David Banks made his first appearance as a Cyberleader; he was to play Cyberleaders in the following three Cyber stories and argued that there was an element of the Cyberleader which survived into all its replacements. He eventually published a book about the Cybermen which theorised about their origins and nature. Cybercontroller Michael Kilgarriff thought the book showed Banks had become a bit too mystical about the whole thing.

The *Radio Times* offered John Nathan-Turner a cover photograph to mark the Cybermen's return. This would have been the first *Radio Times* cover since Jon Pertwee's day, but Nathan-Turner turned it down, preferring to keep the enemies' identity secret until the surprise at the end of episode one. Hence David Banks was credited as "Leader", rather than Cyberleader, in the magazine's cast listings. "Earthshock" was well received but contained some of the worst lines ever to be inflicted on an actor. The Doctor expresses sarcastic surprise that the Cyberleader can understand a word connected with emotion, as they hurtle towards planet Earth:

> Cyberleader: It is a word like any other. And so is "destruction". Which is what we're going to do. To that planet.

273

(They are going to "destruction" it?) The Fifth Doctor lets the linguistic abuse pass: the Fourth picked it up when a Cyberleader said their bombs would "fragmentise" Voga, the planet of gold. "Fragmentise? Oh well, I suppose you can't expect good English. From a machine." A BBC technician also appears on screen in one shot, behind one of the space frieghter's stairwells and he can be spotted if you turn your television brightness setting up high.

"Time Flight", the season's final story, vies with "The Horns of Nimon" as one of the worst ever made. It was apparently commissioned because British Airways offered the BBC some filming on their supersonic airliner, Concorde; somehow, a *Doctor Who* story had to be shaped around the aircraft. This particular black spot fell to Peter Grimwade, who proceeded to turn in the weakest of his three weak scripts for Peter Davison's Doctor. Concorde travels back in time to prehistoric Earth, where the Doctor and his companions meet the Plastmatons and the Master, stroll around a bit and then go back to Heathrow. It seems extraordinary that anyone thought it was possible to realise Concorde landing on prehistoric Earth on the show's budget but the rest of the script is up to the standard of this concept. Veteran British film actor Nigel Stock – who had appeared with William Hartnell in the Boulting Brothers' wonderful film of Graham Greene's *Brighton Rock* (1947) – wanders around looking embarrassed and speaks his lines without attempting to give much of a performance. Tegan is left behind at Heathrow, apparently written out, only to reappear again in the first story of season twenty, "Arc of Infinity", where the Doctor finds her in Amsterdam of all places.

## Season Twenty

Perhaps boosted by the positives of "Earthshock", "Time Flight" managed to gain nine million viewers. Perhaps memories of "Time Flight" caused "Arc of Infinity" to shed almost two million – and three million since "Castrovalva" – from a public which thought that *Doctor Who* was now a bit rubbish. Viewing figures hovered around the seven million mark for the whole of season twenty. Sadly, "Arc of Infinity" (1983) is very poor fare indeed. In the first sign that Nathan-Turner intended to raid the series' back catalogue with a vengeance, "Arc" is set again on Gallifrey with Omega (from "The Three Doctors" (1973)) attempting to return and control the Matrix. The story required viewers to remember Omega from a story transmitted ten years previously, and Gallifrey from stories broadcast in 1976 and 1977. For viewers who couldn't remember, the story was baffling; for those who could, it seemed ridiculous to bring back Omega when he had been so comprehensively destroyed in "The Three Doctors". "Arc of Infinity" is notable for Colin Baker's appearance as Commander Maxil, commander of the Chancellery Guard. There is also a dreadful alien in the Ergon, a giant chicken, and Peter Davison scowls most dreadfully as Omega when the latter copies the Doctor's body. The story's one good moment is a small child smiling at Omega; Omega smiles back at him, remembering what it was like to have physical form and contact with his fellows. Tegan rejoins Nyssa in the TARDIS and the trio go off to Manussa, to encounter the Mara again in "Snakedance", a story that is virtually a retread of "Kinda" minus the religious references, but which does at least include a young Martin Clunes as the bored and spoilt Lon, heir to the throne. This is the best story in a woeful season. Valentine Dyall returns as The Black Guardian in three stories and viewers are expected to remember who he is after four years. The Black Guardian recruits Turlough (Mark Strickson), an alien posing as an English public schoolboy, to destroy the Doctor. He tells Turlough that "I may not be seen to act in this", but doesn't explain why not. The Black Guardian then pops up in the course of the next few stories to gently nudge Turlough along by bellowing such lines as, "In the name of all that is evil! Destroy him!"

Turlough becomes Adric's replacement as a companion and is never entirely trusted by Tegan, although he is fully accepted once the Black Guardian spontaneously combusts in "Englightenment". John Nathan-Turner worried that Strickson's blond hair would make him look too like Peter Davison in long shot, and Turlough was thus manifested as auburn. In keeping with his preference for the regulars to wear a uniform rather than clothes, the producer decreed that Turlough should always wear his school uniform. This stretched credulity to the limit for younger viewers: they could accept dimensional transcendalism and regeneration, but not the voluntary wearing of school uniform. Turlough presumably only had one uniform when he stepped on board the TARDIS, so his presumably was as ripe as Tegan's after repeated wear. Viewers worried about such things and their worry affected their ability to suspend their disbelief. Nathan-Turner, who provided Tegan and Nyssa with a bedroom to highlight the chastity of sleeping arrangements aboard the TARDIS, didn't extend the courtesy – or realism – by allowing them regular changes of clothes.

Turlough joined the series in "Mawdryn Undead", which featured David Collins as the eponymous Mawdryn, an alien stuck in an undead state ("dryn maw" is Welsh for "dead man"). Mawdryn is mistaken for the Doctor after an aborted regeneration by Tegan and Nyssa. In a typical example of Peter Grimwade's crass scripting, they don't consider what tragedy might have caused the Doctor to regenerate: perhaps they thought he had fallen off an exercise bike, the apparent cause for the sixth Doctor's regeneration in "Time and the Rani". Tegan and Nyssa realise their mistake when Mawdryn recovers his true form and they notice his spaghetti-like brain falling out of his head. Mawdryn and his mutant companions seek death, which can only be provided by the Doctor donating the rest of his regeneration cycle to them: the energy of one regeneration will cause the death of one of them. This is an intriguing addition to Time Lord lore in an otherwise uninteresting and poorly developed script. Mawdryn says that donating his regenerations will mean "the Doctor will cease to be a Time Lord. That is the price of compassion." The implication is that being a lord of time lies in the capacity to cheat death through regeneration, rather than to control time as suggested in "The War Games" (1969).[1] The Doctor is willing to make the sacrifice and presumably to die at the end of his fifth incarnation, but the energy is supplied by two versions of the Brigadier meeting in a temporal paradox: as they touch, the energy created releases Mawdryn and his brothers from life. The Brigadier has been brought back for the story as a Mathematics teacher in Turlough's public school. He has a nervous breakdown as a result of the events of the story on his younger self and, when the Doctor meets him seven years after the death of Mawdryn, has forgotten his time at UNIT. The Doctor reunites him with his younger self to complete the time paradox that frees Mawdryn. It is as disappointing to see the Brigadier tamed as a schoolmaster as well as it is unlikely; this can be explained by the original plan to use Ian Chesterton, one of William Hartnell's first companions, as the teacher, but actor William Russell was unavailable and the Brigadier was substituted instead.

Steve Gallagher contributed an intelligent script about space leprosy for "Terminus", named "lazar's disease" after the Middle English word for leprosy. The story is notable for the intelligent designs of the lazars' carers, the Vaneer (based on Anglo-Saxon images of death) and a giant talking dog with light-up eyes, the Garm. Again, the execution let down the script; a problem that had plagued the series as far back as "The Krotons". Space travellers' terror at contracting lazar's disease is spoilt by hysterical overacting from Dominic Guard ("That's it! That's WHAT IT'S ALL ABOUT! WE'RE ALL GOING TO DIIIIIIIIIIIIIE!") and Lisa Goddard wearing a fetching white outfit more suited to *Barbarella*, frizzy hair and a big bubble space helmet. The story attracted complaints from the Leprosy Society for its negative portrayal of leprosy and from the Tannoy company which complained about the word "tannoy"

---

[1] It is a moot point whether "Time Lord" is the name of the species at all. "The Invasion of Time" (1978) implied that Time Lord was the term for Gallifrey's ruling class, not the race itself, and the Doctor's unseen parents worry that he will never become a Time Lord in "Listen" (2014). Does this mean that non-Time Lord Gallifreyans can't regenerate?

being used for the ship's public address system. The company quite reasonably pointed out that "tannoy" was not a generic term but a copyright brand name, in the same way that Hoover is not a synonym for vacuum cleaner. The BBC apologised to the Tannoy company.

The season ended with the lacklustre two parter "The King's Demons", another pseudo-historical by Terence Dudley who had supplied the well-regarded "Black Orchid" the previous season. The Master appears again in disguise ("Oh my dear Doctor, you have been naïve!") and has substituted a shape-changing android called Kamelion for King John in order to carry out a baffling and pointless scheme to prevent the ratification of Magna Carta. Kamelion was an animated, computer controlled robot made by a firm called CP Cybernetics. John Nathan-Turner was enthusiastic about its possibilities as a companion but it quickly became apparent that its capabilities as a mechanical prop, like K9's before it, were very limited. Peter Davison recalled that Kamelion's dialogue had to be pre-recorded and fed into the robot for its lip movements to synchronise with its speech. This meant recording sessions with Kamelion were frustrating and slow and there was no possibility to vary its performance as Davison et al were not interacting with another actor. Although a remarkable piece of work for the time, Kamelion actually looked so human it might as well have been played by a human actor and some viewers were surprised to learn it was actually a robot. Sadly, the only person who understood how to program him died and Kamelion was banished to the realms of the TARDIS corridors. Here, he was largely forgotten for the next season until he was unceremoniously written out in "Planet of Fire" (1984).

"The King's Demons" was to have been followed by a story called "The Return". Of what? Of the Daleks of course, their inclusion being kept as a surprise as the Cybermen's had been in "Earthshock" and as the dinosaurs had been in "Invasion" (part one of "Invasion of the Dinosaurs" (1973), the retitling of which caused much trouble: see chapter six). A strike by BBC electricians put paid to

"The Return", which was held over to the following season where it became "Resurrection of the Daleks" (1984).

"Resurrection of the Daleks" typified the problems of this period of the show. Penned by script editor Eric Saward, the plot seemed to be made up as it went along. One minute we were on Earth, with android policeman controlled by a gangster called Lytton (Maurice Colbourne, who had played Coker in the BBC's excellent adaptation of *The Day of the Triffids* (1981) and who would play the lead in the BBC yachting drama *Howard's Way*), then we were on an Earth ship in the far future under attack by the Daleks; then the Daleks have made androids of the Doctor and his companions, intending to use them to assassinate the High Council of the Time Lords; then the Doctor intends to assassinate Davros... such plot as there was consisted of a series of set pieces sustained by a bunch of cardboard characters. Again, the casual viewer was required to remember chunks of continuity from years-old stories: the Daleks' war against the Movellans from "Destiny of the Daleks" five years previously is discussed (the Daleks lost) and we were expected to know – and care about – what is meant by the High Council of the Time Lords. There was yet another flashback sequence of clips from old episodes: as the Daleks drain the Doctor's memory of his past companions, all are seen on screen, except for Leela, whom the production team forgot to include. These clip sequences were a hallmark of Nathan-Turner's in the eighties: in "Logopolis", the fourth Doctor sees images of his old enemies; in "Earthshock", the Cybermen watch clips from old Cybermen stories to remind themselves of the Doctor; in "Mawdryn Undead", the Brigadier sees clips of his UNIT days. The clips were intended to please the fans, which was very sweet of Nathan-Turner, but arguably meant nothing to other viewers; except perhaps to remind them of happier periods in the show's history or to get a parlour game of the "Who's that?" variety. They certainly slow down the action and were mercifully abandoned by the time Colin Baker became the Doctor.

"Resurrection of the Daleks" also suffers from some very poor acting by co-stars better known for light entertainment, thus, for once, fulfilling the prophecy of fans that some actors were not up to the high drama of the series. Rula Lenska has no character to work with; Rodney Bewes (from *The Likely Lads*) is absolutely without grit as a Dalek agent; Chloe Ashcroft, who often presented *Play School*, is utterly unconvincing as Professor Laird. The Doctor carries a revolver while hunting a Dalek mutant and a blaster when threatening to execute Davros, both anathema to the tradition that the Doctor never carries, or uses, firearms. Some sequences are frankly nasty. The Daleks' allies release a nerve gas that destroys human flesh: one character raises his dissolving hand and asks, "What's happening?" in real distress. *Doctor Who* now seemed to be a show that had lost its way; meandering plots, poor acting and a neglect of the casual viewer would be hallmarks of the show until its cancellation in 1989.

Perhaps mindful of the need to do something to stop the rot, Davison was keen to inject some more humour into the proceedings. He felt that his Doctor was awfully straight-laced. Nathan-Turner, mindful of the horrors of Tom Baker's clowning around, rejected the idea.

### The Twentieth Anniversary Special: "The Five Doctors"

Nevertheless, here were some good stories in the rest of Davison's run. One is the twentieth anniversary special, "The Five Doctors". This was broadcast two days after the actual anniversary on 25th November 1983 as part of the BBC's annual Children in Need telethon appeal. Some regions ran captions over the action detailing the donation hotline number and the amount raised so far. Canada saw the special two days before the British, on the actual anniversary itself.

Robert Holmes was the first person to be approached to write the special. Saward had wanted him because he had written for the show for fifteen years and knew it backwards. Holmes warned Saward that he wasn't sure he'd be able to make the script work and turned in a treatment called "The Six Doctors", in which the Cybermen have made an android copy of the first Doctor which doesn't look entirely like William Hartnell and thus explain the necessary recasting. Holmes eventually abandoned the script, having succumbed to his own fears that it was impossible to write, and Eric Saward turned to another *Who* veteran, Terrance Dicks. Dicks wrote a story akin to a role-playing game, in which an unseen villain removes the Doctors and their companions from time and space and plonks them down in the Death Zone on Gallifrey: an ancient wilderness where the founders of Time Lord society brought aliens to fight each other for their entertainment. This loose structure allowed the script to adapt to whichever actors might be available, although Saward would soon be tearing his hair out to accommodate additions like Caroline John (Liz Shaw), Richard Franklin (Mike Yates), Frazer Hines (Jamie) and Wendy Padbury (Zoe), asked to appear at the last minute by John Nathan-Turner. In the end, all appear as phantoms generated by Rassillon's Dark Tower in the Death Zone. The second Doctor only realises that Jamie and Zoe are illusions by recalling that, as the Time Lords had wiped their memories in "The War Games" (1969), they shouldn't be able to recognise him. This is in fact a continuity mistake and an example of Terrance Dicks's axiom that continuity in *Doctor Who* was like the definition of history in *1066 And All That*: What You Can Remember. The Time Lords wiped Jamie and Zoe's memories of all their adventures with the Doctor *except for the first one*: thus they would have been able to recognise Troughton's Doctor. Robert Holmes made a similar continuity blunder in "The Two Doctors" (1985): the Time Lords use the second Doctor as an agent to do their dirty work, when in fact it had been the third and fourth Doctors who had been used thus. Holmes had forgotten.

Nathan-Turner decided to recast the first Doctor before work on the special began. William Hartnell had passed away in 1975. He chose Richard Hurndall, whom he had seen in an episode of *Blake's Seven* and thought closely resembled Hartnell. Hartnell himself is represented in a clip from the last episode of "The Dalek Invasion of Earth" and Hurndall turns in a good performance, copying a few of

Hartnell's mannerisms but otherwise making the part his own.

The problem of the first Doctor was dealt with; the problem of the fourth Doctor soon arose. Tom Baker had agreed to be in the special and a substantial role had been written for him, but he was having second thoughts. He had only left the show two years previously and appeared to feel it was too soon to return: he also wondered if he would think "Who are all these people?" pretending to be the Doctor. Baker withdrew and Terrance Dicks was left with an almost identical situation to the one he had faced ten years earlier with "The Three Doctors", when a substantial role for Hartnell's Doctor had had to be abandoned. Heather Hartnell, William Hartnell's wife, had telephoned the production office to say that Bill couldn't possibly do all the running around that was required in the script. Dicks cheerfully employed the same solution on "The Five Doctors" that he had employed on "The Three Doctors": the attempt to lift the Doctor from his time stream had been unsuccessful. The first Doctor had been stuck in a travel capsule in a time eddy (in 1973) and the fourth Doctor was stuck in limbo in the new story. John Nathan-Turner got Baker's permission to use some clips from the abandoned "Shada" (1979) to represent his Doctor, and the actor agreed. Mindful of the friction between Pertwee and Troughton in filming "The Three Doctors", Dicks structured the new script to keep the Doctors apart until the final scenes.

"The Five Doctors" is a vastly enjoyable, nostalgic romp and a reminder of how the programme should be made and scripted. It features a Dalek, the Cybermen and the Master as the main enemies, with cameo appearances from a Yeti and a new enemy, the Raston robot. Susan, the Brigadier, Sarah Jane and K9 return as companions as do some Time Lords from "Arc of Infinity", although Colin Baker was replaced as Captain of the Chancellery Guard so that viewers wouldn't be confused when he appeared as the Sixth Doctor at the end of the following season.

Season twenty-one began two months later, with a return to dreadful form in the appalling "Warriors of the Deep" (1984), a Sea Devil and Silurian tale scripted by Johnny Byrne. The season contained two excellent stories in "Frontios" and "The Caves of Androzani". "Frontios" is a fine piece of science fiction by former script editor Christopher H. Bidmead, in which a human colony in the far future is under attack from meteors from the sky – which apparently destroy the TARDIS – and burrowings from underground, which claim colonists' lives. Those responsible are the Tractators, mindless burrowing creatures controlled by the Gravis – a Tractator that has developed extreme intelligence and psycho-kinetic powers – whose control over the other Tractators recalls the Animus's control over the mindless Zarbi in "The Web Planet" (1965). Bidmead was inspired to create the Tractators by a plague of woodlice that kept infesting his flat and the design does recall a woodlouse. Director Ron Jones cast dancers to realise the Tractator movement, but the costumes were unfortunately far too rigid to do much more than shuffle along.

**Spectrox Toxaemia**

Davison's final story is the superb "The Caves of Androzani", by Robert Holmes, a tour de force of excellent writing, directing, acting and design that recalled the heights of the Holmes/Hinchcliffe/Tom Baker years and won a "Best *Doctor Who* story" poll in *Doctor Who* Magazine. Holmes re-used some elements which worked well in his previous stories, but "Androzani" is none the worse for that. On the planet Androzani minor (shades of the third moon of Delta Magna in "The Power of Kroll" (1979)), the scalded and embittered Sharaz Jek lurks in the planet's cave systems (shades of Greel's lair below the theatre in "The Talons of Weng-Chiang" (1977)), holding Androzani major to ransom by keeping sole hold of its supply of spectrox. This precious element slows the ageing process and grants a human being twice his normal life span. "Would you think I was eighty?" the President asks the villainous industrialist Morgus. "Fifty, at most," that worthy replies. Jek has let it be known that the people of Androzani major can have all the spectrox they like, if they give him the head of Morgus in return. He and Morgus were once in partnership but Morgus betrayed him and left him to be hideously scarred by a mud burst in one of the Anrozani caves. Jek's thirst for revenge has become an obsession and driven him to the point of madness. Jek is one of the planet's foremost android engineers and is protected by android troops of his own making, armed by the gun runner Stotz, whom Jek supplies with spectrox in return for weapons. Stotz is himself in Morgus's pay, who receives Jek's spectrox through him and thus has a monopoly on the limited supplies available on Androzani major. Morgus is simultaneously financing the President's armed campaign against Jek, but the Praesidium's troops are bogged down against superior forces. Jek has also kidnapped their General Chellak's deputy Salateen (Robert Glenister) and replaced him with an android duplicate: he thus has a perfect spy in his enemy's camp.

Into this murky world of political intrigue, double-crossing, cave systems and soldiers come the Doctor and Peri. They are first suspected of being gun runners and are then captured, or rescued, by Sharez Jek, who falls violently in love with Peri and allows the Doctor to be taken back to Androzani major by Stotz. Investigating the tunnel systems, both time travellers stumble into a nest of raw spectrox and quickly fall victim to spectrox toxaemia, for which the only cure is the milk of the giant queen bat that lives in the cave system's lower levels. The gun runners, aided by Morgus in person when his treachery is discovered and his business empire collapses (he has murdered the President), over-run Jek's lair and are beaten back by Jek and his androids. Jek murders Morgus and dies of his wounds. The Doctor conserves enough oxygen in his respiratory bypass system (last seen in "Pyramids of Mars", 1976) to enter the airless levels or the queen bat, but there is only enough milk for Peri. He collapses on the floor of the TARDIS and regenerates.

There is much to delight the viewer in "The Caves of Androzani", a story full of guts and high drama. Holmes, believing that there were reserves of untapped heroism in the fifth Doctor, gives Davison some moments of real gusto and physical violence. When Sarez Jek drools over Peri, the Doctor stands up and eyeballs him silently, forcing Jek to divert his attention from his companion; the Doctor defies Stotz in turning the ship back to Androzani minor and runs for his life through the sand dunes as the gun runners machine-gun him; he uses his fists on Salateen when he needs to escape. As Morgus, John Normington gives a performance of Jacobean coldness and villainy, turning to deliver his soliloquys directly to camera in the best traditions of BBC Shakespeare. In fact, this was the result of Normington's misunderstanding of Graeme Harper's direction, but Harper liked it and kept it in. Christopher Gable excels in the Phantom of the Opera melodrama of Sharez Jek, making him both pathetic and genuinely frightening. He turns from ranting to being quietly terrifying on a heartbeat, as in this exchange with the exhausted Peri:

> Jek:  And it is Morgus who has done this to me!  Morgus destroyed my life.  Do you think I'm mad?
> Peri: (lying)  No.
> Jek: I *am* mad.

Never has Peri been in greater peril in the series. Holmes intelligently has her sympathise with her captor and tormentor and Nicola Bryant conveys Peri's physical deterioration as spectrox toxaemia takes hold with great subtlety and conviction. Holmes also re-uses a powerful image from "The Talons of Weng-Chiang" as Jek, like Greel before him, rips off his leather mask to reveal his disfigured face beneath, to the hysterical terror of Morgus and, when she spots him, Peri. Jek jabbers with distress at her fear and hides under the table in a touching and realistic moment: a considerable dramatic achievement in the midst of a battle between humans and androids. Graeme Harper's inventive direction on his first *Doctor Who* story is rightly praised: even small details surprise, as in the holographic viewer in Morgus's office when it would have been so much simpler to use a two dimensional monitor.

Harper was swiftly re-employed to direct "Revelation of the Daleks" in the following season; he would have directed the aborted

BBC Enterprises thirtieth anniversary special "The Dark Dimension", but returned to helm several episodes of the revived series from 2005, including the four Cybermen episodes in David Tennant's first season (2006).

Peter Davison collapses on the floor of the TARDIS, asks "Is this death?" and his features reform – after the inevitable nostalgia sequence featuring his past companions – into the sixth Doctor, Colin Baker.

# 11
# Doctor Wholigan?

Colin Baker is a fine actor and could have been one of the great Doctors, but he was let down by poor scripts and various eccentric decisions by the production team. The other Doctors were all fully committed to the programme and cared deeply about it: Colin Baker shared that commitment, but he went further and was, in effect, a fan. He had watched the first episode when he had been studying the law, before he became an actor; he was always generous with his time in giving interviews to fans and wrote some of the comic strips for his Doctor. Baker was delighted when offered the part. He had been reluctant to play Commander Maxil in "Arc of Infinity" because he thought taking a part in the show meant he would never get a chance to play the Doctor; when Nathan-Turner asked him if he'd like to be the new Doctor, his jaw dropped and he simply said, "Yes please!"

Colin Baker drew on William Hartnell's portrayal of the Doctor in preparing his characterisation. Hartnell, he said, was "the guv'nor", and he wanted to return to his irascibility and alien quality. The sixth Doctor would be inconsolably grieved over the death of a butterfly, Colin said, but might react with indifference to the departure of a companion: "All right. Go then." He wanted to beat Tom Baker's record of seven years in the part and determined to play the Doctor, initially, as somewhat unlikeable: then, as time went on, he would peel back the layers of the character like the layers of an onion, and we would see the real man inside. This perhaps wasn't a good idea as the unlikeable Doctor that Colin portrayed in his first season repelled many viewers: at the end of "The Twin Dilemma" (1984), he turns to Peri, who misses his "sweet" fifth incarnation, and says, "I am the Doctor, whether you like it or not." The trouble was, lots of viewers didn't. Furthermore, by the time we got to the centre of the Doctor's being, he would presumably turn out to be much the same person we had been used to for the past twenty two years.

Events, of course, prevented Colin's plans from being realised.

By this point in the series' history, John Nathan-Turner was attracting almost as much publicity as its stars. He enjoyed being photographed with Davison and Colin Baker, always in his trademark Hawaiian shirts. He attended many conventions in America, where he was as feted as the Doctors themselves, and introduced Colin Baker as the new Doctor to American fans before the British, much to the latter's disgruntlement. British convention organisers in the 1980s were finding it difficult to attract any of the programme's stars to their events; they couldn't match the fees of their American counterparts, and actors understandably thought an event in Los Angeles might be more fun than one in Milton Keynes. There was consequently a certain amount of resentment felt towards American fans and the production team. The inclusion of the American companion Peri was seen as pandering to American fans, which is perhaps unfair (and a bit racist) as almost all the previous companions except Tegan had been unmistakeable British, whether or not they hailed from the planet Earth, and Nicola Bryant gave an excellent performance anyway.

## Clothes and costumes

Pat Godfrey, the costume designer on "The Twin Dilemma" (1984), asked John Nathan-Turner what sort of clothes he would like the new Doctor to wear. Nathan-Turner asked for something "totally tasteless and clashing", like his own Hawaiian shirts. Apparently several designs were sent back as not being outrageous enough, but the eventual hideous look of the Technicolor dreamcoat, striped waistcoat and spotted cravat was settled on. The coat still had the cut of the Edwardian outfits favoured by previous Doctors but the ensemble was manifestly a costume, and criticised by some as drawing attention to the Doctor (although most characters, ridiculously, didn't comment on it) when he should be able to slip in and out of events and places as he pleases. Even Peri says, "You're not serious," when he tries it on. The costume was presumably supposed to be very funny but looked like a parody of previous Doctors' outfits and recalled Verity Lambert's criticism of the later show, that it sent itself up and wasn't taken seriously by its production team. Colin Baker himself wanted to wear black, to emphasise the mystery of the Doctor's character, but was told this wasn't possible as the Master wore black: it was presumably too difficult to adapt the Master's costume accordingly, such was the rigid thinking of the time. Colin said the best thing about his costume was that, as he was inside it, he didn't have to look at it.

Rigidity in costuming was a key feature in Nathan-Turner's tenure: characters tended to wear uniforms that stayed the same from story to story, and any pretence at realism was thrown out of the window. Philip Segal, the executive producer of the Paul McGann TV movie (1996), said one of the worst faults of the original series had been its costume design in its final years. Similarly, one of the designers on J. Michael Staczynski's *Babylon 5* (1994-9), said they wanted their human characters to wear clothes, not costumes[1]. The dullness of the *Doctor Who* costuming in the 1980s was apparently driven by the belief that it was easier for merchandisers if characters always wore the same clothes, as it helped consumers to distinguish between them. Quite why anyone would mistake Colin Baker for Nicola Bryant wasn't explained.

It appears that Colin Baker was encouraged to play up his performance in his first story, "The Twin Dilemma". If other Doctors had suffered from post-regeneration trauma, which had made them somewhat erratic, the Sixth Doctor's regeneration made him positively psychotic. He sneers and snarls at Peri throughout, calls her evil and tries to strangle her. Nathan-Turner elected to change the established pattern of a new Doctor starting a new season

---

[1] *Babylon 5*, while it ran, which was a worthy comfort for the lack of *Doctor Who* and comes highly recommended. Straczynski himself admired and liked *Doctor Who*, which, like *Blake's Seven*, was one inspiration for his five year arc story. Straczynski was amazed when he watched *Blake's Seven* and saw that, unlike *Star Trek*, here was a crew of people who *didn't like each other*: this he carried into the rivalries and feuds between *Babylon 5*'s leading characters. He also tried to get Tom Baker aboard as a guest star.

by appending "The Twin Dilemma" to the end of Davison's final season. This was intended to establish Colin as the new Doctor before the summer break between seasons but proved disastrous as "The Twin Dilemma" is one of the worst stories ever made, although Nathan-Turner apparently thought it was brilliant. While its immediate predecessor came first in the Best Story poll, "The Twin Dilemma" came bottom. The juxtaposition of excellent and execrable highlighted the schizophrenic quality the show was beginning to demonstrate. Watching "The Twin Dilemma" was like watching a different programme; perhaps a particularly bad episode of the children's drama *Captain Zep – Space Detective*. The Doctor goes mad, lands on a planet to cure himself to find it ruled by Mestor, a giant slug, who intends to explode a star to scatter his eggs all over the Universe. The costumes for the human characters – shiny black nylon uniforms – would have been thought cliched in the 1960s; the acting is often appalling, especially from Helen Blatch as Fabian, and the dialogue is excruciating. Blatch gets to utter immortal lines like "May my bones rot" for giving an uncongenial order; the Doctor says ludicrously over-melodramatic lines like "The very core of my being is on fire with guilt and rage!". Denis Chinnery, who had played Gharman beautifully in "Genesis of the Daleks", is that sit-com figure, the father who is out of his depth, trying to cope with boy genius twins called, you've guessed it, Romulus and Remus. The poor lads – identical twins – who were cast as these characters have identical speech impediments and say "w" for "r", but no-one thought to change the characters' names. Distinguished actor Maurice Denham plays retired Time Lord Azmael, an old friend of the Doctor, but excellent actor though he was, even Denham couldn't save the story from being anything other than risible rubbish. The season ended with fans in dismay.

It would be nice to say there was an improvement in Colin Baker's first full season. There were some good stories amidst the dross, but the first story – "Attack of the Cybermen" (1985) – appeared to continue the downward trend of "The Twin Dilemma". Season twenty two was moved back to Saturday evenings, where *Doctor*

*Who* stayed as long as Colin Baker played the lead. For the first time in its history, the series was made as forty five minutes episodes: the standard episode length for the post-2005 revival. The previous season's "Resurrection of the Daleks" (1984) had been re-edited as two forty five minute episodes to avoid programming clashes with the winter Olympics. This was thought to have worked well and a necessity became a virtue as all of Colin Baker's first season was scripted and shot as forty-five minute episodes. Were longer *Doctor Who* episodes staking a claim for the programme to be taken more seriously by the viewing public? Certainly, both the traditional timeslot and the innovative episode length were intended to boost the ratings, but the timeslot – around 5.20 p.m. – didn't help. It was, as *The Guardian* pointed out, too early for families to catch after the Saturday afternoon trip to a local football match; it was also before the six o'clock watershed, which neutered its attempt to move into *Blake's Seven*'s viewing demographic (*Blake's Seven* had always been transmitted after 7.00 p.m.). Furthermore, the timeslot was far too early for the amount of horror and violence contained in the season, both heavily criticised by the fans. In spite of all the effort, season twenty two failed to garner more viewers. It averaged about seven million, the same as Peter Davison's last two seasons; much better than Tom Baker's final season but respectable rather than spectacular. The ratings nevertheless put the lie to Michael Grade's claim that the show was unpopular when his cancellation announcement was made during the broadcast of "The Two Doctors" (1985).

Season twenty two's first story, "Attack of the Cybermen" was another dreadful script which, like "Resurrection of the Daleks", appeared to make things up as it went along. It lurched from set-piece to set-piece, subjecting cardboard characters to all manner of indignities. It has been pointed out that the Cybermen lose their menace as emotionless, dehumanised versions of ourselves if the human characters are equally dehumanised because of bad writing. "Attack of the Cybermen" was written by one Paula Moore, actually a pseudonym for a friend of Eric Saward and Saward himself, working from ideas fed to the production team by unofficial series consultant, Ian Levine. Levine was the fan record producer who had saved many of the black and white episodes from being wiped. He suggested a sequel to "The Tenth Planet" (1966) and "The Tomb of the Cybermen" (1967); all very well, but these serials were long forgotten by the general public and even by the fans. "The Tomb of the Cybermen" was still one of the stories that was lost (it was returned to the BBC from Hong Kong in 1992) and neither was available on the BBC's fledgling home video collection of *Doctor Who*, so there was no possibility of re-watching them to try and make sense of the new story.

"Attack of the Cybermen" is apparently aimed at pleasing the fans with numerous continuity references. Fans, who wanted good, new, original ideas, weren't impressed at yet another raid on the programme's back catalogue. The Doctor lands in I.M.Foreman's junkyard, last seen in the first story "An Unearthly Child" (1963). This might have been exciting if it was tied in with the plot, but it isn't, and so comes across as a gimmick. The production team also spells Foreman's name wrongly, which only served to irritate the handful of viewers who actually got the reference. There are Cybermen lurking in the sewers (as in "The Invasion", 1968) and Lytton is back from "Resurrection of the Daleks" (1985), as scowly as ever. The Doctor distrusts him as he seems to be working for the Cybermen, this time with a bunch of London villains led by distinguished actor Brian Glover, who apparently enjoyed the part enormously. Lytton, however, is inexplicably revealed to be a goodie who was working to undermine the Cybermen all along, and the Doctor regrets misjudging him. So far, so baffling. The Cybermen want to crash Halley's comet (then about to appear in our skies again) into Earth, and so prevent the events of "The Tenth Planet", a story a mere nineteen years old, which we are expected to remember; all this is offered to the viewer with minimal explanation so we can't follow the plot (such as it is). The action then switches to the Cybermen's tombs on Telos (taken from "The Tomb of the Cybermen" again) now redesigned to look the frozen food aisles in a supermarket. The Cybercontroller – from "Tomb" – returns, again played by Michael Kilgarriff in a fan-pleasing piece of casting; not a good idea as Kilgarriff has put on weight and had a cyberbeerbelly. There are various scenes where the Cybermen convert some shouty humans into Cybermen (see most previous Cybermen stories) and then the Doctor defeats them, shooting the Cybercontroller with his own cyber-weapon. One of the story's few effective points is the Cryons, the other inhabitants of Telos, female humanoids who recall the Sensorites in design (see "The Sensorites", 1964) with beautifully choreographed hand movements which I nicked for the witches in a student production of "Macbeth" in 1985. Although production values are high and the story looks great, the script is drivel and should never have been made.

There were, however, three good stories in the season, or two good and one reasonable. The issue of "video nasties" was causing public concern at the time and became the new bête noir of Mrs Whitehouse, now that she had turned her attention away from *Doctor Who*. These were an apparently uncontrolled feature of the wide availability of home video recorders and commercially available video tapes: extremely pornographic and/or violent videos with titles like *Driller Killer* were copied illegally and circulated by video rental shops without certificates. Such was the concern of Mrs Thatcher's second government that a law was passed requiring videos to be classified in the same way as films. The press agonised over what sort of people would want to watch these sorts of horrors and the issue was addressed in playwright Philip Martin's story "Vengeance on Varos", the second of season twenty two. This was an intelligent satire on the media and capitalism that recalls similarly politically engaged stories like "The Green Death" (1973) and "The Sun Makers" (1977). The economy of the planet Varos is drained by its obligations to the reptilian Mentors and their ambassador, Sil (Nabil Shaban). Its main exports are Ztyon 7, a mineral needed to power space and time craft (the TARDIS runs out of Zyton 7, which necessitates the Doctor's visit), and extremely violent videos made to keep a bloodthirsty population dormant and content while living in poverty. These are manufactured in the Punishment Dome by the sadistic Quillam and include burning by lasers, hanging, immersion in acid baths and being eaten alive by cannibalistic, atavistic savages dressed in nappies. The Doctor and Peri are caught up in the Dome and subjected to all manner of horrors as they try to escape. Watching at home are Arak and Etta, a middle aged, apparently working class couple whose function, Philip Martin explained, is the same as a Chorus in a Greek tragedy: they comment on the action beamed from the punishment dome and punch in their appreciation ratings in their interactive control unit. Interactive television was then only in its infancy and largely confined to phone-in chat shows like the Saturday morning BBC children's show *Multi-Coloured Swap Shop* and its successor, *Saturday Superstore*, on which Tom Baker, Peter Davison and Colin Baker had appeared at various times to be quizzed on *Doctor Who* by children at home. Punching in your appreciation of a programme while watching it, or even voting in elections, was the stuff of *Tomorrow's World* in 1985, but Philip Martin's prescient anticipation of such technology is brilliantly handled and worthy of Nigel Kneale. In one sequence, Varos's Governor (Martin Jarvis) subjects himself to the will of the people, whose punch-in electronic votes of approval or disapproval will result in his re-election or live torture on television under green disintegrator beams. If the ratings are bad enough, the beams will eliminate him and ensure the election of his successor. Viewers mused on the excellence of this idea and wondered if it could be applied to some of our own politicians. "Vengeance on Varos" is a satire on human thoughtlessness and cruelty. The Doctor saves the day by telling the Governor the true market price of Zyton 7: this piece of market economics means that Varosians can stop making video nasties and being exploited by Sil, who is so enraged that his translator unit self-destructs.

Martin Jarvis gives a wonderful, silky performance at the Governor, who tries to protect Peri from torture but whose conscience has been worn away by his exposure to such a corrosive political system. Jarvis, who had played a Menoptra in "The Web

Planet" (1965) and Butler in "Invasion of the Dinosaurs" (1973), was pleased to return to *Doctor Who* not least because of his friendship with Colin Baker, who had played Laertes to Jarvis's Hamlet in the theatre. Nabil Shaban is also excellent as Sil. Shaban, an actor with osteogenesis imperfecta (also known as brittle bones disease), had submitted a story idea to the production office with himself cast as the Doctor. He explained in an interview that the idea was the Time Lords, who were really out to get the Doctor this time, forced him into a disabled body for his next regeneration. Nathan-Turner wrote to Shaban explaining that he couldn't play the Doctor but auditioned him for the role of Sil, a role which he clearly relished. Shaban developed a revolting, rattling laugh for Sil by lapping his tongue vigorously against his lips while gurgling. He tried this out in the read-through; there was a stunned silence, then vigorous applause from the other actors. The laugh, Shaban explained, was Sil's catchphrase equivalent of the Daleks' "Exterminate", and would, he hope, "get the kids back behind the sofa where they belong."

The trouble with "Vengeance on Varos" is, that in attempting to show that torture and horror are vile, it shows vile torture and horror and was much criticised at the time. Quillam is a monstrous bully with greasy black hair, a leather costume and a horribly scalded face; the cannibals are frankly very disturbing, nappies notwithstanding, and a sequence where the Doctor and Jondar (Jason Connery, Sean's son) are hanged – we see them fall through the trap door – is real violence of the type not shown in the programme before. That the Doctor and Jondar are immediately shown to be unharmed is presumably an excuse for the sequence's inclusion, but mock hangings are hardly the stuff of family viewing. Peri is transmogriphied into a bird for Sil's slavering pleasure in a sequence that could only be described as kinky. Worst of all for some viewers is that the Doctor is no longer the reassuring figure of moral outrage we could hide behind: Pertwee's Doctor might have mocked the terrors and Tom Baker's Doctor might have raged at their perpetrators, but the unsympathetic harshness of Colin Baker's

Doctor means that the story lacks a reassuring moral centre. Two guards sent to dispose of him in the Punishment Dome are dispatched to their deaths in baths of acid: instead of showing horror or sympathy, the Doctor quips "You'll forgive me if I don't join you," in a psychopathic aside worthy of James Bond. This lack of care and general unkindness on the part of the Sixth Doctor led some to label him Doctor Wholigan. The production team radically toned down his nastiness for the twenty third season, when it eventually appeared, and Colin Baker's Doctor is a much more conventionally likeable figure in his second year.

The uneven tone and quality of the first two stories combined with other extraordinary moments to suggest a production team that had taken its eye off the ball and a series that had lost its way. There was unnecessary and nasty violence in "Attack of the Cybermen" when two Cybermen crush each of Lytton's hands until they bleed copiously. A character is murdered with cyanide powder in "The Two Doctors". Some of the story ideas were just plain odd. Nathan-Turner let it be known that he was going to change the TARDIS's exterior form as no-one knew what a police box was any more. This was a publicity stunt which resulted in mothers writing in asking him to change his mind as their children were in tears. Nathan-Turner had no intention of making such a change permanent, but the chameleon circuit works for a bit in the first story and we have lots of fun, apparently, when the TARDIS appears as a pipe organ (with no door: how does the Doctor get in and out?) and a pair of silver doors in the Cybermen's control centre. It becomes a police box again at the end of the story but only when the gimmick has been milked to maximum viewer irritation. In "Mark of the Rani", a character is transformed into a tree (a ludicrous costume straight out of a pantomime) by the Rani's land mine. Peri is about to step on one but the tree, apparently still sentient, reaches out a protective branch and grabs her. The Borad in "Timelash" was once mistaken for the Loch Ness Monster, which doesn't seem very likely as he's only about six feet tall and *Doctor Who* had already explained that the Loch Ness Monster was the Zygons' Skarasen cyborg ("Terror of the Zygons" (1975)). Some of the ideas are simply poor or cheesy: the tiresome Herbert, whom the Doctor encounters in "Timelash", is H.G.Wells, who gets his story ideas from his trip in the TARDIS (a very unoriginal conceit). The inhabitants of Karfel in the same story have a painting of the Doctor so they know who he is. However, the painting is an American fan's portrait of Jon Pertwee included by Nathan-Turner as a favour; no-one comments on the fact that the Doctor doesn't look like this any more but they are still able to recognise him from the portrait of an apparently entirely different person. "Timelash" also graces the TARDIS with seatbelts attached to the console, which the Doctor and Peri stand upright in, lean back against, and run around as they hit turbulence. Robert Louis Stephenson's workshop in "The Mark of the Rani" has the completed Rocket in the background, just in case we don't know who he is. We have two refugee actors from *Blake's Seven* in the twenty second season. Jacqueline Pearce, who played chief villain Servalan in that series, is very effective as Chessene, the villain in "The Two Doctors". Paul Darrow, who had played Avon, is dreadful as Tekker, the villain in "Timelash"; he admitted he played it as Richard III, complete with limp, and hammed it up ludicrously because he was allowed to. Asked what he thought of the story, Darrow said it was "rubbish". "Timelash" is as bad a story as "The Twin Dilemma" and it makes "Attack of the Cybermen" look like a masterpiece.

And yet, among the dross, and in spite of all their problems, there are good stories in "Vengeance on Varos", "The Two Doctors" and "Revelation of the Daleks". These, however, are not the sure footed, well-written fare of seasons past but succumb to the general silliness or uncertainty of tone of the rest of the season.

Patrick Troughton enjoyed his time in "The Five Doctors" so much that he asked to return again as the Doctor. Nathan-Turner obliged two years later with "The Two Doctors" and turned to Robert Holmes to write it. It is effectively a six parter – three parts in the new format – and Holmes was brought back on board because of his experience in writing six part stories. He was asked to include the Sontarans, which Holmes didn't really want to do as he thought bringing back old monsters was boring (his sentiments in his years as script editor), but went along with it because he hadn't liked the way his creations had been handled in "The Invasion of Time" (1977). Nathan-Turner also hoped to shoot on location in New Orleans, again to please American viewers, and Holmes had to work both New Orleans and the Sontarans into a story. He reasoned that New Orleans was known for its jazz, which might not work well with the Sontarans, but also for its food, which led to the creation of the new aliens, the Androgums, an anagram of "gourmand". Holmes enjoyed anagrams; the name for the Drashigs from his "Carnival of Monsters" (1973) is an anagram of "dishrag". Unfortunately, the American deal fell through and Nathan-Turner elected to shift the action to Seville in Spain instead. Holmes said he had no idea what the connection between gourmands and Spain was, but the script was shot there anyway.

Patrick Troughton is clearly enjoying playing the second Doctor again, this time accompanied by Jamie, who had been scripted into "The Three Doctors" (1973) but replaced by Sergeant Benton when ITV refused to release Frazer Hines from *Emmerdale Farm* (later just *Emmerdale*). The pre-"Five Doctors" TARDIS console reappears for the Troughton TARDIS and the first moments of the story are transmitted in black and white as a reminder of Troughton's original sixties episodes. There is a wonderful turn by John Stratton as Shockeye, the Androgum's chief butcher and cook, who will eat anything, including rat and intends to butcher and serve Peri for lunch ("What a fine, fleshy beast!"). John Stratton was best known at the time for playing Mr Bott, or "Botty", in ITV's children's serial *Just William* (1976-7), based on the books by Richmal Crompton. Mr Bott's daughter was the lisping and spoilt Violet Elizabeth, played by Bonnie Langford who was, it must be said, absolutely superb.

"The Two Doctors" suffers from being the second multi-Doctor story in two years. As with the Master, if the idea is over-used it suffers from the law of diminishing returns. It also succumbs to the flabby padding of many six parters (three parters in the new format) as the final episode is essentially a chase around Seville.

There are some good moments in "The Mark of the Rani". John Nathan-Turner wanted to include a renegade female Time Lord, like the Master, as an adversary and antithesis of the Doctor. The producer wasn't sure what she should be called, although he stipulated that it couldn't be "The Mistress". The title Rani was eventually chosen. The word is Hindi and means a Queen or a Rajah's wife. The word was never explained on screen for those few viewers who didn't know it, but Kate O'Mara's imperious performance fits the title well. This was Pip and Jane Baker's first script for the series and was far better than their later contributions. The Rani, unlike the Master, is an amoral psychopath rather than an evil genius. A brilliant Gallifreyan chemist, she has as much interest in human beings as in laboratory animals and doesn't care whether they live or die as a result of her experiments. This indifference and lack of empathy, recalling the Nazi doctors who experimented on prisoners in concentration camps, is hideously plausible. It was, therefore, something of a mistake to pair her with the Master in the story, who is completely upstaged by Kate O'Mara and comes across as a bumbling and incompetent egotist, as she herself tells him. We also get to see the Rani's TARDIS, a jolly design with a gyroscope instead of a time rotor; the story ends with the Rani and the Master in its console room, powerless to move as her ship hurtles out of control and an embryo tyrannosaurus rex, collected by the Rani on one of her last visits to Earth, starts to grow to adult size... Kate O'Mara's Rani so impressed some American television executives that they offered her a starring role in the glitzy series *Dynasty*, the rival soap to *Dallas*.

The series' final story is Eric Saward's "Revelation of the Daleks". This takes Evelyn Waugh's novel *The Loved One* as its source, a satire on the American "death care" industry which features a lonely undertaker, Mr Joby, as its down-at-heel hero. In "Revelation of the Daleks", Mr Joby becomes Mr Jobel (Clive Swift), the toupeed head of the funeral facility Tranquil Repose.

Here, the rich can deposit their dead loved ones in suspended animation, ready to be awakened when a cure is found for the disease that killed them. Tranquil Repose is in fact run by Davros, who is using the corpses to make a new race of Daleks (the "Revelation" of the title) or turning them into foodstuffs to be shipped to other planets, in another reference to cannibalism of questionable taste. Broadcasting to the dead is the DJ, played by comedian Alexei Sayle, who had once submitted an article to *Marxism Today* entitled "Why I should be the next Doctor Who: the case for a Marxist in the TARDIS". The DJ rejigs his equipment into a weapon and manages to destroy two Daleks with a pure beam of concentrated rock and roll before he is exterminated. Again, the story is well made and, under Graeme Harper's direction, looks great but, in common with many of Eric Saward's scripts, is oddly structured. The Doctor and Peri spend most of episode one trying to get to Tranquil Repose and don't actually engage with the other characters until episode two. In another bit of fan pleasing reference, we have a transparent Dalek, imagined by David Whitaker in his novelisation of the first Dalek story but never realised on screen, and a flying Dalek. The latter was a commercially available model made by Sevans Models. As it is seen for only a few seconds, the flying Dalek didn't have sufficient impact to stamp out, once and for all, the hilarious jokes about Daleks being unable to conquer the Universe because they can't climb stairs.

With the Dalek story, the uneven, good looking, extraordinary season came to a close. But not before a new threat stirred. On the higher floors of Television Centre, a mind immeasurably different from our own, an intellect cold and cool and unsympathetic, regarded the programme with hostile eyes; and slowly, and surely, drew its plans against it.

# 12
# Cancellation, reprieve, cancellation

And so it came to pass that Michael Grade, the Controller of BBC 1, looked upon Colin Baker's first season as the Doctor and liked it not. Grade had come over to the BBC from ITV, Britain's commercial television company, and immediately applied the principles of commercial television to a public service network funded by the licence fee. Grade ruffled feathers at the corporation by a perceived "dumbing down" of the BBC's output: colourful game shows, of the type produced by ITV, were in, and series which didn't garner enough viewing figures were out. Critics wondered why, if competition was so important a motivational and commercial force in Mrs Thatcher's Britain, Michael Grade thought he could compete with ITV by making the BBC's output essentially the same, but Grade ploughed on regardless. He axed the BBC's adaptation of John Christopher's science fiction novels, *The Tripods* (1984-5), after only two of its proposed three series (one for each of the novels), thus leaving the story unfinished. This was the sort of commercial decision only too familiar for commercial television, but it was new at the BBC, and it dismayed some of the corporation's old hands. Such was the comparative innocence of the times in the 1980s.

Grade actively disliked *Doctor Who* and, in a later interview, remembered how appalled he had been at watching scenes of "shop window dummies calmly mowing down shoppers" (a reference to "Spearhead from Space"(1970)). Although the twenty second season of the programme had many problems, it did produce some strong stories. The viewing figures, perhaps helped by the move to Saturday nights and forty five minute episodes, held up well, with an average of seven million per episode, proving that any gloss on the decision to cancel *Doctor Who* on the grounds of declining viewing figures was so much hogwash. But this was not enough to save the show from Grade's pitiless attention. Could it be that

*Doctor Who* was axed, not because it was in decline, but because Mr Grade hated it?

The production team was told half way through season twenty two's run that there was to be no twenty third season.

The immediate effect on *Doctor Who* was to depress the cast and crew thoroughly. Scripts had already been commissioned and partly written for the twenty third season: they were axed (although the audio company Big Finish did eventually release them, in adapted form, as CD plays). The final scene of "Revelation of the Daleks" (1985) has the Doctor wonder where to take Peri next: he triumphantly utters the line, "I know! I'll take you to Blackpool!" This was to have been a lead in to the first story of the new season, "The Nightmare Fair" by Graham Williams, in which Michael Gough would have reprised his role as the first Doctor's enemy The Celestial Toymaker, now operating from Blackpool's pleasure domes. Knowing that this would never be made or broadcast, the production team cut the last word of Baker's line. His speech now ran, "I know! I'll take you to –": the picture froze before the last word. Freeze frames had been used before to excellent dramatic effect in the programme (for example, Sarah falling off a gantry at the end of episode three of "Genesis of the Daleks" (1976)), but it was somewhat bathetic – and baffling – to use one to cover the Doctor's announcement of his next destination.

Richard Marson uncovered much more of the story in researching his biography of John Nathan-Turner. Jonathan Powell, the Head of Drama, was determined to work well with his new boss and said Grade could axe any shows which were already planned for production. Unsurprisingly, Grade plumped for *Doctor Who*, which, Powell said, was an embarrassment, needed three times the money and was a laughing stock. Far from wanting it to succeed, the BBC wanted it to die[1]. Various excuses were made at the time – the budget was needed to launch *EastEnders*, the budget was needed to

---

[1] Pp.223-4 Richard Marson, *The Life and Scandalous Times of John Nathan-Turner*, Tadworth, 2013

launch breakfast television. Neither was true. The programme was cancelled.

## Counter-plot

Ian Levine, a record producer and fan of the series, was working with producer John Nathan-Turner as a script consultant when the cancellation was announced. He recalls that Nathan-Turner briefed him to give the inside story of the cancellation to *The Sun* newspaper. With a circulation of four million copies a day and perhaps twice as many readers, this was Britain's best-selling tabloid. Levine was told to use the alias Snowball, which signalled to *The Sun* that his call was genuine and from the BBC; Nathan-Turner, standing in the same room, fed Levine the line about the cancellation he wanted to be made public. *The Sun* which, for all its faults, had been often supportive of *Doctor Who,* splashed the story across its front page with "*Dr Who* Is Axed In A BBC Plot". Much was made of the corporation's alleged motivation to cut costs in a recession, as a preparation for its new breakfast television service.

Other newspapers quickly picked up the story: *The Guardian*'s leading article pronounced that, while the programme had endlessly recycled plots and was *not* a national institution, it did not make sense to axe a popular show purely on grounds of cost. The BBC became worried about the bad publicity. Fans declared they would clamber into their Daleks and glide to the House of Commons with a flanking guard of Cybermen, in protest at the cancellation. Powell knew that the newspapers would love this and the accompanying photos would make the BBC look ridiculous. The execs reversed their decision. The show hadn't been cancelled at all but was being rested and would return bigger and better than ever, a word which here means, atrophied. What was actually intended was that *Doctor Who* would be run down, starved of resources and reduced to an anachronistic and ludicrous twenty five minute episode length. The season's total screen time was halved. Film, which had greatly enhanced its look for location scenes, was replaced by video. The new American series *Star Trek: The Next Generation* arrived in the UK, with a budget of a million dollars per episode and shot on film. Videoed *Doctor Who* looked ridiculous in comparison and allowed Michael Grade and co to drawl that the Americans had budgets and production values which the BBC couldn't possibly hope to match, not least because he had no intention of giving *Who* either. The comparison became a self-fulfilling, budget starved conclusion and the execs kicked *Doctor Who* until it was dead. The bill for ending the series, paying off writers and production staff, was over £200,000 in today's terms[1], but the BBC considered this money well spent. Much better to use licence fee money not to make the programme than to make it. Such is the wisdom of senior management everywhere.

Colin Baker's contract was not renewed and the BBC put the show up against the ratings juggernaut *Coronation Street* – which regularly harvested over fifteen million viewers a week. Ratings slumped to a disastrous four million. Even Sylvester McCoy said the BBC didn't care about *Doctor Who*. That was an understatement. Interviewed by Richard Marson, Jonathan Powell said he wanted John Nathan-Turner to go away and take his blessed show with him. (Actually, Powell used some other words)[2].

It was made clear to Nathan-Turner that he would not be allowed to produce another show and that, if he wanted to move on as he repeatedly requested, it would be out of the BBC front door and *Doctor Who* would be brought to an end. Nathan-Turner struggled on for another four seasons, eventually serving ten years as producer, far too long for anybody: Barry Letts, the show's longest serving producer to that point, had served five years. Nathan-Turner became increasingly demoralised, although he was bucked by the encouragement of Sylvester McCoy in the original series' final seasons. Eric Saward left as script editor and was replaced by the inexperienced Andrew Cartmel, who hired his twenty-something friends from the BBC scriptwriters' course to provide scripts.

[1] Ibid P.234
[2] Ibid P.235

*Doctor Who* had now almost become an internal training video for newbies, only it was broadcast. Many thought that the infusion of young blood led to a renewal of creativity in the McCoy seasons, and it is true that some of the visuals, special effects and designs were excellent, however ropey the scripts.

The *Daily Mirror* sent journalists to pursue Michael Grade and caught up with him on a skiing holiday. Grade opined that everyone was making a lot of fuss and that the fans were hysterical; he announced that the programme had not been cancelled (which was news to the production team), but was merely being rested. The idea was mooted that a long break would give an exhausted production team time to rethink their approach to the show. *Doctor Who* fans smelt a whole sewer full of giant rats and were not convinced.

## A Time Lord on Trial

The series went into an eighteen month hiatus. Colin Baker, who cared deeply about the programme, was bitterly disappointed. There was a brief respite from the gloom when BBC Radio Four commissioned six ten minute episodes from Eric Saward (an experienced radio writer) to be part of their new magazine show for children, *Pirate Radio Four*. The story, "Slipback", was inflected towards comedy and showed the influence of *The Hitch Hiker's Guide to the Galaxy* on *Doctor* Who yet again in, for example, its ditsy computer with a split personality. Valentine Dyall gave a strong performance as the melancholy spaceship captain and the story ambitiously focused (yet again for the series) on the creation of the universe and its possible prevention. Derivative though it was, "Slipback" was also light hearted and rather good. One of the technical staff who worked on it pointed out that it didn't fully exploit the creative possibilities of radio where, unlike television, there were no budgetary and technical limitations to limit what could be featured. He suggested that the monster should have fourteen penises, but this idea was surprisingly not picked up by the production staff[1].

There were stories that Michael Grade, who had tried to kill off *Doctor Who*, was cross that Radio Four had resurrected the show. Nearly twenty years later, fans' collective stomachs lurched when they learned that Grade was to be the new chairman of the BBC, just after BBC 1 had announced it was re-launching the series with Christopher Eccleston. Was the prize of a new series to be snatched away, after they had waited so faithfully and so long? To calm such fears, Grade let it be known that he had no intention of interfering in the revival; after the first series had screened, he even congratulated everyone concerned and said how much he and his young son had enjoyed it. This was rather like watching the Master deciding that he fancied running a foodbank.

After a holiday, the production team had to decide what to do about the twenty third season. Rumours hit the *Doctor Who* Appreciation Society that the number of episodes was going to be cut. The BBC denied it and pointed out that the new season would have fourteen episodes, one more than the previous season's thirteen. What they neglected to mention was that the new season's episodes were returning to the twenty five minute length that had been standard for the programme: fourteen episodes of twenty five minutes each was significantly less screen time than thirteen forty five minute episodes, and fans sank into a black gloom.

Michael Grade was consulted about what he wanted the new season to be like: the production team were anxious to find out and, if possible, propitiate him if the programme were to avoid his attention in the future. Colin Baker recalled that Grade had opined, "Yes, more humour, less violence." This was exactly the same brief given to Graham Williams after the supposed excesses of season sixteen had drawn down the wrath of Mary Whitehouse. Reluctantly, Saward and Nathan-Turner went back to the drawing board. The scripts which had been already commissioned for the season were axed and a new umbrella theme, emerged. As with season sixteen's Key to Time season, the twenty third season would

---

[1] Conversation with the author.

comprise several – in fact, four, because of the reduced episode count – stories united by a common theme. The Doctor was to be put on trial by his own people for interference in the affairs of other races. This sounded promising to some fans, who recalled it was exactly the same premise as the final two acclaimed episodes of "The War Games" (1969), Patrick Troughton's last story. So obvious was the repetition (perhaps *The Guardian* had a point about the series recycling its plots) that Lynda Bellingham's Time Lord Inquisitor notes in the first episode: "The Doctor [had] been tried for these offences before."

Saward and Nathan-Turner used the trial theme as a cheeky metaphor for the way the show itself was on trial. The season's structure was borrowed from Charles Dickens's *A Christmas Carol*: in the same way that that tale had three ghosts of past, present and yet to come, so the fourteen episode story "The Trial of a Time Lord" would feature three stories taking place in the Doctor's past, present and future.

"The Trial of a Time Lord" is, sadly, generally perceived as a failure and even worse than the season which had preceded it. Powell had commented harshly on all the scripts for "The Trial of a Time Lord": didn't like this, didn't like that, thought that was too silly. Experienced writers like Robert Holmes were unused to such treatment; fans were later aghast when Powell commented that Holmes's name linked to a *Doctor Who* was far from a guarantee of good quality. Sadly, Powell's judgement on this new season wasn't far wrong. Having been shoved around so much, a demoralised producer and script editor couldn't summon up much enthusiasm to revitalise the series. They had no idea if there would be a twenty fourth season and thought that this run of fourteen episodes could well have been the end. The original ending was for the Doctor and the Valeyard, his villainous future incarnation, to fall into the Matrix, locked in mortal combat – who would survive? Would *Who* survive?

Saward had been script editor for four seasons of production. When he mentioned this to Robert Holmes, who was returning to write for the new season, Holmes told him, "You're mad. I did three years and that was enough." The strain of endlessly commissioning, polishing and occasionally rewriting whole scripts had worn Saward down.

"The Trial of a Time Lord" started unambitiously and pleasantly enough with a four part story by Robert Holmes. Some eyebrows were raised by the first shot – the TARDIS is dragged aboard a Time Lord spaceship by a tractor beam – as it was news to the fans that the Time Lords had spaceships at all. The effects shot itself was superb for the time, but used up much of the season's effects budget: something made obvious by the number of times the shot was repeated in the season[1]. There was yet another new arrangement of the theme tune, apparently written and recorded in five days: it was as twinkly as the programme's messy title sequence.

Holmes' story (called either "The Mysterious Planet" for convenience or "The Trial of a Time Lord" episodes one to four) concerns a planet called Ravalox which appears to be Earth in the far future, moved to a different location in space and peopled by an iron age tribe led by *Carry On* star Joan Sims. There were some effective scenes set in a ruined Marble Arch tube station and an amusing Holmes double act called Glitz and Dibber, a pair of con-men who recalled "The Ribos Operation"'s Garron and Unstoffe (1978). The sixth Doctor's relationship with Peri has softened from the previous season and they treat each other like old friends; Colin Baker quite reasonably said that it was entirely believable for two people who had travelled together for so long and, had they continued their abrasive previous relationship, Peri would have left long ago.

Some of the first story's action takes place on Ravalox, the rest on the space station where the adventure is screened as evidence of the Doctor's trial. The Prosecutor is called the Valeyard and was played with relish by Michael Jayston; he knows the Doctor well but the Doctor has no memory of him or of how he came to be in court.

---

[1] The shot was later included in a video publicity package for the *Doctor Who* TV Movie in 1996.

This was all well and poor but the ratings were disastrous: "Attack of the Cybermen", which had opened season twenty two in 1984, garnered over seven million viewers: "The Mysterious Planet" managed just over four million. The decline demonstrated how far the programme had declined in the affections of the public and its transformation from a family show loved by millions to a cult show popularly held in derision, which was just how the BBC execs at the time wanted it. The viewing figures were never to rise above five and a half million until the end of the original series' run in 1989. Some argued that it was inevitable that people wouldn't watch as long as the production values were so poor and the stories so incoherent: yet the production team battled valiantly on.

The second story (sometimes called "Mindwarp") saw the return of the amphibian Mentors and Sil from "Vengeance on Varos"(1985). At this point, the season falls apart. The Doctor is again acting strangely and appears to be evil (a la "The Invasion of Time" (1978)): the Doctor protests to the court that the evidence has been tampered with and that this wasn't how it happened. He appears to betray Peri to the Mentors and sides with a sadistic scientist called Crozier (a wonderfully cool performance from Patrick Ryecart). Colin Baker recalled that he went from writer Philip Martin to script editor Eric Saward asking whether the Doctor was really evil, just pretending to be evil, or whether the evidence had been tampered with. Martin said he had no idea and suggested Baker consult Saward; Saward said he had no idea and suggested Baker consult Martin. The resulting incoherence on screen made for unhappy viewing.

**Privatising the Doctor**

It was at this point in production that the first rumours circulated that the BBC was to relinquish production of *Doctor Who* to an independent television company. The policy of commissioning programmes from independents was the BBC's response to a Conservative government hostile to public service broadcasting and the BBC in particular. Denis Thatcher, the Prime Minister's husband, had once said, "Of course, everybody at the BBC's a Trotskyist"[1]. To head off any attempt to privatise the BBC, it attempted to prove its free market credentials by commissioning programmes from the private sector. The Government was appeased for the time being. Rumours reached the production team that *Doctor Who* was considered ripe for the independent treatment: the team's sense of insecurity deepened overnight. Brian Blessed was playing King Yrcanos in "Mindwarp" and recalled that he had been named as a possible future Doctor in an independently produced show. On set, he reassured a troubled Colin Baker that this was not true. The sword of Damocles, in the form of cancellation or independent production, hung over the show until the end of its run in 1989.

The final straw that triggered Saward's resignation was a dispute about the final story of season twenty three. Set in the Matrix (and retreading – *yet again* after "The Invasion of Time" – the events of "The Deadly Assassin"(1976)), the Doctor was to have battled the Valeyard in a dreamscape. Saward had the two of them fight to the death and fall into the vortex at the end of episode fourteen, a dramatic climax and an inconclusive ending which reflected the uncertain fate of the programme as a whole: would the Doctor, or *Doctor Who*, return? Nathan-Turner rejected the storyline as too negative. Saward, upset at the death of Robert Holmes (who had written episode thirteen), resigned, saying he had had enough, and refused to allow Nathan-Turner to use his script. He then gave a blistering interview with the science fiction magazine *Starburst*, attacking Nathan-Turner as uninterested in the stories of the show and only caring about budget and merchandising. (It is a frequently cited criticism of Nathan-Turner's ten years on the series that the stories are only as good as the current script editor.) The cast, including Colin Baker, comforted and supported an extremely

---

[1] p. 346 John Cole, *As It Seemed to Me*, London, 1995, 1996. The Conservative Cabinet under David Cameron, Conservative Prime Minister from 2010-2016, declared that BBC stood for, "British Bolshevik Corporation".

wounded Nathan-Turner, who now had to find a replacement script for the final episode.

He turned to the writers of the third instalment of "The Trial of a Time Lord", husband and wife Pip and Jane Baker. Arriving at his office, they were somewhat surprised to find a solicitor present. Nathan-Turner explained that a lawyer was required to witness that he did not even breathe a word of plot detail about Saward's cancelled final episode. Pip and Jane Baker had to come up with a replacement on their own.

The final episodes of the season unwound unevenly on screen. Pip and Jane Baker's story, called either "The Terror of the Vervoids" or parts eight to eleven of "The Trial of A Time Lord", was an Agatha Christie-type yarn set aboard the spaceliner Hyperion, in which the passengers and crew are being murdered by intelligent plant creatures, the Vervoids. The story was reasonably engaging but suffered from the gleaming white lighting so beloved of eighties *Who* for spaceship interiors, which reveals only too clearly the limitations of the set and the budget: the Hyperion, for example, looks like an upmarket health club. The Vervoids' design was effective but some viewers drew attention to their penile faces; the crew's guns were called phasers, which presumably infringed a *Star Trek* trade mark. *The Avengers* star Honor Blackman played Professor Lasky, injecting some much needed gravitas into the proceedings, but that was not arguably enough to counter-balance the casting of the new companion. Bonnie Langford made her first appearance as Mel.

Bonnie Langford was best known to British viewers for her wonderful performance as a child actress as Violet Elizabeth Bott in ITV's *Just William* (1976-7). A talented singer and dancer, she was appearing in a revival of *Peter Pan* on stage during the eighteen month hiatus. Nathan-Turner arranged for publicity photos of her and Colin Baker – she in her Peter Pan costume, he in full *Doctor Who* rig: Baker was grinning madly, Langford smiling sweetly, and the pictures were duly printed in the newspapers.

"Terror of the Vervoids" is set in the Doctor's future and he had no memory of its events, including how he comes to be travelling with Mel, whose character brief was "a computer programmer from Pease Pottage". This was almost as feeble as the brief for Peri, which ran, said Saward, to two words: "An American". Mel was a generic companion character and was never given an introduction to the Doctor. Saying goodbye to her at the end of the following season, Sylvester McCoy's Doctor notes, "I haven't even met you yet." Bonnie Langford threw herself into the part and gave an enthusiastic performance, but it was too theatrical for the small screen and confirmed fans' views that Nathan-Turner was interested in generating publicity rather than telling good stories. Nathan-Turner had once remarked that *Doctor Who* was like *The Morecombe and Wise Show*, which some interpreted as meaning he saw it as light entertainment, demonstrated by the later casting of Ken Dodd, Hale and Pace and even Sylvester McCoy: back in 1986, McCoy was best known as the Prof, an eccentric figure who raced around in the BBC's magazine show for deaf and partially-hearing children *Vision On* (was this character's name the inspiration for Ace continually calling the Doctor, "Professor"?). Nathan-Turner later said his remark had been misunderstood. He had meant that everyone wanted to be in *Doctor Who* – something that certainly appeared to be true of the post – 2005 series.

Seeing no alternative, the Doctor eliminates the Vervoids and the Valeyard attempts to keep the lurching plotline going by arraigning the Doctor for genocide. It seems extremely strange that a defendant standing trial for one charge could, in the same trial, be suddenly made to answer another charge but presumably the Time Lords' legal system was as eccentric as the season's plotting: they made it up as they went along. The final two episodes reveal that the Valeyard is an evil future incarnation of the Doctor, somewhere between his twelfth and thirteenth regenerations, though this idea is not explored beyond a throwaway line and anyway, we all know that the twelfth regeneration produced Matt Smith and the thirteenth,

Peter Capaldi.[1] Back in "The Trial of a Time Lord", the Master comes to the Doctor's rescue because he would rather face the Doctor he knows than a rival, evil Doctor. The Doctor saves the day somehow or other and goes off in the TARDIS with Mel, who intends to put him on a strict exercise regime. Colin Baker's final words as the Doctor are the bathetic, "Carrot juice, carrot juice, carrot juice." The Valeyard escapes, grins evilly into the camera, and the season lurched to a halt. Was there to be a twenty fourth season? Back in 1986, I remember asking a BBC production manager if the BBC was keeping *Doctor Who*. "Oh yes, I'm afraid they are," he said, voicing the prevailing BBC sentiment for the show. That was the first I'd heard of it, and I had high hopes.

### Enter Sylvester McCoy

Production wrapped on the twenty third season and Nathan-Turner still didn't know if there was to be a twenty fourth. Colin Baker's contract lapsed. Michael Grade has asked Sidney Newman, *Doctor Who*'s creator, to come up with some ideas for revamping the series; Newman's ideas were basically the same as those he had thought up twenty three years earlier, including a group of companions and a youngster as an audience identification character. They were not acted on.

Eventually, Colin Baker got a phone call from Nathan-Turner. "I've got some good news and some bad news." "Go on," said Baker. "The show is coming back but they want a new Doctor." Grade had taken the simple step of replacing the lead as a panacea for the show's woes. Very unhappy that he was to leave a part he loved, Colin Baker went to see Jonathan Powell. Baker recalled that

---

[1] Those numbered regenerations in full: the first regeneration produced the second Doctor, Patrick Troughton; the second, Jon Pertwee; 3rd, Tom Baker; 4th, Peter Davison; 5th, Colin Baker; 6th, Sylvester McCoy; 7th, Paul McGann; 8th, the War Doctor, John Hurt; 9th, the 9th Doctor, Christopher Eccleston; 10th, David Tennant; 11th, David Tennant again (he had vanity issues, said 11th Doctor Matt Smith in "The Time of the Doctor", 2013); 12th, Matt Smith; 13th, Peter Capaldi; 14th, Jodie Whittaker.

Powell had been charming, said he was quite happy with the actor's performance as the Doctor, but was adamant that it was time for a change. Baker asked if he could do one more season so that he could continue to play a part he loved in a series to which he was committed; then he could leave with some dignity. He was offered one more story. Shooting "Time and the Rani" would have made it difficult for him to find other work; he had to make a living, so, very angry and upset, he opted out of the series. After one complete season, a radio series, eighteen months off, and a curtailed season of fourteen episodes, the era of the sixth Doctor came to an unceremonious end. *The Sun* published an account of the parting under the headline, "Why I'll Never Forgive Gutless Grade, By Sacked Dr Who"[1].

Bonnie Langford was to reprise her role as Mel in the twenty fourth season but a new script editor and Doctor were needed. Scottish actor Sylvester McCoy (born Percy James Kent-Smith in 1943) put himself forward through his agent, auditioned with Janet Fielding as Tegan, and was quickly cast[2]. McCoy was best known for *Vision On* but was an accomplished stage actor, then working in a production of *Antony and Cleopatra* with Timothy Dalton; McCoy recalled that he was cast as the Doctor at about the same time that Dalton, in the same show, learnt he was to be the new James Bond[3]. Fourteen more episodes were commissioned. The ratings had been poor for season twenty three and, after returning to Saturdays for all of Colin Baker's run, the programme was again shifted to a midweek slot. Now up against ITV's *Coronation Street*, then the mightiest ratings winner of all, no doubt to fulfil the execs' plan that the bubble car of *Doctor Who* would be smashed to smithereens by

---

[1] *The Sun*, 6th January, 1987.

[2] Ken Campbell was also under consideration.

[3] History almost repeated itself in 1996. Christopher Eccleston and Daniel Craig starred together in the BBC series *Our Friends in the North*, by Peter Flannery. One went on to become the Doctor, the other, Bond. David Bradley also starred... I'll shut up now.

the juggernaut of *Street*[1].

A replacement for Eric Saward was found in Andrew Cartmel, a young television writer relatively new to the industry who had a background in computer journalism. He amused Nathan-Turner at his interview with his statement that he would like to use *Doctor Who* to bring the government down; Nathan-Turner quietly suggested that the most they could hope for was to make stories which showed good defeating evil. Critics later noted the similarity in looks and vocal range of the dictator Helen A, played by Sheila Hancock in "The Happiness Patrol" (1988), and Mrs Thatcher, but the story's satire of a society in which happiness is compulsory hardly qualified it as leftist criticism of a Conservative government, not least because everybody was very happy indeed under Mrs Thatcher's beneficent rule and no connection could be made between the two rulers.

Cartmel inherited scripts written for Colin Baker's Doctor, which were quickly adapted to McCoy. Pip and Jane Baker had contributed the first story, "Time and the Rani" (1987), execrated by fans and described by Russell T Davies, the 2005 show runner, as "a low point". With Colin Baker unavailable, Cartmel and the Bakers were faced with the problem of how to regenerate the Doctor. Under attack from the Rani, the TARDIS is buffeted about in time and space: while the third Doctor faced his fear and died from radiation poisoning in the cave of the Great One, and the fifth Doctor sacrificed his life to save Peri from spectrox toxaemia, the sixth Doctor apparently regenerates after falling off his exercise bike. It was the silliest regeneration since Romana's in 1979's "Destiny of the Daleks". Sylvester McCoy wore Baker's costume and a blond wig: something very obvious when the regeneration effect begins on a shot of a face that is clearly McCoy's and not Baker's.

---

[1] A deeply satisfying draught for fans is to drink at the wellspring of the ratings for television programmes post-2005, in which *Doctor Who* regularly beats *Coronation* Street, if not to rubble, then convincingly, in the top twenty. Never mess with a Time Lord.

Previous producers and script editors had had traditional career backgrounds in writing and university education: Terrance Dicks once said, "I don't think about it very much any more, but I have a degree in English"; Douglas Adams's scripts were highly literate and informed by his reading English at Cambridge. Andrew Cartmel's background was, at the time, somewhat left field. He drew on comics and graphic novels for inspiration – which were even more sneered at as a genre than science fiction in 1986 – and suggested writers read *Halo Jones* from *2000 AD* to inform the new reading of the Doctor's character. The influence of graphic novels was seen in the shorthand, rapid and hyphenated storytelling of the McCoy episodes, which often jumped from scene to scene without plot threads being fully resolved. Some said that this style was both garbled and incomprehensible, but that is not kind. Graphic novel imagery influenced the new title sequence, which took advantage of advances in computer generated imagery to show a galaxy forming, the TARDIS flying overhead in a bubble (why a bubble?), and McCoy winking at the camera. There was a new logo: the word "Who" tumbled out towards the centre of the screen and the word "Doctor" swished open above it in a handwriting font: merchandisers disliked it as it could only be reproduced against a black background. Oliver Elmes, who created the title sequence, said his inspiration was his thought that *Doctor Who* was like a comic strip; questioned about why the Doctor gave a cheesy wink, Elmes replied that he thought he had always winked in the title sequence. He never had: so much for careful research. There was a new, more serious arrangement of the theme music to replace the twinkling fairy tricks of the previous year's version.

It might be argued that not much of Cartmel's influence could be seen in "Time and the Rani", which had the recognisable Pip and Jane Baker signatures: lots of colour and memorable images, including Bonnie Langford in a bubble trap that careered around a quarry and threatened to explode, and a plot that raced along and tripped over itself. There was the Rani trying to create a giant brain from geniuses of the universe including Einstein (who rather wistfully tries to understand the TARDIS; the Doctor gently tells him, "I'll explain it all later"), some very effective three-eyed bat creatures called Tetraps, and Kate O'Mara giving a wonderful, and very funny, impersonation of Bonnie Langford as she tries to inveigle her way into the confused new Doctor's confidence. Not much made sense but it was colourful hokum.

More troubling was McCoy's uncertain performance as the Doctor. He races around, plays the spoons, gurns, tries on his predecessors' costumes and eventually settles down a little in episode four. Perhaps confused by the mess, only 4.7 million people tuned in; newspaper television critics gave scathing reviews.

Needing new scripts quickly, Cartmel commissioned "Paradise Towers" from a writer called Steven Wyatt, who had sent in some material on spec. The new script editor then turned to his friends from the BBC scriptwriters' course, Malcolm Kohll and Ian Briggs, who each contributed a story. Kim Newman has remarked that many of the McCoy episodes included some interesting ideas (and excellent images and designs), but had no idea how to turn these ideas into a coherent narrative. "Paradise Towers" is a dystopian story set in high rise tower blocks inhabited variously by rival girl gangs, cannibalistic grandmothers, and Richard Briers as the Chief Caretaker. Briers puts on a silly voice, a Hitler moustache and a cabaret costume and proceeds to send the part up. Sylvester McCoy tones down the Doctor considerably and there is a good scene where he persuades his caretaker guards that their instructions are unreasonable and he should be released. "Delta and the Bannermen", the third story, by Malcolm Kohll, features comedian Ken Dodd, who was then linked in the public mind with McCoy as a light entertainer: not perhaps a good idea when McCoy was trying to establish his serious credentials as the Doctor. It is a tale of Chimeron queen Delta who travels back to the 1950s to a Butlins-style holiday camp, pursued by Don Henderson and his bannermen; Stubby Kaye turns up as a CIA agent, the plot bumbles along incomprehensibly, and I switched the television off in disgust for the first time ever during a broadcast of *Doctor Who*.

The final story, "Dragonfire", featured a villain called Kane, a space station called Ice World, and some excellent design: the dragon creature itself resembled the alien from the *Alien* film series and Kane melts at the end as he exposes himself to the sun. The McCoy era saw fans of the show, and members of the *Doctor Who* Appreciation Society, actually work on it: a trend that became the norm with the post-2005 incarnation of the series. Susan Moore, herself a fan model maker, created the effect of Kane's face melting from a sculpt of actor Edward Peel's head. She was briefed that she wasn't to use any red in the effect; cast and crew stayed to watch the head being slowly melted by blowtorches and the speeded-up shot was one of the best effects in the programme to date.

"Dragonfire" also featured an unusually incoherent script: guards have impenetrable conversations as they pursue the Doctor and, in an extraordinary sequence at the end of episode two, Sylvester McCoy climbs over a railing to hang over a cliff by his umbrella for no reason at all. This was apparently an auto-referential joke to a cliff hanger ending (geddit?), and there is a handy ledge for the Doctor to fall onto at the start of part three. Casual viewers expect television drama to make sense and such incoherence in prime time drama is inexcusable. Apologists for Sylvester McCoy's era argue that his stories often have to be watched several times on video (then widely available) for them to yield up their secrets: this is all very well for fans, but it was too much to expect of the general public, who, expecting comprehensible entertainment, couldn't and didn't watch a programme repeatedly. Viewers switched off in droves and the viewing figures hovered around a disastrous four million. I was studying for my PGCE in Oxford at the time and remember some of my undergraduate friends saying, "*Doctor Who* is just so weird now" and refusing to watch it. After viewing part one of "The Curse of Fenric" (1989) at our student house, another snarled, "If that's the best they can do, they might as well cancel it." Quite so, nodded the spirit of Grade. Steven Moffat referenced the cliffhanging scene in "The Name of the Doctor" (2013): a splinter of Clara, the impossible girl, hammers on the glass which overlooks McCoy's

Doctor cliffhanging in a sequence achieved by marrying a clip with new footage. Casing a nut of twaddle in the revived series' chocolatey goodness was an attempt to rehabilitate a notorious scene from the original series, and fans gave wry smiles.

Bonnie Langford left at the end of "Dragonfire", to be replaced by Sophie Aldred's Ace. Ace is a companion much loved by fans of the McCoy era and Aldred herself was dedicated to the show. In scripting typical of the Cartmel era, Ace, whose real name is Dorothy (a reference to *The Wizard of Oz*), arrives at Ice World in a time storm (whatever that is; it is never explained, but is apparently another plot device borrowed from *A Wizard of Oz*). She is a streetwise teenager given to setting off explosives with Nitro-9: how a British comprehensive school student could have access to such things, or to have acquired such knowledge, is never explained in the comic strip shorthand storytelling favoured by Cartmel, but it does mean Ace can produce some pretty bangs and flashes. As a streetwise teenager, Ace should have colourful language, but the timeslot and censorship obviously prevented this, so she is given to calling people "scumbug", "toerag" and so on. She also calls the Doctor "Professor" for no very good reason (unless it is a reference to Sylvester McCoy's role as the Prof in *Vision On*), but reverts to "Doctor" in moments of stress. Does this make psychological or dramatic sense?

Season twenty four came to a close with ratings that were no better than "The Trial of a Time Lord": the shift to a midweek slot had not done the trick. The show was renewed for a new season; Nathan-Turner made one of his periodical attempts to quit but said he was persuaded not to do so by Sylvester McCoy. Anyway, Nathan-Turner knew that, if he left, he would be out of a job and the BBC would cancel the programme.

## The Cartmel Master Plan

Having cut his teeth, Cartmel now started to take firmer control over the series. He attempted to reintroduce mystery to the Doctor's character: perhaps a tall order, given that viewers knew he was a Time Lord from the planet Gallifrey, had two hearts, a respiratory bypass system, could regenerate twelve times, was a member of the Prydonian chapter, had scraped through his degree at the second attempt, and in fact had twenty four years of history behind him. Cartmel proposed rewriting the established continuity of the programme in what would now be called retrospective-continuity, or ret-con, and devised what has come to be called the Cartmel master plan. The Doctor, he decreed, was not just a mere Time Lord, but a survivor of Rassilon's dark time on Gallifrey; he was one of the founders of Time Lord society with Omega and Rassilon, and a stellar engineer on the first TARDISes. The Doctor was to become a much more amoral figure, who would put the lives of his companions in danger if necessary because he would know the ultimate outcome of events. This is an inexcusable reworking of the Doctor's morality, who told Professor Kettlewell in "Robot" (1975) that "The end never justifies the means" and moved him away from a Judaeo-Christian morality to, at best, a utilitarian one.

Nathan-Turner was ambivalent about Cartmel's ideas and, on screen, they amount to little more than irritating hints. In "Remembrance of the Daleks" (1988), the first story of season twenty five, the Doctor tells Ace about the Hand of Omega, "and didn't we have trouble with the prototype." "We?" asks Ace. "They," the Doctor smiles. Some scenes which revealed more of the Doctor's dark history were shot and then edited out of the broadcast version (though they survive as extras on the DVDs). Again in "Remembrance of the Daleks", Davros rants that he will sweep away Gallifrey and its impotent collection of Time Lords: the Doctor, in a cut line, says, "Oh Davros, I am so much more than an ordinary Time Lord"; in the final story, "Survival" (1989) the Master asks the Doctor, "Who are you?" as they battle to the death on the Cheetah people's dying world: the Doctor gives an evasive answer but again the sequence was cut. Ben Aaronovitch includes some intriguing flashbacks to the Old Time on Gallifrey in his novelisation of "Remembrance of the Daleks": here, the Doctor is called "The Other" and works alongside Rassilon and Omega on the eponymous Hand.

Again, the narrative of the series is irritatingly incomprehensible to the viewers, who could make little of Ace's comment "No-one knows who the Doctor is" and "Doctor, who are you?" at the end of "Silver Nemesis" (the Doctor puts his finger to his lips). Perhaps the script writing was influenced by the tendency of the new American series *Star Trek: the Next Generation*, which spent much time exploring its own continuity in the forms of Klingon, Vulcan, Romulan and human culture (this is known by media critics as, going up its own arse), when the original series had told exciting space adventure stories. Although the viewing figures picked up slightly for season twenty five, they collapsed completely for the final season: "Battlefield" (1989) did not even reach four million viewers and only the final story, "Survival", got anything approaching five million after a five minutes to midnight publicity blitz by the BBC, which had finally awoken to the fact it had spent a considerable amount of money on a programme that no-one was watching.

The Cartmel "Time's Champion" version of the Doctor was picked up by Virgin's "New Adventures" series of novels which began after the television series ended. Promoted by their editors as a direct continuation of the television series, the authors enthusiastically took the opportunity to explore the Doctor's origins: but this was for a series of books that sold thousands of copies, rather than for a television series that had to appeal to millions if it was to survive. In book form, the new version of the Doctor flourished; on television, it baffled and confused. When the series was resurrected in 2005, Russell T. Davies and his team quietly ignored the Cartmel masterplan, as they also ignored the Paul McGann TV Movie's revelation that the Doctor was half human, and returned to the original series' notion that the Doctor was a wandering Time Lord.

Things looked up for the season twenty five opener, "Remembrance of the Daleks" (1988), a comprehensively told and well executed story. Set in London in 1963 at Cole Hill School and I.M.Foreman's junkyard[1], both revisited from *Doctor Who*'s first episode "An Unearthly Child", the story featured a conflict between rival gangs of Daleks for the Hand of Omega, a stellar manipulation device brought by the Doctor from Gallifrey before the events of that first story. Ben Aaronovitch's scripts treats it theme of racism with intelligence: the Imperial and renegade Daleks "hate each other's chromosomes" as "impure in their blobbiness", as Ace puts it. Some of the human characters share the racism: Ace leaves her bed and breakfast in disgust when she finds her landlady has put a sign saying "No Coloureds" in the window; the builder Ratcliffe is attracted to the rebel Daleks as he was imprisoned as a Nazi sympathiser in the war. The Emperor Dalek is revealed to be Davros: Ben Aaronovitch noted that this was a late addition and was the idea of Mike Tucker[2] who said, wouldn't it be great if the Emperor Dalek's head swung open to reveal Davros inside?

The show ran into trouble with the design of the Kandyman in "The Happiness Patrol" (1988) which irresistibly recalled Bertie Bassett, then used to promote the sweets liquorice allsorts. Bassett Foods PLC complained to the BBC about copyright infringement but were placated by an assurance that there was no connection between the characters (although viewers instantly made one, to the detriment of the show) and that the Kandyman would not appear in the series again.

### The Twenty Fifth Anniversary Special, "The Seven Doctors" (not really)

The twenty fifth anniversary rolled around in November 1988. Sylvester McCoy said at the time that the BBC didn't care about *Doctor Who* and had no interest in its place in broadcasting history. This was as true as it was depressing. In 1983, the BBC had

---

[1] Was this a good idea? The Doctor had already visited it in "Attack of the Cybermen" three years earlier.

[2] Of the BBC visual effects department. Not the Ambridge milkman.

celebrated *Doctor Who*'s twenty fifth anniversary by commissioning a 90 minute special, "The Five Doctors", shown as near as possible to the anniversary date itself (23rd November, 1983) and featuring all the surviving Doctors. In 1988, the BBC celebrated *Doctor Who*'s twenty fifth anniversary by doing nothing at all, although Noel Edmonds did put a "Happy Birthday *Doctor Who*" card on the set of that week's *Telly Addicts*. An untried writer called Kevin Clarke wrote a Cybermen story called "Nemesis": this was quickly amended to "Silver Nemesis" when it became clear that the story would be broadcast on the silver, twenty fifth, anniversary. Clarke said[1] he had been thinking about anniversary elements and thought that, because it was the silver anniversary, the Cybermen should be in it because they were silver. "Silver Nemesis" was reviled by fans at the time of broadcast as utterly incomprehensible nonsense. Its plot was virtually the same as "Remembrance of the Daleks", two stories previously: viewers were asked to believe again that William Hartnell's Doctor had escaped from Gallifrey with two Armageddon-inducing weapons, the Hand of Omega and, in "Silver Nemesis"'s case, a living statue of a metal called veridium. The statue is pursued by Nazis (compare the fascists in "Remembrance"), Cybermen (taking the place of the Daleks) and a sorceress from the seventeenth century called Lady Peinforte. Once again, the shorthand narrative explanation of comic strips is used to explain (or not explain) how Lady Peinforte came to be in our time: it is apparently by magic. Isaac Asimov once wrote that extremely advanced technology would look indistinguishable from magic. This maxim was employed to good effect in 1972's "The Daemons" and was an explanation which would just about excuse Ace's time storm in "Dragonfire", but, in "Silver Nemesis", magic looked indistinguishable from magic. Magic sat ill with the science fiction elements of *Doctor Who* and only made the narrative – which also featured the Queen, corgis, Windsor castle, Halley's comet and Gallifreyan legend – even stranger. The Cybermen also suffered

---

[1] Interview on an American television documentary, "The Making of *Doctor Who*" – which was subsequently released on VHS with a revised cut of "Silver Nemesis".

from a chrome accessoried redesign; their vulnerability to gold – a criticised plot feature of 1975's "Revenge of the Cybermen" – here became absurd as they were dispatched by Ace with gold coins fired from her catapult.

The final story of the season, when coupled with the name of the programme in television listings magazines, was witty entitled "*Doctor Who*: The Greatest Show in the Galaxy". This concerned a physic circus run by the Gods of Ragnarok, a race of beings who forced performers to entertain them or die. It featured T.P.McKenna as the Captain and Jessica Martin as Mags, his werewolf (in a science fiction programme?) companion. As with Vorg and Shirna in "Carnival of Monsters" (1973) these were mirror images of the Doctor and Jo/Ace, promoting much enjoyment for viewers who spotted the links. Nathan-Turner apparently included a character called Whizz Kid as a parody of the fanboys who had been a thorn in his side. Gian Sammarco, who played him, had recently starred as Adrian Mole on ITV: the casting sardonically emphasised the production office's view of *Doctor Who* fans[1], Whizz Kid is an irritating geek who states that he hasn't seen the early versions of the Psychic Circus, but says that everyone knows they were much better than its present incarnation. This was, of course, a reference to fans who dared to say that the earlier versions of "Doctor Who" were a bit better than the fare that was currently being served up[2]. Like "Shada" in 1978, "The Greatest Show in the Galaxy" was hit by industrial action at the BBC and production was only salvaged when the production team elected to record the circus scenes in a tent in the BBC car park. Sylvester McCoy recalls his back and

---

[1] Nicknamed "barkers" by Nathan-Turner and production manager Gary Downie and "Doable Barkers" if they were sexually attractive. See Richard Marson, *The Life and Scandalous Times of John Nathan-Turner*, Tadworth, 2013.

[2] Commenting on his own script for "The Unquiet Dead" in 2005, Mark Gatiss said that the new version of *Doctor Who* was more like *Doctor Who* than *Doctor Who* had been in its final years (*Doctor Who Confidential* on "The Unquiet Dead", BBC 3, 2005). It is certainly true that the revived series championed the virtues of coherent story telling.

behind being singed from a huge explosion detonated by over-enthusiastic special effects men at the climax of the story.

## Last minute renewal

One more season was commissioned and many fans began to be more optimistic about its quality. Even *DWB* ("*Doctor Who* Bulletin"), a widely circulated fanzine that was blistering in its unremitting criticism of Nathan-Turner's output, remarked that people seemed more cheerful about the programme and things were looking up. The Brigadier returned in 1989's season opener, "Battlefield", a sword and sorcery tale by Ben Aaronovitch which he had pitched to the production office before "Revelation of the Daleks". Again, magic sat uneasily with science fiction as the Doctor is recognised, by knights from another dimension, as the sorcerer Merlin; Morgaine (Jean Marsh) cures a character's blindness with magic and tries to start a nuclear war before she is led off – inexplicably, given her great powers – to prison. There was a near disaster in the studio when Sophie Aldred, as Ace, is trapped in a glass tank filling with water. McCoy saw that the glass was bulging and yelled for Aldred to be pulled clear, which she was, just before the glass broke and water flooded the studio floor.

Marc Platt's second story, "Ghost Light" (1989), was the last story of the original series to be made. Acting again as Time's Champion in keeping his motivation secret, the Doctor returns Ace to a haunted house which had terrified her as a child. Here, Josiah Samuel Smith (Ian Hogg) lives with his Neanderthal butler: it is never explained why he has a Neanderthal butler, but the casual viewer was just expected to accept it. He attracts the attention of the Reverend Mr Matthews (John Nettleton), who questions Smith's interest in the blasphemous theory of evolution and ends up, in a memorable image typical of this period in the show's history, as a monkey clutching a banana in a glass case. An alien called Light is cataloguing life on Earth but destroying that which he catalogues. The story is intriguing, but very complicated.

There were two more stories to go. One is "The Curse of Fenric", which is highly regarded by fans of the McCoy era. Set in a secret base in the Second World War, it features enigma machines, vampires from the future, Viking runes and an enemy of the Doctor from the dawn of time with whom he had played chess (in a reference to the film *The Seventh Seal* (1957), in which a knight plays chess with Death). The story was rushed and confusing, partly owing to the episodes over-running drastically. Cartmel had instructed his writers to write as much as they wanted and not to worry too much about the twenty five minute running time: thus episodes were pruned down in the cutting room, with plot and explanations (such as they were) lost. Cut footage was restored to "The Curse of Fenric" for its VHS release: critics of the story opined that it was still confusing, only longer. Ian Briggs changed vampire lore by stating that it was the vanquisher's faith in the cross of Christ, rather than the cross itself, which allowed him to repel vampires; hence a Russian could repel a vampire through his faith in the Revolution. This piece of atheistic political correctness was matched by Ace asking a character (actually her grandmother Kathleen) if she had had a baby (Ace's mother) with her "boyfriend": it seems highly unlikely that Ace wouldn't know that illegitimacy was a social stigma in the 1940s and that a woman with a child would have been married. It was, in short, bad writing.

The show's final story was written by another newcomer, Rona Munro, who became an accomplished playwright and the first person to write for both the original and the revived series of *Doctor Who*: she wrote "The Eaters of Light" (2017) for Peter Capaldi's Doctor. The script had the working title of "Cat Flap", which cleverly referenced the cheetah people's ability to flip between their planet and ours. Someone thought this was a bit rude and the title was changed to the much duller "Survival". In a comprehensible and intelligent script, Sophie Aldred shone in a story which centred around Ace. In contemporary Perivale, Ace's friends are disappearing to the planet of the cheetah people, who snatch humans from our world to hunt them in theirs. The cheetah people were well conceived and designed, although Alan Wareing, the director, worried at a design meeting: "As long as we don't get Puss In Boots". When he saw the finished costumes, he wryly said that that was exactly what he got. Wareing is a little unfair as the cheetah people are actually very effective. There is a memorable sequence in part one when Ace cowers inside a child's climbing frame as a cheetah person on horseback stalks around its circumference. The cheetah people's planet, shot in a Dorset quarry but enhanced by new video technology as a convincing alien world, exerts an influence on the humans, who become more like the cheetah people themselves and eventually transform into them. Episode two ends with Ace's eyes changing colour, effectively indicating her infection by the planet. Some viewers, like my brother Simon, were still watching in black and white in 1989: not noticing the transformation in eye colour, they missed the significance of the cliff hanger. The Master lurks on the planet, fighting off his own transformation into a cheetah person: in his finest performance as the character, Anthony Ainley battles the Doctor at the end of the planet's life; the Doctor, also transforming, rejects his animal nature and refuses to kill the Master, howling "If we live like animals, we die like animals!" as he is hurled back to Earth, to Ace and to the TARDIS.

A final, late publicity push – somebody at the BBC must have taken his eye off the ball by actually encouraging people to watch *Doctor Who* – saw "Survival" gain the highest ratings of the season, but only to five million viewers. At home, Sophie Aldred got a phone call from Sylvester McCoy. "Are you sitting down?" he asked. "You'd better sit down. The show's been cancelled." There was to be no new season. A monologue was hastily written and recorded for the Doctor, played over the last minutes of "Survival" as the Doctor and Ace walked back to the TARDIS. In a piece of Cartmel-scripted, Tolkeinesque, whimsy, the Doctor reminded Ace that there were planets to visit where people were made of smoke and cities made of song. "Come on Ace," he enthused, "we've got work to do."

The Doctor did not return to television for seven years.

# 13

# Lost in The Time Vortex

## Doctor Who – The Ultimate Adventure

One of *Doctor Who*'s last gasps before it disappeared at the end of the 1980s was the third professional stage version of the show. This was *Doctor Who – The Ultimate Adventure,* commissioned by fan and successful theatre producer Mark Furness in 1988. The BBC production office had the first shout at preparing a script and Andrew Cartmel and Ben Aaronovitch put a draft together, which eventually ran into the sand. Furness turned to the ever-reliable Terrance Dicks, who had written the 1974 stage play *Doctor Who and the Daleks in Seven Keys to Doomsday.* Dicks rolled up his sleeves and got to work. He turned in a cheerful romp called *The Ultimate Adventure.* The play's structure was a version of episodic seventies *Doctor Who*, a logical choice given that the Doctor was going to be played by Jon Pertwee, reprising the role after he'd left it fourteen years previously.

The plot, such as it was, saw the Doctor being summoned to Downing Street and given a mission by the female prime minister, whom Pertwee called "Margaret" and kissed her hand, and Colin Baker, who replaced Pertwee later in the run, less ceremoniously called "Maggie". The companion was a French aristocrat named Jason, saved by the Doctor from the guillotine at the time of the French Revolution. The TARDIS takes off from Downing Street for the Bar Galactica, where the Doctor and Jason meet mercenary Madame Delilah, an alien called Zog and new girl companion Crystal. Crystal and Jason sing a love duet, Madame Delilah sings "Come to Bar Galactica for all Star Mercenaries" while a Vervoid and Draconian dance. Space Mercenary Karl, played by David Banks (the Cyberleader in all the 1980s television stories), is in league with the Cybermen to get the Doctor. The Doctor lands on the Dalek ship and they vow that, as he has defied them for the last term, he will be exterminated, he will be exterminated, he will be exterminated. Crash in the theme tune for the interval, two gins and tonics later and the Doctor has not been exterminated but lo, has escaped! Back to the French Revolution and to 10 Downing Street, where everything has worked out well after the Daleks and the Cybermen have had a bit of a scrap.

*Doctor Who – The Ultimate Adventure* was, as SFX magazine wrote, the most gloriously awful piece of nonsense which started in the cavernous Wimbledon Theatre in London and toured several locations from 23rd March to 19th August 1989. Pertwee played the Doctor for the first part of the run and told Colin Baker that he would find the show exhausting. There was one performance where Pertwee appeared in the first scene, then went off stage, unwell, to be replaced by David Banks, his understudy as the Doctor. Banks wore a Greenpeace t-shirt and apparently played the part like Peter Davison; he said he dried on stage when he couldn't remember the line, "Reverse the polarity of the neutron flow", an in-joke by Dicks who had inserted it as Pertwee's old catchphrase[1]. "Do you know what that Dalek's managed to do?" Banks improvised. "You don't mean it's managed to reverse the polarity of the neutron flow?" asked the resourceful Crystal. "Yes, that's exactly what I'm saying it's managed to do!" the new Doctor declared.

Colin Baker watched the show when it premiered in Wimbledon Theatre and was somewhat dismayed at the production values. The TARDIS was manhandled roughly onto the edge of the stage by stagehands, Jon Pertwee as the Doctor emerged and said crossly, "Well, we *appear* to have arrived" and Baker cringed. I saw the show on a very hot summer day in Brighton's Theatre Royal, with Colin Baker in the lead. It was very well received and the audience laughed and applauded all the way through. Two distinguished

---

[1] Colin Baker's Doctor asked Zog, "Do you like carrot juice?" and the alien burped and spluttered; then the Doctor replied, "No, nor do I." This was another in-joke and reference to the sixth Doctor's last line in "The Trial of a Time Lord" episode 14 (1986).

329

ladies in the bar said how very good they thought the young girl was playing Zog, and they really thought she had made the part her own.

The Cybermen were identical to their television counterparts (were they the same costumes?), although the Daleks had undergone a rather lamentable redesign.Much taller and thinner than the television Daleks, these looked rather like giant washing up liquid bottles, with sixties style bands round their bodies rather than the vertical slats sported since "The Chase" (1965) and eye sticks that lacked the series of concentric circles before the bulb. I feared greatly for the operators on the steeply raked stage of the Theatre Royal. The show featured many minutes of model work projected onto a big screen, the Daleks' scanner, as they caught the TARDIS in their tractor beam. Special effects were very limited and neither the Daleks' nor the Cybermen's ray guns could emit beams: battles were shown by lasers stabbing down from the flies onto the characters below, which didn't quite work. Baker performed with gusto and I particularly relished the moment when the crone threw off her cloak in the French Revolution scene, to reveal the Doctor, who promptly rescued Jason from certain death. One of the Daleks was told off by his fellows, and his eyestick drooped in sadness – much to the audience's amusement. Contemporary audiences relished the line about the Daleks being so evil that they plotted to enlarge the hole in the ozone layer, although the idea of the Doctor taking orders from Mrs Thatcher (never named on stage, but clearly her) was rather too much to take: even the third Doctor, the most establishment of all, would have blanched at obeying a politician, let alone such a controversial one. SFX's assessment – that the play was the most gloriously awful piece of nonsense – was spot on. It was a romp, it was lively, and very funny – a real tonic when the sword of Damocles hung by the slimmest of Metebelis spider thread over the television show.

**The production office closes**

Back at the BBC, Andrew Cartmel had made plans for the new

season. Ace was to have left and, as a subtle contrast to a working class companion, was to be replaced by an upper class companion who was also a safe cracker (interestingly, a premise used for the character played by Michele Ryan in the 2010 special "Planet of the Dead"). There was to have been an atmospheric introductory scene in which the new companion entered a dark building, found the safe, opened it in triumph to reveal the Doctor inside, saying, "What kept you?" Sylvester McCoy would have left at the end of the season.

Instead, the production office closed its doors and Nathan-Turner finally left the BBC. Andrew Cartmel returned eventually to journalism. The word "cancellation", as in 1985, was never actually used by the BBC, but it was fairly clear to fans that this was what had happened. Concerned viewers wrote to the BBC listings magazine *Radio Times*: one wrote that people should realise that "Survival" was the last ever episode of "Doctor Who". Not so, equivocated Peter Cregeen, the new controller of BBC 1, in the *Radio Times* letter pages: there might be a longer wait than usual before a new series, but options were being explored to resurrect the Doctor at some point, when the series would be new and fresh rather than featuring "a battle-weary Time Lord languishing in the backwaters of audience popularity." Cregeen later said there was no intention of reviving the programme and the BBC, relieved at last of a property it despised, looked to new projects. The wait between the twenty sixth and the twenty seventh season was, in fact, fifteen years.

*DWB* confirmed in a late 1989 edition that there would be "No New *Doctor Who* in 1990". Officially, the BBC was looking at independent bids for making the series. Cregeen eventually explained, in the extras to the DVD release of "Survival", that he had come to the BBC to find several old series still in production and haemorrhaging viewers. One was Peter Davison's former vehicle *All Creatures Great and Small*: another was *Doctor Who*. Cregeen considered recommissioning them, but decided that their time had passed. Wary of exasperating fans and recreating the storm of adverse press reaction which had resulted from the 1985 cancellation, the BBC avoided saying that *Who* had been cancelled and kept telling anyone who enquired that it would probably, eventually, be made by an independent company. Why, I even received such a letter myself.

There were some approaches from independent producers to revamp the series. Gerry Davis, the co-creator of the Cybermen and script editor of the Hartnell era, put together a proposal to the BBC; so did Terry Nation, the creator of the Daleks. Neither got anywhere. Derrick Sherwin, Troughton's last producer, proposed a new series featuring UNIT but excluding the Doctor: again, nothing came of it.

### "Lost in the Dark Dimension" is lost in the dark dimension

With the BBC refusing to make the show, the corporation's commercial arm, BBC Enterprises, began to look at options for a straight-to-video thirtieth anniversary special. *Doctor Who* had been kept alive by a very successful series of VHS releases in the 1990s: the newly found "Tomb of the Cybermen" had been rushed into release in 1992 and shot to the top video spot in the retail chain W.H.Smith. *Doctor Who* was a merchandising cash cow, and BBC Enterprises was grateful. They wanted to "give something back to the fans" and considered a documentary, then a drama. Tom Baker expressed an interest in playing the Doctor again and was swiftly signed up to the project. Fan Adrian Rigelsford wrote a script for a story called, variously, "The Dark Dimension" or "Lost in the Dark Dimension". This featured all the surviving Doctors but centred on Tom Baker's and Sylvester McCoy's. It also featured a character called Summerfield, presumably Bernice Summerfield, a companion from the Virgin novels, and the Doctor's funeral: his body is pushed out to sea on a Viking long boat and then set on fire. (This striking image was coincidentally used by Steven Moffat in the opening scenes of "The Impossible Astronaut" in 2011.) The premise was that the fourth Doctor had not regenerated at the end of "Logopolis" (1981) and had to reunite himself with his seventh incarnation if he was to remain whole. On the way, he meets his other selves, Daleks, Yeti, Cybermen and a villain who was to have been played by Brian Blessed.

Graeme Harper, who had directed "The Caves of Androzani" (1984) and "Revelation of the Daleks" (1985), was appointed as the special's director; Tony Harding, who had designed K9, was the visual effects designer and started work on revamping the special weapons Dalek from 1988's "Remembrance of the Daleks". Designs were completed, locations chosen, studios booked, the cameras were ready to roll and several hundred thousand pounds were spent on preparing the project.

However, Colin Baker, Peter Davison and Jon Pertwee were far from happy that their Doctors were only to appear as cameos. They also noted the naivety of BBC Enterprises, which was a merchandising, rather than a production, company, in writing directly to them about their involvement in the special rather than contacting them through their agents. It seemed unlikely they would agree to the script as it stood. Meanwhile, BBC 1 got wind of the production and expressed an interest in screening it; they also offered to put up much of the budget. Other parts of the BBC protested at Enterprises making programmes, which was not its role, and "The Dark Dimension" started to flounder on rights issues and BBC internal politics. It was eventually vetoed by Philip Segal, who was unhappy about a BBC produced *Who* clashing with his version of the show (which eventually became the 1996 TV movie), and the BBC closed the project down. There were some attempts by Enterprises to remount it: Tom Baker was still under contract and the film could be made as a straight-to-video release with only one Doctor, but by then it had run into the sand. Fans who had read eagerly of the production learnt glumly, and with a sense of inevitability, that it was not going to happen after all: "Disinterest [sic] Kills The Dark Dimension", stated *DWB*.

## "Dimensions in Time"

The disappointment of fans was not appeased by the BBC's replacement special, two short segments in 3D for its annual *Children in Need* telethon called "Dimensions in Time". This did feature all the surviving Doctors and as many companions as could be found, including the Brigadier, Leela, Victoria and Romana II, in an incomprehensible skit shot on the *EastEnders* lot. Kate O'Mara returned as the Rani with as many monsters as could be found and the cast did their best with a preposterous and appalling script. There were two versions of episode two, in which one of two characters from *EastEnders* helped the Doctor: viewers were invited to phone Noel Edmonds and vote on which version they wished to see. Only one version was shown and nobody much cared to see the other one. The escapade confirmed the contempt the series was still held in by some at the BBC.

The BBC's thinking in the early 1990s is somewhat opaque and documentary evidence is not readily available, but it seems that it was interested in two approaches to revamp the programme. A company called Lumiere Pictures (later Green Light) wanted to produce at least one feature film. Scripts were written by Johnny Byrne, who wrote "The Keeper of Traken" (1980) and "Arc of Infinity" (1983), and featured, at various times, K9, an alien companion called Pog, Amelia Earhart, Shakespeare, the Master and a replacement renegade Time Lord called the Mandrake. Negotiations continued into 1995; some design sketches were completed; the company released a publicity leaflet for the film, now called "Last of the Time Lords", with the strapline: "Doctor Who: the man: the myth: the motion picture." It seems that the negotiations culminated in a three film deal to start shooting in 1996 with Pierce Brosnan (soon to be cast as James Bond) as the Doctor. The deal collapsed when the BBC opted to go with the Universal/Fox TV movie with Paul McGann, and Green Light took them to court for breach of contract. They got nowhere.

# The TV Movie (1996)

The other approach that the BBC was considering was a new television series, co-produced by an American network, and linked with Steven Spielberg. This decision was a culmination of the decades old criticism that *Doctor Who* couldn't compete with the production values of American science fiction series: the budget for two episodes of *Star Trek: the Next Generation* was about the same as a fourteen episode season of *Who*. Furthermore, the BBC had been impressed by the popularity of *Doctor Who* in the States. An American co-production for a US network, the BBC mused, could take advantage of the show's stateside publicity and attract the sort of budget that Nathan-Turner et al could only dream of.

In fact, Spielberg was only involved on the peripheries of the negotiations, although he was aware of *Doctor Who* and liked it. In 2009, he accepted Steven Moffat's resignation as chief scriptwriter on the Tintin movies when Moffat was offered the post as showrunner on *Who*: Spielberg gave him his blessing and told him that the world would be a poorer place without *Doctor Who*. The driving force behind the American negotiations was Philip Segal, an executive producer on such science fiction shows as *Seaquest DSV*. Segal had grown up in the United Kingdom and had happy memories of sitting on his grandfather's knee to watch William Hartnell as the Doctor. He produced a series bible for the new show, purportedly written by Cardinal Borusa (who had featured in the four Tom Baker/Peter Davison Gallifrey stories) as the Doctor's mentor. Segal touted it around American television companies saying, "Isn't this fantastic?" He wryly recalled that the reply was, "To you, maybe; to us it's just gobbledegook."

Segal moved employers several times in the 1990s and took his *Doctor Who* proposal with him. In the UK, meanwhile, a champion for the programme was found in Alan Yentob. As controller of BBC 2 in the early 1990s, Yentob had endeared himself to fans by agreeing to a repeat season of classic stories including "The Time Meddler" (1965), newly returned to the archives, and "Genesis of the Daleks" (1975); now, as controller of BBC 1, he sanctioned more repeats and a documentary in 1993, "Thirty Years in the TARDIS". Interviewed at its conclusion, Yentob was asked if it was true that he was in discussion with Steven Spielberg about *Doctor Who*. Quoting from *House of Cards*, then running on BBC1, Yentob replied: "You might think that. I couldn't possibly comment." He then relaxed and said "You know what the American networks are like, so there are no promises." For the first time in four years, the BBC was making something like positive noises about the show's return. In private, Yentob was trying to hammer out a deal with Segal. Several networks had turned the project down as a television series; Segal took it to News International's new network, Fox TV, which declined to commission a series but agreed to a one-off television movie. This could act as a back door pilot to a series. Universal Television was to make the film for Fox with support from BBC Enterprises: thus three companies had had to be fully satisfied before the project could go ahead and it was something of a miracle that it did.

Once the film had been given the green-light, things moved very quickly. Before *Doctor Who* fans were fully aware that there was indeed to be a television movie, they learnt that it had already begun shooting in Canada and Paul McGann was playing the Doctor. The BBC was pleased with the choice: McGann was an accomplished actor who had given an acclaimed performance in the BBC's First World War series, *The Monocled Mutineer*. Segal had the choice of two possible scripts. One, which he preferred and wondered later if he should have made, effectively pressed the reset button on the series and took the Doctor back to Gallifrey, where his brother, the Master, was in charge and his father, the great explorer Ulysees, was lost in time. Pursuing his father is the Doctor's motivation for leaving Gallifrey, and the story featured both Davros and redesigned Daleks. Dramatic blockbuster though it would have been, this was a far more radical reimagining of the series than the 1960s Peter Cushing movies had ever been and would, perhaps, have been too much for British viewers to accept. McGann's audition tape, which survives, appears to have been taken from this script: he is great, but the script sounds appalling.

In the end, Segal opted for a script by the British writer Matthew Jacobs, who was briefed to introduce the series to an American audience which might be unfamiliar with it, while simultaneously including "kisses to the past" for a British audience who knew it backwards. As well as squaring this circle, Jacobs was briefed to tell a simple story. The Master was chosen as the main villain, as with several scripts for the Green Light/Lumiere movie: this may have been because copyright for the Master was owned by the BBC and could easily be included in the film's rights package. Other monsters, such as the Daleks (who made a cameo offstage appearance in the TV movie), were owned by their creators or by their creators jointly with the BBC, thus creating tiresome rights issues for anyone who wanted to use them again[1].

Strangely for a movie that was supposed to introduce the programme to a new audience, Segal and Jacobs elected to include Sylvester McCoy as "the Old Doctor" and make the film a regeneration story. The BBC weren't happy with the inclusion of a Doctor from a period of the show that they disliked and asked for Tom Baker instead. Segal, who had more of a sense of the programme's continuity than the corporation, insisted on McCoy and the BBC eventually concurred.

The film was shot in Canada to take advantage of various tax deals, and Vancouver doubled for San Francisco. The BBC faxed over designs for the police box exterior of the TARDIS and Segal enthused that "our carpenters have done a wonderful job" when the prop was finished. Daphne Ashbrook, an actress who had appeared in *Star Trek: Deep Space Nine,* was cast as Grace, the female companion, a doctor working in the emergency room when the seventh Doctor is brought in, dying from gunshot wounds. Lee Jee Tso played Chang Lee, a young Asian gangster companion, and Eric

---

[1] Green Light had apparently thought that the Master was not available in their rights package; they replaced him in some draft scripts with a similar character called the Mandrake.

337

Roberts, brother of Julia, was cast as the Master. Roberts was much better known in the States than in the UK and Fox's promotional material for the film featured his Master much more prominently than McGann's Doctor. "Two time travellers arrive in San Francisco on December 31$^{st}$ 1999: only one will leave alive", growled the movie poster. The British poster featured the cheery strapline: "Time Waits For No Man... Except One". Roberts knew McGann, having trained with him at RADA, and the two actors apparently enjoyed each other's company on the shoot.

The film's budget was set at five million pounds: enough for five seasons of McCoy *Doctor Who*. A voiceover from Paul McGann introduces the story. The Master has been put on trial by the Daleks on Skaro and exterminated. The seventh Doctor has been charged by the Daleks to take Master's ashes away from their planet. Unfortunately, the Master's remains are only dormant; a timing malfunction forces the TARDIS to land in San Francisco on December 30$^{th}$, 1999. The Doctor leaves the TARDIS, only to be shot down by a hail of bullets intended for Chang Lee. The Master's casket is by this time broken open and his essence, a transparent goo, leaks from the TARDIS's keyhole. Ambulanceman Bruce (Eric Roberts) takes Chang Lee and the Doctor to the hospital. Grace tries to operate but is unfamiliar with the Doctor's alien physique and the seventh Doctor dies on the operating table. He regenerates in the morgue, terrifying the mortuary assistant as he rises from his slab, and steals some fancy dress clothes from hospital lockers in a sequence inspired by an identical scene in "Spearhead from Space" (1970), Jon Pertwee's first story. (Steven Moffat repeated the scene again in "The Eleventh Hour" (2010) with Matt Smith's newly regenerated Doctor.) Meanwhile, the Master's essence has taken over Bruce, who dies, rises as the Master, kills Bruce's wife and declares that he must have the Doctor's body: Bruce's is already decaying.

The rest of the story is essentially a chase around Vancouver/San Francisco, with the Master and Chang Lee haring after the Doctor and Grace. Both are captured, the Doctor is strung up in a device that resembles Christ's cross and crown of thorns (the film uses Resurrection imagery throughout in its treatment of regeneration) and the Master prepares to take over the Doctor's body. He kills both Chang Lee and Grace; the Doctor is freed and throws the Master into the Eye of Harmony, the energy source at the heart of the TARDIS. (This contradicted "The Deadly Assassin", which established that the Eye of Harmony is situated on Gallifrey and all TARDISes draw their power from it.) In an incomprehensible twist, the TARDIS then decides it likes Chang Lee and Grace so much that it rolls back time and brings them back to life. This "get out of jail free" card had been outlawed by 1970s script editor Douglas Adams, who forbade writers from letting the Doctor return to a point in time to prevent the cataclysmic events of the story from happening in the first place. Adams wisely saw what Jacobs and Segal missed, that this plot line could be used to save the day in every single adventure. The Doctor drops his new companions back to Earth and asks Grace to come with him: "You come with me!" she replies, and they part. The TARDIS spins off into the vortex and *Doctor Who* was again absent from British television screens; this time, for nine years.

Well-acted and well made, the TV movie had much going for it and gained nine million viewers on this side of the Atlantic: proof that there was still an audience and affection for the programme. Perhaps the BBC had been wise to rest *Doctor Who* if it could be so welcomed when it returned? There were some problems. Segal and Jacobs came to the conclusion that, as the Doctor kept returning to Earth and loved the planet so much, he must be half human (like *Star Trek*'s Mr Spock); in a shorthand for American viewers, the chameleon circuit[1] was renamed a cloaking device (another

---

[1] Peter Capaldi's Doctor called it a cloaking device in "Smile" (2017). This was another example of Steven Moffat's view that, if it was said on screen, it was canonical: hence his contribution to the series that the Doctor had actually adopted the name "Who" and was "Doctor Who" from Matt Smith's Doctor onwards. It might more truthfully be said that Moffat referenced the canonical bits that he liked: the revelation that the Doctor was half-human was buried thoroughly, never to be heard again. Joke: One viewer asked why, in "The Five Doctors" (1983), the Master is not wearing a cloak in the High Council's chamber but, when he is

reference to *Star Trek*) and the evolution of a Time Lord, in which Paul McGann suggests he, like the Master, can transform into another species at the end of his regeneration cycle, was derided by fans. Some fans were unhappy that the previously asexual Doctor kissed his female companion in a definitely non-avuncular manner: this was too radical a departure from the paternalistic figure they had grown up with and gay fans, who made up a large percentage of the programme's followers, felt understandably excluded by this identification of the Doctor as exclusively heterosexual.

Critical opinion was similarly divided and some argued that, in attempting to appeal to both American and British viewers, it had pleased neither. *The Guardian*'s television critic wrote that the film had been stuck mid Atlantic like the isle of Rockall and was "about as interesting"; the *Independent* said that the best word to sum up the film was "derivative" and cited its similarities to the *Terminator* films, not least in Eric Roberts's leather coat and dark glasses. Another *Independent* writer lavished praise upon the attractive figure of Paul McGann ("Doctor FWhooaaarrrr") and said that the BBC would be mad not to commission a series. Asked what he thought of the movie at its premiere screening, Terrance Dicks said it was "incoherent crap" and then wondered if he should have been a little more frank; Barry Letts said the execution of the story was "bad, bad, bad"; Waris Hussein, who had directed the first story "An Unearthly Child" in 1963, said that the movie showed the Americans didn't understand *Doctor Who*.

In the States, the TV movie was scheduled against the final episode of ratings champion *Roseanne* and did very badly. Many felt that there was far too much new information for new American viewers to take in – the first five minutes ask viewers to absorb the concepts of the Time Lords, the TARDIS, regeneration, the Daleks – and it was felt a mistake to have two actors playing the leading role. In 2005, Russell T Davies avoided this problem: he did not script a regeneration scene for Paul McGann and "Rose" only features

---

teleported from there to the Death Zone, he is suddenly wearing one. Answer: the teleport was clearly fitted with a cloaking device.

Christopher Eccleston as the Doctor. Davies stated it would be far too confusing for new viewers to have McGann shot by a laser bolt in the first five minutes, only to be replaced by Eccleston: viewer loyalty should be immediately attached to one hero, not two.)

Fox declined to make another movie or to commission a series from this "back door" pilot. It became apparent to fans very soon after the TV movie was shown in May 1996 that there was to be no more *Who*.

Segal was disappointed. Before the rights to the series reverted to the BBC, Yentob wrote to Segal to tell him that the rights to the Dalek movies *Dr Who and the Daleks* and *Daleks: Invasion Earth 2150 A.D.* had come up and that Segal was welcome to remake them. Segal was less than enthusiastic, noting that these movies were themselves adaptations of existing television stories ("The Daleks" (1963) and "The Dalek Invasion of Earth" (1964)) and that he was being asked if he would like to make a remake of a remake. He declined.

By the end of 1996, it looked as though the BBC had taken its best shot at bringing back *Doctor Who* and had failed. It seemed very unlikely that the programme would return. Fans consoled themselves with the BBC's series of novels based on the eighth Doctor: following the TV movie, the BBC had taken back the rights to the novels from Virgin. Terrance Dicks wrote the first novel, "The Eight Doctors", as a direct continuation of the TV movie: Paul McGann's Doctor finally finishes reading *The Time Machine*, which he had been reading in the film, and goes back in time to meet his other selves. "*Doctor Who* Magazine" continued to be published every month as a consolation: but it looked as though the Doctor's career on television was over. There was *Babylon 5* and the UNIT-like set up of *The X Files*, but it just wasn't the same…the exhibits in the Longleat *Doctor Who* exhibition looked more and more tired, the Yeti slumping over listlessly, the "Tribute the 'The Invasion'" display, featuring Cybermen in a mock-up of London, featuring eighties Cybermen… it was all wrong, wrong, wrong. The commercial company Big Finish started producing some very good audio CDs featuring Peter Davison, Colin Baker and Sylvester McCoy but, good as these were, they weren't new screen stories.

But, in late 2003, there was a surprise…

# 14

# Resurrection: New *Who*, 2005

Seven million people listen to BBC Radio Four's *Today* news programme, broadcast six days a week from six to nine in the morning. In November 2003, many listeners dropped spoons into their cornflakes in astonishment at the announcement, at the end of the six thirty a.m. news summary, "And *Doctor Who* is coming back." There was a short feature explaining that a new series had been commissioned, that Russell T. Davies was to be the producer, that the Doctor hadn't yet been cast and that nothing would appear on our screens until 2005. Clayton Hickman, the editor of "*Doctor Who* Magazine", was interviewed on *Today* and said that he and his team had been dancing on their desks.

Several planets moved into a favourable conjunction to create a change of heart at the BBC. Many of the corporation's executives, who now had the power to commission programmes, had watched and enjoyed *Doctor Who* as children; the programme's detractors, like Peter Cregeen and Jonathan Powell, had long since moved on. Lorraine Heggessey had been appointed as controller of BBC 1 in 2000 and had made some positive comments about wanting to bring back the show, perhaps with a female Doctor (a female Doctor? What's that all about?) played by someone like Judy Dench. Fans had heard it all before and grunted non-commitally. The BBC was anxious, in 2003, to beef up its Saturday evening schedule against competition from ITV: it considered which programmes had been popular in the past. One had been *Doctor Who*. Why not do something like *Doctor Who*? In fact, why not just do *Doctor Who*? Proposals for a feature film had grumbled on through the early 2000s, going back and forth, not really getting anywhere, and Lorraine Heggessey said she eventually said, "Enough!" She and Mal Young, the BBC Controller of Continuing Drama Series, agreed that plans for a movie had had their chance; Young said that

*Doctor Who* wasn't a movie, it was a television show, and that was how it should return.

The choice of Russell T. Davies to produce the new series was, Mal Young said, a "no brainer". Davies had written several very successful series and plays for commercial television, including Channel Four's *Queer as Folk*, which had prompted questions in Parliament about its supposed obscenity and had featured a gay *Doctor Who* fan who watched the programme because it made him happy. Davies had long been a *Who* fan and had written the novel *Damaged Goods* for the Virgin New Adventures range. Working for Granada Television in the 1990s, Davies had suggested the company should bid for *Doctor Who*, only to be slapped down by a boss who said, "Why should we make that rubbish?" The time was still not right. In 2000, Davies was courted by the BBC to write for them. He held out for *Doctor Who* and submitted a proposal for revising the series: the proposal was headed, "*Doctor Who* 2000". The BBC passed on the idea, but Davies remained optimistic, assuring "*Doctor Who* Magazine" of his confidence that the series would come back one day.

Knowing that Davies was a fan and a brilliant writer, Heggessey and Young wooed him to join the BBC and produce the new series. Like most fans, Davies was somewhat sceptical at first: he said that he wrote programmes that were going to be made, and was not interested in writing a *Doctor Who* story that would end up as one episode on BBC 3 or as a webcast on the official *Who* website. Such had been the case for Paul Cornell's 2003 webcast, "Scream of the Shalka", featuring Richard E. Grant as the Doctor (claimed by the BBC at the time as the official Ninth Doctor), Derek Jacobi as the Master and David Tennant (who he?) as the Caretaker. The BBC reassured Davies: there would be a full series on television, initially planned at seven episodes, and it really would happen.

Davies climbed on board. In execution and storyline, the new series was much influenced by American series like *Buffy the Vampire Slayer* (1997-2003) and *The X Files* (1993-2002, 2016, 2018), not least in its production management. Davies was to be the showrunner of *Doctor Who* in much the same way that Joss Whedon was the showrunner on *Buffy*: unlike previous producers and script editors, Davies effectively combined the two roles as showrunner. He would write the bulk of the scripts and have control over the others: he would outline stories to other writers and rewrite the scripts as necessary to meet the new house style. Davies also persuaded the BBC to commit to thirteen, rather than seven episodes, arguing that it would be much easier to sell a package of thirteen episodes to overseas stations and, not least, to the United States. Once again, the BBC had its eye on selling *Doctor Who* to an American network: a prize that had eluded the series in its original twenty six year run.

## Casting the ninth Doctor

Press speculation now turned to casting the new Doctor. Many fans wanted Paul McGann, who had instantly made the role his own in the TV movie and had not, they felt, been given a fair crack of the whip. McGann himself did not rule it out. Unsurprisingly, Davies wanted to cast his own Doctor, perhaps with the intention of making a clean break with the past. Christopher Eccleston had played the Son of God in Davies' television movie *The Second Coming* (2003). Interested in news reports that Davies was to be writing again for "children's television" (Eccleston's description), Eccleston went out for his daily run and decided to put his name forward. Davies said, "Of course I'll audition you". Other actors were seen but Eccleston's extraordinarily intense performance was acclaimed by Davies and executive producers Mal Young and Julie Gardner, and Eccleston was cast.

The casting was greeted with some surprise by the press: Eccleston had a reputation as an actor who chose his roles carefully, often opting for gritty realism in drama. He had been one of the leads, with Daniel Craig, in the 1996 mini-series *Our Friends in the North* and cited *Doctor Who*, with its thirteen episodes filmed over nine months, as a similar "challenge". *The Guardian* broke the story with the headline, "Shakespeare actor Eccleston reincarnated as Doctor Who" – a reference to Eccleston's recent performance as Hamlet in 2003. In emphasising that the new *Who* was to take the show seriously and eschew the pantomime inflection of the McCoy years, Eccleston's casting was a bold and wise move. It was also an example of Davies's understandable liking for working with actors he already knew: David Tennant, the tenth Doctor, played the lead in Davies's 2005 BBC 3 series, *Casanova* (an experience which Tennant described as "an extended audition for *Doctor Who*").

## Movie standard special effects

The press returned to the theme, common in lazy writing about the series, that its special effects were poor and its sets wobbled (a charge which always made fans cross; they pointed out that any 1970s BBC drama had wobbly sets, as witnessed by episodes of *Fawlty Towers* and *The Fall and Rise of Reginald Perrin*, but no-one ever listened). Davies joked that he was six foot four and would lean against the sets to ensure they wouldn't wobble. Quoted in *The Guardian*'s feature on Eccleston, a "BBC source involved in the production" said the production values would be high and they were making the show with serious money: modern audiences wouldn't accept the cheap and cheerful production values of the original series. How much money was not entirely clear and the BBC didn't release details of the budget: it wasn't, it seemed, as much as a million pounds per episode but was at the higher end of the BBC budget for drama. Certainly, it was proportionally more than the budget allocated to the programme in its original run, when producers had been expected to produce science fiction on a cop show budget.

As for the special effects, advances in CGI (computer generated imagery) were such that excellent, movie standard effects could be created relatively cheaply. The ghost of "laughable" special effects (another charge lazy writers levelled against the original series) was laid to rest. Several effects companies – staffed, perhaps understandably, by *Doctor Who* fans – scrambled over each other to bid for the CGI contracts; some were willing to undercut their usual fees because, as one said, "This is *Doctor Who!*" The contract was eventually awarded to The Mill, a London based effects company which had provided CGI for the Oscar winning film *Gladiator* (2000). In its pitch, the Mill produced an animated version of the octopoid Nestene consciousness that had adorned the cover of the Target book *Doctor Who and the Terror of the Autons* in 1975 (the Nestene on television had appeared as a fluttering lighting effect that looked like rubber gloved hands waggling under a spotlight). This creature was eventually seen as the Bane in the first episode of the spin-off series *The Sarah Jane Adventures* in 2007.

BBC politics of 2005 were radically different from those of 1989, when the show had last been in regular production. Then, all episodes of *Doctor Who* (bar "Horror of Fang Rock" (1977)) had been made in London: initially at Lime Grove studios (much to Verity Lambert's disgust) and eventually in the new BBC Television Centre. Under pressure to justify its licence fee from successive Conservative and now Labour governments, the BBC had started to move its programme making away from London. *Doctor Who* was to be made by BBC Wales in Cardiff. New producer Phil Collinson enthused about the excellence of Wales as ripe in locations within easy reach of the studio: there were stately homes (seen in *The Girl in the Fireplace*, 2006), Victorian streets (*The Unquiet Dead*, 2005), rugged hills and valleys (doubling as the Highlands of Scotland in *Tooth and Claw*, 2006) and Cardiff's Temple of Peace (doubling as a space station, a Berlin restaurant, the Silurian parliament, and an art gallery in *The Sarah Jane Adventures*). There was to be a London shoot for the first episode, "Rose", as the ninth Doctor and his new companion race across Westminster Bridge, flanked by double decker buses: Davies was keen to establish the series' British credentials and wanted its imagery to be as British as the yellow school bus was American in stateside science fiction shows. The BBC's policy of moving out of London continued into the late 2000s as many productions moved up to Manchester and BBC Television Centre itself was sold off in 2012.

## The Daleks are *not* back?

Having dealt with wobbly sets, special effects and the casting of the Doctor, the press wanted next to know if the Daleks would be in the new series? In 2003, the audio company Big Finish had produced an audio story called "Jubilee" by the playwright Rob Shearman, a friend of Sir Alan Ayckbourn. The story concerned a single Dalek that is imprisoned and tortured and begins to question its existence. Davies commissioned Sherman to rewrite the piece for *Doctor Who*: it eventually became the fifth episode, "Dalek". Mal Young suggested that the Daleks should feature in the first episode: Davies successfully argued that they should be held back until half way through the season, which would allow the series effectively to relaunch itself. In fact, "Dalek" was broadcast at the time of the 2005 general election: the *Radio Times* cover reprised an iconic image from 1964's "The Dalek Invasion of Earth", now featuring the redesigned Daleks gliding over Westminster Bridge under the headline, "Vote Dalek!"

It was during the writing of "Dalek" that the series hit its first serious trouble. Terry Nation's agent, Tim Hancock, was allegedly unhappy about the treatment of the Daleks in the script and withdrew his permission for their use. *The Times* of 5th August 2004 reported that talks between the BBC and Nation's estate had broken down over issues of editorial control and that the BBC hadn't consulted them carefully about their plans for the Daleks. BBC Wales carried an interview with Davies in 2004 outside "Henrik"'s department store in Cardiff, where shooting was underway for the shop scenes of "Rose". The presented asked enthusiastically about the new series and commented, "But no Daleks?" "Well, never say never," Davies replied.

In fact, Shearman had been asked to rewrite his episode without the Dalek and to replace it with the Sphere: this was the Toclafane, which Davies had been saving for a future season. Shearman called his redraft "Absence of the Daleks". Eventually, Hancock and the BBC came to an agreement and "Dalek" went into production.

## Family and realism

Of the fans who had welcomed the casting of Eccleston, some were less happy when they heard that the new companion, Rose Tyler, was to be played by Billie Piper. Piper had been a pop star in her late teens and had had a number one hit with "Because We Want To": fans feared celebrity casting and thought it would be Bonnie Langford all over again. They were reassured by Billie Piper's performance as Alison in the BBC's *Canterbury Tales* in 2004, and accepted that she could actually act.

The treatment of the companion was another change from the original series. American series like *Buffy the Vampire Slayer* had surrounded the lead character with family and friends, or friends-as-family. Perhaps following this lead, Davies gave Rose a boyfriend, Mickey, and a mother, Jackie, to ground the companion's character on Earth and to make real to the audience the consequences of travelling with the Doctor. It was argued that viewers would no longer accept that human beings could drop homes, families and jobs to take off in the TARDIS or that their lives afterwards could be unaffected by their experiences. To be fair, the original series had sometimes touched on these matters: in the last episode of "The Hand of Fear" (1976), Sarah's final scene has her longing for her lost life on Earth:

> I want a bath, I want my hair washed, I just want to feel human again.

"Zeus plug!" calls the Doctor, repairing the TARDIS console and, as usual, not listening.

Rose's family was a backbone to the plotting and themes of the 2005 season. She has to choose between her "stupid boyfriend" (the

349

Doctor's words) and travelling with the Doctor; Mickey, utterly distraught after his experiences of being captured by the Autons and duplicated by the Nestenes, can only hold onto her like a toddler and beg her not to go into the TARDIS. In "Aliens of London", episode four of the new series and the first to be filmed, the Doctor returns Rose to Earth twelve months after they left. He had imagined it to be twelve hours but the TARDIS is as unreliable as ever. In this time, Rose has become a missing person and the Doctor is horrified to find posters asking "Have you seen Rose Tyler?" stuck around the estate. Mickey has been questioned as a murder suspect and Jackie smacks the Doctor hard when he returns Rose to her; so does Martha's mother, Francine, in the 2008 season ("It's always the women!" the Doctor grumbles).

Realism was considered essential in making an otherwise fantastical series acceptable to a modern television audience. Insisting on realism, and further insisting that all the first season's stories should be set on or near Earth, Davies was returning to the successful template established in "An Unearthly Child" (1963), itself influenced by literary science fiction. Such writers as John Wyndham had made science fiction mainstream by adding only one or two fantastic elements to an otherwise realistic world: thus the London of *The Day of the Triffids* is very much the contemporary London of the 1950s, although, granted, there are all these carnivorous, semi-sentient plants wandering about everywhere. Indeed, David Whitaker, *Doctor Who*'s first story editor, greatly admired Wyndham's work and invited him to write for the series. Nothing came of it, but the series produced its own version of the triffid in the 1976 serial "The Seeds of Doom".

## Sex and sexuality in the TARDIS

If realism was to be a keynote, Davies had to address the other perennial issue repeatedly asked by the series' original viewers: was there hanky-panky in the TARDIS? Most viewers had at least wondered about the Doctor's predilection for attractive young women: science fiction and *Star Trek* writer Harlan Ellison opined that the relationship was never satisfactorily explained for those like him with a nasty, suspicious turn of mind[1]. Tom Baker had once said it was all about "Shagging. Yes, shagging." Davies addressed the matter by having Rose gradually fall in love with the Doctor over the course of the series; he becomes a substitute for Mickey but the relationship is never consummated. A policeman in "Aliens of London" (2005) asks if travelling together for a year meant that theirs was a sexual relationship: both Rose and the Doctor are incredulous and reply, "No" in unison. Nevertheless, the Doctor appears jealous of Rose's affection for Mickey and refers to him as "your stupid boyfriend" or "Rickey". Steven Moffat develops the theme further in his first two scripts for the series, the wonderful "The Empty Child"/"The Doctor Dances" (new *Who* had returned to the early Hartnell practice of giving each episode individual titles: Davies argued that if a story carried the label "part two", those who had missed part one wouldn't watch it). Here, the Doctor is jealous of Rose's infatuation for the handsome Jack Harkness, described in Steven Moffat's script as having the jaw of Dan Dare and the smile of a bastard. Dancing is used as a euphemism and symbol for sex in episode two when the Doctor tells Rose that, in nine hundred years, she might imagine he has at some point *danced*. The Doctor's sexuality had never really been explored in the original series, although some in the 1980s production team were apparently uneasy about the suggestion that Susan really was the Doctor's granddaughter as it would mean he had had sex; surely, they tremblingly suggested, "grandfather" was her name of endearment for him? Steven Moffat settled the matter by arguing that the Doctor was sexual but chaste: something he undermined in his second story "The Girl in the Fireplace", in which David Tennant's Doctor triumphantly declares, "I've just snogged Madam de Pompadour!" and seems content to settling down to a life with her when he is separated from the TARDIS. Eccleston finally gets to kiss Rose in

[1] "Introducing *Doctor Who* – amenities performed by Harlan Ellison", *Doctor Who and the Talons of Weng-Chiang*, Pinnacle Books, New York, 1979.

his final episode, but only to draw the time vortex out of her which, in turn, triggers his regeneration.

Having established sexuality in the TARDIS, Rose declares her love for the Doctor in "Doomsday" (2006); he is about to say that he loves her, but the link that allows him to communicate with her across universes is broken. A tear courses down the Doctor's cheek in the TARDIS but this tender moment is broken by the materialisation of Catherine Tate as Donna who demands to know what the hell is going on. Rose is eventually rewarded with a half human regeneration of the Doctor in "Journey's End" (2008) and they settle down to a lovely life together in a parallel universe.

Following the two season story of mutual love, Davies opted for a theme of unrequited love for the third season. Martha is in love with the Doctor but he won't even look at her; finally accepting that he won't love her, she leaves at the end of the season. Some fans were by now tired of the companion mooning around after their hero and wondered if it was the production team who was most in love with the Doctor; some longed for the days when the Doctor and his companion loved each other – arguably the case with the third Doctor and Jo, or the fourth Doctor and Sarah – but the show accepted it rather than dwelt on it and got on with telling the adventure story. Perhaps realising this seam had been sufficiently mined, Davies opted to make Donna emphatically uninterested in the Doctor in season four. When the Doctor says he needs "a mate" to travel with, Donna is aghast: "You're not mating with me, sunshine!" There are repeated and very funny sequences in which characters assume that the two are together and the Doctor and Donna deny it in unison. Donna tells Martha that the Doctor is so skinny, if you "hug him, you get a paper cut" ("The Sontaran Strategem" (2008)).

Some wag[1] suggested in the *SFX* letter pages that the Doctor was now as veteran a snogger as James T.Kirk and you couldn't imagine Hartnell behaving like that: Moffat said that he wasn't trying to make the Doctor like Kirk at all but the sexual tenth Doctor was the

---

[1] Actually it was me.

Doctor we had. When he became showrunner in 2010, Moffat didn't give Amy a romantic interest in the eleventh Doctor. She does, at one point, try to get him into bed: Karen Gillan, who played Amy, said this was justified as Amy is an ordinary young woman with ordinary sexual desires; a correspondent to the *Radio Times* disagreed and said Amy was behaving like a tuppenny tart. Otherwise, Amy and the Doctor's relationship is one of a more profound, chaste love. This does not placate Amy's fiancé, Rory, who understandably perceives the Doctor as a rival in the 2010 season. Moffat's decision to move away from the Doctor as a romantic figure was perhaps inspired by his wish to stamp his own mark on the series, not least, by pushing the reset button so that many events in the Davies years never happened. Amy does not recognise the Daleks, for example. Ending the romance might also have been a response to the casting of the gangling Matt Smith as the Doctor, who moves, according to Moffat, like a drunken giraffe and is arguably less conventionally attractive than the dashing David Tennant. The eleventh Doctor is uncomfortable with sexual matters and is embarrassed to think that Amy and Rory conceived River Song on board the TARDIS. It seemed that Moffat was returning to the original series' Doctors in shearing him of his sexuality.

Davies continued to bring the new series into the twenty first century by reflecting contemporary attitudes to race and sexuality. Casting regardless of colour was common: Mickey is black and Martha was acclaimed by the press as the first black companion (presumably they hadn't noticed Mickey). This was quite a departure from the original series which had treated race sensitively but had a predominantly white cast for much of its run. Bob Baker and Dave Martin had been surprised when a West Indian actor had been cast as Cotton in "The Mutants" (1972), a story which satirised apartheid South Africa in its depiction of separate development for the native Mutts and the colonising Overlords. The Mutts are mistreated and kept in poverty while the Overlords live like kings. In the DVD commentary, the writer and social commentator Bidisha applauded the story's attempt to tackle racism but was amused by the contrasting depiction of the Doctor: as a Chap, he was a fellow you could trust.

Again reflecting changes in contemporary attitudes, Davies introduced gay characters into the show: another contrast to the original series which, perceived by many as a children's programme even to the end of its run, barely touched on characters' sexuality and, if it did, suggested they were heterosexual. In "The Curse of Fenric" (1988), for example, the Doctor is surprised when Ace tells him she's "not a little girl" and proposes to use her sexuality to distract a guard. Davies' insistence on including gay characters was, of course, partly determined by the fact that he is gay, but also as a perfectly logical extension of the Doctor's, and the programme's, championing of individual freedom against oppression and prejudice. At a press launch for the 2005 series, a journalist from the gutter tabloid *The Daily Star* asked if the new series would be camper than the original. Davies replied that he thought the journalist was being very rude, that he was only asking that question because he knew he was gay, and that he could fuck off. The Doctor's sexuality, such as it was, had been identified as heterosexual (in keeping with Paul McGann's revelatory kissing of Grace in the 1996 TV movie), and the main companion was traditionally attractive, female and heterosexual, but Davies did introduce an "omnisexual" companion in Captain Jack Harkness. Jack is from the fifty third century and Davies reasoned that, by that point, interest in people's sexual orientation would no longer be of interest. In his spin-off series *Torchwood*, Jack criticises twenty first century human characters for their narrow distinctions in sexual matters and pursues vigorous liaisons with male and females. In a very touching scene in "The Parting of the Ways" (2005), Jack kisses Rose and then the Doctor in exactly the same way to say goodbye before he goes to face his death by the Daleks.

Times had changed. In the early 1990s, fans of *Star Trek: the Next Generation* had petitioned Gene Roddenberry to include a gay couple on the bridge of the Enterprise. Like Davies, Roddenberry reasoned that humanity would have transcended arguments over sexual orientation in the future: unlike Davies, he used this as a reason not to include homosexual characters. This was a cop out: Roddenberry had ignored the southern Bible belt's objection to a black character on the bridge in the person of Lieutenant Uhura, but he would not champion a gay one.

## "Rose": season ~~twenty-seven~~ one

"Rose" debuted on BBC 1 at 7.00 p.m. on 26th March 2005. The new series was shot in widescreen on video, and then "filmised" to give it a look indistinguishable from film. It was an immediate critical and popular success: 10.8 million people tuned in. There was a technical problem when sound from Graham Norton's new show *Strictly Dance Fever* bled over the sequence where Rose explores the department store's cellars and the Autons come slowly to life behind her, although some viewers assumed this was part of the soundtrack. Finding that the episode under-ran, the production team decided to feature a "Next Time" trailer for "The End of the World". This featured Cassandra, a creature Davies had conceived when watching the Oscar ceremony's parade of women who had had so many facelifts that they could barely speak. Cassandra has had several hundred slimming operations and was now a stretched piece of skin bolted to a metal frame. Rose calls her a "bitchy trampoline". *The Guardian*'s television critic, new to *Doctor Who*, was enthusiastic and wrote, "I'm damned if I'm going to miss that."

Nearly eleven million viewers was an outstanding achievement in the fragmented age of multi-channel television and the BBC was delighted. It was perhaps inevitable that the second episode dropped two million viewers: after all, people had tuned in to see what the new Doctor, and the new series, was like, and a pattern of falling off in viewers for episode two had been common in the 1970s. Some fickle commentators, including Richard Ingrams in *The Observer*, crowed. Davies had said that he absolutely hoped the new series would work and that a second would be commissioned on the basis of strong viewing figures: a system which, he said, he absolutely supported. He also said that, privately, there was a little voice in his head which whispered "four million", and he had prepared a defence to say that public service broadcasting didn't necessarily have to mean high viewing figures, that the BBC's duty was to serve the public, and so on. It was the BBC's status as a public service broadcaster which had ensured the longevity of the original run: the BBC stuck with the series through troughs of poor viewing figures – at least, before Michael Grade arrived – in, for example, Tom Baker's final season, because it believed in serving a significant section of the public. Contrast Paramount's treatment of the *Star Trek* franchise, the world's second longest running science fiction brand, where various incarnations of the series were axed when their viewing figures dipped. It is highly unlikely that *Doctor Who* would have lasted even to the end of the 1960s if it had been made by commercial television.

## Gone after only one season

Davies and the production team were delighted; the fans were thrilled; the BBC confirmed that there would be a second series before "The End of the World" was broadcast. It was at this press conference that the show came off the rails for the first time after the wrangling over the rights to the Daleks. The BBC bungled a question about whether Eccleston would be returning for the second series. In fact, fans had had their suspicions since his appearance on a special *Doctor Who* themed edition of the BBC's quiz show *Mastermind.* John Humphrys, the show's host, asked if he could call Eccleston "Doctor Who" and the actor replied, "You can for now"; he had said "I can't answer that" when asked if he would return for a second series on BBC News. Eccleston had been offered a second season during the filming of the season's final story "Bad Wolf"/"The Parting of the Ways", but had said he wanted to leave. Nick Briggs, who supplied the Dalek voices, prepared to make the Daleks say, "Christopher Eccleston has filmed his last scene on *Doctor Who*. He will now be exterminated!" on the actor's last day on set, but forgot to perform the joke in the pressures of the studio day.

Thus, when the new series was only two episodes old, the audience learnt that the new Doctor would be gone before they had a chance to get used to him. The press ran some silly stories about crisis in the new series, coupling the reduction in viewing figures with the news of Eccleston's departure; fans reacted grumpily and blamed him for harming the prospects of the fledgling series. The BBC quickly steadied the boat and announced that David Tennant would be the new Doctor in series two and in a Christmas special for 2005. Again, some fans had picked up the intimations of Tennant's casting, noting that he had provided the voice-over for the documentary "The Story of *Doctor Who*", screened on BBC 1 before "Rose" was broadcast.

It wasn't entirely clear at the time why Christopher Eccleston had left after only one season, but it was reported then that he saw the part, and the intensive shoot, as a similar challenge to *Our Friends in the North* (1996) or a one year run of a stage play. The BBC put out a statement, without consulting him, that he had feared being typecast, and then withdrew it with an apology. More details trickled out over the years. Eccleston suggested that he had been unhappy with how some of the crew had been treated on the set. In 2011, he added that he had left the show because he couldn't get along with the senior people, didn't agree with the way things were being run or with the culture that had grown up around the series. He left, he said, over a principle[1].

Eccleston returned to the subject in March 2018. Why hadn't he spoken out before? the *Radio Times* asked. Because, said Eccleston, he had made an agreement with Russell T Davies in 2005 not to say anything that would damage the show, so he "didn't criticise anybody". Perhaps he felt, thirteen years on, that he could break his silence. Eccleston said the BBC had mishandled his resignation

---

[1]    https://www.theguardian.com/tv-and-radio/tvandradioblog/2011/jul/21/doctor-who-christopher-eccleston

(which was certainly true) and that "What happened around *Doctor Who* almost destroyed my career." He said he had been blacklisted by the BBC at the time and his agent had advised him to go to America, where he made a series of duff films which were as much fun, he said, as cutting his throat every day. He had found making *Doctor Who* an unhappy experience even when shooting the first batch of episodes, and he blamed himself: he didn't feel comfortable playing a lighter role[1] (it must be said that Eccleston tended to appear in gritty dramas, hence the general surprise when he was cast as the Doctor) and he was out of his comfort zone. Billie Piper, he said, was brilliant but very, very nervous and inexperienced and "then you had me"[2]. He was carrying around his own insecurities while making *Doctor Who* as it was something he had never done before[3].

In his *Radio Times* interview of March 2018, Eccleston went further. He said that his relationship with his three immediate superiors – the showrunner, the producer and the co-producer – broke down in the first block of filming and never recovered. He would never again have a working relationship with Russell T Davies.

Eccleston, to his credit, stuck to his agreement to say nothing for years. He appears to be a man who guards his own privacy and that of others: spilling the beans on the backstage tensions would have involved some violation of other people's private lives and behaviour. Even the revelations of March 2018 lacked salacious detail. Fans were often cross with him, but Eccleston is clearly a decent man. He was always courteous when he played the Doctor,

---

[1]    http://www.radiotimes.com/news/tv/2018-03-19/doctor-who-christopher-eccleston-russell-t-davies/

[2]    ibid

[3]    https://www.theguardian.com/culture/2018/mar/11/christopher-eccleston-macbeths-very-insecure-about-his-masculinity-i-am-most-men-are    Eccleston was interviewed about his role as Macbeth for the Royal Shakespeare Company's 2018 production in Stratford upon Avon.

revealing how carefully he had researched the show in his interviews for BBC 3's *Doctor Who Confidential*. He thought carefully about returning for the fiftieth anniversary special "The Day of the Doctor" and had friendly discussions with Steven Moffat. If he had had found making *Doctor Who* a miserable experience, it is no wonder he didn't want to go back. Long after he had left the series, he agreed to a fan's request to help him propose to his girlfriend in a restaurant: there is a lovely video of Eccleston telling the lady concerned that he has parked the TARDIS round the back and was here to help her boyfriend propose. It was disappointing that he left after only one season, but he had been unhappy and how many of us are obliged to stick at a job that makes us miserable if we have a chance of moving on?

Back in 2005, people wrote letters of complaint to the papers; the director Joe Ahearne wrote to *The Guardian* in the actor's defence, ironically asking how Eccleston dared leave a programme after one year of giving such a committed performance to return to other work, and working on the show with such courtesy and patience.

Eccleston's performance as the Doctor was certainly radically different from his predecessors'. His was a darker Doctor even than Sylvester McCoy's, bearing the burden of survival guilt as the last of the Time Lords and spitting with rage at the Dalek in Van Statton's cell. Some of the humour didn't always sit easily with his portrayal and some cast members – like Camille Coduri – while praising Eccleston's performance, hinted in 2005 that David Tennant would much more in keeping with the public's traditional conception of the Doctor.

It is, however, clear that securing the services of such a respected actor as Christopher Eccleston was a major reason for the audience to take the new series seriously, even if he wasn't necessarily everyone's idea of what the Doctor should be. Eccleston had helped to get the new series made and renewed for a second season. Some fans couldn't forgive him for not being a fan of the show, unlike David Tennant, for declining requests for interviews about his time as the Doctor and for saying, when asked if he would return, "No.

Never bathe in the same river twice." But we now had a tenth Doctor and it was time to move on.

## A wanderer in space and time

Davies had changed much of the back story for the Doctor. He argued that viewers knew too much about him and there were too many proper nouns: he was a Time Lord, a member of the Prydonian Chapter, a renegade... It was time to sweep away the complications and return, in many ways, to the simplicity of the character as originally played by William Hartnell. The Doctor would again be a solitary wanderer in time and space. The Time Lords were no more. As the season unfolded, we learnt they had been destroyed in the Time War against the Daleks: the Doctor had destroyed both races to bring it to an end. These were all unseen events which presumably took place in the gap between the TV movie and "Rose" and had, we imagined, caused the Eighth Doctor to regenerate. The ninth Doctor seems to be a new regeneration ("Not too bad. Look at the ears!") and post regeneration trauma – established in "Robot" (1974-5), Tom Baker's first story – might combine with survivor guilt to produce his erratic behaviour. "Not made of plastic are you?" he asks Rose, tapping her on the forehead. "No. Bone head. Bye then." Davies had determined back in his Granada Television days that the Doctor's costume should be modern: in 1996, he had asked a senior colleague what he had thought of the TV movie. "Too much fancy dress", was the reply, and Davies agreed. The ninth Doctor was therefore scripted as wearing jeans, a sweater and a leather jacket. The Edwardian or eccentric outfits of his predecessors were no more nor, much to the fans' relief, was the silly question mark motif which had featured on all the Nathan-Turner Doctors' costumes. Reading Davies's outline for the season, Lorraine Heggessey worried that the end of the Time Lords would mean no return for the Master. She needn't have worried: Davies had worked out how he could be resurrected and the Master returned for the last three episodes of season three.

Mark Gatiss, the writer of the third episode "The Unquiet Dead", said that the revived series was much more like *Doctor Who* than *Doctor Who* had been at the end of its original run. This was true: garbled story telling was gone, the Doctor was no longer half human, the Cartmel master plan, thank goodness, was ignored. Part of the explanation for the clarity of storytelling lay in the experienced Davies' overall control of the series as chief showrunner: all the scripts were polished by him to fit in with the house style and the season's overall arc. Seventies script editor Terrance Dicks laughed when he was asked if he would like to write for the new series: "What, and do eight drafts?" Shearman's "Dalek" (2005) had reached eight.

As the programme returned, so did much of its cultural legacy – and even baggage. In its initial research for the relaunch, the BBC had found that adults thought it an old show and children thought of it as their parents' show, making them unlikely to watch it. Pre-broadcast, specially shot trailers, pitched *Doctor Who* as a new series, sometimes from Rose's point of view: "I've got a choice. Stay at home with my mum, my boyfriend, my job, or chuck it all in for danger, and monsters, and life or death…" she said, standing next to a silent Doctor and giving viewers their first glance at the new TARDIS interior. Eccleston recorded a special trailer which featured him racing away down a corridor from an approaching fireball and directly inviting the viewers to join him on his travels. The Eccleston trailer laid fans' fears about special effects to rest, featuring the movie standard footage of the Slitheen's spaceship slicing through Big Ben and crashing into the Thames. Rather sweetly, it also recalled Peter Cushing's gentle trailer for the 1965 movie *Dr Who and the Daleks*: "Come with us into that strange new world. I cannot guarantee your safety, but I can promise you unimagined thrills." These specially shot trailers – or special scenes – were hallmarks for all of the new series Doctors.

**Family viewing**

The BBC's pre-broadcast research proved erroneous. Parents who had enjoyed the series as children watched it with their children. The concept of families watching a programme together on a Saturday night returned: *Doctor Who* was one of the few programmes which appealed to all ages. The BBC had assumed that family viewing was dead: to their surprise and pleasure, *Doctor Who* brought it back and the corporation celebrated their clean sweep in the Saturday night ratings. *Doctor Who* was a hit and so was *Strictly Dance Fever*. The latter evolved into the top rated show *Strictly Come Dancing* in 2006, *Doctor Who* was renewed and the BBC commissioned *Robin Hood* and later *Merlin* as family-friendly replacements for when the programme was off the air. All were strong ratings winners for Saturday nights. The perennial taunt that fans had endured for the programme's original run – that *Doctor Who* is a children's programme – was silenced by the new series' inflection as family viewing. Adults appreciated the subtext of some witty dialogue; children (and adults) enjoyed the monsters, which Davies, preparing the series, had insisted should always be simple enough for children to draw. As an example of subtext: the Prime Minister in "World War Three" announces that the Slitheen's mother ship contains "massive weapons of destruction – capable of being launched in forty five seconds". This was a reference to the US Republican and British Labour governments' claim that Saddam Hussein's troops could launch weapons of mass destruction in forty five seconds, used as a justification for the Iraq War in 2003. In "World War Three", The Doctor wonders if the people will believe a lie. "Why not? They did last time," says Rose.

Is *Doctor Who* for children, for adults, or for everyone? In 2012, Steven Moffat said that if you enjoy the programme, it's for you. Perhaps it is part of the British sensibility to be dismissive of science fiction. Like satire, it has never been seen as a respectable genre in the minds of sophisticates or of some sections of the general public, and dismissing *Doctor Who* as a children's programme, even in its more sophisticated incarnations, is a way of keeping an unrespectable genre in its place. Perhaps the British sensibility is inclined to cynicism, irony, a refusal to take things seriously and a fear of being too enthusiastic: by contrast, the American audiences of *Star Trek* in the 1960s never saw it as a children's programme, in spite of some of the merchandising. I had a mighty fine Captain Kirk's Space Communicator set, based on the old children's toy of two yoghurt pots linked by a string: two blue plastic globs replaced the yoghurt pots and it looked nothing like the series' communicators.

## Let's not be beastly to Daleks

Another part of *Doctor Who*'s heritage was its capacity to disturb and terrify children, at least according to the newspapers. Fans gleefully rejoiced at reports that "The Unquiet Dead" had prompted dozens of concerned parents to complain to the BBC because it was too frightening. *The Times* reported viewers' concern about a sequence in the pre-credits teaser in which a dead grandmother's hand shoots out of a coffin and strangles her grandson. I was watching this with my small daughter, not yet three, who burst out laughing. Gatiss skilfully doused down the terror in any case with undertaker Mr Snead's comic attempts to jam the coffin down on the old lady ("Gwyneth! Get down here! We've got another one!") and any horror is of the *Carry On Screaming* variety ("The stiffs are getting lively again!"). The BBC rather fumbled its response to the concerned parents, perhaps because it had been a long time since it had handled such complaints about *Doctor Who*. It said at first that the programme shouldn't be watched by under-eights and then said it should. Fans recalled David Coleman fronting the BBC viewers' response programme *Points of View* in 1967: parents had written in to complain about "horrific" sequences in "The Tomb of the Cybermen" and Coleman cheerily introduced the item by presciently asking, "Is *Doctor Who* too frightening for children? Or should that be, is *Doctor Who* too frightening for adults?"

Matters came to a head with the release of season one/twenty seven on DVD. The British Board of Film Classification took exception to scenes in which the Doctor "tortures" a Dalek ("Dalek" (2005)). However cross one might be with a Dalek, the BBFC opined, torturing it is no way to behave; children's identification with the Doctor might lead them to imitate him; the DVD must not be supplied to anyone under the age of twelve. In a display of how quickly the new *Doctor Who* had become part of mainstream British culture, *The Times* took up all of its third page to run the story. In its leading article of 16th May 2005, "Let's not be beastly to Daleks"[1], *The Times* quite rightly ridiculed the BBFC's decision and wondered if a creature intent on exterminating all mankind might not deserve a taste of its own medicine. Championing the series as a piece of serious children's fiction on a par with Harry Potter and Roald Dahl, *The Times* concluded that the message of *Doctor Who* was that sometimes violence was necessary to defeat evil, and good could only triumph if it asserted itself. This had always been the theme of the original series: that is was clearly the theme of the revival was reassuring and proof that the theme was as vital now as it had ever been.

---

[1] A reference to Noel Coward's satirical post Second World War song, "Don't let's be beastly to the Germans".

# 15
# Christmas Time – Sycorax and Wine

What should we call Christopher Eccleston's season? "The Christopher Eccleston months", some wag suggested. BBC documentation and DVD releases treated the revived *Doctor Who* as an entirely new series and went with "series one". American writer Harlan Ellison, growled that it was the twenty seventh season, so it should be called the twenty seventh season. Steven Moffat complicated things further when BBC documentation referred to Matt Smith's first series as "series one". He explained to pedantic fans that no-one talked about season eight, they talked about Pertwee's second season, which was why he'd opted for the new naming: we could then talk about Matt Smith's second season and so on. The DVD range stuck with "series five", however.

It appears that David Tennant had been cast as the Doctor before Christopher Eccleston's season had even aired. Tennant had played the lead in Russell T Davies's *Casanova* (2005) on BBC3. Davies asked him if he would like to play the Doctor almost at the same time; Tennant was incredulous and laughed heartily. He was a fan of the programme and, as a child, had queued to get Tom Baker's autograph when the actor had visited Scotland. Tennant had been inspired to become an actor because of his love of the show and had a successful career in television and theatre, not least with the Royal Shakespeare Company. Davies said he understood Tennant's reaction as it was too much to take in; he left him to think it over. Like Peter Davison before him, Tennant partly took the part because he couldn't bear the idea of someone else doing it when he'd been offered it. He also eventually came to terms with the idea that it was fine for a fan to play the Doctor.

Russell T Davies suggested to Tennant that he should change his native Paisley accent; Tennant said this was fine, as he spent half his life speaking with an English accent anyway. Davies was anxious to avoid what he called "a tour of the regions" after Eccleston's northern accent, which had caused some controversy amongst some unimaginative people who reasoned that Time Lord was a lord and should therefore have an educated southern English, or Received Pronunciation, accent. Davies wrote the issue of the accent into "Rose" (2005), when our eponymous heroine asks him, "If you're an alien, how come you sound like you're from the north?" "Lots of planets have a north," the Doctor huffs. In "World War Three" (2005), Harriet Jones (MP for Flydale North) makes the same comment when told the Doctor is alien and Rose, showing how she has accepted the Doctor and his accent, repeats his earlier explanation: "Lots of planets have a north". The tenth Doctor adopts a mild East London accent, which cut dialogue from "The Christmas Invasion" (2005) indicated was imprinted on him by his contact with Rose. Matt Smith spoke in the Received Pronunciation accent we are used to from most of the original series' Doctors; Peter Capaldi kept with his Scottish accent and Jodie Whittaker uses her native Yorkshire accent.

Tennant's debut was in the 2005 Christmas special, another first for the revived show. Commissioning an hour-long special was an early mark of confidence from the BBC in the new series. Fans hoped for, and got, a Christmas Day slot, and the Christmas special has been a fixture of the new series ever since. There had been one Christmas episode in 1965 entitled "The Feast of Steven" after the companion played by Peter Purves. This was the seventh instalment of the twelve episode epic "The Daleks' Master Plan" but, as it contained neither Daleks nor much of the surrounding plot line, is effectively a separate story. It is basically a good-natured romp in which the TARDIS lands in a 1920s Hollywood studio, where the crew are chased by Keystone Cop-a-likes, and the Doctor is investigated by 1960s police in Liverpool. Director Douglas Camfield had hoped to persuade the actors of the popular Liverpool-based police series *Z-Cars* (1962-1978) to play the policemen, but they refused. The Doctor produces champagne for Steven and Sara, who was to be aged to death in episode twelve, and Hartnell then wishes the viewers at home a very happy Christmas. Donald Tosh, the story editor, was apparently furious, saying Bill deserved to be shot as the line wasn't in the script but was just something he'd thought up. Another version of the story is that the line was actually scripted but this breaking of the fourth wall, the riff on *Z Cars* and the pause in the science fiction Dalek adventure, all failed to find favour with the public: audience research suggested they hated the episode. "The Feast of Steven" was the only Hartnell episode not to be telerecorded, and "The Daleks' Master Plan" was presumably sold abroad without it. Without being able to see it, it's hard to judge how good – or bad – it is.

The first Christmas special of the new series, "The Christmas Invasion" (2005), was well received by ten million viewers. Davies was enthusiastic about Christmas specials, saying that he loved seeing familiar characters surrounded by tinsel, presents and Christmas cheer; he intended to bring this all to *Doctor Who* and the subsequent Christmas specials to date have all been set at Christmas time. Davies said he had thought of the title – "The Christmas Invasion" – even before he started writing it.

In the same way that Sarah Jane bridged the transition between the third and fourth Doctors, and so helped viewers accept Tom Baker after five years of Jon Pertwee, so Rose stayed on into a second season to help viewers accept David Tennant: a crucial decision as the programme had only been on the air for three months and a new Doctor was being introduced far too early into its run. "The Christmas Invasion" focuses its first half on the familiar characters of Rose, Jackie and Mickie. The Doctor is in a troubled sleep or coma and looked after by Jackie and Rose, who put him to bed in the pyjamas he wears for the rest of the story. Rose tells her mother about his two hearts; Jackie asks, "He hasn't got two of anything else, has he?" When it looks as though the regeneration is failing, the Doctor is restored to health by the scent of the tea dripping from Jackie's thermos. Rose had greeted her mother's insistence on bringing tea on board the TARDIS by sarcastically saying, "The answer to everything": a good piece of dramatic irony, because of course, it is.

It's a brave decision to keep Tennant in the background for so much of the story, with the result that, when he does appear on the Sycorax ship, his entrance is all the more dramatic, and Rose's – and the viewers – sense that all is going to end well, is heightened.

As with so much of the original series, "The Christmas Invasion" takes ordinary objects and makes them strange or sinister. Rose and Mickey are wary of a band of masked Santa Claus (Clauses?) playing Christmas carols on their brass instruments in a very Salvation Army fashion. The Santas duly turn their tubas towards the pair and fire them as flame throwers. Jackie's Christmas tree starts to spin and advance towards her, its separate sections apparently razor sharp: whereas the Santas are sinister, the Christmas tree is great fun and entirely in tone with a Christmas special. Both Santas and tree reappear in the following special, "The Runaway Bride" (2006), with some surprises: the Santa abducting Donna (Catherine Tate) is seen to be a robot under the Father Christmas mask, and the tree at her wedding reception launches its baubles to burst as small grenades amongst her wedding guests.

Davies kept the plot of "The Christmas Invasion" simple, reasoning that people didn't want to be taxed after Christmas dinner and too much booze. The Sycorax are scavengers who want to abduct humans. Davies named them after Caliban's mother in Shakespeare's play *The Tempest*. He remembered studying *Antony and Cleopatra* at school and being pleased with Cleopatra's line, "Give me to drink Mandragora" as it reminded him of the 1976 Tom Baker story "The Masque of Mandragora". He wanted to prepare a surprise for school based *Doctor Who* fans reading *The Tempest*, then a standard text for Key Stage Three students (aged 13) in England, Scotland and Wales. The other Christmas present buried in the script is the names of the two children suffering from the Sycorax's massed hypnotism, blood control; they were named after Davies' niece and nephew and he said this was a Christmas present to them.

Having recovered, the newly regenerated Doctor asks Rose if he is ginger; he hasn't yet seen his reflection.  Told he has brown hair, he is bitterly disappointed and says how much he wanted to be ginger. Is this a reference to Billie Piper's former husband, DJ Chris Evans, a famous ginger celebrity with whom she remained close friends? The eleventh Doctor (Matt Smith) similarly pulls down a lock of hair for inspection and murmurs, "Still not ginger". This line provoked complaints from some viewers as being anti-ginger, and one correspondent asked why didn't the BBC realise this ridicule of ginger haired people would only reinforce the teasing experienced by some ginger children at school? The BBC sent a soothing reply saying no offence had been intended. The complainants obviously hadn't remembered "The Christmas Invasion" or noted that Donna was a redhead (and so was Amy, but she hadn't appeared yet), and that it was absurd to accuse the programme of redheadphobia.

Davies makes intelligent use of the Christmas dinner, a staple of all Christmas drama specials, to show the differences between the tenth Doctor and the ninth. Invited by Rose and Jackie to supper, the ninth Doctor tells her "I don't do that" and waxes lyrical about visiting some fantastic galactic phenomena instead. The tenth Doctor is clearly more sociable than the ninth, and has moved away from his survivor guilt to interacting comfortably among humans. He also doesn't appear to be quite so anti-social and rude. Eccleston, like Colin Baker, had been somewhat unapproachable and spiky; Tennant was warm, funny, reassuring and – particularly according to his legions of female fans – extremely handsome and sexy[1].

The episode ends with another traditional Christmas special image – snowfall, although this has the alarming cause of being the fallout from the destroyed Sycorax ship. Similiarly alarming, and not the usual staple of Christmas drama, are the UNIT personnel reduced to smoking piles of bones by the Sycorax leader's whip ("Oi," says the new Doctor, "You could have someone's eye out with that.") The

---

[1] I arranged a school trip for A level students to see Tennant as Hamlet at the RSC in 2009: the scramble for tickets amongst female students was, for some reason, phenomenal. I had never seen anything like it since a similar rush for tickets for Jude Law playing Dr Faustus at the theatre a few years earlier.

Doctor loses his hand in a broadsword fight with the Sycorax leader, only to grow a new one from his residual regeneration energy. "Witchcraft," breathes the Sycorax leader, aghast. "Time Lord," the Doctor corrects. His severed hand falls down to London below, where it is eventually picked up by Jack Harkness and preserved on his desk in the spin-off series *Torchwood*. Jack eventually reunites it with the Doctor, who siphons off more regeneration energy into it in "The Stolen Earth"/"Journey's End" (2008); it eventually grows into a human clone of the Doctor, which comes in handy for defeating the Daleks. In "The Christmas Invasion", The Doctor saves the day with a satsuma – always, he remarks, left over at the end of Christmas – which he bungs at a control button: the Sycorax ship's wings retract and the Sycorax leader falls to his death. The "next time" trailer was a montage of clips from the new season and a cause of great excitement for viewers. We got our first look at the cat people and the redesigned Cybermen. Cheers abounded through the land when the last clip at the end of "The Runaway Bride" was of the black Dalek Sec, proving that the Daleks would indeed be back in series three. Or twenty nine.

### Donna

The 2006 Christmas special was "The Runaway Bride". It opened with the sudden materialisation of Donna in the TARDIS reprised from the last moments of "Doomsday" (2006) which temporarily startles the Doctor out of grieving for Rose. Having Catherine Tate as Donna was a serious piece of star guest casting arguably only topped by securing Kylie Minogue as Astrid for the 2007 Christmas special. Catherine Tate had her own series on BBC2; Davies thought it possible she wouldn't want to be in *Doctor Who*, but she was enthusiastic. At the press launch for "The Runaway Bride", Catherine Tate was asked if she would like to return as a regular companion – she elects to return to her family at the end of the special – and she said, "I'd love to, but no-one has asked me." Davies did ask her when Martha left and Tate joined the cast for the fourth (or thirtieth) season. She slightly toned her performance down for her regular role, thus silencing some critics who'd found her too raucous in "The Runaway Bride". Donna, it seems, has regretted her decision not to go with the Doctor and has been looking for him ever since. She eventually runs into him while they separately investigate Adipose Industries in "Partners in Crime" (2008) and slightly alarms him by revealing the cases she keeps in her car, including a hatbox, fully packed for climbing aboard the TARDIS. Catherine Tate's performance as Donna was widely praised by viewers and she was celebrated as a mature woman, rather than a young woman, aboard the TARDIS. Tate joked that being buxom made the endless running scenes a bit uncomfortable and it was all right for David Tennant because he didn't have breasts. Being busty had apparently been seen as a problem with the first actress to be cast as Sarah Jane Smith, who had been paid off after a few rehearsals, although this might have been attributable to Jon Pertwee's failure to gel with her.

Again, Davies opted for a simple plot for the second Christmas special. The Racnoss, a giant spider-humanoid creature, is attempting to awaken its young, imprisoned at the Earth's core since the dawn of time. Neil Gorton, whose firm Millennium FX made most of the physically realised monsters for the new series, assumed that the Racnoss would be CGI and was surprised when the production team instead elected for a prop, into which an actress could be fitted. The Racnoss prop was so huge that it couldn't be assembled in the workshop and had to be put together for the first time on location. Sarah Parrish played her, standing in the front section of the fifteen-foot-diameter spider; she understandably found filming somewhat uncomfortable and cut the inside of her lip on her prosthetic teeth. Although the Racnoss prop was brilliantly designed and could lurch up and down, it couldn't walk or scuttle, which disappointingly – or mercifully – robbed it of some of the alarm factor of a real spider. The Racnoss's children climb towards her out of the pipe that leads to the Earth's core. We never see them as the budget wouldn't run to that, but the Doctor drains the Thames into the pipe, thus flushing them down the plughole, and the Racnoss herself is killed. Donna is alarmed at the Doctor's callousness in dispatching so many, and the Racnoss's shrieks of distress are genuinely affecting. Later, Donna tells the Doctor that he mustn't travel on his own: "You need someone to stop you." This sets up an intelligent theme of the revived series, that the Doctor needs the company of human beings to civilise him and to remind him of his conscience. The human cloned Doctor in "Journey's End" (2008) has had no such contact with human beings and little conscience; the tenth Doctor tells Rose that he is effectively like the ninth Doctor we met in "Rose" (2005), traumatised and almost amoral after the terrifying slaughter of the Time War. It is the cloned Doctor who kills all the Daleks in "Journey's End". This is very convenient as then our peace-loving Time Lord Doctor then doesn't have to, thus proving Davros's point that he never has to carry a weapon because others do his slaughter for him.

In "The Angels Take Manhattan" (2012), Matt Smith's Doctor asks River Song to travel with him after the loss of Amy and Rory, knowing that he shouldn't be on his own. River, presumably hyperbolically, says that one psychopath per TARDIS is enough. The eleventh Doctor responds by withdrawing into a depression or sulk in Victorian England, refusing to become involved in saving the world until he encounters Clara (Jenna-Louise Coleman) and the Snowmen ("The Snowmen" (2012)).

**Kylie's Voyage**

Kylie Minogue was the guest star in "Voyage of the Damned", the 2007 Christmas special. Perhaps remembering the tendency for ITV and the BBC to show blockbuster movies over Christmas when he was a child – with James Bond films and *Towering Inferno* (1974) particular seasonal favourites – Russell T Davies opted to merge the disaster movie with *Doctor Who*. The result is a version of *The Poseidon Adventure* (1972), with the Titanic now a space liner controlled by a creep called Max Capricorn, who swivels Davros-like in his wheelchair and intends to crash the ship into Earth to bankrupt the travel company that has betrayed him. Securing the services of Kylie Minogue was another coup for the show; as an international star, Davies hoped that people around the world who had never heard of *Doctor Who*, but who loved Kylie, would tune in, and it seems that this is indeed what happened. Thirteen million viewers watched in the UK, making this the highest rated episode of the revived series to date[1]. Kylie Minogue played Astrid, a waitress aboard the Titanic who wants to see the Universe and is set up as the replacement companion for Martha. She dies disposing of Max Capricorn, which is a good thing as Kylie couldn't make the filming dates for the thirtieth season. Fans quickly noticed that "Astrid" is an anagram of "TARDIS" and speculated that Kylie would play the TARDIS in human form: they had to wait until Neil Gaiman's "The Doctor's Wife" (2011).

"Voyage of the Damned" is visually exciting but pretty thin on plot. There are some good ideas. Series regular Jimmy Vee plays a cyborg called Bannakaffalatta; Davies draws some parallels between the emergence of homosexual equality in the twentieth century and rights for cyborgs in this story. The Titanic's guests are served by robot Angels called the (Heavenly) Host, which some Christian viewers might find slightly profane, but the revived series under Davies often got in some jolly digs at Christianity. Davies had pretended to be cross with Steven Moffat for including angels in his script for "Blink" in the previous season, since Davies wanted to use them in "Voyage of the Damned", but it is the Weeping Angels that are remembered from the two sets of angels in 2007. There were some complaints from families of survivors of the real Titanic disaster, presumably stirred up by the press, who said it was wrong to create entertainment out of a terrible tragedy. The BBC pointed out that the Titanic in the story was a spaceship and not the original. Clive Swift played Mr Copper, a tour guide to Earth who is woefully informed about his subject; he was interviewed by *Doctor Who Magazine* about the series and television viewers in general, was very rude to his interviewer, Benjamin Cook, and the magazine

---

[1] September 2018.

printed most of the interview in full. The Doctor manages to stop the Titanic from crashing into Buckingham Palace and the Queen appears for the first time since "Silver Nemesis" (1988); she waves and thanks the Doctor for saving the day.

Bernard Cribbins has a cameo role as a newspaper seller, originally called Stan, in "Voyage of the Damned". He reappeared as Donna's grandfather Wilf in the 2008 season and in Tennant's final two episodes. Wilf's role in the season was originally to have been taken by Howard Attfield, Donna's father Geoff in "The Runaway Bride". Howard Attfield managed to shoot a few scenes with Catherine Tate – included as extras on the series four DVD box set – but sadly passed away from cancer. As Bernard Cribbins' newspaper seller had never been named on screen, the production team was able to rename him as Wilf and insert him into Donna's household as her grandfather. Bernard Cribbins's witty and realistic performance, and Davies's scripting, made Wilf one of the most popular characters of the Tennant years.

Great fun and froth though the specials were, Davies made brilliant use of them in "Turn Left" (2008). This was a "Doctor lite" episode focusing on Donna; the production schedule required two of its episodes to be made at once for the Tennant seasons and in 2008, the Doctor hardly appears in "Turn Left" and Donna hardly appears in "Midnight". "Turn Left" begins with an alien returning Donna to the time immediately before she met the Doctor. Instead of turning her car right and taking a job where she will eventually encounter him, she turns left, gets another job and they never meet. The events of the revived series unravel. Donna was never with the Doctor when he destroyed the Racnoss, so he is killed before he can escape the deluge and the inferno. As there is no Doctor aboard the Titanic spaceship, it crashes into Buckingham Palace in a nuclear explosion which kills millions and pollutes the whole of southern England. France and other countries close their borders and refuse to accept any more refugees; Donna and her family are sent to hugely overcrowded digs in Leeds. In the poverty and unemployment, resentments build and an Italian family living with Donna are taken away to "resettlement camps". Wilf, Donna's grandfather (Bernard Cribbins), is near tears: "That's what they called them last time". Establishing concentration camps in England is worlds away from the cheery Christmas specials and shows how wildly the tone of the series can vary: the crazy plunge from glee to horror and darkness covers the whole gamut of human emotion, thus deeply embedding a fantasy/science fiction show into the viewer's consciousness.

## More Specials

The 2008 Christmas special is "The Next Doctor", arguably the least successful of the eight. It is effectively two stories. In the first, the Cybermen stomp around Victorian London and wire a lady called Mercy (Dervla Kirwan) into the Cyberking, a giant robotic cybership along the lines of the AT-ATs, the walking ships in *Star Wars*. In the second, much more successful, part of the story, David Morrissey played Jackson, a man who believes he is the Doctor after being imprinted with Cybermen data technology. The tenth Doctor is fooled for a while, believing Jackson to be a future regeneration suffering from post-regenerative trauma. Jackson eventually recalls his real identity and the Doctor deals with the Cybermen.

It was at this point in the revived series that some felt Davies was both losing his way and his ability to distinguish between a good idea and a terrible one. "The Next Doctor" played on the press and public's obsession with the casting of the leading man in the series. David Tennant noted that, as soon as he arrived, journalists were asking him how long he would be staying; once he had left, they asked him when he would be coming back. The press and fans' unease about a new Doctor was presumably a manifestation of the insecurity felt at Eccleston's departure after only one year; perhaps it went back to the TV movie, when Paul McGann only made one story. David Tennant had now been in the part for three years and was taking a break in 2009 to play Hamlet at the Royal Shakespeare Company. Instead of a regular series, there would be five specials in 2009-10. There was much speculation about a change of Doctor and

"The Next Doctor" teased us that David Morrissey would be the eleventh. Asked if this was true on breakfast television, Morrissey gave an evasive reply. By the end of the episode, we knew that Tennant would be back.

The special also highlighted the production team's, and Russell T Davies's, love of spectacular visuals which, by this point of the series, weren't always accompanied by explanations in the script. We have some pretty visuals of Victorian orphans in a Cyberman workshop (or workhouse) straight out of *Oliver!* (film, 1968). The Cyberking stomping over London closely resembles the giant gingerbread man menacing the castle in *Shrek 2* (2004). Steven Moffat wisely pressed the reset button when he became showrunner in 2010, wiping out many events from Davies's time including – thank goodness – the Cyberking.

David Tennant had appeared in the BBC's *Who Do You Think You Are?* in 2008, a series which invites celebrities to investigate their family tree. At one point, Tennant held up a skull, which prompted Royal Shakespeare Company director Gregory Doran to think he would be a great Hamlet. Tennant would play the Dane for a long run in 2009. The first fans got to know about this was when the RSC released advanced publicity for its new season. If Tennant was in *Hamlet*, he couldn't also do *Doctor Who*. With echoes of its fumbling over the announcement that Eccleston was leaving, the BBC belatedly explained that, as Tennant was otherwise engaged, there wouldn't be a full season of *Doctor Who* in 2009 but some lovely specials instead to keep us all happy. It felt a bit like the 1985 cancellation/hiatus to fans who were old in the tooth. Some asked why, if Tennant were otherwise engaged, didn't they just recast the Doctor? Rumours filtered through that the production team needed a rest to rethink the show. This was one of the reasons given by the BBC when the show was cancelled, then rested, in 1985, and fans were unhappy. The fact the rest and rethinking story was just a rumour was confirmed when we learnt that a new production team, headed by Steven Moffat as showrunner, would take over for 2010. In late 2009, David Tennant announced he was leaving the series live on television from the interval of a performance as Hamlet at the Royal Shakespeare Theatre in Stratford upon Avon; the live announcement had been intended to ensure that the news didn't leak. Again, some wondered why Tennant hadn't left and a new production team hadn't taken over a year earlier, giving us a full series in 2009. The letters pages of genre magazines brimmed with unhappiness. Someone wrote in *SFX* that a two year gap between seasons was nothing; we had once had to wait fifteen years...

The specials of 2009 were variable in quality. The Easter special – "Planet of the Dead" (2009), the first to be shot in high definition, was dreadful. Some of the ideas worked well. The Tritovores were a well-designed species of humanoid fly, looking, perhaps unsurprisingly, like the mutant human-fly hybrid in both film versions of *The Fly* (1958 and 1986). They trade with other planets, offering to take away its waste (on which they feed) in return for technology. Arriving on the planet San Helios, the Tritovores find a desert. This is all that is left of the planet's ecosystem, destroyed by ravening stingray-like aliens who create wormholes, devour a planet, and move on to the next. Their next target is to be Earth. So far, so good. This story is framed by a nonsensical introduction to the one-off companion Lady Christina de Souza, played by Michelle Ryan, formerly of *EastEnders* and the cancelled revival of *The Bionic Woman* (2007). She is a master cat burglar pulling off the heist of the century in a sequence that baffles and irritates and comes straight out of a *Pink Panther* film. The whole concept is another example of the later Davies era going for pretty visuals, regardless of plot, sense or consideration of whether the sequence fitted into the programme as a whole. The Doctor and Christina are transported to San Helios on a double decker bus, where they hook up with the Tritovores. The bus itself was transported to the United Arab Emirates – the great looking location for San Helios – by sea and the upper deck was smashed to bits on the voyage. Davies hurriedly wrote the damage into the script: this, he said, is what happens to a bus when you pass it through a wormhole. The bus returns to Earth, now augmented with Tritovore technology, and can fly. Lady

Christina de Souza evades the police by flying off in it in a sequence that appears to have been borrowed from a *Harry Potter* film.

The autumn special, "The Waters of Mars" was a return to form. On the first manned Mars base, the water is turning hostile; if you touch it, you turn into a ravening, mutated beast (shades of "Planet of Evil" (1975)). Water being water, it can get in almost anywhere, as anyone who has had a leaking shower can testify. Lindsay Duncan guests as another strong, mature woman and the companion character for this episode, Captain Adelaide Brooke. The Doctor knows that he has entered a fixed point in time, which cannot be changed. Brooke destroyed the base, killing herself and everyone on board, to prevent the infection from spreading. By this point, the Doctor has been travelling alone for so long that he has become wayward again. Announcing that he is "the Time Lord victorious", he argues that, as the last of the Time Lords, he can make time bend to his will. He rescues Adelaide and brings her home but she shoots herself, thus making time resume its accustomed course and graphically showing the Doctor that he is not all-powerful.

The final David Tennant special was the two part story "The End of Time", broadcast on Christmas Day 2009 and New Year's Day 2010. Russell T Davies asked Steven Moffat, his successor, if he could use the Daleks; Moffat replied that he would like them in the new season (in "Victory of the Daleks" (2010)) and Davies opted for the Master instead. A single Dalek appears at the bedroom window of the young Adelaide Brooke in "The Waters of Mars". Instead of exterminating her, it flies off, thus indicating the Daleks' knowledge of Brooke's importance to history and the time line. "The End of Time" was the first, and to date the only, story of the new series to be specifically billed as a two parter: Davies had previously eschewed the practice by arguing that someone who had missed part one wouldn't bother to watch part two. Presumably the viewer's knowledge that this was Tennant's last story, plus the favourable scheduling, encouraged Davies to think that the labelling would work as a one-off. Again, "The End of Time" is a curious tale, the excellent juxtaposed with the execrable. John Simm returns as the

Master, resurrected as a peroxide blond which was apparently Simm's idea: he later thought it was a bad one. The Master uses the power of stolen alien technology to duplicate himself into every human being, thus changing the human race into the Master race and proving that he has finally gone completely nuts. The Doctor, Wilf and Donna are unaffected. The Time Lords are back, with Timothy Dalton as Rassilon, who helps defeat the Master, and the tenth Doctor dies absorbing the radiation which would otherwise kill Wilfred Mott. Davies inevitably goes for unexplained visual thrills, as the resurrected Master can now bounce hundreds of feet in the air (why?) and throw fireballs from his hands (why?). Apparently *Doctor Who* was now in the same stable as *Spiderman* as well as the *Pink Panther* and *Harry Potter*. The programme could now attract Hollywood actors like Timothy Dalton and Brian Cox, who voices the Ood leader, which is impressive, but the script doesn't make it clear who Rassilon is or why his return is a big deal. He was, of course, a founder of Time Lord society who discovered the Eye of Harmony as a power source for time travel (see "The Deadly Assassin", 1976), and the Second Doctor suggests in "The Five Doctors" that he wasn't as pure as history painted him. Dalton kills Time Lords who oppose him and barks "On your knees, mankind" as he appears on Earth. Rassilon returned, regenerated, in the Peter Capaldi story "Hell Bent" (2015), now played by Donald Sumpter[1]. Again, no reference was made to him being a legendary figure in Time Lord history and he might just have well have been called something else.

Tennant's Doctor holds off regeneration long enough to say goodbye to his companions, including Sarah Jane and her adopted son Luke from *The Sarah Jane Adventures*; not necessarily a good idea as the spin-off was watched by about a fifth of the audience as the parent show, and many viewers would not have known who Luke was. Rose appears yet again as the Doctor meets her on New

---

[1] Sumpter was a familiar figure on British television. He had played the submarine captain Commander Ridgeway in "The Sea Devils" (1972) and Maester Lewin in the first two seasons of *Game of Thrones* (2011, 2012).

Year's Day 2005, just before she runs off with his ninth incarnation. On board the TARDIS at last, the Doctor says, "I don't want to go" – presumably voicing David Tennant's ambivalence about leaving – and he regenerates into Matt Smith who, like Tennant before him, instantly makes the part his own with four lines of monologue. Such is the incredible force of volcanic energy released by the Doctor's regeneration that the TARDIS control room blows up for no reason at all, which is fine as it looks jolly spectacular. After filming Tennant's last line, Russell T Davies and his team left their chairs and left the set; the chairs were then filled by new show runner Steven Moffat and his team, who handled the final post-regeneration minutes of the episode. This scene was re-enacted in 2017, when Moffat and Capaldi handed over to Chibnall and Whittaker: Chibnall wrote and oversaw the last few minutes of "Twice Upon A Time" (2017), which introduced the thirteenth Doctor.

### Sardick, Arwell, Vastra and Strax

The Christmas specials were by this time a fixture of BBC 1's Christmas Day schedules, and Matt Smith duly appeared in three more. Such is the influence of Charles Dickens' *A Christmas Carol* on our conception of Christmas that three of the episodes made full use of Victorian imagery and two were actually set in Victorian England. 2010's special was actually called "A Christmas Carol", with both Steven Moffat and the Doctor acknowledging Dickens's role in its plotting. The tale of Scrooge had been used twice before in the programme: it provided the past, present, future structure of "The Trial of a Time Lord", Colin Baker's second season; Dickens himself, played by Simon Callow, had appeared in "The Unquiet Dead" (2005), performing the story at a public reading in Cardiff, which is rudely interrupted by the phantasmagorical Gelth. In *Doctor Who*'s "A Christmas Carol", the tenth Doctor uses the paradoxes of time travel to soften the heart of Kazran Sardick, a miserly Scrooge figure who rules an Earth-like planet that favours

Victorian fashion and design. Sardick is played by Michael Gambon in another triumph of casting. Back in 1967, Innes Lloyd had been asked if Laurence Olivier would soon be in the programme after he succeeded in attracting top names to appear: in 2010, we had Michael Gambon and in 2012, Ian McKellen. The story's only disappointment is its monster, a somewhat uninspiring giant shark.

Having borrowed thoroughly from Dickens, Moffat borrowed from C.S.Lewis for the 2011 special, "The Doctor, the Widow and the Wardrobe", whose title obviously references C.S.Lewis's novel *The Lion, the Witch and the Wardrobe* (1950). The pastiche on Narnia is inspired and cleverly used in the story. It might also be a reference to Lewis's novel's influence on the genesis of the series, with parallels between the wardrobe and the police box as doors into another world. Lewis, who died in 1963, never saw *Doctor Who* but might well have liked it: he enjoyed H.G.Wells' science fiction, wrote three science fiction novels of his own and was no literary snob. He had seen the original *King Kong* movie (1933) with his brother Warnie and had enjoyed it enormously. In the special, Moffat used the novel's imagery of the wardrobe and the snow clad forest; the castle containing the immobile wooden king and queen recalls the White Witch's castle in the novel and the petrified forms of her enemies, including giants, which litter the courtyard. Madge Arwell and her three children arrive at a vast and deserted country house to escape the bombing, just as the Pevensie children do in the novel. There is an eccentric and wise figure in the house: Professor Kirk in the novel, who has been to Narnia himself, and the Doctor in the special. The Doctor is spending time on his own after dropping off Amy and Rory from their regular travels in the TARDIS.

Moffat also drew on the imagery of the recent film version of *The Lion, the Witch and the Wardrobe* (2005), which opens with German bombers swarming towards London to deliver the Blitz. In the special, these become a single Lancaster bomber piloted by Alexander Armstrong as Reg Arwell, whom the Doctor reunites with his wife, thus un-widowing her. The wife, Madge Arwell, is played by Claire Skinner, immediately identifiable as Sue from the

BBC comedy *Outnumbered* (2007-2014), which also rolled out its Christmas specials from year to year.

Previous specials had taken the seasonal icons of Santa Claus and Christmas trees and made them sinister; in "The Snowmen" (2012), Moffat reached for the Christmas card staple of snowmen, gave them piranha teeth and had them devour humans in Victorian England. Also present were a wonderful cast of characters first seen in "A Good Man Goes to War" (2011): the Silurian Madame Vastra, now established as a private detective; her maid and lover Jenny and their Sontaran butler Strax, who gets some of the best lines in the programme ("Do not attempt to escape, or you will be obliterated. May I take your coat?"). The villainous Dr Simeon was played by Richard E. Grant, who had starred with eighth Doctor Paul McGann in *Withnail and I* (1987). Grant had twice played the Doctor in BBC spin offs "The Curse of Fatal Death" (by Steven Moffat (1999)) and "The Scream of the Shalka" (2003), a webcast that had briefly seen him hailed by the BBC as the ninth Doctor before Christopher Eccleston was cast. Dr Simeon is apparently in charge of the Snowmen, but answers to a giant globe which issues him with his instructions. The globe's design recalled the snow globe ornaments which you turn upside down to cause a snowstorm: another witty use of snow and Christmas imagery. The Doctor, dressed and hailed as Sherlock Holmes, breaks into Dr Simeon's lair: this is a reference to Moffat's other BBC series *Sherlock* (2010-2017), in which Sherlock (Benedict Cumberbatch) makes brilliant deductions from fragments of evidence. The Doctor, by contrast, makes wildly inaccurate deductions from similar fragments.

The episode's conclusion reveals there is more to the title than a pleasing reference to the Christmas villains of the piece. The voice in the globe is that of the Great Intelligence, the disembodied entity that controls the Yeti in the much loved Patrick Troughton stories "The Abominable Snowmen" (1967) and "The Web of Fear" (1967). The 2012 special's title refers back to the title of the first Great Intelligence story and the plot of "The Snowmen" implied that the Great Intelligence gets the idea of using the Yeti from the

Snowmen favoured by Dr Simeon. This return of an old adversary is beautifully and intelligently handled, in complete contrast to, say, the return of Omega in "Arc of Infinity" (1983); in "The Snowmen", it doesn't matter to casual viewers if they don't know who the Great Intelligence is, as knowledge of the entity isn't necessary to follow or enjoy the story: if you didn't know who Omega was in 1983, you were completely lost. For the fan, the return of the Great Intelligence was exciting and pleasing, as was the news, issued late in December, that it was to be voiced by Ian McKellen. For an English graduate and English literature teacher like me, the credit "Voice of the Great Intelligence – Ian McKellen" was one of the best Christmas presents of the year (I also liked the socks thank you). McKellen's beautiful voice is entirely suited to the Great Intelligence's malevolence. In the treatment of time paradoxes that is one of his contributions to *Doctor Who*, Moffat revealed that this is the Doctor's third encounter with the Great Intelligence but its first encounter with him. To top it all, the Doctor, now one thousand years old (the newly regenerated ninth Doctor had been nine hundred, so the Doctor had aged one hundred years in the eight years of the revived series) can't remember the Great Intelligence: "Doesn't ring a bell", he says. This line is a really tricky reference to a plot detail in "The Abominable Snowmen": in an untelevised adventure, the Doctor was given the holy ghanta (a small bell) of the Tibetan Det-Sen monastery for safe keeping. In "The Abominable Snowmen", he returns it, only to encounter the Yeti and the Great Intelligence. "Doesn't ring a bell" is a reference to the ghanta. Again, Moffat skilfully gives the uber-fan a treat without alienating other viewers. This is surely the way to write *Doctor Who*, true to Moffat's guiding principles as a showrunner: he has said that he has to ignore the fans and write for the other ten million viewers. It is when the programme is directed at the fans, with the tail wagging the dog – as it was for much of John Nathan-Turner's time as producer – that it loses its way.

# 16
# The Fiftieth Anniversary

Preparing auditions for the eleventh Doctor, Steven Moffat intended to cast an older actor than Tennant. This was perhaps as an attempt to return to the Doctor as more of an authority figure, as William Hartnell or Jon Pertwee had been. An actor who crossed his mind briefly was Peter Capaldi, best known as the foul mouthed Malcolm Tucker in Armando Iannuncci's splendid satire *The Thick of It*; Iannucci himself wondered if Capaldi might be the new Doctor; Moffat considered Capaldi but thought the time for him was not yet ripe. Moffat's intention to cast someone older than Tennant contrasted with Russell T Davies's view that an older actor could no longer play the Doctor because the hectic schedules and lengthy shoots would simply exhaust him. There is a poignant extra on the season twenty seven (season one) DVD when Christopher Eccleston, looking exhausted and fed up on the TARDIS set, turns to the camera and says, "It's three o'clock in the morning!" Moffat's intention was almost immediately overturned when he saw Matt Smith as about the second actor to audition; when Smith started his piece, Moffat thought, "That's him!" Smith, with his gangling body language and wonderfully eccentric reading of the character, immediately captured the essence of the Doctor. The auditions continued, but Moffat felt they had found their man.

The announcement of the eleventh Doctor was made in a special edition of the behind-the-scenes companion series *Doctor Who Confidential*. This usually ran on BBC3 immediately after the broadcast of a new *Doctor Who* episode on BBC 1, but the announcement was considered big enough news to run on the flagship channel. Matt Smith, like Tom Baker, was a virtual unknown, and was introduced by Moffat as the youngest actor to have played the Doctor: he was twenty seven; Peter Davison had been two years older. Although not a household name, Smith had starred in *The Ruby in the Smoke* with ex-companion Billie Piper and had played Danny in the 2007 series *Party Animals*. He was also an experienced theatre actor, having performed in Alan Bennett's acclaimed satire *The History Boys* at the National Theatre, which also starred James Corden, soon to guest in *Doctor Who* as Craig in "The Lodger" (2010) and "Closing Time" (2011). Smith was a talented football player and had wanted to turn professional, but a back injury led him to pursue his alternative career as an actor. If the fifth Doctor was a fine cricketer ("First class bowler and a demon bat", according to Lord Cranleigh in "Black Orchid" (1982)), the eleventh was a wonderful footballer, demolishing the opposing pub team in "The Lodger", much to Craig's increasing glumness, and performing impressive "keepie uppies" in "The Power of Three" (2012).

Matt Smith's Doctor was joined by Amy (Karen Gillan) in his first story, "The Eleventh Hour". Pre-broadcast photos had shown Amy in a policewoman's uniform with a rather short miniskirt, which led some to grumble about sexism. Moffat wittily revealed that Amy is a kissagram and this is one of her outfits: "It's a laugh," she shrugs. The Doctor first encounters Amy as a young girl, played by Karen Gillan's cousin Caitlin Blackwood. Karen hadn't met Caitlin before they introduced themselves on the set. The Doctor's first scenes with the young Amelia are charming and hilarious; he is starving after his regeneration and demands food ("You're Scottish. Fry something."), eventually settling on fish fingers and custard. The fish fingers were actually coconut cakes and the scene is referenced in later episodes. Amy, knowing that the Doctor will die in the future in "The Impossible Astronaut" (2011), tells his earlier self that she can't reveal the future and he will have to trust her. When she swears on "fish fingers and custard", the Doctor trusts her: "My life in your hands, Amelia Pond." Rory, Amy and the Doctor eat fish fingers and custard together in "The Power of Three".

Amy's fiancé Rory (Arthur Darvill) is another recurring character who became a full companion in Matt Smith's second season. In the first, he appears when the TARDIS returns Amy and the Doctor to Earth. In contrast to Rose and Martha, Amy is not wildly and romantically in love with the Doctor; rather, Moffat makes her relationship with him more like Jo's and Sarah's. She does love him but does not see him as a romantic partner. The eleventh Doctor is much more uncomfortable about sexual relations that his predecessor, spluttering when kissed by River Song and squirming when Amy tries, on one single occasion, to seduce him. This is a return to the more asexual Doctor, and the more chaste friendship with his companion, of the original series: they love each other, but the Doctor's love isn't sexual. Moffat, however, creates dramatic play from the suggestion that Amy and the Doctor are romantically involved, not least because we are encouraged on occasions to see their relationship through the Rory's eyes, who is understandably jealous of Amy's relationship with another man. It's even hinted that the Doctor is the father of Amy's baby, although of course it is Rory. Amy gets increasingly impatient with Rory's failure to believe that she is in love with him, and not with the Doctor. The events of "Journey's End" (2008) suggest that Time Lords and humans might not be biologically compatible anyway, at least as far as breeding is concerned. The Doctor tells Donna, suffering because she has a Time Lord's intellect in her head, that there are no Time Lord-human hybrids "because there can't be."

Moffat has much fun with Rory's character, and sometimes at Rory's expense. He seems to die as many times as Kenny in *South Park*. He turns to dust in the dreamworld of "Amy's Choice" (2011); is consumed by the time rift in "Cold Blood" (2010); returns as a Roman Centurion who is also an Auton in "The Pandorica Opens"/"The Big Bang" (2010); guards Amy in the Pandorica for two thousand years while still an Auton; returns to human form in "The Big Bang"; is aged near death in "The Doctor's Wife" (2011), ages to death in "The Angels Take Manhattan" (2012) and is finally zapped back in time with Amy by a Weeping Angel in that story, to live out his life with Amy and to die in twentieth century New York. Rory also takes on the mystical persona of the Centurion from time to time, and the persona seems to be enough to cow a fleet of Cybermen into revealing where Amy is imprisoned in "A Good Man

Goes to War" (2011).

Following the established practice of Russell T Davies' time as showrunner, Rory is given a family and a job. His father Brian, wonderfully played by Mark Williams, appears in "Dinosaurs on a Spaceship" (2012) and "The Power of Three" (2012). Even more of a dignified geek than Rory, it's easy to believe Brian and Rory are father and son. Amy's mother and father appear and disappear according to which timeline we are in, but they attend her wedding to Rory in "The Big Bang" (2010).

## Hello Sweetie

One of Steven Moffat's most loved characters is River Song, first played by Alex Kingston in the David Tennant story "Silence in the Library" (2008). Professor Song is an archaeologist whose first words to the Doctor are, "Hello sweetie". She clearly knows him well but the Doctor has no memory of her. River's timeline and the Doctor's run in different directions. The first time he meets her is the last time she meets him and River laments that, every time she meets the Doctor, he knows her less well; there will come a terrible day when he doesn't know who she is. This is the case in her first story: River dies in "The Forest of the Dead" (2008) and the Doctor grants her a form of immortality as part of the computer matrix that sustains the library. In a moment of crisis in the story, River urgently needs the Doctor's trust and proves that she knows him by whispering something in his ear. From the Doctor's shock and silence we know that it's his name, which he never reveals to anyone. Donna asks if River Song is his wife, and the Doctor gives a non-committal reply.

River was intended as a one-off character. Davies and Moffat were delighted to get Alex Kingston to play her. Alex Kingston had been praised in the United Kingdom for her performance as the lead in Andrew Davies's adaptation of Defoe's *Moll Flanders* (1996); she then moved to the States and played Dr Elizabeth Corday in *ER* (1994-2009). Bringing River Song back depended on Alex

Kingston's availability, but she was delighted to return as the character for ten episodes with Matt Smith's Doctor and one with Peter Capaldi's. River Song's story gives Moffat a chance to indulge his delight in time paradox stories which we first saw in "Blink" (2007).

In "The Time of Angels"/"Flesh and Stone" (2010), River is simply "Dr" Song and is thrilled to learn that she will one day be a Professor. She is accompanied (and guarded) by military clerics, who have allowed her freedom from her prison, where she is held for killing a good man. Which good man? "Spoilers", she smiles, using her catchphrase. Perhaps drawing on the first six seasons on the show for inspiration, which had seen the answer to the question "Doctor who?" endlessly deferred, Moffat continually asks, and doesn't answer, the question who is River Song? We speculate that she is the Doctor's wife. Is she a Time Lord? Is she his mother? How can she be his mother if the mysterious woman played by Claire Bloom in "The End of Time" (2009-10) was his mother? "A Good Man Goes to War" answers the question for us. Amy and Rory's baby is named Melody Pond. Lorna Bucket, a human soldier from the Gamma forests, gives Amy a piece of cloth on which is her baby's name embroidered in gold. This is the tradition among her people. However, and in fulfilment of the cryptic prediction "The only water in the forest is the river", made by Idris in "The Doctor's Wife" (2011), there is no word for "pond" among her people. The TARDIS telepathic circuits eventually translate the embroidery from "Melody Pond" to "River Song", thus proving that River is Rory's and Amy's daughter. We thus have the fun of an apparently older person being the daughter of two apparently younger people; an image familiar from the apparently younger Doctor being much older than many of his friends and companions.

Amy and Rory are in the process of divorce in "Asylum of the Daleks" (2012), not least because Amy can't give Rory children as a result of her incarceration and forced childbirth on Demon's Run (see "A Good Man Goes to War"). They save their marriage in "Asylum". In a scene scripted but not filmed for the season seven (season thirty three) DVD release, Chris Chibnall revealed that Amy and Rory had another child, a son, in New York after they were sent back in time by the Weeping Angel.

River was conceived on Amy and Rory's wedding night in the TARDIS; having absorbed the energy of the time vortex, she is part Time Lord and able to regenerate. River's story is an example of the fiendishly complicated plotting favoured by Moffat, who answered criticisms of its difficulty by saying that you had to pay attention to *Doctor Who* and couldn't watch it while having a conversation or texting or whatever. Moffat's plotting can be followed by the viewer who is paying attention and it is a pleasure to do so. River as a child was brought up by Madame Kovarian as a weapon to kill the Doctor. As a child, she inhabits the space suit in "The Impossible Astronaut" (2011), is injured when Amy shoots her to prevent the Astronaut from killing the Doctor, and regenerates in an alley into Mels[1]. As Mels, River attends Rory and Amy's school ("Let's Kill Hitler", 2011), goes back to Berlin in 1939 and regenerates into Alex Kingston. Looking a little older than she did in "Silence in the Library", River says that she may take the age down a bit; thus is continuity satisfied. River shoots the Doctor, who is dying, and then overcomes her programming by saving him with her remaining regeneration energies. She is thus no longer able to regenerate and is no longer part-Time Lord: this was to have been the Doctor's fate in "Mawdryn Undead" (1983), where donating his regeneration energy to the mutants to free them from life would rob him of his power to regenerate. The Doctor partly returns the favour to River by healing her broken wrist with some of his regeneration energy in "The Angels take Manhattan" (2012). The idea that regeneration energy can be accessed at will is new and a bit too much like magic for some viewers' tastes. Regeneration in the rest of the series always results from some massive trauma and River herself is furious at the Doctor for "wasting" his regeneration energy. She yells that he has embarrassed her, and storms off.

---

[1] This regeneration isn't the first to show that the process can change skin colour; one of Romana's trial bodies in "Destiny of the Daleks" (1979) is also black.

After Berlin, River trains to become a Doctor of Archeology and is recruited again by Madame Kovarian and the Silents. She is returned to the space suit which we saw rising from the lake to shoot the Doctor in "The Impossible Astronaut": an event that is a fixed point in time and cannot be changed. It then appears that the Doctor she shoots is not the Doctor but a shape-changing machine containing miniaturised humans and the Doctor himself, the Teselecta. It is this machine, taking the Doctor's form, that River marries in "The Wedding of River Song" (2011), rather than the Doctor himself, which makes the question of whether she actually is the Doctor's wife or not a moot point. (Neil Gaiman and Steven Moffat play with the question further by entitling a 2012 episode "The Doctor's Wife", who is eventually revealed to be the TARDIS in human form. "Did you wish really hard?" asks Amy.)

The Doctor's "death" at the hands of the impossible astronaut allows him to drop out of history. He is, he says, becoming too big, hailed as a legend and saviour by almost everyone he meets. The Doctor's quest for anonymity is boosted by his wiping all data on himself from the Daleks' collective hive database[1]. River has been freed from her incarceration in the Stormcage facility for the murder of the Doctor. Apparently he has wiped himself from all databases in the universe, so she cannot be imprisoned for the murder of someone who doesn't exist.

## Return of the Brigadier, Sarah and the Cybermen

The revived series resurrected several characters from the original show. Sarah Jane Smith, of course, returns in "School Reunion" (2006), back in her role as investigative journalist. Sarah was now scripted according to the new approach of the revived series. She

---

[1] That there is such a thing as a hive intelligence for the Daleks is perhaps borrowed from the Borg in *Star Trek: the Next Generation*. However, as *The Next Generation* probably based the Borg on the Cybermen anyway, *Doctor Who* was only doing a little minor pilfering compared with *Star Trek*'s a dirty great theft, and Trekkers should hang their heads in shame. So there.

mourns the loss of the Doctor and asks if she did something wrong, as he just dumped her on Earth. "You were getting on with your life," the Doctor smiles. "You were my life," she replies. In a pleasing addition for fans, she reveals that the Doctor didn't leave her at her home in South Croydon in "The Hand of Fear" (1976), but in Aberdeen. "That's near Croydon, isn't it?" the Doctor offers hesitantly. Sarah comes to terms with her new Earth-bound role in the course of the battle against the Krillitanes and, in a parallel to Elisabeth Sladen's refusal to rejoin the show in the late 1970s, turns down the offer of travelling again with the Doctor (Mickey goes instead). Elisabeth Sladen only agreed to return as Sarah if the character was treated with respect and not just seen in a fleeting cameo. She was evidently delighted with "School Reunion" and returned – occasionally with K9 – in her own-spin off series *The Sarah Jane Adventures* (2007-2011) on the children's channel CBBC. The tenth and eleventh Doctors guested; so did Katy Manning as Jo Jones (née Grant) and Nicholas Courtney as the Brigadier.

Davies planned for Courtney to return to *The Sarah Jane Adventures* for a second story, but Courtney wasn't well enough to appear. He died in 2011 and his death is marked twice in the *Doctor Who* story "The Wedding of River Song". In a sequence which shows how much Courtney and the Brigadier were loved by viewers and the production team, the Doctor phones the Brigadier's nursing home only to be told that his old friend has passed away. The Brigadier had always kept two glasses of scotch by his table to the end, in case his old friend the Doctor happened to drop by. The Doctor, shaken and saddened, is shocked into accepting that he must face his own death by the impossible astronaut.

All of Madame Kovarian's team in "The Wedding of River Song" apparently wear eyepatches; in fact, sophisticated devices called eye-drives wired into the brain which allow the wearers to remember, and interact with the Silents. The Silents cannot be remembered after they have been encountered: an evolutionary advantage which makes them as dangerous as the Weeping Angels and has allowed them to live alongside mankind for hundreds of thousands of years without being detected. The eye-drives are inspired by a favourite story of Nicholas Courtney's which he trotted out for interviews and conventions. Asked what funny things had happened during filming of the show, Courtney recalled that he had played the Brigade Leader, the Brigadier's fascist counterpart in a parallel universe, in "Inferno" (1970). He had had to swivel round in his chair to reveal the Brigade Leader was without moustache but with a scar on his cheek and an eyepatch. Jon Pertwee and Caroline John decided to make him laugh during a take; when Courtney swung round, he was confronted by the Doctor and Elizabeth Shaw wearing eyepatches. Courtney carried on "as cool as a cucumber" and it was Pertwee and Caroline John who burst out laughing. (Apparently director Douglas Camfield was not pleased at the prank, which wasted studio time and money.) Courtney had told the story so many times that most fans knew it by heart. At one convention, he entered the hall to find the fan audience facing him were all wearing eyepatches, which he thought a good joke. The eyedrives in "The Wedding of River Song" are an affectionate reference to the story and a remembrance of Nicholas Courtney.

*Doctor Who* clearly misses the Brigadier. Unable to revive the character with Courtney in the role, and presumably unwilling to recast him, the revived show has his daughter Kate Stewart (Jemma Redgrave), successor to the Doctor as the scientific adviser to the British branch of UNIT from "The Power of Three" (2012) onwards. In "Twice Upon A Time" (2017), the World War I officer who wanders aboard the TARDIS (Mark Gatiss) eventually reveals his name as Archibald Hamish Lethbridge-Stewart, an ancestor of the Brigadier. The Brigadier himself appears to be given a questionable new life as a Cyberman in "Death in Heaven" (2014).

Both the Cybermen and the Daleks returned in the revived series. The Cybermen originally appear in a parallel universe story, "Rise of the Cybermen"/"The Age of Steel" (2006). This is effectively a version of "Genesis of the Daleks" (1975), but with Cybermen; Roger Lloyd Pack plays their Davros-like creator, John Lumic. Like

Davros, he is crippled and confined to a wheelchair; like Davros, he has a fanatical desire to perpetuate himself in his creations. The new Cybermen are fashioned by Cybus Industries (Lumic's company) and thus have a large C on their chest units: the Cybus industry logo. Davies apparently decided to source his new race of Cybermen from a parallel universe in order to sidestep the complicated, and contradictory, history of the Cybermen established in the original series: necessary if their genesis was to be told. Some fans were unhappy that these were not "real" Cybermen, although Davies was careful to have the Doctor note that "there are Cybermen in our Universe". These don't appear until Matt Smith's era, when a lone, partially dismembered Cyberman attacks Amy in the Pandorica vault ("The Pandorica Opens" (2010)). In a continuity error, this Cyberman still has the C Cybus industries logo on its chest. Perhaps it had fallen through from the parallel universe. Cybermen from our universe, with the C plate replaced by a blank circle, lurk beneath the department store in "Closing Time" (2011) and attempt to turn Craig (James Corden) into their Cybercontroller. The Cybermats, last seen in "Revenge of the Cybermen" (1975), make an effective re-appearance. They now sport vicious teeth and are clearly a cyborg based on an animal, tying them in effectively with the Cybermen (cyborgs based on humans) and solving the mystery of their nature which had been bugging fans for years. Steven Moffat asked the props department if the Cybermen could be seen as battered and broken for "Closing Time". The props department told him that, after six years of being worn, blown up and bashed about generally, the costumes looked like that anyway. Partly as a response to the need for new props, Moffat took advantage of the Cybermen's battered condition to have them redesigned for their reappearance in Neil Gaiman's story "Nightmare in Silver" (2013). The retooled Cybermen, like so much else in the revived series, took their design inspiration from the 1960s black and white episodes and closely resembled the Cybermen of "The Moonbase" (1967) and "Tomb of the Cybermen" (1967), although the chest unit was replaced by integrated armour and a central, electric blue light. This colour also alluded to the Cybus industries Cybermen, whose mouths flashed electric blue when they spoke[1]. Neil Gaiman said one of his intentions in this, his second story, was to make the Cybermen terrifying again; they can certainly move with superhuman speed and are creatures of few words, like their 1960s counterparts. Their relative silence certainly makes them more alarming: they obviously know what they are up to but, because they don't tend to tell us, our anxiety, like the characters', goes through the roof. Perhaps Cybermen have a point about emotions curtailing our efficiency.

The Daleks were also redesigned in Mark Gatiss's 2010 story "Victory of the Daleks". The hybrid Daleks created by Davros reactivate the Dalek progenitor, a device which generates and duplicates Daleks composed of pure Dalek DNA. The bronze Daleks seen up to this point in the revived series are various bastardised mixes of tissue sourced from humans or Davros himself: as Ace said in "Remembrance of the Daleks" (1988), they are "impure in their blobbiness". As racial fanatics, the bronze Daleks accept their impurity and are happy to be exterminated by the Dalek paradigm, a new race of Daleks. These apparently partly came about because the toy company Character Options asked the production team if it had plans to introduce new types of Daleks which it could sell as models. The production team responded enthusiastically by creating five types, or colours at least, of new Dalek. Mark Gatiss, like most fans of his generation, had considerable affection for the Peter Cushing Dalek movies of the 1960s and suggested that the new generation of Daleks in "Victory…" should be like them. In the script, they are described as "big buggers". There are five types: the red Drone (shades of the Borg again): the white Supreme Dalek (Supreme Daleks had previously been black so this is radical stuff); the blue scientist; the yellow strategist and an orange Eternal Dalek. Gatiss named the first four in the script but told Moffat he had no idea what to call the fifth. Moffat suggested "eternal". Neither knew what it meant but both agreed it sounded great.

---

[1] Electric blue was apparently one of Russell T Davies's favourite colours, which is perhaps partly why it appears so often in the Eccleston and Tennant stories.

The new Daleks were designed by Peter McInstry, who had also designed the red Dalek supreme for "The Stolen Earth"/"Journey's End" (2008). They were not popular with fans, who disliked the disruption of the Dalek silhouette which had been maintained into the revived series. It also seemed odd that, while the bronze Daleks seen from "Dalek" (2005) onwards had included much more intricate surface detail than their classic series counterparts, the Dalek paradigm had much less: and this in the first Dalek story to be filmed in high definition. These Daleks had four, not three, discs in the neck section, which was supposed to be "concertina" up and down but never did on screen (although it closely resembled a laundry basket); they also swapped the vertical slats of the shoulder section for the horizontal bands last seen in "The Dalek Invasion of Earth" (1964) and sported a blank back panel with a spine running down its middle. It was apparently planned that this panel would conceal extra weapons which could be whizzed around the shoulder section to give the Dalek more firepower, but this was never seen on screen either. The bright colours of the paradigm encouraged some fans unkindly to dub the new Daleks "Teletubbies".

The production team eventually acknowledged that the new design was not an unparalleled success and restored the bronze variety to prominence in "Asylum of the Daleks" (2012), although the paradigm Daleks appear in the background. The Dalek paradigm are banished altogether from the 2013 anniversary special "The Day of the Doctor" and the 2013 Christmas special "The Time of the Doctor": it is the bronze Daleks who invade Gallifrey in the former (actually quite right for continuity purposes, as this was the Time War) and come to gloat over the Doctor's end on Trenzalore in the latter. The paradigm Daleks were nowhere in sight for the Capaldi stories.

### "Dasssss Boot"

The Daleks, the Cybermen, the Sontarans, the Master and Davros had all been resurrected for the revived series after 2005; fans were growing restive about the non-appearance of the Ice Warriors, who, after all, had had as many stories as the Sontarans in the original series – four apiece – and were as fondly remembered, not least for being more terrifying. A Sontaran is a short troll and can appear somewhat absurd; the recurring character Strax (Dan Starkey) is often played for laughs, getting over-excited in "The Crimson Horror" (2013) after wolfing down Jenny's sherbet and muttering, as he is sent off the killing fields by Madame Vastra for misbehaviour, that he is going to play with his grenades. An Ice Warrior, on the other hand, is a lumbering giant and, once it has your wrist in its pincer, you aren't going anywhere in a hurry. Steven Moffat wasn't apparently convinced by the Ice Warriors and was lukewarm about reviving them: Neil Gorton, the new series' principle monster designer, disliked the original design. They eventually returned in the 2013 story "Cold War" by Mark Gatiss; Gatiss loved the Ice Warriors and convinced Moffat that he could do something new with them; they wouldn't just be lumbering up and down corridors in the T-mat base or on the planet of Peladon while the Doctor and his companions ran rings around them.

"Cold War" (2013) is set on a Russian submarine in the 1980s, at the height of the stand-off between the Soviet Union and NATO. Gatiss joked that the working title was "Dasssssss Boot", a reference to the German mini-series *Das Boot* ("The Boat", 1981), which followed the fortunes of a U-boat crew in the Second World War. For all that Gatiss wanted to do something new with the Martians, the teaser to the episode condensed much of part one of "The Ice Warriors" (1967) in a few minutes, thus emphasising the breakneck pace of the new series in comparison to its earlier incarnation. In both stories, a mysterious giant figure is found encased in solid ice; the curious scientists, who don't know this is a very bad idea because they have never seen *Doctor Who* on account of the fact they are in it, bring the frozen creature into the base/sub and start to defrost it. Grand Marshall Skaldak, like Varga in 1967, is quickly awoken and, in Gatiss's story, immediately dispatches the hapless crewmember who foolishly tries to thaw him out with a blowlamp.

The new features of the Ice Warriors, which perhaps enabled Gatiss to sell the story to Steven Moffat, are arguably the most disappointing aspects of the story. Having waited for years to have the Ice Warriors back, and delighted to see one break out of his chains and stomp around as of old, some fans were disappointed when Skaldak leaves his exoskeleton to go zooming around the ship like the woosenpoof (aka The Fuzzy Worm) from *Vision On*. This real form of the Ice Warrior is an etiolated – and not particularly convincing – CGI mandrake which returns to his cyborg suit at the end of the story and makes his last threats to the Doctor, red eyes glowing and sharp teeth glittering, without his helmet on. The Doctor observes that he has never seen an Ice Warrior without his suit before. Nor had we, and it was a bit of a disappointment. There is a slight contrast here with Bernard Bresslaw's Varga, the original Ice Warrior, which suggested that the exoskeleton was fused with the flesh as a tortoise is fused with its shell (Bresslaw would pull his head, tortoise-like, into his collar when Varga was upset) and an Ice Warrior couldn't therefore leave his suit. On the other hand, if the Daleks and Cybermen could evolve, why not the Ice Warriors? *SFX* magazine suggested the Ice Warriors should replace the Sontarans as the new series' Big Bad monsters as the Sontarans were now principally played for laughs, although Strax briefly regained his genocidal and racist tendencies in "The Name of the Doctor" (2013). Gatiss resurrected a full hive of Ice Warriors for "Empress of Mars" (2017), the first story to feature a female, Queen, Ice Warrior. There was a cameo from the mono-eyed hermaphrodite hexapod Alpha Centauri, last scene in "The Monster of Peladon" (1974). Actress Ysanne Churchmann, now in her nineties, was astonished and pleased to be asked to reprise the voice of Alpha Centauri, which she duly did.

The submarine in "Cold War" was a miniature model made and shot by Mike Tucker's effects company. The underwater sequences – although the model actually went nowhere near water – recalled the submarine sequences from "The Sea Devils" (1972). These had also employed a miniature submarine, although this one, in deference to the show's budget, was a retooled Airfix kit. As the third Doctor's exile stories were supposedly set in the near future, the visual effects team elected to enlarge the sub's propeller to suggest enhanced technology. A few weeks after the original broadcast, director Michael Briant answered a knock on his door: two men in suits from the secret service wanted to quiz him about the sub, whose larger propeller apparently had led them to suspect that the *Doctor Who* team had had a squint at plans for a new, top secret, upgraded submarine for the Royal Navy. In the bizarre times of the Cold War, truth was stranger than science fiction. Briant convinced the spooks that *Doctor Who* was not real and the BBC Visual Effects Department's upgraded submarine's resemblance to the Ministry of Defence's was a coincidence. Persuaded, the spooks duly faded away.

Mike Tucker had worked on the original and the revived series, providing effects shots for the Sylvester McCoy stories and the model footage of the Slitheen spaceship slicing into Big Ben for "Aliens of London" (2005). The BBC disbanded its visual effects department in 2006, preferring to buy in its effects from outside companies in deference to the prevailing and unquestionable orthodoxy that as much should be privatised as possible, and thereby making Tucker and his team redundant. That the BBC should buy from Tucker's own company is something of an irony, but no doubt the provision of special effects from a private company rather than a BBC department vastly improved their quality. Private good, public bad. As a freelancer, Mike Tucker returned to provide miniature effects in 2013, including the sequence when the War Doctor's TARDIS crashes through a wall and into three Daleks in "The Day of the Doctor" (2013). This effect was achieved using eighteen inch interactive Dalek toys from Character Options and recalled the similar use of toy of commercially available model Daleks in "Revelation of the Daleks" (1985), which used a Sevans Model Dalek kit for the flying Dalek, and the highly inaccurate Marx toy Daleks in "The Evil of the Daleks" (1967) and "Planet of the Daleks" (1973). Brought up making Airfix models and playing with

Dinky Toy Thunderbirds, it was immensely satisfying for this writer to see the return of miniatures to the show, not least because I haven't the foggiest how CGI works (how, for example, can you light something that doesn't even exist?), but also because the old ways are the best and, as my wife said, models remind us that "this is something you can do at home".

## Zygons

Another alien race which the production team fondly recalled from the original series was the Zygons, whose single appearance in 1975's "Terror of the Zygons" was etched onto fans' collective memory by the fine script, design and John Woodnutt's performance as Commander Broton. If Neil Gorton disliked the Ice Warriors, he was enthusiastic about the Zygons, saying their design – based on a foetus – was perfect and, other than being made from new materials, would require hardly any updating for the new series. The Zygons were name-checked in "The Pandorica Opens" (2010) as one of the races that comes to corner the Doctor in Stonehenge, but didn't reappear until "The Day of the Doctor" (2013). Indeed, so enthusiastic did the production team appear about their return that the Zygons were featured on the second wave of publicity photos from the special after the Doctors themselves. The return of the Daleks was kept in the background until much later in the summer of 2013. Some have argued that these new Zygons were actually less impressive, from a design point of view, than the originals. They were of a uniform brick red and frankly looked rubbery: the original Zygons had been differentiated by the moulding of the masks to the face of the actor; these new Zygons had pointed teeth, like the new Ice Warrior, and dribbled; the originals appeared to have no teeth at all and the habit of one of the actors, by forming his mouth into an O for his lines, suggested effectively that the mouth was another of the Zygons' sucker-like protuberances.

Still, Moffat has lots of fun with the Zygons in their reappearance. David Tennant's Doctor has rigged together another ramshackle device, like his timey-wimey detector in "Blink" (2007), to detect shape-shifters, but it's as unreliable as the first Doctor's TARDIS. Thinking she is a Zygon, the tenth Doctor proposes to Queen Elizabeth I in the hope that the proposal will shock it into revealing its true nature: as the Zygon has shape shifted as the horse and Queen Elizabeth really is the genuine article, he ends up having his proposal accepted. There is a brief and very funny wedding scene for the Tenth Doctor, looking somewhat embarrassed, later in the episode, while the eleventh and the War Doctors (John Hurt) look on and Clara (Jenna Coleman) throws confetti. "Is there a lot of this in the future?" the War Doctor asks, bemused. Moffat makes the tenth Doctor's failure to spot Zygons a running gag in the early parts of the special; Tennant's machine leads him to paraphrase his menacing speech from "Voyage of the Damned" to a rabbit ("Whatever you've got planned, forget it. I'm the Doctor. I'm 904 years-old. I'm from the planet Gallifrey in the constellation of Kasterborous. I'm The Oncoming Storm, the Bringer Of Darkness, and... you are basically just a rabbit, aren't you?") One of the Zygons grumbles about assuming the form of Osgood who has asthma: "I so hate it when I get one with a defect," he says. The Zygons returned in the Capaldi two-parter, "The Zygon Invasion"/"The Zygon Inversion" (2015).

## Iconic Imagery

The original series gave popular culture enduring and iconic images: the Daleks gliding over Westminster Bridge; the Yeti lumbering through the London Underground; the Sea Devils rising from the waves; giant maggots hissing from the coal face of a Welsh mine. The revived series has added equally effective images which, according to my secondary school students, have burned themselves into the consciousness of new viewers: a child with a gas mask for a face asking, "Are you my mummy?"; clockwork robots in eighteenth century costumes, striding towards us as French courtiers scream in terror; statues that move when we don't look at them;

Munch's painting *The Scream* come to life in a towering Silent, sucking the life force from a middle aged woman in the White House washroom. Beautifully designed and realised, these are all products of Steven Moffat's imagination. The Weeping Angels were voted the favourite monster by fans in a recent poll, unseating the Daleks for the first time ever. They first appeared in the Doctor-lite story "Blink" in 2007, menacing a pre-fame Carey Mulligan (Sally Sparrow) in an abandoned house called Wester Drumlins (named after a house Moffat used to live in), and more or less came about by accident. Moffat was too busy to write a promised two-episode Dalek tale for the third (twenty ninth) season, so, in propitiation, he offered to do the Doctor-lite one instead for Davies. Davies agreed.

Moffat's script for "Blink" was based on a short story he wrote for Christopher Eccleston's Doctor in the 2005 *Doctor Who* annual called "What I did in my Christmas holidays, by Sally Sparrow". Sally is much younger in the short story and receives a message from the Doctor on an old VHS tape, telling her how to bring the TARDIS, stuck in her time, back to him where he's stranded a few years earlier. The Weeping Angels were inspired by the children's game of grandmother's footsteps, in which a group of children creep up on a single child, the leader, while her or his back is turned. If the child whirls round and spots the others moving, they have to go back to the beginning (the origin of the Weeping Angels sending their victims back in time?). The game ends when one of the creepers touches the leader. The Weeping Angels, visually represented as the sort of angels one might see on a sentimental Victorian tomb, are quantum-locked and can only move when they are not being looked at. They are also unbelievably fast and can cover many metres in the time it takes you to blink: hence the episode's title and the tendency of children to hold their eyes open as long as possible when playing the episode in the playground. The Angels can be beautiful and look serene, but their true faces are revealed as feral and vicious when they attack. If they reach you, they send you back in time and feed off the energy of the days you would have lived in your own time line. Moffat had no idea how to end the story and asked Mark Gatiss to suggest some solutions. In the end, the writers realised that the four scavenging Angels could be placed one on each side of a TARDIS wall; when it dematerialised, they would be looking at each other and so would be quantum-locked and harmless.

Moffat was pleased with his story but said it would never win a season poll. He was right: it came second in the following Best Story poll of *Doctor Who* Magazine, ceding first position to "The Caves of Androzani" (1984). The episode was so highly thought of that American *Who* fans suggested on BBC America that people new to the programme should watch "Blink" as a first taste of *Doctor Who* because it encapsulated the series' imaginative brilliance and introduced its concepts. After watching it, the new viewers could bombard the fan viewer with questions ("What's with the phone box?" etc.). "Blink" implied that all statues might be Weeping Angels in its final montage of images, thus making statues as terrifying for children as shop window dummies had been by the Autons (my daughter wouldn't go past a shop with tailors' dummies in the window for about five years). "The Angels take Manhattan" (2012) confirmed that any statue could be inhabited by a Weeping Angel. "The Time of Angels"/"Flesh and Stone" (2010) showed their malevolence and cruelty as they torment Amy into thinking she is turning to stone, telling the Doctor they are doing it "for fun".

## The Fiftieth Anniversary and the Twelfth Doctor

2013 was, of course, the fiftieth anniversary year and shops were deluged with new merchandise and books. The Forbidden Planet shop in Cambridge moved to new, airier premises and exhibited a full sized, original series Dalek and police box (see photograph on the next page).

News of Matt Smith's departure was rumoured – I first heard it from one of my year nine pupils – and then confirmed. As with David Tennant's announcement that he was leaving, Smith's resignation led to a storm of media speculation about who would be the new Doctor. Benedict Cumberbatch, Chiwetel Ejiofor and Rory Kinnear were hot tips; even Helen Mirren was mentioned as an outsider and my brother lost a fiver betting on her. The smart money at the bookies was on Kinnear, until the actor felt obliged to issue a statement saying he hadn't been approached[1] .

Just a week before the casting was confirmed, Ladbrooke's stopped taking any more bets when Peter Capaldi's name came forward as a front runner. Someone knew something; Steven Moffat has said on several occasions that it is virtually impossible to keep all news about *Doctor Who* under wraps, especially when it's such a popular show and so many newspapers, not to mention the fan bloodhounds who follow the crew around locations, are falling over themselves to publish stories about it. The executive producer explained that it is sometimes necessary just to ask people, like the press at preview screenings, not to give away plot details because it will spoil the show; the press often agrees and keeps schtum. In this way, the production team kept the secret of Jenna Coleman's appearance as Oswin Oswald (one of the versions of Clara) in "Asylum of the Daleks" (2012). This was quite a change from the way major spoilers had found their way into the *Doctor Who* Appreciation Society

---

[1] History repeated itself in 2017: Phoebe Waller-Bridge, who wrote and starred in the sitcom *Fleabag* (BBC 3, BBC 2, 2016-), had to issue a similar statement when the media confidently predicted that she had been cast as the thirteenth Doctor. At least they got the gender right.

newsletter *Celestial Toyroom* in the 1970s: "Surprise news has filtered through that the megalomaniac Davros will make a return", one piece ran in 1979, thus spoiling the cliffhanger of part two of "Destiny of the Daleks" (1979) and torpedoing the best bit of the whole lacklustre story[1].

The casting of the twelfth Doctor was announced, as Matt Smith's had been, in a special BBC programme, this time on 4th August 2013, entitled *Doctor Who Live: The Next Doctor.* Hosted by Zoe Ball, this was a showy piece of razzmatazz featuring Peter Davison and Bernard Cribbins, as well as some celebrities who had nothing at all to do with the programme but told us all how much they liked it. The new Doctor was announced at the end of the show by an exuberantly excited Zoe: "Please welcome the twelfth Doctor, a hero for a whole new generation... it's Peter Capaldi!" The theme tune struck up, the crowd went wild, the laser show began, canny punters licked their lips in anticipation of their Ladbrooke's winnings, and Peter Capaldi emerged on stage, waving and smiling. He gripped his lapels at one point in an imitation of one of the favourite habits of the first Doctor and an indication that he knew the programme inside out. Capaldi made a subdued and modest speech on *Doctor Who Live*, praising and thanking everyone who had ever worked on the show and saying that it belonged to everyone who watched and enjoyed it. He had apparently been driven into the studio in a people carrier, lying down on the back seat so that no-one could spot him before he was unveiled to the world, over a year before his first full series would air on BBC 1.

Capaldi, like Tennant before him, was a fan of the show. He had been five years old in 1963 and said in an interview that there had been no time when the series hadn't been part of his life. Aged

---

[1] Douglas Adams had cavalierly rewritten the script to make the Daleks pure robots, much to Terry Nation's annoyance. The next time the Daleks appeared, in "The Five Doctors" (1983) and "Resurrection of the Daleks" (1984), they spewed Kaled mutants a-plenty in a rebuttal of Adams and as an insistent reminder of their true hybrid nature.

fifteen, he had written to the *Radio Times* praising the *"Doctor Who* Tenth Anniversary Special" magazine, which had featured (highly inaccurate) plans to build a full sized Dalek (my brother and I had followed these to build two, distinctly wonky, Daleks). The plans had been intended as a project for secondary woodwork and metalwork departments, and Capaldi speculated in his letter that the nation would be invaded by an army of school built Daleks: "Ah, but we would have Dr Who to protect us, wouldn't we?" Capaldi had appeared as Caecilius in the David Tennant story "The Fires of Pompeii" (2008) and was best known as the foul mouthed spin doctor Malcolm Tucker in *The Thick of It* and its movie spin-off, *In The Loop*: several edits featuring Malcolm Tucker as the Doctor were posted on You Tube immediately after Capaldi's casting, some of them very funny. Steven Moffat explained that he hadn't held auditions for multiple actors but, as with John Nathan-Turner in casting the fifth and sixth Doctors, had had one actor in mind for the new Doctor; when Moffat had suggested Capaldi as the Doctor to BBC management, they had said yes: all agreed he was the right fit for the part. Capaldi recorded some specially written test pieces at Steven Moffat's house, one featuring the Doctor refusing to part with a spaceship's cargo of human beings to a Cyberleader that demands its stock back.

**"The Day of the Doctor"**

*The Guardian* in November 2013 wondered if there was a danger of OD'ing on *Doctor Who* (is it possible to do such a thing?). November brought a plethora of special programmes to all the BBC channels, and half hour features on each of the Doctors, originally made by BBC America, played on the digital channel Watch. Professor Brian Cox, who had appeared in "The Power of Three" (2012) as himself, speculating on the nature of the ubiquitous black cubes, presented *The Science of Doctor Who* on BBC 2; Matthew Sweet presented an excellent *Culture Show* special on the series. Of course, the major event was the seventy five minute special, "The Day of the Doctor" (2013), a tour de force of an episode broadcast on BBC 1 and simultaneously across the world in ninety four countries, earning the show another place in the *Guinness Book of Records* (alongside its place as the world's longest running science fiction series) as the largest ever worldwide "simulcast" of a television drama. The special was made in 3D, which meant more time than usual had to be set aside for Milk (the successor to The Mill) to complete its CGI effects. The 3D effects were principally appreciated in the three-dimensional painting *No More* or *Gallifrey Falls*; "Time Lord art," explains the Doctor, "Bigger on the inside."

The special played in several hundred cinemas across the world. Extraordinarily, "The Day of the Doctor" was one of the biggest box office hits for that week in the United Kingdom and the United States, placed third in the UK for that week after Hollywood blockbusters *The Hunger Games: Catching Fire* and *Gravity*. Box office takings accounted for £1.7 million in the UK and $10.2 million worldwide. With Wagnerian inevitability, the dusty engine of *Who* film rumours, which had stood idle for all of two years, shuddered into life: if BBC Worldwide could make this much money showing a television episode in the cinema, how much more could it make if it actually made a feature film? (Fans thought: here we go again). Appropriately and happily as a fiftieth anniversary special (how many other programmes have notched up that achievement?), "The Day of the Doctor" was the most highly rated programme on British television for that week, netting 12.8 million viewers. The Christmas special "The Time of the Doctor" (2013), Matt Smith's swan song, was second in the weekly twenty, with the last five minutes – the regeneration scene – pulling in the biggest television audience on Christmas Day in the United Kingdom. It was proved again, to a delighted BBC, that there was still life in a show that had run for eight years in its new form and twenty six in its original series: an extraordinary achievement. Steven Moffat swiftly confirmed that Peter Capaldi's first season, the show's eighth or thirty fourth, would be shown uninterrupted (that is, without a season break, unlike the thirty second and thirty third seasons), probably from the autumn of 2014. This was Moffat's favoured time slot for *Doctor Who*, bringing agreeable tea time terror to dark winter evenings as had Tom Baker's seasons as the Doctor, and, with luck, boosting the show's audience when it was not competing with glorious summer days: what could be nicer, on an early Saturday evening, when the football was over and it was a bit early to go to the pub, than to settle down with the family to watch *Doctor Who*? A thirty fifth season was confirmed for 2015.

"The Day of the Doctor" was a delight. David Tennant stepped back into the Doctor's shoes as though he had never been away. His scenes with Matt Smith had a tone of cheerful friendliness and banter, rather than the scrapping between incarnations of "The Three Doctors" (1973) forty years before. Billie Piper returned as the Moment, a Time Lord weapon so sophisticated that it has developed a self and a conscience. The Moment tries to take the form of Rose Tyler to communicate with the War Doctor (John Hurt) but gets it wrong and appears as the Bad Wolf: thus in the special, Billie Piper speaks with a received pronunciation, rather than a London, accent. In behind the scenes footage, she noted that David Tennant's old suit still fitted him; Davison, returning for the Children in Need special "Time Crash" (2007), said he was now unable to do up his old coat.

Moffat had had some meetings with Christopher Eccleston to see if he would be interested in reprising his role as the Doctor; the meetings were friendly but Eccleston, who had found working on the series an unhappy experience, eventually declined. Moffat reasoned that the ninth Doctor's absence was correct from the point of view of continuity: his had clearly been a new regeneration in "Rose" (2005) and the ninth Doctor couldn't therefore have fought in the Time War, which provided the bulk of the plot of "The Day of the Doctor". Moffat also said he couldn't see Paul McGann's eighth Doctor as ruthless enough to bring the Time War to an end by wiping out both the Daleks and the Time Lords. Making a virtue out of necessity, Moffat reasoned that there might be incarnations of the Doctor that he had kept hidden, or forgotten: a "mayfly" Doctor, who had flourished only briefly and had ended the Time War. Thus the War Doctor was born and revealed at the end of season thirty three's "The Name of the Doctor" (2013) as John Hurt. Hurt had hesitated before playing the part, but said his wife had pushed him into it with the words, "This is fucking Doctor Who!" He loved playing the Doctor and being associated with the series; he reprised his role as the War Doctor in audio plays for Big Finish before his untimely death in January 2017.

Hurt gave a wonderful performance, sporting a worn leather jacket, a beard (which he had asked Moffat if he could keep) and a world (or universe) weariness as he reluctantly concludes that the Time War can only be ended with genocide. In this incarnation, he doesn't even call himself "The Doctor": his eleventh self has supressed all memory of him, but his tenth remembers the number of children there were on Gallifrey when the Moment was activated. This is the question the Moment herself asks the War Doctor, testing his conscience and his reliance on the Just War theory to justify his decision. Hurt beautifully conveys the Doctor's reluctance to end the Time War and a pragmatism that borders on despair: he also allows glimpses of the Doctor's old self and humour to shine through as he tries to activate the Moment: "Why is there never a big red button?" Moffat's script has the War Doctor rehabilitated as the three Doctors rewrite history. They refuse to activate the Moment and call on all their other selves to use their TARDISes (actually, of course, the same TARDIS) to hide Gallifrey in an instant of time. This is a joyous moment for the viewers, as multiple police boxes barrel down onto Gallifrey and all the Doctors' past selves appear on the Time Lords' scanners. Most fantastic of all is the first appearance of Peter Capaldi as one of the Doctors; seen in extreme close up of his eyes and distinctive eyebrows scowling in concentration, cheers let rip throughout the land and at the BBC's huge convention in London's Excel centre, where thousands of fans gathered to celebrate the series and to watch the special on the big screen.

If this were not enough, and in another moment which the production team had managed to keep as a surprise, Tom Baker appeared in the closing minutes as the Curator of the Tower of London/UNIT headquarters exhibits. He is clearly a version of the Doctor, presumably from a different time stream where he has not regenerated but aged instead, thus following Queen Elizabeth I's instructions that the Doctor should look after her collection in the tower. Fans swooned in excitement.

And the other Doctors? Paul McGann appeared in a mini-episode, "The Night of the Doctor", in which the eighth Doctor, at some point in the Time War, comes to the aid of a distressed spaceship. The Doctor tries to save its pilot but she refuses to come with him, saying the Time Lords are as bad as the Daleks and preferring to go down with her ship. The eighth Doctor crashes on Karn, affectionately remembered by fans from "The Brain of Morbius" (1976); here, the Sisterhood of the Flame (led by RSC actress Claire Higgins – but fans were now getting blasé about distinguished actors appearing in the show) aid his regeneration into John Hurt: "Make me a warrior," the eighth Doctor breathes. Fans of the show were now drowning in milk and honey: could it really be true that the eighth Doctor was back on screen after an absence of sixteen years? And of course, it was

There was more. Peter Davison, understanding that it was unlikely he would appear in "The Day of the Doctor", proposed a special to Steven Moffat which the latter enthusiastically embraced. This was the half hour play *The Five-Ish Doctors Reboot*, written and directed by Davison and starring himself, Colin Baker and Sylvester McCoy. The three actors played versions of themselves, desperate to appear in the anniversary special and eventually disguising themselves as progenitor Daleks to sneak onto the set. There are some very funny moments with Baker and Davison grumbling about McCoy's success in *The Hobbit*, whose director, Peter Jackson[1],

---

[1] Jackson was a fan of *Doctor Who* and apparently owned two full sized Daleks. He was quoted as saying he wanted to direct some episodes of the show.

appears to tell Ian McKellen that McCoy won't be able to shoot a scene as Radagast the Brown; McKellen suggests that McCoy's absence might actually improve the scene. John Barrowman appears as himself, unable to appear in the "The Day of the Doctor" because he has a secret: a car full of little girls and a wife, again proving Barrowman's good-natured ability to laugh at himself.

*The Five-Ish Doctors Reboot* aired as a red button episode at anniversary-tide in November 2013; Moffat rejoiced at the appearance of the older Doctors on the new TARDIS set (itself based on the 1970s and 1980s designs piloted by those Doctors), enthusing about how good it was to feature them in the anniversary celebrations. He also noted that the spin-off circumvented the need for him to explain their ageing in the script for the special proper.

Moffat had even considered referencing Peter Cushing's Dr Who character from the 1960s Dalek movies; in his head, he explained, the Dalek movies existed in the *Doctor Who* universe as garbled, urban myth versions of the Doctor's adventures. The posters from the films were to be hung next to the photographs of past companions and Doctors Clara is shown by Kate Lethbridge Stewart; but, irony of ironies, the BBC couldn't afford the rights to posters from its own show's spin-offs.

## David Bradley plays William Hartnell

Another major event of the anniversary year was Mark Gatiss's play *An Adventure in Space and Time*. Taking its title from *Radio Times* tagline for the 1960s episodes, this was a beautifully written, acted and directed biopic of William Hartnell, Sidney Newman and Verity Lambert. Gatiss had, he said, wanted to write it for ten years and has considered it for the fortieth anniversary; but then, the show had been off the air and the likelihood of his play being commissioned was small. The play went through several drafts. One early version featured Terry Nation and Ray Cusick, the writer and designer of the Daleks respectively. If, as Esslin wrote, the root of all drama is conflict, then the relationship between these men contained the germ of an excellent drama: Cusick, arguably largely responsible for the Daleks' success, hadn't received a penny for his design while Nation made a fortune. In shaping the play, Gatiss realised that he had to cut and cut: Nation and Cusick disappeared, as did story editor David Whitaker. In the end, Gatiss centred on four people: Waris Hussein, who had directed "An Unearthly Child" (1963), the first producer Verity Lambert, creator Sydney Newman and William Hartnell.

The play is a delight and was even appreciated by those who were not particularly fans of *Doctor Who*. One of my teaching colleagues praised its insistence on the show's radicalism: she hadn't realised *Doctor Who* had been one of the first dramas to be produced by a woman, Verity Lambert (a wonderful performance by *Call the Midwife*'s Jessica Raine); it had also been directed by an Asian, and gay, man (acknowledged by the interest shown in Waris Hussein by one of the young men propping up the BBC bar) and created by a Canadian. David Bradley towered as William Hartnell, encapsulating the man's contradictions: his vanity, his sadness at the direction his career had taken, his enthusiasm for this new programme and his love of the character. The play lovingly celebrated *Doctor Who*, recreating iconic moments: old style Daleks trundled over Westminster Bridge in a scene shot in February 2013 and photographs of them appeared in broadsheet newspapers the following day; actors dressed as Menoptra and a "Tenth Planet" Cyberman wandered into shot, reading the paper and smoking between takes. Gatiss said he would have liked to feature the Zarbi but they couldn't afford them. The play's first shot is of a car which stops at last on foggy Barnes Common, near the comforting lights of a blue police box. This is, of course, a reference to the first chapter of the first novelisation, *Doctor Who* [taglined] *In An Exciting Adventure with the Daleks*: Ian Chesterton, frustrated by his failure to secure a job as a rocket scientist, is forced by the fog to stop on Barnes Common. The moment is a delight for fans and a visualisation of a scene which they had often played in their imagination but had never, until now, appeared on television. Anneke Wills (Polly) and Jean Marsh (Sara Kingdom) appeared as guests in the scene of Verity Lambert's farewell party; William Russell, the great Ian Chesterton, played Harry, a stuffy BBC jobsworth; Carole Ann Ford featured as a mother calling in her children to watch that new series they loved; Mark Eden, who had played Marco Polo in the eponymous 1964 adventure directed by Waris Hussein, had a cameo as Donald Baverstock (the Controller of BBC 1), who instructs Sydney Newman (Brian Cox) to kill the new series because it is too ambitious and too expensive. In a play full of poignant moments, a late scene showed Hartnell at the TARDIS console, about to record his final scene; the camera cuts away to Matt Smith as the Doctor, who smiles at him, thus reassuring him that the series will have a long and happy future: something which Hartnell's friends said would have delighted him.

A debate in the Australian Parliament praised *Doctor Who* and noted the contribution of Australians to the making of the series[1]; the MP sponsoring the debate invited the BBC to repeat its success in filming the show overseas by bringing the TARDIS to Australia, where the show had been a hit since 1965. Not to be outdone, the House of Lords in the United Kingdom praised the show and minuted its success.

**Regeneration 2013**

2013 ended with the Christmas special "The Time of the Doctor", thus completing the trilogy that had begun with "The Name of the Doctor" in May 2013. For the first time since "The Tenth Planet" (1966), we saw the Doctor reach the natural end of his regeneration, as the tenth Doctor grows old as the protector of the town of Christmas and Matt Smith is progressively aged by prosthetics and make up. Daleks, Cybermen, the Silents and the Weeping Angels featured in the special, which addressed the continuity question of

---

[1] Anthony Coburn, who wrote the first story "An Unearthly Child" (1963), was an Australian. He was also a Catholic and named Ian Chesterton after the Catholic novelist G.K.Chesterton.

how many regenerations could a Time Lord actually have, and how many has the Doctor had? The appearance of the War Doctor had thrown a spanner into the works, suggesting that Christopher Eccleston's Doctor was the tenth, not the ninth, and causing headaches for continuity hounds who thought they would have to renumber the lot. In *The Sarah Jane Adventures*, Russell T Davies had amused himself by having the eleventh Doctor tell Clive that a Time Lord can have hundreds of regenerations, when "The Deadly Assassin" (1976) and the TV movie (1996) had both insisted on twelve. The question was settled in "The Time of the Doctor" when the Doctor explains that the regeneration into the War Doctor counted, as did the tenth Doctor's regeneration into himself in "The Stolen Earth"/"Journey's End" (2008): that incarnation had "vanity issues", says the Doctor. Thus, the eleventh Doctor is actually the thirteenth, on his final regeneration and waiting to die. The Daleks eventually break through to Christmas to gloat at his death, but Gallifrey comes out of hiding and the Time Lords grant the Doctor a new regeneration cycle in a puff of gold breath from the crack in the universe that had featured from Matt Smith's first story, "The Eleventh Hour", in 2010. The Time Lords had offered Anthony Ainley's Master a new regeneration cycle as a reward for helping the Doctor escape the Death Zone in 1983's "The Five Doctors", so there was a precedent in the original series; casual viewers like *The Guardian*'s television reviewer said they found all this hard to follow.

Such is the force of the eleventh Doctor's regeneration that it blasts the Dalek ship out of the sky. Regeneration in the revived series seems to have very destructive properties: River Song knocks down a patrol of Nazi soldiers as she regenerates in "Let's Kill Hitler" (2011), the TARDIS blows up when the tenth Doctor regenerates and one wonders if Time Lords had to pay very high building insurance premiums on Gallifrey to cover regeneration demolition damage. Clara sees the young form of the tenth Doctor again in the TARDIS before he says goodbye to her and to an image of Amy – a cameo from Karen Gillan – and, in a surprise change from the volcanic regenerations of the revised series, Matt Smith simply flips into the form of the twelfth Doctor, Peter Capaldi. The new Doctor is clearly confused and suffering from post-regeneration trauma. Advancing on Clara, he asks, "Do you happen to know how to fly this thing?"

The first publicity photo of the twelfth Doctor in his new costume was issued by the BBC in January 2014. Capaldi sported a navy frock coat with dashing red lining, black trousers, an elegant, button down shirt (but no bow tie) and highly polished Dr Marten boots. Capaldi commented, "No frills, no scarf, no messing, just 100 per cent Rebel Time Lord". Fans were quick to spot the similarity in pose and costume to Jon Pertwee's third Doctor and hoped for a similar dynamic, action hero. They got one.

# 17

# A darker Doctor: twelfth knight

It might be said that the twelfth Doctor got off to an uncertain start. After three young a dynamic Doctors, we returned to an older actor playing the part. Peter Capaldi was fifty five when his first season aired. Perhaps acknowledging such difficulty as there was, Moffat wrote Clara in "Deep Breath" (2014) finding it hard to accept the new Doctor because he seemed so old. "Did you think he was young?" Madame Vastra asks her, and Matt Smith even appears in Capaldi's first episode telephoning Clara from the past and asking her to look after his successor, who is going to be frightened and alone.

Capaldi took some getting used to for the viewers. He had something of the spikiness and anger of the first, sixth and ninth Doctors, which was fine except that he was no longer funny and approachable like the tenth or eleventh, and made some viewers as wary of him as Clara. Like Tom Baker in "Robot" (1974), Capaldi is giving an excellent performance as the Doctor in his first story, "Deep Breath", suffering from post-regeneration trauma, wandering around Victorian London in his nightshirt and confused by his new Scottish accent. It is, however, a performance and Capaldi arguably doesn't quite settle into the part until later in his first season. Some of my secondary school students began to drift away from the programme at this point, missing the comforting, quirky Doctors of Tennant and Smith; some said they were getting fed up with the increasingly convoluted plots and Moffat's love of tangled time paradoxes. As Capaldi moved into a second and a third season as the Doctor, he increasingly called to mind Jon Pertwee's avuncular Doctor: not least because of the similar costume and his increasingly long, curly grey mop of hair.

Clara stuck around to ease the viewer into the new run of episodes with a new Doctor, as Ben, Polly, Sarah Jane, Tegan, Adric, Nyssa, Peri, Mel and Rose had done before her. This was a fine strategy as far as it went and had worked well in the past, but it arguably wasn't entirely successful here because Clara herself wasn't entirely likeable. She was clever, able to look after herself, devoted to the Doctor, brave, resourceful... in fact, as a commentator wrote in *The Guardian*, she ticked all the boxes but the production team had forgotten to make her likeable. She wasn't allowed to be funny or cheeky, like Amy before her, and sometimes came across as somewhat pert and pleased with herself. Thus season thirty four began with a difficult new Doctor and a so-so established companion: it was a good thing that Strax, Vastra and Jenny were on board to welcome the twelfth Doctor into the world ("Deep Breath", 2014).

In the same way that Russell T Davies had been fascinated by Rose, it seemed that Moffat and his team were far more interested in the companion than the viewers were. Rose kept turning up after leaving the Doctor[1] in Norway in "Doomsday" (2006): Clara hung around for three seasons, as long as Jo or Sarah Jane in the 1970s. As Clara's story arc as the Impossible Girl, splintered in time in several incarnations to help the Doctor, was really played out by the end of "The Name of the Doctor" in 2013, there wasn't much reason for her to stick around. Jenna Coleman had thought hard about moving on at the end of her second year and Clara was written out in "Last Christmas" (2014). In a very touching scene, Clara appeared as an elderly woman who has lost all strength in her hands: the twelfth Doctor has to help her pull a Christmas cracker[2]. Moffat said in 2018 that he thought he hadn't really finished with Clara and that Jenna would stay on: as indeed she did, for another season.

Moffat had prepared a replacement companion in case Jenna Coleman decided to leave early. This replacement was, he said, to have had some of the characteristics which were eventually found in

---

[1] Actually, it was a projection of him and he was burning up a sun to send it. Such is love.

[2] This referenced, and reversed, a scene in "The Time of the Doctor" (2013), when Clara helps the elderly eleventh Doctor to pull a Christmas cracker.

Bill[1], Capaldi's final companion, but she remained forever in the time vortex of possibilities with Penny, the companion Russell T Davies had scripted as a replacement for Martha before Catherine Tate's return as Donna was secured[2]. Clara was given a job as an English teacher at Cole Hill School (Chairman of Governors: Ian Chesterton) – where Susan Foreman had been a pupil back in 1963 – and a boyfriend, Danny Pink, later transformed into a Cyberman. She also had a flat in what appeared to be the same block as Rose. Moffat introduced another companion, Ashildr, into season thirty five (season nine). Here, *Doctor Who* cashed in on the popularity of *Game of Thrones* (2011-) in casting Maisie Williams as Ashildr[3], which was fine except that she was a bit wooden and her character was terribly dull. Eventually, she and Clara slip off together in a Hartnell-control-roomed TARDIS to explore the universe ("Hell Bent" (2015)). The Doctor has subjected himself to a mindwipe and forgets Clara.

When Capaldi's first episode was aired, Steven Moffat had been showrunner for some five years and *Doctor Who* seemed – a little – to be losing its way. The production team wasn't always clear in distinguishing between a good idea and a terrible one. This isn't to say that there weren't some excellent stories – there were some crackers – but there was a bit of a wobble after Matt Smith left, accompanied by a falling off in the viewing figures, of which more later. At the end of 2015, the BBC kindly lent a hand by taking the show off the air, yet again, for a year: there was only one episode in 2016, the Christmas special "The Return of Doctor Mysterio"[4]. This was the fourth year that there had not been a full run of episodes since the show's return in 2005 and it royally browned off fans and merchandisers.

---

[1] Interview for *The Fan Show*, BBC online
[2] Donna returned in "Partners in Crime", the first story of season thirty (season four).
[3] She played Arya Stark in *Game of Thrones*.
[4] *Doctor Mysterio* is what the show is called in Mexico. Moffat liked it and used it in the script as the title the Doctor would have had if he had been a Superman-type superhero.

## Attack of the Ideologues

The reasons for the pause between seasons in 2016 are buried deep in the Lost Scrolls of Rassilon, but the perennial need to save money was a likely motivator. So too, for the BBC, was a sense of being once again under political siege. The Conservative Party had been unexpectedly returned to power with a small majority in 2015 and the new culture secretary, John Whittingdale, was a neocon who opposed all publicly owned bodies on principle, particularly the BBC, which was full of Bolsheviks who failed to trumpet the achievements of the previous Conservative-led government. Whittingdale served notice on the BBC that it was not to expect an easy ride under this new administration and there seemed to be a possibility of the Corporation being broken up and privatised. Certainly, a plan was – and is – in place to require the BBC to "outsource" all its programmes. All radio and television programmes, including *Doctor Who*, could expect to find themselves put out to tender. The BBC, it was generously decreed, could bid to make its own programmes itself: hence the tagline which started to appear at the end of BBC shows stating that this was a BBC Studios Production, the newly-formed umbrella organisation which would eventually bid to make BBC programmes. For the first time since 1990, fans were wondering if, to quote the BBC line from the time, that *Doctor Who* would probably, eventually, be made by an independent company[1].

Whittingdale was not a particularly popular figure within the Conservative Party. Former party chairman and Cabinet minister Chris Patten said he was a ridiculous ideologue – and Theresa May sacked him when she became Prime Minister in 2016. The BBC held its breath. Talk of programmes being farmed out to compulsory tender went quiet as the new government prepared for the EU referendum, the fallout from Brexit (every bit as complex and dangerous as moves to take the planet Peladon in and then out of the

---

[1] BBC letter to author, 1994.

Galactic Federation[1]), and the loss of its majority in the 2017 general election. The government was too busy to worry too much about the BBC – although, unlike the Peladonians, it didn't have to contend with martial law imposed by a rogue group of Ice Warriors. We think. The BBC Studios logo remains and concluded season thirty six (season 10) *Doctor Who* episodes in 2017, but the show remained a BBC production into season thirty seven (season 11) with Jodie Whittaker.

This political pressure reportedly created a sense of unease and even siege at the BBC, with employees wondering whether there would be a BBC to employ them in a few years' time. The Conservative-led governments after 2010 loudly rejected any requests for an increase in the BBC's television licence fee, and the BBC's source of revenue was uncertain: hence the perceived need to save money, which could presumably be facilitated in part by resting *Doctor Who* in 2016. Again, this wasn't necessarily a sensible move on the Corporation's part. The show paid for itself many times over in overseas sales – but the money came back into the coffers of BBC Worldwide, an organisation disliked by the Conservative Party. The Tories had said that the BBC should generate revenue other than the licence fee, but BBC Worldwide was a victim of its own success and the government disapproved. It wasn't fair to have a publicly funded body making money from a stake paid initially by taxpayers through the television licence, putting, as it did, poor little impoverished private companies like Rupert Murdoch's Sky TV at a disadvantage. The BBC couldn't win, but the Conservative Party and its allies (like Rupert Murdoch) didn't want it to. Was the problem with *Doctor Who* that it was *too* successful? If it made too much money for Worldwide, would the government start bashing the BBC again? If any programme was ripe for privatisation, it was the internationally successful, profit-generating *Doctor Who*. Ironically, the best way for the BBC to keep the show in house was to rest it.

---

[1] See "The Curse of Peladon" (1972) and "The Monster of Peladon" (1974), in which High Priest Hepesh and delegate Arcturus are clearly members of UKIP: Unilateral Kingdoms on Independent Planets. No?

Once again, with no show on the air, merchandisers had no platform from which to launch their wares. *Who* toys and models had been staples of toyshops and supermarket toy departments in the Eccleston and Tennant years: now they were banished to specialist shops and online order. This is a big deal: BBC Worldwide announced in early 2018 that over eighteen million DVDs, twelve million action figures and four million sonic screwdrivers had been sold since the show returned in 2005[1]. Something like seventy companies held active merchandising licences[2] and the lack of a series inevitably imperilled their revenue. Once again, the standing sets in TARDIS were left dark. When we consider what are the existential threats to *Doctor Who* as a television series, and wonder how many years it will still be on our screens, one of those threats is the Conservative Party, which always wages war against the public sector: the Labour Party and the Liberal Democrats support publicly owned, public service broadcasting. Perhaps the Labour Party's fortunes would improve if it adopted a poster campaign headlined, "Vote Conservative: Kill Doctor Who". As long as the Conservative government is distracted by its own troubles, the BBC, and *Doctor Who*, appear reasonably safe.

**Enter Bill**

The 2016 break did have the effect of giving the production team a chance to rethink and reinvigorate the show: something Russell T Davies had said was always the plan when the revived show took its first break in 2009[3]. Capaldi's final season was a much more confident and exciting beast than his first two, when it finally burst onto our screens in 2017. Its success was not least due to a softening

---

[1] The news that over four million sonic screwdrivers have been sold since 2005 is my second favourite statistic unearthed since I began researching this book. My favourite will always be Mat Irvine's revelation that the special effects budget for each episode of *Blake's Seven* was fifty quid.

[2] BBC Worldwide brand and licensing update in *Toyworld* magazine, early 2018. The figure of seventy companies applies to January 2018.

[3] Was this the real reason or the whole truth? Hmm.

in the Doctor's character: he has now been a lecturer at St Luke's University for many years (St Luke was a doctor, so this is a pun). Hailed as a brilliant teacher who has been there for longer than anyone can remember: shades of Professor Chronotis, the Cambridge University don in "Shada" (1979). The Doctor is now 2000 years old, so he has aged 1100 years since Christopher Eccleston accosted Rose in the department store ("Run!") in "Rose" (2005). The TARDIS is parked in the Doctor's study, he is attended by the bald alien Nardole (Matt Lucas) as his batman, and he guards the creature in the vault from prying eyes. The Capaldi Doctor has reverted back to Tom Baker's description of the character as a benevolent alien with secrets. Again, the Doctor shows his liberal and all-embracing ideology in befriending his new companion and inviting her to take his classes: this is a working class woman who serves chips in the canteen, Bill Potts.

That this is a rejuvenated show was admitted by Steven Moffat in the changing of the name of episode one from "A Star in Her Eye" to "The Pilot". Bill is a major factor in the show's new energy and confidence. Pearl Mackie's performance is a joy. Bill is funny, clever, full of life and bursts with enthusiasm at the sight of every new alien wonder: "It speaks emoji!" she cries on seeing the first "proper" robot in "Smile" (2017). Mackie's Bill is also warm, affectionate and a real person. She startles both the Doctor and the viewer when she asks, "Can I use the toilet?" in "The Pilot" – a good joke when the TARDIS's lavatories haven't been mentioned before. Nardole has just used it, however, and tells Bill, "I'd give it a minute if I were you." In so saying, Nardole marries that British institution *Doctor Who* with that even longer lived British institution, toilet humour. Moffat skilfully tops the joke with realism as Bill explains quietly, embarrassed, to a Time Lord who presumably has a different (or no?) excretory system, "I've had a fright. I need the toilet." The realism is perfect and the link between the science fiction and the real world, fundamental.

There is similar engagement with reality (whatever that is) in Bill's sexual identity as a lesbian. She has several girlfriends in the course of the season, not least the water-pouring, time and space hopping Heather, with whom Bill is reunited in the final story and saved from eternal conversion into a Cyberman. First Danny Pink, then the Brigadier, now Bill: travelling with the twelfth Doctor clearly carries a high risk of cyber conversion or death. And they almost converted Craig in "The Lodger" (2010). Even Clara is killed in "Face the Raven" (2015), before she is saved between breath and breath by Ashildr. Are Bill and Heather named after William Hartnell (Bill) and his wife, Heather[1]?

Moffat and producer Brian Minchin were adamant that Bill was to be a black companion and only black actresses were auditioned. Peter Capaldi commented that, as he was an actor, he understood what they were going through and wanted to cast them all[2]. Pearl Mackie came to the auditions from a run in the Royal National Theatre production of *The Curious Incident of the Dog in the Night Time* and delighted the production team with her freshness and energy. She was duly cast and, as usual with *Who*, instructed to tell no-one. Pearl recalled her audition[3] and thinking, well, it's fun, it's *Doctor Who*, but I'll never get it; then she was told she'd got the part and, thrilled, had to do a matinee that day and keep schtum.

Pearl Mackie had seen hardly any *Doctor Who* before and the team invited her to watch previous episodes to familiarise herself with it. She said she didn't want to, as the world of the programme was new to Bill and she wanted it to be new to herself. This acting choice pays off in the final programme in Bill's spontaneous delight, fear and absolutely convincing reactions to each new world. All contributed to make Bill one of the best and most loved companions in the whole of the series' run. We can only lament that she lasted a single season, but the new team under Chris Chibnall had,

---

[1] John Smith's parents are similarly named in "Human Nature" (2007) as Sidney and Verity, after *Doctor Who*'s creator Sydney Newman and its first producer, Verity Lambert, who surely have a claim to be the parents of John Smith/Doctor Who. (John Smith has been the Doctor's alias since "Spearhead from Space" (1970)).

[2] Season Ten Blu Ray Extra, BBC Worldwide, 2017.

[3] ibid

understandably, to clear the decks for the accession of Jodie Whittaker.

## The stories

The range of stories told in the twelfth Doctor's era is as broad as ever. From medieval myth in "Robot of Sherwood" (2014) to science fantasy in "Mummy on the Orient Express" (2014); experiments in form from "Listen" (2014) and "Heaven Sent" (2015), in which the Doctor, respectively, expresses his paranoia in tracking an invisible and intangible menace, then repeats his actions billions of times in the only story ever to feature the Doctor as the sole character (although he is menaced by the cowled figure of the Veil).

"Robot of Sherwood" played up the comical and mythical possibilities of the series' format. Striding out of the TARDIS, determined to prove his point to Clara, the Doctor declares: "No damsels in distress, no pretty castles, no such thing as Robin Hood." An arrow immediately thuds into the TARDIS and we cut to the story's other immortal hero, the Earl of Loxley himself, who gives a cheeky wink. The timing of the story was a little unfortunate as it inevitably recalled *Robin Hood* (2006-2009), the BBC's replacement family show when *Who* was off the air, and we blinked at the new cast for the Merrie Men when we'd got used to Jonas Armstrong[1] and co.. But the story was great fun and gave Jenna Coleman a chance to do some comedy when captured by the Sheriff of Nottingham (Ben Miller, fresh from his BBC sketch shop *Armstrong and Miller*). Clara endures his boasting and tries to keep up:

> Sheriff: Once upon a time, there was a brave and clever and handsome man.
> Clara: I can almost picture him. I don't even have to close

---

[1] Robin in *Robin Hood.*

my eyes.

In "The Caretaker" (2014), writer Gareth Roberts took us back to the scenario of the Doctor assuming a human role, as he, Roberts, had in "The Lodger" (2010) and "Closing Time" (2011), here lurking in Cole Hill School as a caretaker to keep an eye on Clara and her possibly shifty new boyfriend Danny Pink. That an English teacher (Clara) should be above reproach and a Maths teacher (Danny) somewhat suspect and strange is entirely according to the natural order of the universe. These stories were fun but, like others of the episodes in season thirty four (eight), were actually a bit forgettable and lacklustre among that year's few gems. "Mummy on the Orient Express" (2014) was a fantasy set on a train in space which recalled the space liner Titanic in "Voyage of the Damned" (2007); "In the Forest of the Night" (2014) had London overgrown with forest and the Doctor protecting a group of schoolchildren. One of the problems with the first Capaldi season was its lack of real evil. *Doctor Who* often works best when it is about an elemental clash between good and evil: this season, there was an overabundance of whimsy and of the revelation that the aliens were not actually evil at all but had a different motivation from the humans and were misunderstood. The aliens in "Deep Breath" (2014) harvest human organs but only because they wish to survive; the Sheriff of Nottingham's ambitions are small beer in "Robot of Sherwood" (2014); there is no evil enemy at all in "Listen" (2014) or "Kill the Moon" (2014). Even Rusty the Dalek is good (sort of) in "Into the Dalek" (2014). As the Doctor says in "Twice Upon A Time" (2017), "I don't really know what to do when it isn't an evil plan," and the programme becomes a little bit dull. It's fine to have some whimsy and misunderstood aliens – they're not evil, they just have different values from us – in some stories. It's a big drain on the drama if there is too much of either.

And the gems? "Flatline" (2014) was a beautifully realised and inventive story concerning two dimensional aliens who destroy by converting our three dimensional world into their two dimensions.

The Monks trilogy in 2017 overflowed with creative ideas. In "Extremis", we discovered that the Doctor, Nardole and Bill who investigate the Veritas – a book which sends anyone who reads it, mad – are actually computer simulations in a wargame modelled by the alien Monks. In "The Pyramid at the End of the World", the Doctor helps scientist Erica to destroy a GM-modified bacteria which, if released into the atmosphere, would destroy all life on Earth. The Doctor is blind, trapped in the laboratory which is about to blow up, and unable to see the combination of the door lock which Erica recites to him. The Monks can save him and humanity, but only if they are invited to do so and invited out of love. They have already dispatched two sets of supplicants, who have crumbled to ash (an example of the upping of the horror imagery in Capaldi's era) because their requests for help were impure. Bill asks them to save the Doctor by restoring his sight: they judge that she acts out of love and grant her request. But the Doctor has warned Bill that the Monks' price will be too high. In "The Lie of the Land", the Monks are now the rulers of a convincing dystopian Earth. Writer Toby Whithouse cleverly exploits the propaganda of totalitarian governments in contrasting the propaganda ideal with the miserable reality[1]. The Doctor's uplifting broadcasts about the Monks' beneficence – "Two species, sharing a history as happily as they share a planet, humanity and the Monks are a blissful and perfect partnership" – contrasts with the grey skies and the humans' drab black and navy blue clothes. Bill, who is usually so colourful and effervescent, is dressed thus and has had her hair severely tied back. A woman is arrested for possession of an article which contravenes the Memory Crimes Act of 1975; a child is sent to a prison camp for ten years' hard labour for possession of a box of comics. The Doctor

---

[1] *Doctor Who* has employed a similar contrast several times, notably in episode one of "The Armageddon Factor" (1979). The episode starts with an heroic, brightly lit television drama, in which a heroine says farewell to her heroic husband, going off to fight the war "so that Atrios might live". We cut to the miserable reality of war: bombed hospitals, civilians cowering underground, the blimpish military dictatorship fighting on when they have already lost.

appears to have joined the Monks and, for the third time in the series (after "The Invasion of Time" (1978) and "Mindwarp" (1986)), appears to be evil.

This is the first ever three part story – or six part story of the original series – to have its three episodes written by different writers. In his final episode, Toby Whithouse mined deeply from that seminal dystopian text, *Nineteen Eighty-Four* by George Orwell[1], which is no bad thing: if you are going to borrow, borrow from the best. The Monks have only been on Earth for six months, but their mind control convinces almost everyone they always have been here, benevolently guiding humanity from the time of our ancestors' first emergence as amphibians from the seas. This, of course, is "The Lie of the Land" and the Monks, like the Party in *Nineteen Eighty-Four*, have used propaganda to rewrite history. With the Party, they could claim that:

> Who controls the past controls the future: who controls the present controls the past.[2]

In the end, it is love which defeats evil. Bill's love for her mother blots out the lies broadcast from the Monks' control pyramid, the Monks are destroyed, and humans – much to the Doctor's despair – demonstrate their inability to learn from history by forgetting the lot.[3]

---

[1] First published in 1948: Orwell named the novel by reversing the last two numerals. Presumably if he had finished it the next year it would have been called, *Nineteen Ninety-Four*. The naming emphasised the fact that the novel was a satire on the present day. It was a good thing he didn't finish it in 1950.

[2] *Nineteen Eighty-Four*, Part III, Chapter ii.

[3] The Monks are horrific, corpse-like creatures whose mouths form into an O when they speak. Tim Bentinck, who voiced the Monks, said fans had asked him how he had researched their cavernous, dead voices. He explained that he had watched the finished visuals, seen what the Monks looked like and how they opened their mouths, and immediately provided a voice which suited the O. (Conversation with the author, 2017)

The theme that love defeats evil, that goodness always wins eventually, runs through Capaldi's final season and triumphantly emphasises the Christian morality of the series. Christ suffered but defeated evil through his loving sacrifice of himself: Bill and the Doctor suffer but their repeated acts of self-sacrifice save the world. In "Twice Upon A Time" (2017), the first Doctor (David Bradley) wonders why goodness should ever prevail when evil is more powerful: "Evil should always win. Good is not a practical survival strategy. It requires loyalty, self-sacrifice and love. So why does good prevail?"[1] His question is answered in the previous episode, "The Doctor Falls" (2017), with the meeting of two incarnations of the Master, John Simm and Michelle Gomez. Both Missy and the Master demonstrate treachery, self-interest and hatred: they stab each other in the back, which they both think is hilarious, and limp off to death and regeneration. The two Doctors, the first and the twelfth, work together selflessly: instead of turning on each other, their energy is directed outwards to find beneficial solutions. The first Doctor's question is also addressed in the twelfth's advice to his imminent successor: "Hate is always foolish and love is always wise."

There were other excellent Capaldi stories. Rona Munro returned as a writer with 2017's "The Eaters of Light". River Song returned in "The Husbands of River Song", the 2015 Christmas special. Here, she fails to recognise the twelfth Doctor and Capaldi gets a hilarious scene when she invites the Doctor into the TARDIS and he runs around, open-mouthed, in imitation of almost every previous companion: "Oh. My, God! Oh, it's bigger on the inside than it is on the outside." The Doctor eventually reveals who he is to River and they live in married bliss for twenty four years at the Singing Towers of Darillium: from here, River tells the tenth Doctor in "The Forest of the Dead" (2008), the Doctor, in tears, sent her to the

---

[1] Madame Kovarian harps on the same theme in "A Good Man Goes to War" (2011). The good Doctor's disadvantage in the fight against her evil is that "good men have too many rules".

Library and her death. Seven years on from her first appearance, River's timeline comes to its end.

"The Husbands of River Song" also features a servant called Nardole, played by Matt Lucas, whose head is eventually cut off and mounted on a giant robot once inhabited by River's ex-husband, Hydroflax. Matt Lucas reprised the role for "The Return of Dr Mysterio" (2016) and the whole of the 2017 season, his character slightly toned down into the mildly fussy and irritable valet to the Doctor. As such, Nardole continually nags him about his duty to attend to the Vault and not go gallivanting off into time and space (shades of the third Doctor and the Brigadier). Matt Lucas is an international star who lives in Los Angeles and was starting a Hollywood career: he appeared as Tweedledum and Tweedledee in Tim Burton's *Alice in Wonderland* (2010) and its sequel, and had a small role in *Bridesmaids* (2011). Steven Moffat said that Lucas was more than happy to give all this up and live in Cardiff for a year, just so that he could be in *Doctor Who*. Why on earth, mused Moffat, wouldn't we then want to bring Nardole back?

**Declining popularity…?**

In spite of all the creativity and dedication to *Doctor Who* by international stars, in spite of the best companion to have graced the show for years, there was a decline in its viewing figures in the United Kingdom. This wasn't anything like as severe as the British press loved to make it appear: a preposterous story in *The Guardian* pronounced that the viewing figures had halved from ten million under Tennant to five million under Capaldi, a conclusion which could only be arrived at by taking the top rated Tennant story and comparing it with the lowest rated Capaldi's story. Nevertheless, there was some decline. Five or six million viewers was not unheard of even in Tennant's or Matt Smith's time, but Tennant's seasons averaged 8.4 million viewers in the UK, Smith's averaged eight million and Capaldi's, 6.4 million[1]. On the other hand, we are not fully comparing like with like as the way ratings are calculated has changed to reflect, more or less, the new ways in which people watch television. Eccleston's and Tennant's seasons were repeated on BBC 3, and these repeat figures could be added to the original broadcast to create a final viewing figure; BBC 3 then went online only. From 2007, viewers could watch *Doctor Who* on its online catch-up service, BBC iPlayer, but only those who watched iPlayer on a television counted towards the viewing figures, not those who watched iPlayer on a computer or a tablet, nor those who watched the programme more than seven days after its first broadcast. To look on the positive side, *Doctor Who* still regularly made the top twenty programmes of the week and never, under Capaldi, fell below the week's top thirty. Nine of Capaldi's episodes hit the top ten and "Twice Upon A Time" netted 7.92 million viewers and a number eight place in the week's top forty programmes. There has been a decline, and even some falling off in the average viewing figures of each of Capaldi's seasons, but the programme still does well and the viewing figures are more than respectable.

When will the ratings decline so much that they hit the danger zone when *Doctor Who* is under threat? What is the danger zone anyway? Four million viewers? As the BBC is a public service broadcaster, the decision to make or axe a programme isn't driven purely by ratings alone. You have to wait for an exec like Michael Grade to show up ha ha. A show *can* continue to be made even if its ratings decline, although draining viewing figures will usually cause even the generous BBC to look carefully at a programme's viability. *Doctor Who* is an international hit which makes huge sums for BBC Worldwide (just think of the millions of sonic screwdrivers sold) and pays for its budget – apparently at the top end of the BBC budgets for Drama – many times over. But what if Worldwide makes too much money and attracts the ire of a reforming Conservative government? Could the Doctor be *too* successful? Would the programme's success internationally be enough to save it

---

[1] "Public Image", *Doctor Who Magazine* no. 522, March 2018.

from the axe if viewing figures in the home market declined? International success should be sufficient, but we live in crazy times.

How safe is the programme? Who knows? Steven Moffat said in 2010 said it was as secure as any television programme could be. Perhaps a new Doctor and a new production team will regenerate the franchise again in 2018. For every person who has vowed that They Will Never Watch The Programme Again now that the Doctor is female, as many more have expressed enthusiasm about the Doctor's new persona and have vowed to tune in to Jodie Whittaker's first season. As we approach the thirty seventh season and the programme's fifty fifth year, the question remains: How safe is *Doctor Who* on television? Well, time, as the Doctor once said, will tell. It always does.

# 18

# Hate is Always Foolish
# and Love is Always Wise

In January 2017, Peter Capaldi announced that he would be leaving the series after three seasons. This was a calendar total of four of our Earth years, given that there was only one new episode in 2016. Capaldi summed up his time in the part in December 2017:

> For me, it's been an amazing trip. I went to the end of time. I met fantastical creatures. And I blew them up.[1]

Ever enthusiastic about a show business story (and perhaps bored with Brexit?), the media rumour mill ground into predictable action and threw up names which had been "leaked" by "a BBC insider": that is to say, were made up by some TV editor at his desk. Kris Marshall was often mentioned. He had starred in later series of the light BBC detective show *Death in Paradise* (2011-present), where his performance as Humphrey Goodman and boyish good looks suggested he might be reminiscent of Peter Davison's fifth Doctor. Sacha Dhawan was another name in the running. He'd been in the original production of Alan Bennett's play *The History Boys* (Royal National Theatre, 2004) and was noted by *Doctor Who* fans for his performance as Waris Hussein in *An Adventure in Space and Time*. Stephen Moffat had revealed that a black actor had, at one point, been asked to play the Doctor and had turned it down, so Dhawan was a hot favourite. Moffat had already established that regeneration could bring about a change in skin colour as the episode "Hell Bent" (2015) had seen the white Time Lord General regenerate into a black woman. This Moffatian addition to the series' mythology was in addition to his revelation through Missy/the Master that Time

---

[1] Quoted on thedoctorwhocompanion.com 18.12.17

Lords could also change gender at regeneration[1] and the rumour mill confidently and simultaneously predicted that the new Doctor would be a black male woman. "BBC insiders" in the press poo-poohed a change of gender and said it was just a rumour designed to whip the tabloids into a frenzy, as had a similar rumour in 1981 when Tom Baker wished his successor luck – "Whoever he or she might be." [2]

There was no repeat of the slightly silly television special which had announced Peter Capaldi's casting as the twelfth Doctor in 2013. Instead, the BBC announced on 14th July, 2017 that the new Doctor would be revealed immediately after the Wimbledon Men's Singles Final on 16th July, 2017. This was following the precedent of the introduction of Pearl Mackie as Bill Potts, which had been screened in the interval of the FA Cup semi final on 23rd April, 2016.

The 2017 special scene opens on a wood. A hooded figure, wearing a long coat, is seen from the back. The costume hides the gender, although – are the hips wide for a male? The figure wears Capaldi-style boots and we hear breathing. A long shot of the figure walking with wide steps, a rusting cannon wheel in the foreground. We see a broken stone wall: was this the site of a battle in the distant past? A shot of the figure raising its hand – are the nails manicured? – and we hear the familiar TARDIS materialisation sound[3] as the ship's key appears in its palm. There is an extreme close up of an

---

[1] The 1996 TV movie showed that Time Lords could change species at regeneration by transforming the Master into a spectral CGI cobra. This terrible idea was buried in the post-2005 revival, as was the "revelation" that the Doctor was half-human. *Doctor Who* has a habit of moving swiftly on from terrible ideas in its continuity: for example, the young and nervous Dalek who said "er, er" in "The Chase" (1965) was never resurrected.

[2] This had been producer John Nathan-Turner's idea, whose strengths as a producer included a talent for generating interest in the show by laying false trails for the press. In 1984, he let it be known that the exterior of the TARDIS would change from being a police box, as no-one knew what police boxes were any more. He never had any such intention, but the story ran for several weeks.

[3] A series of thirty second teasers as to the thirteenth Doctor's identity had run on the BBC in 2017, showing the TARDIS key materialising in various locations like the summit post of a hill. It eventually materialised in Whittaker's hand in the scene shown on 16th July, 2017.

eye, heavily fringed, its iris green-brown, full of depth. A one second view as the figure starts to push back its hood, then a cut to a front view as the new Doctor is revealed as – a woman. Beautiful, she has short cropped golden hair and dark eyebrows. The new Doctor smiles slowly as she sees the TARDIS and she walks towards the breach in the broken wall. The lamp on the TARDIS beams in welcome. A caption in three stages:

Introducing
Jodie Whittaker
The Thirteenth Doctor

Many viewers jumped up and down in excitement as the new Doctor pushed her hood back and there are some lovely videos on You Tube of fans watching the special scene: one shows a little girl wide-mouthed with delight, who exclaims "It's a girl!" Other viewers, sadly, were dismayed and a minority of fans were quick to reject the casting: the Doctor was a male character, it was just political correctness to cast a woman, and so on and so on. Social media and fan sites went wild and Monday morning's newspapers led with the story, which was partly the BBC's intention.

Amid all the fuss, the point was made that *Doctor Who* had been in something of a decline for the past few years. True, the show was still a huge hit internationally. Overseas enthusiasm for more *Doctor Who* was again confirmed when Chinese television signed an order in May 2017 for the next five seasons: this didn't indicate, of course, that the BBC would commission another five seasons but that, were they made, the Chinese broadcaster Shanghai Media Group Pictures (SMG) would snap them up. Yet in the United Kingdom, it seemed that fewer people were watching *Doctor Who* year on year and the show needed a shot in the arm if it was to survive.

Depending on how you interpreted them, it could be argued that the viewing figures had declined from an average of some eight million in 2013 to six million in 2017. The radical and imaginative casting of Jodie Whittaker certainly generated the hoped-for excitement and publicity. Many couldn't wait to see her as the Doctor. The BBC had other ideas and, having thoroughly whetted our appetites, allowed the excitement to dissipate. Instead of cashing in on the enthusiasm by broadcasting a new series in, say, March 2018, the corporation let it be known that Jodie Whittaker's first season would not be screened until the autumn[1]. Still, it all drummed up interest in the 2017 Christmas special "Twice Upon A Time". This was described by director Rachel Talalay as "a fanboys' dream" and featured three Doctors: the twelfth, the first (played now by David Bradley) and the thirteenth, as well as appearances by the re-cast original companions Ben and Polly[2].

**Ideology and the new Doctor**

Reactions to the casting of the thirteenth Doctor were sometimes both extreme and diametrically opposed. To understand them, we need to look both into current ideological divisions and back into the show's history. Piers D. Britton writes[3] of the Doctor's status as a figure of authority and even aristocracy. Like Jason King, Brett Sinclair[4], John Steed and Adam Adamant, the Doctor in the classic series had often been of the upper classes or upper middle classes. He was a whiggish adventurer, welcomed by the working classes as a sympathetic champion who was at once one of them and socially above them. Britton emphasises the "Lord" of "Time Lord" in the Doctor's character: he is a paternalist who champions the weak against the strong but retains his distance in social status. This is particularly the case in the persona of Jon Pertwee's third Doctor, but holds for the fourth and fifth Doctors: the latter, for example, slips easily into his place as batsman for an upper-class cricket team in "Black Orchid" (1982) and the fourth leads the workers to

---

[1] The BBC made the same mistake when it announced Capaldi's casting as the twelfth Doctor in August 2013, a year before his first full episode was screened.
[2] Last seen in "The Faceless Ones" (1967)
[3] Piers D. Britton, *TARDISbound*, London, 2011
[4] In, respectively, *Department S* (1969-1970) and *The Persuaders!* (1970)

revolution in "The Sun Makers" (1977). We might think of a figure like Anthony Wedgewood Benn, who renounced his title as the second Viscount Stansgate to become plain Tony Benn, the aristocratic socialist who drank mugs of tea, was a welcome visitor at the annual Durham Miners' Rally (as the Doctor was welcomed by Welsh miners in "The Green Death" (1973)) and a mentor of the Labour Party leader, Jeremy Corbyn. The classic series Doctor might have been a plummy-voiced toff, but he was a decent toff, our toff, who championed the working classes. Britton's identification of the Doctor as an aristocratic interventionist can be taken further: from the early sixties to the early eighties, the role of aristocratic interventionist was seen as an exclusively male one.

It may well be, then, that the visceral objections to the Doctor being female come from socially conservative people (men?) who are happy to take instructions from a man, but not from a woman. Such women as have held positions of power in late twentieth century Britain have had to assume masculine personae. The writer John Mortimer's objection to Mrs Thatcher was that she was altogether too masculine and aggressive, and Germaine Greer once suggested that Mrs Thatcher's popularity as a strong, strident and authoritarian Prime Minister was attributable to *le vice Anglais*: masochism. Greer's point was recently echoed in an episode of *The Crown*. Elizabeth II is furious that her advisers, and the Prime Minister himself, have hidden from her the fact that Churchill has had a stroke. She is inclined to give them a good dressing down but wonders if it is inappropriate from someone of her age, education and gender. "Why?" her tutor replies, and goes on to say that they are male, upper class and English. A telling off from nanny is what they would like best in the world.[1]

It seems, then, that some socially conservative viewers would only accept a female authority figure who demonstrates some masculine, aggressive qualities. It also seems clear that Jodie Whittaker's

---

[1] *The Crown* stars Matt Smith as Prince Philip. He was initially reluctant to take the role in another long running series with a punishing filming schedule, so soon after finishing his run on *Doctor Who*.

thirteenth Doctor, far from being Mrs Thatcher in the TARDIS, is going to retain her femininity. There is a certain type of person (man?) who won't accept a feminine woman in a position of authority, particularly one who intervenes in such male preserves as leading corrupt regimes, like the Governor in "Vengeance on Varos" (1985) or planning megalomaniac schemes of universal male domination, like Morbius: such tyrants in *Doctor Who* are, after all, predominantly male. This is the same mindset that doesn't like a satnav set to a female voice or objects to women priests, not on the grounds of Biblical teaching but on the grounds that they are women. In the mid-1990s, someone told me, "I would rather see that grinning idiot Blair in Number Ten than see a totty serving Mass." It is a mindset which is as visceral as it is impervious to reason. We can only hope that Jodie Whittaker, a superb actor, will win them over with her performance: if they can ever bring themselves actually to watch her episodes.

As Britton points out, the issue of the Doctor's femininity is in fact one that stretches back into the 1970s. The third Doctor, with his love of velvet jackets, frilly shirts and silk-lined capes, hardly dresses as a He-Man; many of the Doctors, even the aggressively masculine persona of the sixth Doctor[1], adore their clothes – a predilection which has traditionally been seen as feminine. Britton quotes Jennifer Craik: "Men who dress up are peculiar (one way or another)." Britton has further written of the queering of the character of the Doctor, not in that he is identified as gay, but in the "friction between gravitas and camp"[2] in his portrayal. This is most marked, Britton writes, in Matt Smith's performance as the Doctor. We might suggest, therefore, that the thirteenth Doctor's identification as a woman is little more than a further development of the feminine that has been part of his character since at least 1970.

The clamorous objections to the Doctor becoming a woman can also be attributed to as the polarisation of political ideologies since

---

[1] Britton notes that, even in the revival, "the Doctor's patriarchal authority remains intact, if not quite unquestioned" (ibid, p.93)

[2] Ibid, p. 93.

the 2008 banking crash. The resulting decline in living standards for all but the rich led to a scrabble to assign blame: in the United Kingdom, the Conservatives ludicrously but successfully pinned the blame on the then Labour government, which had apparently caused a collapse in worldwide banking. One manifestation of this furious opposition to the Left in general was the Right's assault on that supposed Left-wing shibboleth, political correctness. The wave was ridden by the new United Kingdom Independence Party, UKIP[1], whose call for a return of old, sexist certainties was effectively encapsulated by *Private Eye* as "chaps no longer obliged to do the washing up". The political and ideological climate of 2017 was as febrile it was in 2008: the Conservatives moved ever rightwards, the Labour Party ever leftwards; the former only just clung on to power in the 2017 general election, the Labour Party scented blood and both sides hated each other like poison.

In this rolling broil of warring ideology, it was inevitable that so many would lament Jodie Whittaker's casting as a manifestation of hated political correctness gone mad. The Doctor had always been a chap, sir, a chap, and a decent Tory chap at that[2], and to make him into a filly was humbug sir, humbug, bah, brrr, pass the scotch and mind my gouty foot. The Left counter-attacked these right wing reactionary objections all the more ferociously, applauding the casting of Jodie Whittaker as championing resurgent feminism. Why, even Prime Minister Theresa May – another woman under siege in a prominent role – let it be known that she was "very pleased" that Jodie had been cast, not that anyone much was listening to her.[3] Mrs May amplified her remark in December 2017,

---

[1] UKIP campaigned for Britain to leave the EU and to cut immigration drastically. Some claimed the party was of the reactionary right.

[2] Paul Cornell once wrote, of Jon Pertwee's third Doctor: "They exiled the Doctor to Earth and made him a Tory."

[3] David Cameron, the previous Conservative Prime Minister had been fulsome in his congratulations at the time of *Doctor Who*'s fiftieth anniversary, in spite of his half-joking threats to close the BBC at the time of its perceived (by Conservatives) biased reporting at the time of the 2015 general election. Cameron had been asked about David Tennant's support for the Labour Party and had said, "Well, you can't

by saying that she always enjoyed the *Doctor Who* Christmas special (presumably a welcome escape to a saner world than the preposterous and fantastical business of running her government) "and I think this is a great move forward for girl-power that there is going to be female Doctor Who, and one day there should be a female James Bond."[1] Let us all hope that women in these iconic roles have an easier ride than this particular prime minister.

## Slavering tabloid hootings

These cataclysmic ideological divisions were demonstrated in British newspapers' coverage of the casting of the thirteenth Doctor. The papers responded to Whittaker in line with their politics and such ideology as they had. Thus *The Sun* and the *Daily Star* immediately torpedoed the casting with revolting sexism, publishing stills of Whittaker appearing nude in the 2006 movie *Venus*. This film centred on the relationship between the elderly Maurice (Peter O'Toole) and Whittaker's twenty-something Jessie. As Jessie was an artists' model, she might sometimes be expected to have posed in the nude, but this was ignored by the slavering tabloids. Jessie had originally been written as a Londoner but screenwriter Hanif Kureishi had declared, "That girl Jodie is amazing". He was persuaded by her, first, that Jessie should be a northerner and, secondly, that she should be played by her[2]. All that mattered to the tabloids, however, was her body: the new Doctor "flashed her boobs and bum" in a "saucy screen past", opined *The Sun* and the *Daily Star* called her "Doctor Rude": "Time Lady Jodie's Topless Shocker", the report chortled derangedly, opining that "fans of the series" (all sexual innocents who have never seen a naked woman,

---

win them all" before revealing that he was more a Jon Pertwee/Tom Baker man than a follower of the revived series.

[1] https://www.theguardian.com/tv-and-radio/2017/dec/24/jodie-whittaker-regenerating-as-doctor-who-will-be-life-changing

[2] "She is exactly the sort of person you want to go on an adventure with", *The Guardian*, 22nd July 2017

even if they were women themselves) "will be shocked to discover Jodie Whittaker has already made her mark in a topless role"[1]. This was a bit rich from a paper which carried advertisements for the pornographic channel Television X on the same day and invited its readers to enjoy a film entitled *Hard Brexxxit* (a political satire?) in the same edition.

The Labour-supporting *Daily Mirror* welcomed the casting in its opinion page: "It's about time Doctor Who regenerated as a woman...[she] can always point her sonic screwdriver at any outdated blokes who object – and bring them into the 21st Century"[2]. The *Mirror* then rather undermined its welcome by publishing a photo of two Daleks chanting "Ex-fo-li-ate!" under the caption "First Female Dr Who" and a small nude photo of Whittaker from *Venus*. The *Mirror* at least contented itself with one small, nude back view: *The Sun* filled half a page with three nude shots ("Dalektable!", hooted the headline). The *Daily Mirror* included comments from two of its writers, one in favour of the casting and one mildly raising the question of political correctness[3] with a joke implying the new Doctor would be a woman driver and would crash the TARDIS (sigh...). *The Sun*'s TV critic Ally Ross was plain nasty, sneering and snarling that, "the mass outbreak of PC virtue had begun" with female Labour MPs welcoming Jodie, and further writing that "they could appoint a horse to the role and I still wouldn't much care"[4]. Strangely, Mr Ross couldn't find room to note that Tory Prime Minister Theresa May had also welcomed the casting. The coherence of *The Sun*'s position was reinforced by its opinion column, *The Sun Says*, which welcomed the casting as an inspired choice at the right time.

So much for the tabloids. The Conservative broadsheet the *Daily Telegraph*, which loves *Doctor Who*, carried a picture of Jodie on its

[1] "It's Dr Rude!", *Daily Star*, 17th July 2017
[2] "Doctor's Orders" in "Voice of the *Daily Mirror*", *Daily Mirror*, 17th July 2017
[3] "Fans were ready for a change" and "This Doctor may stall the Tardis", *Daily Mirror*, 17th July, 2017
[4] "Time Travel Fave Gets a Time Lady At Last", *The Sun*, 17th July 2017.

front page on 17th July, 2017 and the accompanying article was friendly. So was the feature which ran the next day, "Why is a female Doctor so hard for men to accept?"[1] Author Michael Hogan made the entirely reasonable point, which was taken up by other papers and magazines, that male fans happily accepted a 2000 year old alien who travelled in time and space in a phone box, but found it much harder to ponder the nature of a fictional character's genitalia or that it should now be a woman saving the planet. *The Guardian*[2] applauded the way that television drama reflects life back at us: it was more than time for the Doctor to be a woman, to show that a female Doctor is as able as a male to handle baffling alien technology while dodging life-threatening attack. Would she be able to think her way out of violence before landing herself in it? She should, *The Guardian* advised, have "loyalty and intelligence as well as astonishing physical power".[3] The paper sighed over the sexism of some of the media coverage, such as the Twitter picture which circulated immediately after the casting announcement of the TARDIS crashed into the wall of the building. The new Doctor, the paper opined, will surely save the world, but wouldn't on her own be able to make it gender blind.

Michael Hogan argued in an excellent *Telegraph* article that *Doctor Who* has long been considered a left-leaning show, extolling the virtues of pacifism (not quite correct: the first Doctor rejects the Thals' pacifism in "The Daleks", 1963), tolerance and co-operation. Hogan suggested it was therefore ironic that some Whovians reverted to unreconstructed views, and that their objections were to a perceived feminisation of a culture men considered they owned,

---

[1] *Daily Telegraph*, 18th July 2017.

[2] "Everyday sexism: Nurse Who?", leader in *The Guardian*, 18th July 2017.

[3] This comment is reminiscent of Robert Holmes's reasoning for giving the fifth Doctor some fisticuffs in "The Caves of Androzani" (1984). Peter Davison's Doctor had usually been more apt to reason and think his way out of a crisis, but it was, Holmes indicated, right to remind us that he was also capable of resorting to brute force when necessary. The Doctor must have an element of danger, however suppressed.

"that this is 'ours' not 'yours'"[1]

It is true that *Doctor Who* has sometimes leaned to the left politically and has been at one with the liberal consensus. The show has always been suspicious of Power and the Doctor has always championed the weak against the strong. Governments are nearly always presented as vicious, greedy and corrupt, whether on Earth or another planet. Chinn, the man from the Ministry in "The Claws of Axos" (1971), is a greedy little creep who will stop at nothing to obtain Axonite because it will make Britain rich and great again; The Company in Robert Holmes' incomparable "The Sun Makers" (1977) runs Pluto, rules through fear, works the Work Units (human beings) to death and then obliges their relatives to pay death taxes. Given the leftward leanings of producers and show runners Barry Letts, Russell T Davies and Steven Moffat, and the intertwining of feminism and the left, it was perhaps only a matter of time before a female Doctor appeared. Back in 2002, the then-Controller of BBC 1 Lorraine Heggessey had suggested it would be fun to bring *Doctor Who* back with "someone like Judi Dench" in the role.

The feeling that it was time to have a female Doctor – a belated manifestation of feminism – also combined with commercial reality. With the perceived decline in viewing figures, a radical shake-up was needed to renew interest in the show. It seems unlikely that the required excitement would have been generated by casting yet another man as the thirteenth Doctor, however good or famous an actor he might be.

A minority of fans still found it hard to accept Jodie as the Doctor, before a frame of her stories had been broadcast. Fans who remember the original series on its first broadcast, let alone the black and white episodes, were now in their middle or early old age, when our attitudes harden as much as our arteries (this author is 52 and can remember "Spearhead from Space" on its first broadcast, laddie). Simply put, some people, particularly older people, dislike change. The writer Kingsley Amis once said that people become

---

[1] "Why is a female Doctor so hard for men to accept?", *Daily Telegraph*, 18th July, 2017.

441

more right wing as they become older because they become older. It is perhaps unkind and unfair immediately to judge those who had reservations about Jodie Whittaker's casting as sexist, misogynistic, right wing, fascist dinosaurs. It has been said, by no less a personage than seventies *Who* producer Graham Williams, that *Doctor Who* fans are naturally conservative (with a small c) anyway and dislike change[1]: this appears to have been proved by the negative reaction of some to the outrageous radicalism of the new lamp on Whittaker's TARDIS and the disappearance of the St John's Ambulance badge. Some people were upset about the casting not because they were sexist, but because they dislike change anyway (although, as Michael Hogan argued, such dislike could have an ideological basis). Older fans had seen such a reaction at least twice before. There were similar fans grumbles in 1981 when Peter Davison was announced as Tom Baker's replacement after Baker had completed seven seasons in the part[2]. Davison was, some opined, "the beginning of the end"[3] and "the wet vet" – a reference to his role as the veterinarian Tristan Farnon in *All Creatures Great and Small* (BBC, 1977-1980, reprised from 1988-1990). We Will Never Watch The Show Again, said a minority in 1981, before they became engrossed in the new stories. Then again, in 2005: fans who had loved the original series deplored the revival and, in the pages of *Doctor Who Magazine*, said that They Would Never Watch The Show Again. This was the watchword of those who rejected Whittaker's casting. More depressingly, some objected with equal vigour to the casting of new companions Mandip Gill (Yasmin) and

---

[1] He was commenting in 1979 on the unscreened seventeenth season, script edited by Douglas Adams, which divided fandom.

[2] A bit of a far cry from the number notched up by actors in the revived series: Eccleston stayed for one season; Tennant for three seasons and a year of "specials"; Smith and Capaldi for four years but three seasons apiece.

[3] David J. Howe and Stephen James Walker argued that Davison's tenure did indeed herald a decline, and saw a shift from *Doctor Who* as a much loved family show with eight million viewers to a cult show watched by a relative handful (*The Fifth Doctor Handbook*, London, 1995).

Tosin Cole (Ryan) in October 2017: this was horrible racism, under the guise of opposition to political correctness.

There is nothing new under the sun and, if the show sheds viewers, it will no doubt gain new ones. Fans resistant to change could rejoice at the inclusion of a white, male, middle aged companion in Bradley Walsh (Graham), the first such companion since Mark Williams' brilliant Brian in 2012; others noted it was rather wonderful that the white, male, middle aged actor wasn't playing the Doctor. There are other auspicious signs for the older fan: Jodie Whittaker shares a surname with *Doctor Who*'s first story editor, David, who did so much to shape the programme (although she has an extra "t"); even better, Jodie shares a hairstyle with the first Doctor himself. In her first press statement, released to coincide with her casting, Jodie pleaded with fans not to be put off by her gender. She, like Tennant and Capaldi, loves *Doctor Who*, cares for it deeply and is beyond thrilled to have been cast as the Doctor.[1]

Yet the row, such as it was, rumbled on through the summer of 2017. There was a huge cheer at the 2017 San Diego Comic-Con when Jodie Whittaker was name checked by the *Doctor Who* panel. Speaking at the same event, Stephen Moffat said that the idea that male fans rejected her was drivel. Colin Baker congratulated Chris Chibnall on the casting, expressed sadness at the loss of some fans who would never watch the show again, and wrote that they would be replaced by many more. Baker found it heartening that it would not only be little boys in the playground – and bigger boys in the acting profession – saying, "I want to be the Doctor one day"[2]. A little girl I know told me she was thrilled at the casting because, "Now I can be the Doctor" in playground games of *Doctor Who*. Peter Davison expressed cautious sympathy for those who were upset by the casting, saying that he felt "a bit sad" about the "loss of a role model for boys who I think *Doctor Who* is vitally important for". He qualified the comments by suggesting "maybe I'm an old

---

[1] "Doctor Who: Jodie Whittaker becomes 13th Time Lord, urging fans 'not to be scared by my gender'". *Daily Telegraph*, 17 July 2017.
[2] "A female Doctor? About time", Colin Baker, *The Guardian*, 18th July, 2017.

fashioned dinosaur" and that Whittaker was a terrific actress who would do a wonderful job. Colin Baker immediately responded that Davison was talking "absolute rubbish" as the Doctor would continue to be a role model anyway, regardless of her gender: "Can't you be a role model as people?" Davison's Twitter account was deluged with negative and abusive comments and, as a result, he ended it.

### Gender pay disparity at the BBC

The churning about the Doctor's gender coincided with the revelation of huge disparities in pay between male and female stars at the BBC. This report had been commissioned by the Conservative government, anxious as ever to find sticks with which to beat the corporation. The press fell upon the report, and its findings were disheartening: John Humphrys, the Rottweiler interviewer on BBC Radio 4's *Today* programme, had an annual salary of £600,000 when his co-presenter Mishal Husain had to scrape by on a salary of between £200,000 to £249,000. Peter Capaldi was listed as one of the corporation's more highly paid stars, in the same pay band as Husain. Some wags immediately suggested that casting Jodie Whittaker was a ploy to enable the BBC to save money on a female, rather than a male, star for *Doctor Who*. Apparently galled by the joke, BBC let it be known that Whittaker would be on the same salary as Capaldi.

Although the gender gap at the BBC in pay was alarming, it was evidential of the gender pay gap in British society as a whole. That the commissioning of the report was humbug was demonstrated by ITV's refusal to release the pay details of its employees, or by the lack of any similar investigation into any private company. The whole matter was perhaps put into perspective by a correspondent to *The Guardian*, who wrote that he couldn't get excited about some rich people being paid more than other rich people as the hourly rate for his public sector job was less than £9, but he was nevertheless looking forward to his pay rise of almost 9p an hour in 2018.

# Chris Chibnall

Among Whovians, Chris Chibnall and Mark Gatiss had both been floated as probable successors to Steven Moffat. Gatiss had written nine successful stories; as an actor as well as a writer, he had appeared in three episodes. He and Moffat had also co-created and co-written *Sherlock* (2010-2017) for the BBC. Chibnall had a somewhat lower *Who* profile. He had written five episodes for *Doctor Who* plus several mini-episodes (such as, the very funny "Pond Life") for DVD or red button release. He had also script-edited the Jack Harkness-led spin off *Torchwood* (2006-2011). Like Russell T Davies and Steven Moffat before him, Chibnall is a life-long fan of *Doctor Who*. One of his first associations with the programme was an appearance on a BBC discussion programme called *Open Air* in 1986. Chaired by Patti Coldwell, this show gave viewers a platform to air their comments on BBC programmes, often to the programme makers themselves. 1986 was a time when the show served up such horrors as "Time and the Rani" and was generally loathed by fans. Producer John Nathan-Turner had appeared previously to argue that it really was as good as it had ever been and that fans who claim the older episodes were better were quite wrong as "the memory cheats". By this stage, fans had access to most of the show's back catalogue through shared VHS recordings, often copied from off-air American or Australian screenings, and could tell that Nathan-Turner was talking nonsense. As Nathan-Turner described fans as "barkers"[1] (short for, barking mad) and had a low regard for them in general, perhaps he didn't unduly care that his argument was hardly cast-iron.

Chris Chibnall appeared on *Open Air* to argue that *Doctor Who* was now really very poor. He debated with "Time and the Rani" writers Pip and Jane Baker, who afterwards said that they had enjoyed working on *Doctor Who* up to this point but would do so no

---

[1] See Richard Marson, *The Life and Scandalous Times of John Nathan-Turner*, Tadworth, 2013.

longer, now they'd been exposed to such fannish hostility. Chibnall apologised and he and the Bakers became friends.

Chibnall moved on from *Doctor Who* and *Torchwood* to create the hugely successful and popular *Broadchurch* (2013-2017), which starred David Tennant and a host of other actors who had appeared in *Who* (including Jodie Whittaker). Fox TV remade the series as *Gracechurch* (2014) and Tennant again starred. Chibnall was now hot property in television and securing his services for *Doctor Who* was something of a coup for the BBC.

It was while filming the final series of *Broadchurch* that Chibnall asked Jodie Whittaker if she would like to play his Doctor. Whittaker was delighted and accepted. Tennant and Capaldi, and most of the other members of the revival's production teams, were huge fans of the series; Whittaker, it seemed, was less steeped in its lore but liked it very much. As ever, her casting had to be kept completely secret: even an unguarded word in public could make its way into the media. Walls have ears. And Dalek eavesdropping technology. Preparing for the show's return in 2005, Davies and his team had referred to it as "Torchwood", an anagram of *Doctor Who*, to put the hounds off the scent: similarly, Whittaker and Chibnall used the code "George Clooney" to talk about her casting. Whittaker even had to use the code with her husband.

## "Twice Upon A Time": the Christmas special, 2017

Steven Moffat said at the 2016 Comic-Con that the best multi-Doctor story would be with the original Doctor, William Hartnell, which was unfortunately impossible. The idea of re-casting the first Doctor as David Bradley was, Moffat said, Peter Capaldi's, who followed up on Moffat's remark by saying, "We could get David Bradley to play him, though, couldn't we?" The penny dropped for Moffat: "Oh yeah…" Bradley had played Bill Hartnell (and Bill Hartnell playing the Doctor) in the 2013 television film, *An Adventure in Space and Time*.

The episode, when it came along on Christmas Day 2017, was first class: beautifully crafted in tone, structure and story and perfect for Christmas Day. Steven Moffat had insisted that the first Doctor was not a grumpy, sharp tongued old man, but a kind and gentle person. David Bradley gave a beautiful performance, channelling Hartnell through his looks, the language of the script – which caught the first Doctor's speech style perfectly – and his mannerisms: not least, repeated grasping of the lapels. He and Capaldi's Doctor interacted wittily rather than repeating the bickering multi-Doctor encounters of, for example, "The Three Doctors" (1973).

As far as structure was concerned, the episode followed an established *Doctor Who* pattern: mystery – confrontation with the enemy – investigation. The Doctors discover there isn't really a threat at all and the scheme to archive memories at the moment of death[1] is beneficial rather than evil. As the Pilot explains in her institute's promotional hologram, the subject is removed from time just before death, her memories recorded and her body returned so that she could die. The memories live on as an invaluable resource to historians; the person can be recreated by marrying the memories with a glass avatar. Thus the Bill Potts who meet the Doctor again both is and isn't Bill. She argues that she is, as a person is the sum of her memories[2]; the twelfth Doctor initially thinks she is an impostor and a copy, much to her annoyance, and the first Doctor wants her to give the TARDIS a jolly good spring clean. When he discovers the truth, the twelfth Doctor is nonplussed: "I don't really know what to do when it isn't an evil plan."

The twist in the tale is beautifully in tune with the kindliness of Christmas Day and Christmas evening: people sitting happily with their families after presents and dinner wouldn't perhaps want the

---

[1] This premise is very like the season one episode of *Babylon 5*, "Soul Hunter" (1994), in which an alien arrives just before the death of a prominent person to harvest her soul and to preserve it for ever. If there was an actual influence on "Twice Upon A Time", it was reciprocal: *Babylon 5* showrunner and creator J. Michael Straczynski had cited *Doctor Who* as an influence on *Babylon 5*.

[2] A reference to "The Five Doctors" (1983): the fifth Doctor says, "A man is the sum of his memories, you know. A Time Lord even more so."

typical *Who* fare of universal armageddon. When it arrives half way through this episode, the specifically Christmas themed material isn't the Doctor sitting down to turkey with Rose and Jackie, or Clara, but a very moving and appropriate re-enactment of the Christmas Day of 1914. The theme of reconciliation, and recognition that other human beings are your brothers and sisters, aligns itself quietly with the Christian themes of Christmas and brings more than one tear to the eye, as does the fine rendering of the carol "Silent Night" by German and British troops. The Doctor himself is named "The Doctor of War" by the archive Institute, but, as he has a hand in orchestrating the truce, is so in the sense that he dilutes its violence. The first Doctor continues the Christian theme and muses that Good should be ineffective as a weapon[1]: Evil should win because Good requires loyalty, self-sacrifice and love. These laudable qualities are ineffective in war, so why does Good prevail? Contemplating the Christmas truce makes him think otherwise. The show once again re-states its perennial alignment with the Christian doctrine of the Just War, and the Doctor's championing, in all his lives, of its central tenet that evil must be fought and that goodness will eventually triumph. And, as this is a regeneration episode, we again have the parallels between Christ and the Doctor: the Doctor sacrifices his own life so that others might live, and rises again.

So Steven Moffat, an atheist writer, writes a script in tune with Christianity and the real meaning of Christmas, managing to make it fun, understated and without preaching: "Hate is always foolish," says the dying twelfth Doctor. "Love is always wise." "Twice Upon A Time" is different from previous Christmas episodes, with their inoffensive use of commercial Christmas card imagery – turkey, snow, Victorian costumes, lampposts shining in the darkness and so on. The only snow here is the bitter snow of the 1914 trenches and of the South Pole. This viewer was left open mouthed with admiration at Moffat's endless inventiveness: after seven years as

---

[1] This seems to be a reference to Madame Kovarian's similar sentiment in "A Good Man Goes to War" (2011): the disadvantage of virtue in a warrior, she argues, is that "good men have too many rules".

show runner and chief writer, longer in post than any previous show runner or script editor, he can still write first class scripts and the quality shows no signs of flagging. "Twice Upon A Time" is one of his best contributions to the series and a fine story on which to bow out.

And of course, there are the witty references to past stories which please the fans who get them but don't alienate the more occasional viewer – of whom there are more than usual at Christmas. The caption "Previously on *Doctor Who*" blends into "…709 episodes ago" – a witty use of the familiar "Previously on…" tag, and an affectionate tribute to the show's longevity. There is a technically splendid blending of Hartnell's face into David Bradley's – "Have you no emotions sir? Hmm?" – which apparently took the effects technician six weeks to complete. Ben and Polly appear briefly, both in original footage and as played by new actors; so does Rusty the good Dalek (last seen in "Into the Dalek" (2014)) and the scuttling horrors of Dalek mutants outside their shells. One launches itself onto the Captain's face and chokes him – a reference to the 2014 episode "Last Christmas" and its source, the face-hugger monster in *Alien* (1979). Moffat even addresses the differences between the police box exteriors of the TARDIS, which some fans had accepted as attributable to replacement props rather than part of the show's narrative: the interior dimensions have bled into the exterior over two thousand years, so the police box has swollen in size. "You try holding your tummy in [for that long]," says Capaldi's Doctor. [1]
The Captain, thinking he is going to die, asks the Doctors to look in on his wife and boys: the first Doctor promises to do so and asks his name: "Archibald Hamish Lethbridge-Stewart".

---

[1] This is fun but doesn't explain everything: the colour of the windows changing from white to blue and back again; the police box's lantern changing shape and even becoming a police car's spinning light in season sixteen; the disappearance of the St John's Ambulance sign in Hartnell's era, its reappearance for Smith and Capaldi's era, and its apparent disappearance in Whittaker's, if pre-season 37 images are anything to go by. Maybe the Chameleon Circuit is ticking over a bit after all. I'm going to have a lie down now.

There are some very funny gags about the first Doctor's sexism, referencing the ideologies of the early and mid-sixties: Polly needs to dust the TARDIS, the twelfth Doctor must miss Bill because his TARDIS needs a spring clean, and the glass woman avatar is of no surprise because "Well, aren't all ladies made of glass, in a way?" The Captain (Mark Gatiss) chortles along: "Very good, sir, very good," and Bill withers both by saying that she *really* knows women. The man from 1914 and the first Doctor are left wordless as they contemplate lesbianism. Capaldi's Doctor continually tries to douse the flames of his predecessor's daft sexism, which culminates in the latter telling Bill if she doesn't stop swearing he will give her "a jolly good smacked bottom" (a quotation from "The Dalek Invasion of Earth" (1964)). Capaldi's Doctor uneasily asks Bill never to remember this and that this wasn't the mentor-mentee relationship he had envisaged at all when he took her on as a student at the start of season thirty six. Bill bursts out laughing. This is presumably a late addition to the script and a reference to the scandals of sexual abuse in Hollywood, showbusiness and the House of Commons which sank the careers of many in 2017 (David Bradley said the actors had to learn the script quickly, not least because they kept being handed revisions).

The sexism of the first Doctor's attitudes and the twelfth's response of cringing embarrassment prepare for the regeneration. Peter Capaldi's eyes blend into Jodie Whittaker's. The thirteenth Doctor sees herself reflected in the TARDIS monitor and has two words – "Oh! Brilliant!" – before the force of her regeneration sees the TARDIS control room disintegrate, as it did when Tennant changed into Matt Smith in 2010, and she falls through space, gesturing at the TARDIS, both its doors open and now in flames, as she hurtles towards – what? Presumably Earth.[1]

---

[1] Speaking on the BBC *Today* programme on Boxing Day 2017, Carole Ann Ford said her son in law had commented, "Typical woman driver" at this point. Presenter Nick Robinson said he was glad she, not he, had made the joke. Oh dear…

## The Doctor's Accent

Jodie Whittaker keeps her Yorkshire accent as the Doctor, which is as it should be: McCoy and Capaldi had their Scottish burr, Eccleston his Salford accent ("Lots of planets have a north!") and Tennant adopted Rose's East London accent in preference to his native Scottish Paisley. Six of the original Doctors, from Hartnell to Colin Baker, spoke some variation of Received Pronunciation (RP): the only Doctor since Colin Baker to speak some sort of RP was Matt Smith. The shift in the Doctor's accent is another manifestation of the wider cultural shift in British society. Received pronunciation is traditionally rooted in the geographical triangle of London (the seat of government and the Crown), Oxford and Cambridge (the seats of learning). It is the language of the middle classes or even the ruling classes: Brits thought they'd seen the last of the latter until Eton-educated, plummy voiced David Cameron became Prime Minister in 2010, with Eton-educated Boris Johnson and St Paul's educated George Osborne waiting in the wings to succeed him[1]. The BBC in the 1920s onwards had insisted that newsreaders and announcers speak RP and Lord Reith even instructed that they should wear dinner jackets while reading the news on the radio: perhaps the attire reminded them to maintain certain standards. The prevailing culture dictated accents in *Doctor Who*. 1960s companion Dodo was not allowed to keep the accent she had in filmed inserts, and she became altogether more RP in studio scenes. The show was dragged into the more egalitarian 1960s in 1966 – we now had a Labour Government – when Ben became the first companion with a regional, Cockney accent, but the Doctor had to remain RP. BBC announcers into the 1980s had defiantly RP voices, often at odds with the programmes they promoted. As class divisions began to break down, RP became more identified as "posh" and even

---

[1] Opprobrium directed against posh accents was even found in the Conservative Party: Conservative MP Nadine Dorries once said that PM Cameron and Chancellor of the Exchequer Osborne were a couple of posh boys who didn't know the price of a pint of milk.

patronising – a patrician voiced Doctor like Jon Pertwee (called variously "a Tory" by Paul Cornell and "a chap" by Bidisha) would have been considered old hat by the time Sylvester McCoy's became the Doctor. A plummy-voiced Doctor would be unthinkable in the current series, not least, perhaps, because actors speaking RP have cornered the market as villains in American movies [1] and an RP Doctor might jar in the States.

## Press and Critical Reaction

The hashtag *#Doctor Who* took the world number one spot on Twitter minutes after the Doctor's regeneration, beating even "Happy Christmas". "Jodie" and "Capaldi" were in third and fourth place[2]. Those who said *Doctor Who* was in decline humbly ate Twitter statistics. On the BBC Radio 4 *Today* programme on Boxing Day, Carole Ann Ford (Susan) said how excited she had been when she had learned that Jodie was to be the new Doctor. Ford had bought and devoured the box sets of *Broadchurch* as soon as she had heard the announcement. Presenter Nick Robinson speculated on how Jodie would play the role, and that Jodie Whittaker apparently didn't want the writers to make too much of her gender: she was Doctor Who, not a female Doctor Who[3]. Ford argued that the new production team, knowing how different the casting was, would have considered carefully how to write for the new Doctor and would hardly be making it up as they went along.

---

[1] For example: the Harrovian- educated *Sherlock* star Benedict Cumberbatch played Kahn in the movie *Star Trek – Beyond* (2013). Khan had been originally played by the Italian-American actor Ricardo Montalban: his reinvention as a Brit satisfied the Hollywood stereotype that posh British accent = patronising, distant, emotionally cold, patrician, probably evil. Nothing could be further from the truth...?

[2] www.doctorwhonews.net 25.12.17

[3] A similar sentiment was expressed by Peter Capaldi in 2017: he became more accustomed to playing the part when he accepted that he wasn't playing the *twelfth* Doctor, he was just playing The Doctor.

Sam Wollaston praised the episode in *The Guardian*[1] saying only a Cyberman would be dry-eyed as Capaldi bowed out. "Twice Upon a Time" was funny and full of good stuff for the non-fundamentalist Whovian to enjoy; it was charming, sad, full of good jokes, was about death and the fear of death and showed that there can be hope even in humanity's darkest hours. The twelfth Doctor's final words – "Hate is always foolish. Love is always wise. Laugh hard. Run fast. Be kind." – were far from naïve, but, in a violent and divided world, important, relevant and essential.

The other paper of the left, the *Daily Mirror*, similarly loved the episode. Reviewer Daniel Jackson took the references to "The Tenth Planet" as a celebration of the show; the episode itself, he wrote, was funny, uplifting and full of kindness and heart[2]

The *Daily Telegraph*'s reviewer Michael Hogan had written a thoughtful and entirely fair piece on the casting of Jodie Whittaker in July 2017, but, perhaps at the bidding of the sub-editor decreeing that *Telegraph* readers would like some lazy right-wing criticism, said in his review that "Twice Upon A Time" was overindulgent, bafflingly plotted and tried to do too many things at once. The fan-pleasing references got in the way of telling a good story. The *Daily Mail* lambasted the Christmas special for "right-on smuggery"; full of "sanctimonious piety", achingly worthy and deep in self-pity[3]. While *The Guardian* praised Capaldi's final words as necessary to today's world, the *Daily Mail* dismissed them as over-pious "hand-wringing". This frankly nasty review ended on the image of the TARDIS tipping out Jodie Whittaker: perhaps, sneered reviewer Christopher Stephens, the TARDIS didn't want a female Doctor Who either. The *Telegraph*'s Michael Hogan interpreted the final images differently: would the reams of paper streaming through the

[1]   www.theguardian.com/tv-and-radio/2017/dec/25/doctor-who-christmas-special-review-time-gentlemen-now-its-jodies-turn

[2]   http://www.mirror.co.uk/tv/tv-reviews/doctor-who-twice-upon-time-11750282 26.12.17

[3]   www.dailymail.co.uk/tvshowbiz/article-5212005/Christopher-Stevens-reviews-Doctor-Christmas-TV.html   26.12.17

open TARDIS doors would symbolise the end of overly wordy scripts? Not, that Hogan noted, the episode was without its pleasures: he praised the regeneration scene, the interplay between the two Doctors and the smart running gag about the first Doctor's saying un-PC things. In *The Times[1]*, Carol Midgley praised the day's Christmas specials as seriously entertaining with a dose of reality. War and the meaning of life weren't the usual stuff of Christmas Day fare, but this was what "Twice Upon A Time" gave us. It was one of the first *Doctor Who* episodes Midgley had, she said, understood for ages: it was simple and profound. Capaldi managed to make his final lines ("Hate is always foolish...be kind.") "not cheesy". As a Christmas message, Midgley wrote, it would never catch on. It certainly didn't at the *Daily Mail*.

It's interesting that the left-leaning papers professed a liking for "Twice Upon A Time" whereas two out of three right wing papers positively disliked it. "Hate is always foolish. Love is always wise. Be kind" might not be entirely in tune with the *Daily* Mail, a newspaper which had supported Mussolini and the British Union of Fascists in the 1930s and had moved to the right ever since. The *Mail* and *Telegraph* reviewers perhaps did their readers a disservice by saying that this episode had been far too convoluted and difficult to follow[2] and thereby implying they were too stupid to understand it. The world at the end of 2017 was as socially and ideologically divided as ever, and, sadly, it looked as though Jodie Whittaker would not be given an easy landing as the first female Doctor in 2018. All the more important, then, that *Doctor Who* should promote gender equality in a divided and fractious world.

---

[1] www.thetimes.co.uk/edition/news/tv-review-christmas-specials-get-seriously-entertaining-with-dose-of-reality-knw7sc6k9 26.12.17

[2] This is a perennial press complaint about the Moffat-helmed and Moffat-written episodes and constitute what Kim Newman has called "lazy writing" about *Doctor Who*. Moffat admitted early in his tenure as show runner that viewers had to pay attention to the plots and couldn't watch the show with only half an eye. It seems odd that some critics seem to want simple froth and escapism rather than thoughtful and challenging scripts: when they get the froth, they criticise the show for being twaddle.

## And the future…?

The Doctor is, as Terrance Dicks said, an old fashioned hero. He is good and he fights evil. This is a morality which will never grow old and has ensured the Doctor's appeal over six decades. As a character, he is as immortal as Robin Hood, Sherlock Holmes or Jeeves. He is less respectable than Sherlock Holmes because he was created for television, and some people are sniffy about television as a lesser art form than literature. He is not taken seriously by others, who would think this book about him is ridiculous, because he comes from the unrespectable genre of science fiction, as damned as satire as a genre that is neither nice nor respectable. Yet *Doctor Who* continues the tradition of Jonathan Swift in *Gulliver's Travels*, of holding up a mirror to the human race. *Doctor Who* stories comment on human goodness, wickedness, compassion and greed with characters and aliens we can recognise in ourselves, our history and the world around us. Gene Roddenberry thought romantically that human beings were perfectible, and that by the time of the starship Enterprise we would have eliminated poverty, racism and all forms of conflict: such things would only be found outside the human family, among those nasty Klingons who were just like the Soviets anyway. Since 1963, *Doctor Who* has adopted a less romantic, more British cynicism – or realism – in its depiction of the human race in all its forms and symbols, showing that there will always be evil but triumphantly insisting on the moral message that good must fight evil and, when it does so in the person of the Doctor and his allies, good will always, eventually, win. This is a theme that can never become obsolete and will ensure the Doctor's survival long after any television series has ended. The stories of the Doctor continued in book, audio and comic form in the hiatus between 1989 and 2005; I think that people will always be returning to the Doctor as a source for stories and as a figure of moral inspiration.

Let him – and her – always be there.

# Appendix
## *Doctor Who* Episode Guide

This very skimpy episode guide is intended to help people new to *Doctor Who* to see where the stories discussed in this book fit into the history of the programme, and to suggest which might be worth watching. I have scored them shamelessly according to my own preferences. These views are as good as yours, so please disagree with them as what do I know anyway.

I haven't scored stories which no longer exist in the archives as I'm not able to assess a story I haven't seen: listening to a soundtrack and looking at surviving pictures doesn't seem to me a reliable critical substitute. I've made exceptions for those stories which have been restored with animation and so on for DVD/Blu-ray release.

The ratings are as follows:

★★★★★ Excellent
★★★★ Very good
★★★ Good
★★ Poor
★ Dire

## William Hartnell as the Doctor

### Season One

An Unearthly Child ★★★★★                                        1963
Schoolteachers Ian Chesterton and Barbara Wright allow their curiosity about pupil Susan Foreman to lead them to a junkyard, the TARDIS, and a traveller in time and space known only as the Doctor. He kidnaps them and takes them back to a terrifying power struggle in the Stone Age.

The Daleks ★★★★★                                                1964
The survivors of a neutronic war, the Daleks, scheme to leave their travel machines

and exterminate their ancient enemies, the Thals.

## The Edge of Destruction ★ ★ ★ ★
The TARDIS malfunctions and the disorientated crew harbour paranoid and murderous suspicions.

## Marco Polo
The Doctor and his companions join explorer Marco Polo on his journey to Cathay, face death and encounter the mighty Kublai Khan. The first story to be junked in the purge of the BBC archives.

## The Keys of Marinus ★ ★ ★
A different peril every episode as the Doctor must collect the six keys of the Marinus conscience machine when opposed by Yartak, leader of the alien Voord.

## The Aztecs ★ ★ ★ ★
Barbara is hailed as the reincarnation of the Aztec god Yetaxa and uses her power to try and change history. The Doctor is appalled: "You can't change history. Not one line."

## The Sensorites ★ ★ ★
Humans are subjugated by the Sensorites and the Doctor must find the cure to the human disease which is killing them.

## The Reign of Terror ★ ★ ★
In revolutionary France, the time travellers become embroiled in rival plots and Barbara and Susan become guests of Madame Guillotine.

## Season Two

## Planet of Giants ★ ★
The TARDIS crew arrives on twentieth century Earth but, as they are only one inch high, don't find it very congenial. They encounter giant cats, perils in sinks and a plan to market a deadly insecticide.

## The Dalek Invasion of Earth ★ ★ ★
Arriving on Earth in the twenty second century, the Doctor is dismayed to find the planet smashed and Londoners cowering in cellars. The Daleks are in control.

## The Rescue ★ ★ ★ ★                                    1965
The murderous alien Koquillion stalks a crashed spaceship and terrorises Vicki, one of the survivors. But all is not as it seems…

458

The Romans ★ ★ ★
The Doctor meets Emperor Nero, who is as daft as a brush, and Ian is sold as a galley slave. Rome burns in one of the first stories inflected towards comedy.

The Web Planet ★ ★ ★ ★
Controlled by the power of the Animus, the giant ant-like Zarbi war against the Menoptra for control of the planet Vortis. The only original series *Doctor Who* story to feature no humanoid characters other than the regular cast.

The Crusade
In the first Crusade, the Doctor mediates between the mighty opposites of Saladin and King Richard the Lionheart. One of the only Hartnell stories not to be sold to Saudi Arabia.

The Space Museum ★
Starts well with the TARDIS crew finding themselves exhibits in an alien museum, then becomes a silly runaround with rebels vs aliens.

The Chase ★ ★
The Daleks build a time machine and a robot copy of the Doctor to chase after the enemy who has thwarted their schemes so many times (actually, only twice so far). Part six is good: Daleks battle with Mechanoids.

The Time Meddler ★ ★ ★
Peter Butterworth brilliantly plays the Time Meddling Monk, who wants to give King Harold atomic bazookas to win the Battle of Hastings. The Monk is the third member of the Doctor's race to appear in the series and has his own TARDIS. The first pseudo-historical story which mashes up science fiction with the historical.

**Season Three**

Galaxy Four
Beautiful Drahvins and ugly Rills face off on an alien planet. Vicki is tickled pink by cuddly robot Chumblies.

Mission to the Unknown
The first episode not to feature the regular cast. Kert Gantry tries to warn the universe of the Daleks' master plan but gets exterminated.

The Myth Makers
The Fall of Troy. Vicki falls for a bloke called Troilus and changes her name to Cressida, which doesn't sound very auspicious.

The Daleks' Master Plan                                                    **1966**
A twelve episode epic. The Daleks create the Time Destructor but the Doctor nicks
its central component. The Daleks pursue him through all time and space to get it
back. Peter Butterworth returns as the Monk, now working for the Daleks, and new
companion Sara Kingdom (Jean Marsh) is aged to death by the Time Destructor.
Director Douglas Camfield said this epic was "far too long" and "it wasn't much of
a story anyway".

The Massacre of St Bartholemew's Eve
A curious historical story featuring the Massacre of Protestant Huguenots by French
Catholics. Hartnell doubles as the conniving Abbot of Amboise.

The Ark ★ ★ ★ ★
The human race lives in a huge spaceship, waited on by their Monoid servants.
When the TARDIS revisits the post-revolutionary Ark in the future, it is to find the
Monoids are the masters. Look out for the Monoids' Beatles hairdos.

The Celestial Toymaker
The bored immortal Toymaker forces the time travellers to play his games or die.

The Gunfighters ★ ★
The Doctor has toothache and goes back to the Wild West to find a dentist, Doc
Holliday. Wackiness ensues.

The Savages
The seemingly ideal society of the Elders is founded on slavery and exploitation.
Leader Jano desires the Doctor's knowledge, but the brain drain imbues him with
the Doctor's conscience. Companion Steven stays behind to help in the rebuilding
of society.

The War Machines ★ ★
Giant cardboard boxes equipped with sledgehammers take over London. Ben and
Polly join the TARDIS crew.

**Season Four**

The Smugglers
In seventeenth century Cornwall, Pirate Captain Pike enters an alliance with the
local Squire to search for the buried treasure of his former captain, Avery, and is
willing to kill everyone in the village to find out where it is hidden. The Doctor
knows exactly its location. This was the lowest rated serial until 1986. Producer
Innes Lloyd concluded Hartnell was so unwell when filming this story that his
contract couldn't be renewed. Captain Avery appears in the 2011 story, "The Curse

of the Black Spot", played by Hugh Bonneville.

## The Tenth Planet ★ ★ ★
A new planet, Mondas, appears in the solar system and starts to drain Earth of its energy. Its inhabitants, the Cybermen, arrive on Earth to convert humankind into themselves. Exhausted and old, the Doctor collapses and regenerates.

# Patrick Troughton as the Doctor

### The Power of the Daleks ★ ★ ★ ★
On the planet Vulcan, scientist Lesterson revives a dormant Dalek, who declares it is his servant. The Dalek starts a Dalek production line and all human beings are to be exterminated, annihilated and destroyed. Daleks conquer and destroy.

### The Highlanders                                                          **1967**
The Doctor becomes involved in aftermath of the Battle of Culloden. Jamie McCrimmon joins the TARDIS crew.

### The Underwater Menace ★ ★
Nutter Professor Zaroff decides to drain the world's oceans into its molten core to blow it up. Humans are converted into fish people. Nuthink in ze vorld can schtop me now!

### The Moonbase ★ ★ ★ ★
In the far future, a multinational crew of humans mans the Gravitron, which controls the Earth's weather. The Cybermen infiltrate the base to use the Gravitron as a weapon.

### The Macra Terror
In the distant future, human beings live joyous lives on perpetual holiday. The Doctor is unconvinced by this apparent utopia. Giant grab creatures emerge at night.

### The Faceless Ones
The Chameleons, aliens without features, kidnap humans to give themselves faces. Features extensive location filming at London airport. Ben and Polly depart.

### The Evil of the Daleks
The Daleks kidnap Victorian scientist Waterfield's daughter and force Waterfield to help them develop the Human Factor, which, implanted into the Daleks, will make them invincible. The action moves to Skaro where the Doctor encounters the Dalek Emperor and humanised Daleks who want to play trains. A Dalek civil war ensues.

The Dalek race is finally destroyed because Terry Nation wanted to start a new Dalek series in America.

## Season Five

### The Tomb of the Cybermen ★ ★ ★ ★ ★
An archaeological expedition in the far future uncovers the last tomb of the long extinct Cybermen. But they are not as dead as they seem…

### The Abominable Snowmen
In 1930s Tibet, the Doctor is accused of murdering a member of an English expedition looking for the Yeti. The Yeti are robots controlled by the unbodied Great Intelligence, which seeks form and conquest.

### The Ice Warriors ★ ★ ★ ★
The Ioniser is a device which holds back a glacier in a new ice age. It also thaws out the Ice Warriors, long entombed in the glacier and now hungry for conquest.

### The Enemy of the World ★ ★ ★                                        **1968**
Troughton doubles as Salamander, a would-be world dictator who impersonates the Doctor and tries to steal the TARDIS.

### The Web of Fear ★ ★ ★ ★
Engulfed by a glowing amorphous web and fog, London is invaded by the Yeti. In the London Underground, the humans desperately fight back. Nicholas Courtney makes his first appearance as Colonel (later Brigadier) Alastair Gordon Lethbridge Stewart.

### The Wheel in Space
The Cybermen invade a space station and astrophysicist Zoe Heriot joins the TARDIS crew.

## Season Six

### The Dominators ★ ★ ★
Stony-faced humanoids the Dominators seek to enslave the pacifist, shower-curtain wearing Dulcians with their robot walking fridges, the Quarks.

### The Mind Robber ★ ★ ★ ★
The Doctor enters the Land of Fiction, a fantasy void peopled only with fictional characters like Gulliver, Medusa, and the Karkus, a superhero from year 2000 comic strips. Frazer Hines (Jamie) had chicken pox and the void cheerfully conjures up another actor to play him (Hamish Wilson).

The Krotons ★★                                                                              1969
The Krotons, a crystalline race of giant egg boxes, seek to reanimate themselves
using the superior intelligence of selected Gonds. As the Gonds are pretty dim, this
plan doesn't work too well. Unfortunately, the Doctor and Zoe are high brain
enough to bring the Krotons back to life.

The Seeds of Death ★★★★
On another moon base, the Ice Warriors do pretty much what the Cybermen did in
"The Moonbase".

The Space Pirates
The space lanes are being menaced by pirates, who destroy the space beacons
necessary for navigation. The military, a mining corporation and the pirates struggle
for ascendancy. This is the last story to have missing episodes.

The War Games ★★★★★
The TARDIS land in No Man's Land during World War One. Or does it? Captured
armies from Earth fight to the death in the War Lords' war games, designed to
select only the strongest survivors for an army of galactic domination. Unable to
defeat them on his own, the Doctor turns to his own people, the Time Lords, who
put him on trial. Found guilty, the Doctor is sent into exile on Earth, the secret of
the TARDIS taken from him, and his appearance changed again...

## Jon Pertwee as the Doctor

### Season Seven

Spearhead from Space ★★★★★                                                                  1970
The Nestenes have been colonising other planets for a thousand million years. Now
they have come to colonise the Earth.  Shop window dummies are activated as
Autons – the Nestenes can control anything plastic – and gun shoppers down.

Doctor Who and the Silurians ★★★★
Millions of years ago, a race of reptile people went into deep shelters to escape
global catastrophe. Awakened by an experimental laboratory, they find Earth
inhabited by revolting mammals and seek to reclaim their world.

The Ambassadors of Death ★★
David Whitaker was *Who*'s first story editor and this, his final script, was rewritten
by Terrance Dicks and Malcolm Hulke. It is a mess. Alien astronauts are captured
by a xenophobic army officer; they escape and wreak havoc.

Inferno ★ ★ ★ ★ ★

Professor Stahlman intends to harness the power of the Earth's core through his Project Inferno; the Doctor hopes to use it to get the TARDIS working again. Inferno mutates humans into primitives, the Primords, and the Doctor is catapulted to a parallel Earth where the Brigadier and Liz Shaw are fascists in a totalitarian Britain.

## Season Eight

Terror of the Autons ★ ★ ★ ★                                                      1971

The Master makes his debut, aiding the Nestenes in a second attempt to invade Earth.

The Mind of Evil ★ ★ ★ ★

The Keller machine is an apparently benevolent device which drains the aggression from hardened criminals, enabling them to become useful members of the society. In reality, it houses a vicious alien parasite controlled by the Master.

The Claws of Axos ★ ★ ★

Good script, dreadful execution. Benevolent golden aliens, the Axons, offer humanity untold riches through axonite, a substance that accelerates growth. Axonite is in fact an organism which will devour the world. The Master allies himself with the Axons.

Colony in Space ★ ★ ★ ★ ★

In the far future, colonists escape from an overcrowded Earth to start a self-sufficient community on a distant planet. The Interplanetary Mining Corporation arrives to gut their world and ruin their colony in pursuit of mineral wealth. But the planet contains an ancient civilisation and a terrifying doomsday weapon, sought by the Master.

The Daemons ★ ★ ★ ★

The white witch of the village Devil's End dislikes the new vicar, the Reverend Mr Magister (guess who). The Master unleashes the power of Azal, last survivor of the cruel and powerful race of Daemons which guided humankind's development. The Doctor is captured by Morris Dancers.

## Season Nine

Day of the Daleks ★ ★ ★ ★                                                        1972

Guerrillas from the future arrive in our time to assassinate peace delegate Sir Reginald Styles. Jo and the Doctor travel to the guerrillas' time to find the Daleks have successfully invaded again...an impressive achievement, given that there are

464

only three of them. The DVD special edition includes specially shot scenes to augment their numbers to at least six.

The Curse of Peladon ★ ★ ★ ★
The primitive planet of Peladon seeks to join the new galactic federation; other alien factions have other ideas and the Ice Warriors turn up again to stir the pot. The first *Who* story to predict Brexit.

The Sea Devils ★ ★ ★ ★
Serving life imprisonment for his crimes, the Master contacts a race of undersea Silurians, the Sea Devils, who harass the Royal Navy and seek to wipe out the plague of apes. Again.

The Mutants ★ ★ ★
The Time Lords send the Doctor to broker a peace between the Solonians and their tyrannical human overlords in an apartheid society. The Solonians evolve into hideous insect creatures and the racist Marshal wants to wipe them out.

The Time Monster ★ ★ ★
Professor Thascales (he's tried a Latin alias so now adopts a Greek one) seeks to harness the power of yet another all-powerful alien, the chronovore Kronos. The Doctor and Jo pursue the Master to Atlantis, where he has dethroned the King and seduced the Queen.

### Season Ten

The Three Doctors ★ ★ ★                                                    1973
Omega, a founder of Time Lord society, seeks revenge on the race he believes abandoned him. Their very existence imperilled, the Time Lords summon the first two Doctors to assist the third in the universe of anti-matter.

Carnival of Monsters ★ ★ ★ ★ ★
Jo and the Doctor arrive on a cargo ship in 1926. Or do they? A plesiosaurus rises from the waves and, on the planet Inter Minor, the showman Vorg presents his zoo of miniaturised aliens to a sceptical audience. One of the best Pertwee stories: Vorg and his assistant Shirna act as comic mirror images of the Doctor and Jo.

Frontier in Space ★ ★ ★ ★
The space empires of Earth and Draconia are on the brink of war. The Master, now in league with the Daleks, seeks to push them over the brink.

Planet of the Daleks ★ ★ ★
Pursuing the Daleks to the planet Spiridon, the Doctor discovers the Daleks are experimenting with invisibility – and have hidden an army to invade the Galaxy.

The Green Death ★ ★ ★ ★ ★
Giant maggots spit a lethal green slime and a petrochemicals firm seeks to enslave the world.

## Season Eleven

The Time Warrior ★ ★ ★ ★ ★                                1974
Crash-landed in medieval England, the Sontaran Lynx kidnaps twentieth century scientists to work on repairs to his spacecraft. The Doctor follows him to Irongron's castle but there is a stowaway in the TARDIS: journalist Sarah Jane Smith. Bob Hoskins was pencilled in as Irongron.

Invasion of the Dinosaurs ★ ★ ★ ★ ★
London has been evacuated after an invasion of prehistoric monsters. The Doctor, Sarah and the Brigadier uncover a diabolical environmentalist plot to roll back time. Kklak!

Death to the Daleks ★ ★ ★
On the planet Exxilon, Daleks and humans seek a cure for a plague which is decimating their colonies. A living city, one of the seven hundred wonders of the universe, seeks to frustrate their efforts. Features extraordinary incidental music by the London Saxophone Quartet.

The Monster of Peladon ★ ★ ★ ★
The Doctor returns to Peladon to find a miners' strike and an attempt to break away from the Galactic Federation. Corrupt mining engineer Eckersley, in league with the Ice Warriors, employs the spirit of Aggedor to convince the Peladonians to secede. The second seventies story to predict Brexit.

Planet of the Spiders ★ ★ ★ ★ ★
The giant spiders rule the humans on the planet of Metebelis III. They establish a link with a Tibetan meditation centre in England and influence the embittered sales manager Lupton to join them in a conquest of Earth.

# Tom Baker as the Doctor

## Season Twelve

### Robot ★ ★ ★ ★                                                          1975
The newly regenerated Doctor aids UNIT in investigating a series of murders and robberies. The SRS, a fascist would-be totalitarian group, employs Professor Kettlewell's intelligent robot to blackmail the world by threatening a nuclear war.

### The Ark in Space ★ ★ ★ ★
Survivors of the human race wait in suspended animation aboard the Ark, the former Nerva Beacon. But the Ark has been infiltrated by the giant wasp-like Wirrn, who devour the humans and absorb their intellect...

### The Sontaran Experiment ★ ★ ★
On a deserted Earth, the Sontaran Styre tortures humans to discover their weaknesses: to fear, to water deprivation, to suffocation... Kevin Lindsay, who played Lynx in "The Time Warrior", plays Styre. Lindsay, who had a heart condition, found Lynx's mask suffocating and asked for Styre's to be lighter in weight.

### Genesis of the Daleks ★ ★ ★ ★ ★
After a thousand years of war, the Thal and Kaled civilisations on the planet Skaro are on the point of collapse. The Kaled scientist Davros seeks to ensure the survival of his race by creating a travel machine for their final mutational form: the Dalek. One of the best *Doctor Who* stories in six decades.

### Revenge of the Cybermen ★ ★ ★
The Doctor, Sarah and Harry return to Nerva Beacon to discover its human crew are dying from a space plague. In truth, the plague is engineered by the Cybermen, who invade Nerva to launch an attack on Voga, the planet of gold.

## Season Thirteen

### Terror of the Zygons ★ ★ ★ ★
The Brigadier summons the Doctor to Earth to investigate the destruction of North Sea oil rigs by a monster of terrifying size and power. It is controlled by the Zygons, who have emerged from their spaceship under Loch Ness to conquer the world.

### Planet of Evil ★ ★ ★ ★ ★
The planet Zeta Minor contains untold mineral wealth, sought by the humanoid Morestrans. But the planet is on the border between our universe and the universe

of anti-matter, and the anti-matter creature, wanting the Morestrans gone, begins to devour them. The author slept for a week with the light on after watching each episode.

## Pyramids of Mars ★ ★ ★ ★ ★
In 1911, the Doctor and Sarah encounter robot mummies and fanatical servants of the god Sutekh, in truth an Osiran super-being trapped beneath a pyramid in Egypt and now ready to wreak his vengeance.

## The Android Invasion ★ ★ ★
The Doctor and Sarah land in the pleasant English village of Devesham. Or do they? The coins in the pub's till all show the same date, the dart board has never been used, and the locals are uncannily unfriendly. The rhino-like Kraals are creating android copies of the humans to investigate their ability to resist invasion.

## The Brain of Morbius ★ ★ ★ ★ ★                                    1976
The renegade Time Lord Morbius led his army to Karn, promising his rabble the elixir of eternal life. There he was executed and his army destroyed. But the mad Dr Solon has preserved his brain and seeks a head to house it. The head of the Doctor would do so well...

## The Seeds of Doom ★ ★ ★ ★ ★
An Antarctic survey team discovers a pod frozen in the permafrost. The Doctor identifies it as a Krynoid, a galactic weed. On most planets, the animals eat the plants: on planets where the Krynoid becomes established, the plants eat the animals... and the pod feeds on a human scientist to establish the Krynoid on earth.

## Season Fourteen

## The Masque of Mandragora ★ ★ ★ ★ ★
In fifteenth century Italy, the Mandragora Helix seeks to halt humanity's development at the Dark Ages. Court astrologer Hieronymous leads the cult of Demnos and Count Frederico plots the death of his nephew, Duke Guiliano. Portmeirion in north Wales, previously used as The Village in *The Prisoner* (1967), doubles for Renaissance Italy.

## The Hand of Fear ★ ★ ★ ★
A fossilised alien hand is found in a quarry. Dormant, it yet exerts a mesmeric influence over Sarah and reactivates itself. Eldrad must live.

## The Deadly Assassin ★ ★ ★ ★ ★
The President of the Time Lords is assassinated and the Doctor is framed for the murder. The corpse-like Master lurks in the vaults, only clinging to life in the hope

that he will see his old enemy die in ignominy and disgrace. Nothing else matters. NOTHING.

The Face of Evil ★ ★ ★ ★ ★                                    1977
The Doctor is hailed as a god and as the Evil One by the descendants of a long-dead Earth expedition. Two tribes are at war and the Doctor comes to realise that the killing is a consequence of a terrible mistake he made long ago in his past. Working title: "The Day God Went Mad".

The Robots of Death ★ ★ ★ ★ ★
A whole society is founded on robot labour, the humans secure in the knowledge that the robots must serve and never harm them. Then, on a Sandminer, the Doctor realises the murder of a human by a robot heralds the end of this civilisation...

The Talons of Weng-Chiang ★ ★ ★ ★ ★
Young women disappear off the streets of 1880s Whitechapel. A depraved phantom lurks under the Palace Theatre. Hideously mutilated corpses are hooked out of the Thames. Leela and the Doctor are embroiled in a foul scheme hatched by the Butcher of Brisbane, Marcus Greel, posing as the god Weng-Chiang. One of the best stories of the original series.

## Season Fifteen

Horror of Fang Rock ★ ★ ★
A tale of a building menace and a menaced building. The inhabitants of a nineteenth century lighthouse are picked off one by one by a murderous alien.

The Invisible Enemy ★ ★
The age of man is over! The age of the space virus has begun! A miniaturised and cloned Doctor and Leela must seek answers in the Doctor's own brain. K9 assists.

Image of the Fendahl ★ ★ ★ ★ ★
A hiker is murdered and his body decomposes overnight. An ancient evil is resurrected through a five million year old human skull. Followers of an ancient religion in twentieth century England seek to harness the power of the Fendahl, a legendary enemy of the Time Lords.

The Sun Makers ★ ★ ★ ★ ★
The human workers on Pluto are worked and taxed to death; the Doctor leads a revolution. A delight.

Underworld ★ ★                                                  1978
A planet forms around a stricken spaceship. A rebels vs baddies runaround on green

screen sets.

## The Invasion of Time ★
Gallifrey is invaded by aliens disguised as silver foil and the Sontarans stomp around the TARDIS, now revealed to be made of brick. The Doctor goes bad and the viewers give up.

## Season Sixteen

## The Ribos Operation ★ ★ ★ ★ ★
Conmen Garriff and Unstoffe scam a demented warlord, the Graff Vynda-K, into buying the planet Ribos. The Doctor and his new assistant Romana are given a task by the White Guardian: to find the six segments of the Key to Time.

## The Pirate Planet ★ ★ ★ ★
The Doctor tries and fails to land the TARDIS on the planet Calufrax. Romana takes over and lands perfectly, but the Doctor says that this planet wasn't here when he tried to land. On Zanak, the mines fill up with new riches when they have been exhausted, the Captain rules a passive population and the demented Queen Xanxia holds back death with the time dams...

## The Stones of Blood ★ ★
On twentieth century Earth, the cult followers of yet another ancient religion worship yet another pagan god who is actually an ancient alien. The stone circle comes to life and feeds on human blood.

## The Androids of Tara ★ ★ ★ ★
Romana is the exact double of the Taran princess Strella, which suits the schemes of Count Grendel down to the ground. The Doctor is employed as an android engineer to thwart him.

## The Power of Kroll ★ ★ ★                                                1979
The people of the lakes worship Kroll, a giant mutated squid. Vicious refinery chief Thawn plans to wipe them out. All Romana and the Doctor have to do is to find the fifth segment of the Key to Time. Philip Madoc thought his agent had secured the role of Thawn for him, but found himself down to play Fenner, a minor character, instead.

## The Armageddon Factor ★ ★ ★ ★
The Doctor and Romana arrive on the planet Atrios, engaged in the last desperate days of a nuclear war with its neighbour, Zeos. The Black Guardian's agent, the Shadow, waits for the Doctor to deliver the Key to Time to him and to his master, that darkness and night might reign.

## Season Seventeen

Destiny of the Daleks ★ ★
In order to break the stalemate in their war with the Movellans, the Daleks return to Skaro to resurrect Davros and see if he has any good ideas. Romana regenerates. Production values collapse under high inflation.

City of Death ★ ★ ★ ★
A Jagaroth spaceship explodes on prehistoric Earth. The Mona Lisa is stolen by the suave Count Scarlioni, who also appears as Leonardo da Vinci's employer in fifteenth century Italy. The Doctor, Romana and the detective Duggan are embroiled in an art theft which, if ultimately successful, will ensure that the human race never existed in the first place. Douglas Adams rewrote an original script by David Fisher.

The Creature from the Pit ★
A green blob lurks in a pit. That's about it.

Nightmare of Eden ★ ★ ★ ★
Two spaceships collide and drug smugglers try to offload supplies of Vraxoin, the most dangerous and addictive drug in the universe. The Doctor must contend with a scientist with an unstable electronic zoo, giant monsters killing the crew of a passenger liner, and being arrested for drug smuggling.

Horns of Nimon ★                                                    1980

Where to start? The Nimon are a race of galactic locusts who promise technology to gullible rulers, strip the planet of its wealth and move on. A good script ruined by extraordinary and ludicrous execution, which damaged *Doctor Who*'s reputation for years.

## Season Eighteen

The Leisure Hive ★ ★ ★ ★
The Argolin Leisure Hive is a haven of peace, learning and recreation established after a terrible nuclear war. But the Argolins' old enemies the Foamasi want to buy out the Hive and Argolin hothead Pangol wants to restart the war…

Meglos ★
A giant cactus plots universal domination.

Full Circle ★ ★ ★

On the planet Alzarius, the descendants of a crashed starliner prepare for a departure that never comes. Romana is taken over by the indigenous reptiles the Marshmen, and mathematical genius Adric joins the Doctor in his travels.

State of Decay ★ ★ ★

The tanks of an ancient Earth ship aren't full of rocket fuel. They are full of blood. The original crewmembers have survived but have evolved into vampires. An ancient enemy of the Time Lords – yes, another one - stirs into life.

Warriors' Gate ★ ★ ★ ★ ★                                              1981

In a void between universes, a crew of malcontents waits for their ship to take off. Their pilot is a time-sensitive alien, Biroc, who escapes to find the TARDIS. The spaceship's crew are slavers and Biroc is a member of the Tharil race, who once enslaved the humans. Time slips abound and there seems to be no escape from the void. No Tharil shall outlive the day of the feast.

The Keeper of Traken ★ ★ ★ ★

The Traken Union is kept in harmony by people being terribly nice to each other, overseen by an all-powerful and benevolent Keeper. But the Master has infiltrated Traken society and installs himself as the new Keeper.

Logopolis ★ ★ ★

The universe is on the point of collapse and is preserved only by the calculations of the Logopolitans. The Master suspends their mathematics, the universe hurtles towards destruction and the Doctor falls to his death from a radio telescope on Earth.

# Peter Davison as the Doctor

### Season Nineteen

Castrovalva ★ ★ ★                                              1982

Seeking to recuperate after a failing regeneration, the new Doctor lands in Castrovalva, a dwelling of tranquility. Guess who is lurking in the shadows...

Four to Doomsday ★ ★ ★

An Urbankan starship makes periodic visits to Earth every few centuries in order to collect human specimens. Monarch, the Captain, believes that he will be able to return to the beginning of the Universe to find himself: God, the creator.

Kinda ★ ★ ★ ★ ★

The beautiful planet of Deva Loka is despoiled by human imperialists who treat the inhabitants as savages. The Mara, a demonic alien, manifests itself through the Doctor's companion Tegan and threatens to destroy this Eden of Deva Loka.

The Visitation ★ ★ ★
Alien Terileptils use an android figure of death to terrify seventeenth century villagers while they figure out how to return home.

Black Orchid ★ ★ ★ ★
Arriving in 1920s England, the Doctor is hailed as a cricketing saviour by the local gentry and invited to stay in their charming country house. But the house holds a dark secret. The first purely historical story since 1967.

Earthshock ★ ★ ★
The Cybermen re-emerge on an Earth space freighter, which they intend to crash onto the planet in furtherance of their goal of galactic conquest. Adric is blown to smithereens. A nation rejoices.

Time Flight ★
Concorde is sent back to prehistoric Earth and the Doctor discovers the Master is disguised as a magician. Oh dear.

## Season Twenty

Arc of Infinity ★                                                      1983
Omega seeks corporeal form and the Doctor must return to Gallifrey to stop him. Watch out for the Ergon, a giant space chicken.

Snakedance ★ ★ ★ ★
Tegan asks if she will ever be free of the Mara. It is within her and manifests itself again on the planet Manussa. Features a very young Martin Clunes.

Mawdryn Undead ★ ★ ★
Mutants led by Mawdryn seek death. The Doctor can only grant it by surrendering his remaining regenerations and ceasing to be a Time Lord. That is the price of his compassion. Brigadier Lethbridge Stewart has left UNIT after a nervous breakdown and become a maths teacher at a boys' boarding school. The alien Turlough, in thrall to the Black Guardian, joins the TARDIS crew.

Terminus ★ ★ ★
The Doctor and his companions arrive at Terminus, a space station dedicated to the cure of Lazar's disease. Nyssa has been infected and space pirates cause problems.

Enlightenment ★ ★ ★ ★
Creatures who live for ever while away the time with space races in sailing ships, crewed by humans from different periods of Earth history. The ultimate prize is Enlightenment, but no-one quite knows what Enlightenment is. The Doctor joins the deadly race to find out.

The King's Demons ★ ★
The Master tries to stop Magna Carta from being signed. The Doctor and his companions are claimed as demons by King John, who is actually a robot, Kamelion.

## Twentieth Anniversary Special

The Five Doctors ★ ★ ★ ★
The first five Doctors are transported to the Death Zone on Gallifrey, a place where the Time Lords entertained themselves by making aliens fight each other to the death. The Doctors face Cybermen, Daleks, a Yeti and the Raston Robot before unmasking the real traitor.

## Season Twenty One

Warriors of the Deep ★                                                    1984
In 2084, the Sea Devils and Silurians try to start a nuclear war. Breathtakingly bad.

The Awakening ★ ★ ★
Civil war games on contemporary Earth awaken the Malus, a malevolent alien which feeds on human aggression. Very rushed in two episodes and would probably have worked better as a four parter.

Frontios ★ ★ ★ ★
A human colony in the far future is menaced by meteorite bombardment and the TARDIS is destroyed. Burrowing giant woodlice-like aliens, the Tractators, are responsible. The Earth is Hungry.

Resurrection of the Daleks ★ ★ ★
After ninety years in suspended animation, Davros is released on board an Earth ship. He recruits a team of Daleks to serve him. The Daleks intend to use an android copy of the Doctor to assassinate the High Council of the Time Lords. Sickened by the violence, Tegan leaves the TARDIS.

Planet of Fire ★ ★
Sarn is a hot world and ruler Timanov demands obedience. Lanzarote is pretty hot too and Peri Brown makes a bid for freedom from her father, who is overseeing an

archaeological dig there. The Master has been miniaturised and turns up on Sarn. Turlough's history is revealed. Dull.

### The Caves of Androzani ★ ★ ★ ★ ★
Spectrox is the most valuable element in the universe, doubling the normal human life span. But the supply is controlled by demented android engineer Sharaz Jek, who will let the Androzani people have as much as they want if they give him the head of Morgus, who betrayed him, on a plate. The Doctor and Peri are catapulted into plot and counter plot and the Doctor sacrifices his life for his companion. David Bowie was approached to play the role of Sharaz Jek. The best *Doctor Who* story of the 1980s.

## Colin Baker as the Doctor

### The Twin Dilemma ★
A giant slug prepares to send its eggs throughout the galaxy. The new Doctor tries to strangle Peri, so severe is his regeneration trauma. There are some identical twins. Veteran director Douglas Camfield watched the story being made and commented, this is *not* what *Doctor Who* is all about.

### Season Twenty Two

### Attack of the Cybermen ★      1985
In a retread of previous stories, the Cybermen hide in the London sewers and attempt to convert people from their tombs on Telos. The Doctor gets the TARDIS chameleon circuit working again.

### Vengeance on Varos ★ ★ ★ ★
The planet Varos is bled dry by the extortion of Sil, a sadistic alien from Thoros Beta. To keep its population quiet and to help its balance of payments crisis, the Varosians export torture videos from the Punishment Dome, which is where the TARDIS has landed...

### The Mark of the Rani ★ ★ ★
The Rani conducts experiments on humans in the nineteenth century and is displeased by the interference of the Master and the Doctor in her work.

### The Two Doctors ★ ★ ★
The second Doctor is sent by the Time Lords to halt the time experiments of Dastari, who is in league with the Sontarans and the omnivorous Androgums to find the Rassilon Imprimature, which allows the Time Lords to travel in time. The sixth Doctor is to be dissected and Jamie and Peri are prepared for the table.

**Timelash** ★

People are thrown down a tinsel tunnel called the Timelash, H.G.Wells joins the TARDIS crew and a dinosaur tries to eat Peri. Paul Darrow, who starred as Tekker, said the story was rubbish. He understated the case.

**Revelation of the Daleks** ★ ★ ★ ★

Why not store your dying loved ones in Tranquil Repose, until a cure can be found for the disease which afflicts them? Then Davros can turn some of them into foodstuffs and the others into a new generation of Daleks.

## Season Twenty Three

**The Trial of a Time Lord episodes 1-4 (aka The Mysterious Planet)** ★ ★ ★    **1986**

The Time Lords again put the Doctor on trial for interference in the affairs of other worlds. He will see the evidence of three adventures: one from his past, one from his present and one from his future. In the first, he arrives on the distant planet of Ravalox whose society is based on the London Underground network.

**Episodes 5-8 (aka Mindwarp)** ★ ★ ★

The Doctor joins with Sil to revive Lord Kiv, a small matter which will involve transferring Kiv's essence into the body of Peri, who dies. In the courtroom, the Doctor suspects the evidence has been tampered with.

**Episodes 9-12 (aka Terror of the Vervoids)** ★ ★

The Vervoids, intelligent plant creatures, wreak havoc on the space liner Hyperion. Mel joins the Doctor after the apparent death of Peri.

**Episodes 13-14 (aka The Ultimate Foe)** ★ ★

Prosecutor the Valeyard is revealed to be an evil future incarnation of the Doctor. The sixth Doctor battles him in the dreamscape of the Matrix. Peri turns out not to be dead after all but married to Brian Blessed. The Valeyard escapes.

# Sylvester McCoy as the Doctor

## Season Twenty Four

**Time and the Rani** ★    **1987**

The Rani builds a super-brain and pretends to be Mel to entrap the Doctor, who has regenerated after falling off his exercise bike.

**Paradise Towers** ★ ★

The sealed world of Paradise Towers is home to vicious girl gangs, cannibalistic old ladies and a creature in the cellar that calls out its hunger. Very similar to *High-Rise*, the 1975 dystopian novel by J.G.Ballard, and very nearly a good story.

Delta and the Bannermen ★
Aliens go back to a 1950s English holiday camp, where CIA agents wander about and Chimeron queen Delta is hunted by the Bannermen. Or something. Dire.

Dragonfire ★
Kane rules Iceworld and a dragon contains a powerful crystal. Earth teenager Ace, real name Dorothy, has arrived there in a time storm. The Doctor climbs over a cliff.

**Season Twenty Five**

Remembrance of the Daleks ★ ★ ★ ★                                      **1988**
In 1963 London, two factions of Daleks battle to find the Hand of Omega, a stellar manipulator brought by the first Doctor from Gallifrey when he first landed there. Fascist humans aid the Daleks.

The Happiness Patrol ★
Happiness is compulsory on Helen A's world and the TARDIS gets painted pink. A humanoid creature made of candy entraps the Doctor in his Candy Kitchen.

Silver Nemesis ★
The Cybermen repeat the plot of "Remembrance of the Daleks".

The Greatest Show in the Galaxy ★
Performers have to entertain the Gods of Ragnarok in the Psychic Circus or die.

**Season Twenty Six**

Battlefield ★ ★ ★                                                       **1989**
Medieval knights roam the English countryside and the Doctor is assumed to be Merlin. The Brigadier emerges from retirement to fight the sorceress Morgaine.

Ghost Light ★ ★
In nineteenth century England, the alien Light conducts a survey of life on Earth and destroys that which is catalogued. Ace has nightmares about a haunted house so the Doctor takes her there.

The Curse of Fenric ★
Russians attack a top secret English base in World War Two. So do sea vampires. And a being from the dawn of time. A vicar loses his faith. Highly regarded by fans

who admire the McCoy stories.

## Survival ★ ★ ★ ★

The Cheetah people abduct humans and take them to their home world. Here, humans devolve into Cheetah people: the Master is already infected, so is Ace and so, later, is the Doctor.

# Paul McGann as the Doctor

Doctor Who (aka, The TV Movie) ★ ★ ★ ★                                   **1996**
In 1999 San Francisco, the seventh Doctor dies in a hail of bullets intended for young gangster Chang Li. The Doctor regenerates. The essence of the Master, which was in his care, escapes from the TARDIS and finds a new temporary home in the body of ambulance driver Bruce. But the body starts to decay and the Master must effect a permanent transfer into the Doctor's body to survive.

# Christopher Eccleston as the Doctor

### Season Twenty Seven (season one)                                   **2005**

### Rose ★ ★ ★ ★ ★

Shopgirl Rose is attacked by walking tailors' dummies in the basement of her department store. She is rescued by an alien traveller in space and time known only as the Doctor.

### The End of the World ★ ★ ★ ★

The Doctor takes Rose to witness the end of the planet Earth from an orbiting space station. But its shields are down and, when the Earth explodes, the space station and its population of VIP aliens will go up with it.

### The Unquiet Dead ★ ★ ★ ★ ★

Victorian undertaker Mr Sneed is irritated when another of his corpses goes walkabout. Rose and the Doctor join Charles Dickens in investigating the cause; the alien Gelth plead with the Doctor to give them the human corpses they need if they are to survive.

### Aliens of London/World War Three ★ ★ ★ ★

The TARDIS returns Rose to Earth, one year after she has left. Rose is now a missing person, boyfriend Mickey has been arrested for her murder, and giant green aliens infiltrate 10 Downing Street in the bodies of corpulent humans.

### Dalek ★ ★ ★ ★ ★

Billionaire Henry van Statten collects alien artefacts and has one living specimen to show the Doctor. It is the last surviving Dalek from the Time War. The Dalek escapes and follows its primary order: to exterminate every living thing which is not Dalek.

### The Long Game ★ ★ ★
Rose, the Doctor and Adam travel to Satellite Five in the far future. But the technology is wrong and humankind's development has been retarded by the Editor and his boss, humanity's guiding light, the Mighty Jagrafess of the Holy Hadrojassic Maxarodenfoe (he calls him, Max).

### Father's Day ★ ★ ★ ★ ★
Rose persuades the Doctor to take her back in time to the moment of her father's death. When she saves him, she makes a gash in the fabric of time – and the Reapers come to sterilise the wound.

### The Empty Child/The Doctor Dances ★ ★ ★ ★ ★
In the middle of the Blitz, a young woman flees from a child in a gas mask who keeps asking, "Are you my mummy?" Rose is rescued by time travelling con man Jack Harkness and the Doctor discovers physical injury as plague.

### Boom Town ★ ★ ★ ★
Hoping for a break, the TARDIS crew visits contemporary Cardiff, but the new mayor is Margaret Blon Fel Fotch Slitheen, who plans to destroy the city to make good her escape from Earth.

### Bad Wolf/The Parting of the Ways ★ ★ ★ ★ ★
Returning to Satellite Five, the Doctor finds himself in the Big Brother house and Rose plays The Weakest Link. But contestants who lose are vaporised and the Doctor discovers that this Game Station is a front organisation for the Emperor of the Daleks and his new army.

## David Tennant as the Doctor

### The Christmas Invasion ★ ★ ★ ★
Christmas special. Jackie is nearly murdered by a deadly Christmas tree; Rose and Mickey are attacked by Santas with flame throwers. All are precursors to an invasion by the Sycorax, but the new Doctor is in a coma and the humans are powerless against them.

### Season Twenty Eight (season two)

New Earth ★ ★                                                                    2006
The Doctor takes Rose to the planet New Earth, settled by the humans after the

destruction of Earth. In the city of New New York, the Sisters of Plenitude – cat people – are infecting humans with diseases so that they can discover a cure. Cassandra, the villain from "The End of the World", returns.

Tooth and Claw ★★
Rose and the Doctor meet Queen Victoria and a werewolf.

School Reunion ★★★★★
The Doctor poses as a physics teacher to investigate strange goings on at a secondary school. Also investigating is journalist Sarah Jane Smith and K9, reunited with the Doctor after many years.

The Girl in the Fireplace ★★★★★
French courtiers in pre-revolutionary France are attacked by beautiful clockwork robots, who seek Madame du Pompadour: but she is under the protection of her imaginary friend, the Doctor.

Rise of the Cybermen/The Age of Steel ★★★★
On a parallel Earth, billionaire John Lumic proposes to upgrade all citizens into a new species: the Cybermen.

The Idiot's Lantern ★★★★
The Coronation Day for Queen Elizabeth II is to be televised and millions of Britons have bought sets to watch the event. But the alien Wire drains the essence of the viewers who switch on, leaving them as faceless zombies.

The Impossible Planet/The Satan Pit ★★★
Humans on a distant planet use their slave race, the Ood, to assist them in their investigations. Toby, one of the humans, is possessed and the Doctor encounters a giant horned creature who appears to be the Devil.

Love and Monsters ★★★
A motley crew of enthusiasts gathers to exchange information about the Doctor. A vile creature called the Abzorbaloff infiltrates the group and attempt to gain control of the Doctor and the TARDIS.

Fear Her ★★★
A young girl draws in her sketchbook and her nightmarish drawings come to life.

Army of Ghosts/Doomsday ★★★
Translucent ghosts appearing around the globe fully manifest themselves as Cybermen. An elite group of Daleks, the Cult of Skaro, is released from the Torchwood Institute. As the Cybermen fight the Daleks, the planet Earth

480

approaches its end.

## Season Twenty Nine (season three)

The Runaway Bride ★ ★ ★ ★
Christmas special. Grieving for the loss of Rose, the Doctor is astonished when a bride called Donna appears in the TARDIS. Returning to Earth, he finds a giant spider-humanoid creature, the Racnoss, is now ready to awaken her children from their long sleep.

Smith and Jones ★ ★ ★ ★                                                      **2007**
Medical student Martha Jones encounters an eccentric patient, the Doctor, on her rounds. Her hospital is transported to the Moon by the Judoon, rhino-like alien police in pursuit of an alien murderess. Russell T Davies named the aliens "Judoon" as the double o sound was the one English vowel Paisley-born David Tennant couldn't say easily. He also gave him the line, "Judoon platoon upon the moon."

The Shakespeare Code ★ ★ ★ ★
The Doctor takes Martha back in time for a performance of *Love's Labour's Lost* by Shakespeare's theatre company. A trio of witches is very keen that Will should finish the sequel, *Love's Labour's Won*: but why? When Shakespeare first sees Martha, the script said he should be "pure Leslie Phillips" in his delivery of, "Hey, nonny, nonny".

Gridlock ★ ★
Martha becomes stuck in an eternal traffic jam of flying cars, in which the passengers grow old before they reach their destination. The first *Who* story to feature a gay female couple.

Daleks in Manhattan/Evolution of the Daleks ★ ★ ★
The ultimate experiment of the Cult of Skaro is the fusion of two races into a Human-Dalek hybrid, Dalek Sec. Disgusted at this pollution of their DNA, the other Daleks mutiny.

The Lazarus Experiment ★ ★ ★ ★
Professor Lazarus intends to change what it means to be human through his rejuvenation experiments: instead, he transforms himself into a hideous monster which evolution had rejected as unworkable for human beings.

42 ★ ★ ★
The Doctor and Martha have forty two minutes to save a spaceship before it is overwhelmed by catastrophe. "Burn with me."

Human Nature/The Family of Blood ★ ★ ★ ★ ★
Escaping from the Family of Blood, the Doctor transforms himself into a human being, John Smith, with Martha as his servant and protector. Smith works as a teacher in a boys' boarding school in the early twentieth century and falls in love with the school matron. But the Family has pursued the Doctor to Earth...

Blink ★ ★ ★ ★ ★
The Weeping Angels are fast. Unbelievably fast. Don't blink. Blink and you're dead.

Utopia ★ ★ ★ ★
The last humans in the Universe prepare to embark to the planet Utopia aboard a giant rocket ship developed by kindly Professor Yana. But, unknown even to himself, Yana has a hidden identity and the Master is reborn.

The Sound of Drums/Last of the Time Lords ★ ★ ★
For the benefit of all humankind, new Prime Minister Harold Saxon (in truth, the Master) invites the benevolent aliens the Toclafane to Earth. The Toclafane decimate the population and usher in the Master's reign of terror.

## Season Thirty (season four)

Voyage of the Damned ★ ★ ★
Christmas special. The luxury space liner the Titanic has been sabotaged and hurtles towards Earth. Unless the Doctor can save them, everybody on board will be killed.

Partners in Crime ★ ★ ★ ★                                    **2008**
The Doctor and Donna are reunited as they separately investigate Adipose Industries, a sinister organisation promoting miracle diet pills. The fat just walks away!

The Fires of Pompeii ★ ★ ★ ★
Donna and the Doctor arrive in Pompeii on the eve of the eruption of Vesuvius. Alien fire creatures dwell in the volcano and Donna is to be sacrificed by a fanatical cult. Peter Capaldi plays Caecilius, whose body is copied by the Doctor for his twelfth physical form.

Planet of the Ood ★ ★ ★ ★
The Ood, the slaves of the humans, are prepared for service on their home planet. Some Ood fall victim to the rabid disease Red Eye: mutiny ensues, and the Doctor and Donna are caught at the centre of a terrible battle.

The Sontaran Stratagem/The Poison Sky ★ ★ ★ ★
ATMOS is a device fitted to cars to reduce their poisonous emissions. The Sontarans use ATMOS to choke the world with poison gas as a prelude to invasion.

The Doctor's Daughter ★ ★ ★
The Doctor is cloned to create another soldier for the endless war between the Hath and the humans. The clone calls him Dad; the Doctor says she is a generated anomaly and so Donna names her, Jenny.

The Unicorn and the Wasp ★
The Doctor and Donna meet Agatha Christie.

Silence in the Library/The Forest of the Dead ★ ★ ★ ★ ★
Shadows in the library devour the members of a humanoid expedition and the Doctor meets a woman who claims she is his wife: Professor River Song.

Midnight ★ ★ ★
The Doctor leaves Donna to relax by the pool while he goes on a voyage in a sealed vehicle on a planet called Midnight. What could possibly go wrong?

Turn Left ★ ★ ★ ★ ★
A time sensitive creature persuades Donna to turn left instead of right at a t-junction. As a consequence, she never meets the Doctor and the history of Earth unravels.

The Stolen Earth/Journey's End ★ ★ ★
The Earth is stolen by the Daleks and moved into deep space. The Dalek Supreme orders the destruction of the TARDIS and the Doctor is held prisoner of Davros.

**Specials**

The Next Doctor ★
Christmas special. A giant Cyberman stomps on Victorian London. A Victorian gentleman imagines himself to be the Doctor.

Planet of the Dead ★                                        **2009**
A cat burglar joins the Doctor on a dead planet. She flies off in a flying double decker bus. Giant flies eat excrement, but sadly overlooked this script.

The Waters of Mars ★ ★ ★ ★
A human base on Mars in 2059. Anyone who touches the water is transformed into hideous virus creatures, the Flood.

The End of Time ★ ★ ★                                                    2009/2010
Christmas and New Year special. The Master returns to turn all human beings into
copies of himself: the Master race. The Doctor sacrifices himself to save Donna's
grandfather, Wilfred Mott.

## Matt Smith as the Doctor

### Season Thirty One (season five)

The Eleventh Hour ★ ★ ★ ★                                                     2010
The newly regenerated Doctor is looked after by ten year old Amelia Pond, who has
a crack in her wall. The Doctor hears a voice calling through the crack: "Prisoner
Zero has escaped". Prisoner Zero manifests itself on Earth. Silence will Fall.

The Beast Below ★ ★ ★
Survivors of Earth in the far future are borne through space on the back of a giant
creature, tortured by the humans to provide them with propulsion.

Victory of the Daleks ★ ★ ★ ★
Churchill is delighted with chief scientist Bracewell's design for the Ironside
machines, with which Britain will win the war. The Doctor spots a problem: the
Ironsides are actually Daleks.

The Time of Angels/Flesh and Stone ★ ★ ★ ★ ★
River Song and a team of military clerics try to immobilise the Weeping Angel in a
crashed spaceship. The Doctor discovers that hundreds of Angels are returning to
life in the planet's cave system…

The Vampires of Venice ★ ★ ★ ★
Venice in 1580: the Doctor, Rory and Amy discover the pupils of an exclusive
girls' school appear to be vampires.

Amy's Choice ★ ★ ★ ★ ★
The TARDIS crew is tested by the Dream Lord, a humanoid echo of the Doctor
who appears to emanate from the TARDIS. He shares the Doctor's sense of
mischief, but not his morality.

The Hungry Earth/Cold Blood ★ ★ ★
Human scientists are drilling deep into the Welsh soil. The trouble is, the Silurians
are drilling up…

Vincent and the Doctor ★ ★ ★ ★ ★
Amy and the Doctor meet Vincent van Gogh, who is haunted by a hideous creature

and by his suicidal depression.

## The Lodger ★ ★ ★ ★
Locals are disappearing into the second floor of Craig Owen's house in Colchester.
The Doctor takes a room as a lodger to investigate, posing as a human being to
avoid alerting any alien suspicions.

## The Pandorica Opens/The Big Bang ★ ★ ★ ★
The Pandorica is a prison designed to hold the most dangerous criminal in the
universe. The Doctor is tricked by an alliance of his greatest enemies into
inhabiting it.

## Season Thirty Two (season six)

## A Christmas Carol ★ ★ ★ ★
Christmas special. Amy and Rory are trapped on a spaceliner which is about to
crash into an Earth-type planet. Miser Kazran Sardik can save them, but snarlingly
refuses to do so. Why?

## The Impossible Astronaut/The Day of the Moon ★ ★ ★ ★ ★          2011
On contemporary Earth, the Doctor is shot and killed by an astronaut which rises
from a lake. Dismayed, River, Rory and Amy return to a local diner, where they
find the Doctor alive, well, and completely unaware of what has happened. The
NASA moon landings and President Nixon are embroiled in the Silents' scheme to
enslave the human race.

## The Curse of the Black Spot ★ ★ ★ ★
A becalmed pirate ship is attacked nightly by a siren; if it puts the black spot on
your hand, you're dead.

## The Doctor's Wife ★ ★ ★ ★ ★
The TARDIS achieves physical form as Idris, a beautiful woman; searching for an
old friend, the Doctor discovers a graveyard of Time Lords, lured to their doom by
an alien called House.

## The Rebel Flesh/The Almost People ★ ★
Human workers are copied and the clones are abandoned when injured in
dangerous work. The clones then insist on their right to survive.

## A Good Man Goes to War ★ ★ ★ ★ ★
A vicious conflict between Madame Kovarian and the Doctor reaches its climax.
She springs a trap but the Doctor is ready for her with an army of aliens who owe
him their allegiance. River reveals her true identity.

Let's Kill Hitler ★ ★
Mels, a previous incarnation of River Song, takes the Doctor, Rory and Amy back to Berlin on the eve of war in 1939.

Night Terrors ★ ★ ★ ★
A child has terrible nightmares and Amy, Rory and the Doctor become prisoners in a doll house. Amy is transformed into a walking, wooden doll.

The Girl Who Waited ★ ★ ★
Amy is abandoned in an alien hospital and grows to embittered middle age. A parallel, younger Amy meets her but only one of them can be saved.

The God Complex ★ ★ ★
Each of the rooms in an alien hotel contains the greatest fear of each of its guests.

Closing Time ★ ★ ★
The Doctor revisits Craig Owens and takes a job in a department store. But the Cybermen have infiltrated the shop and force Craig to become their new Cybercontroller.

The Wedding of River Song ★ ★ ★ ★
A parallel Earth, the Silents, Madame Kovarian, Charles Dickens and time paradoxes lead the Doctor to his apparent marriage to River Song.

The Doctor, the Widow and the Wardrobe ★ ★ ★ ★
Christmas special. The Doctor becomes guardian to a widow and her children in an old country house in the Second World War.

## Season Thirty Three (season seven)

Asylum of the Daleks ★ ★ ★ ★                                            2012
The TARDIS lands in the heart of the Dalek parliament and the Doctor is astounded when the Daleks beg him to save them.

Dinosaurs on a Spaceship ★ ★ ★
A huge spaceship is almost empty, save for two bickering robots, some dinosaurs and a crippled trader called Solomon. But where is the original crew? David Bradley, the first Doctor in "Twice Upon A Time" (2017), plays Solomon.

A Town Called Mercy ★ ★ ★ ★
The American frontier. An alien gunslinger terrorises the good people of Mercy and demands that they hand over to him Kahler-Jex, an alien scientist and sometime war criminal who has saved them from cholera.

The Power of Three ★ ★ ★
Earth is invaded by millions of small black cubes, which do nothing and stay dormant. The Doctor discovers that they are the instruments of pest control planted by the alien Shakri, who will activate them to purge the world of humankind. UNIT intervenes, now run by scientific adviser Kate Stewart, the daughter of Brigadier Alastair Gordon Lethbridge-Stewart.

The Angels Take Manhattan ★ ★ ★ ★
The Weeping Angels have infested New York. They can be defeated, but only if Amy and Rory become their victims.

The Snowmen ★ ★ ★ ★
Christmas special. Grieving for the loss of Amy and Rory, the Doctor has retired to Victorian England. Strax, Vastra and Jenny attempt to stir him from his lethargy with tales of strange goings on at the house of Dr Simeon. Simeon is in the thrall of the Great Intelligence, and razor toothed snowmen attack.

The Bells of St John ★ ★ ★ ★                                         **2013**
Human consciousnesses are being uploaded to an alien database by the Great Intelligence. The Doctor, now united with Clara Oswald, investigates.

The Rings of Akhaten ★ ★ ★
The hugely powerful entity Akhaten demands the sacrifice of memories from the people of its neighbouring planetoids. A small girl called Merry is to sing to Akhaten, and the Doctor and Clara try to save her.

Cold War ★ ★ ★ ★
A Russian nuclear submarine takes aboard an Ice Warrior, entombed in a block of ice. Unwisely, one of the crew decides to thaw him out.

Hide ★ ★ ★
Professor Palmer and his assistant Emma Grayling are investigating supposed hauntings in Caliburn House in 1974. The Doctor is intrigued and Emma warns Clara against the Doctor: he has "a sliver of ice" in his heart…

Journey to the Centre of the TARDIS ★ ★ ★
The TARDIS is damaged by the tractor beam of a giant salvage ship. The Doctor agrees to let the ship's crew repair the TARDIS, but they are more interested in gutting it. The TARDIS fights back.

The Crimson Horror ★ ★ ★ ★
Strax, Vastra, Jenny and the Doctor investigate the apparently utopian community of Sweetville, run by Mrs Gillyflower and the never-seen Mr Sweet. Meanwhile,

corpses are found dumped in the river and all of them have bright red skin... Diana Rigg guests as Mrs Gillyflower and her daughter Rachael Stirling plays Gillyflower's daughter, Ada.

Nightmare in Silver ★ ★ ★ ★
The TARDIS arrives in an intergalactic theme park, now closed. Some of the exhibits are Cybermen, now a long extinct race. The Doctor discovers tiny robotic insects, Cybermites, who reactivate the Cybermen.

The Name of the Doctor ★ ★ ★ ★ ★
Clara discovers her identity as the Impossible Girl, splintered into many selves in time and destined to save the Doctor. The Doctor's grave has been discovered, the one place he can never visit. Of course, he visits it...

## Specials

The Day of the Doctor ★ ★ ★ ★ ★
The tenth and eleventh Doctors revisit the Time War on Gallifrey, where a previous incarnation, the War Doctor, decided the war could only be ended by activating the Moment and wiping out every living Time Lord and Dalek in the universe. Sir John Hurt guests as the War Doctor.

The Time of the Doctor ★ ★ ★ ★
Christmas special. The Doctor grows old in the town of Christmas, unable to leave because doing so would start a new time war. As the Daleks, Cybermen and Sontarans attack, the Doctor accepts he has reached his last regeneration and he must now die. But the Time Lords have other ideas...

## Peter Capaldi as the Doctor

### Season Thirty Four (season eight)

Deep Breath ★ ★ ★ ★                                                        2014
A giant tyrannosaurus rex brings the newly regenerated Doctor back to Earth. Vastra, Strax and Jenny try to help him through his regeneration trauma and an alien cyborg harvests humans for their organs.

Into the Dalek ★ ★ ★
Miniaturised, the Doctor, Clara and a crew of human soldiers go inside a Dalek to discover why it has apparently become "good". The Doctor nicknames it "Rusty".

Robot of Sherwood ★ ★ ★
Clara says she has always wanted to meet Robin Hood and the Doctor takes her to medieval Nottingham to prove there is no such person. An arrow immediately thuds into the TARDIS, fired by Robin himself.

Listen ★ ★ ★
Clara's relationship with her new boyfriend, Maths teacher Danny Pink, is troubled. The Doctor takes her to meet Danny as a child and Clara bonds with him. Clara meets another child, sleeping fitfully in a barn, his parents worrying that he is unfit to be a Time Lord.

Time Heist ★ ★ ★ ★
The Doctor and Clara receive instructions from a mysterious figure: they must break into the impregnable Bank of Karabraxos and steal three items from its heart.

The Caretaker ★ ★ ★
The Doctor poses as the caretaker of Coal Hill School, to keep an eye on Danny Pink and Clara. The Skovox Blitzer, a war robot, creates havoc in the school.

Kill the Moon ★ ★ ★
A suicide mission is sent from Earth in 2049 to destroy the moon. The mission's crew, the Doctor and Clara are attacked by hideous spider-like creatures and the Doctor realises that the moon is a living entity.

Mummy on the Orient Express ★ ★ ★
Humans in the future ride on the pleasure spacecraft, the Orient Express, a copy of the ancient train. An alien mummy is activated and begins to kill the passengers.

Flatline ★ ★ ★ ★
Two dimensional aliens attempt to make sense of our world by converting three into two dimensions. The TARDIS is affected and goes into siege mode, and the Doctor realises that the aliens' intentions are far from benign.

In the Forest of the Night ★ ★ ★
London becomes a forest and the Doctor has to protect a party of children from Clara's school.

Dark Water/Death in Heaven ★ ★ ★ ★
The Cybermen invade Earth and Missy reveals her identity: well, she couldn't very well go on calling herself the Master, now could she?

Last Christmas ★ ★ ★ ★
Christmas special. Santa Claus enters the TARDIS and humans at an arctic base are

attacked by face-hugging aliens.

## Season Thirty Five (season nine)

The Magician's Apprentice/The Witch's Familiar ★ ★ ★ ★                    2015
Davros summons the Doctor to Skaro to witness his death. Missy and Clara come
along for the ride and Clara becomes a Dalek.

Under the Lake/Before the Flood ★ ★ ★
In an undersea Earth base in 2119, human scientists investigate a long-abandoned
alien craft. One by one, they fall victims to its blank-eyed ghosts, who silently
chant, "the dark, the sword, the forsaken, the temple". The Doctor travels to the
time of the craft's arrival, 1980, where the Fisher King, an alien warlord, sets these
future events in motion and plans to summon an armada to conquer Earth.

The Girl Who Died ★ ★ ★
The Doctor is hailed as Odin by the Vikings, who are attacked by the alien Mire.
Ashildr, a young Viking woman, aids the Doctor, but is killed by the modified Mire
helmet he makes her wear. The Doctor saves her with a chip from the helmet,
which curses her with immortality.

The Woman Who Lived ★ ★ ★
England in 1651. The Doctor encounters a highwayman, who turns out to be
Ashildr, 800 years old and so alone that she now calls herself Me. She has lost her
three children to the Black Death and, embittered, hands the Doctor over to the
authorities to be hanged as a highwayman.

The Zygon Invasion/The Zygon Inversion ★ ★ ★ ★
Since the events of "The Day of the Doctor", the Zygons have lived in peace with
the humans. As they have taken human form, it is impossible to distinguish them
from their neighbours. But a rogue faction of Zygons attempts to rouse their kinfolk
to war.

Sleep No More ★ ★ ★
An episode told through found video footage. Scientist Rassmussen has been
developing the Morpheus device, which compresses a night's sleep into a few
minutes: but a side effect is the creation of the murderous, shambling sandmen.

Face the Raven ★ ★ ★ ★
The Doctor discovers that trap streets, fictional streets inserted into maps as a
signature by individual cartographers, are real.  One houses an asylum for aliens,
and it is here that Clara must face the raven: her death.

Heaven Sent ★ ★ ★ ★ ★
The Doctor endures billions of years in a time loop, pursued by the deathly figure of the Veil, and determined to discover the secrets of the castle that is his prison.

Hell Bent ★ ★ ★ ★
The Doctor returns to Gallifrey, hell bent on uncovering the identity of the Hybrid, a creature which prophecy says will conquer Gallifrey and destroy it.

The Husbands of River Song ★ ★ ★ ★
Christmas special. River Song is up to her deceiving ways again, apparently married to King Hydroflax and unable to recognise the Doctor. Hydroflax is reborn as a murderous robot and the Doctor reveals his identity to River.

The Return of Doctor Mysterio ★ ★ ★ ★                                    2016

Christmas special. In New York in 1922, the Doctor inadvertently gives a young boy superpowers. Grown to adulthood and established as a superhero called The Ghost, the Doctor meets him again in 2016. Brain-swapping aliens attack.

## Season Thirty Six (season ten)

The Pilot ★ ★ ★ ★ ★                                                        2017
Bill Potts, a young woman who works in the canteen of St Luke's University, is intrigued by a brilliant lecturer called the Doctor. The Doctor invites her to attend his lectures and to travel with him. Bill's new friend Heather is apparently consumed by alien water and pursues Bill and the Doctor through time and space.

Smile ★ ★ ★ ★ ★
The Doctor and Bill arrive at a human colony in the far future, but there are no humans to be seen. There are only the emoji robots, who industriously prepare the colony for the humans' arrival, and smile, smile, smile.

Thin Ice ★ ★ ★
Georgian England. In a frost fair on the frozen River Thames, the Doctor and Bill encounter a giant aquatic alien and a villainous aristocrat who imprisons and exploits it.

Knock, Knock ★ ★ ★ ★
Seeking cheap accommodation, Bill is delighted when a friendly landlord offers her spacious lodgings with her friends in an old house. But the house is haunted and the friends are picked off one by one… David Suchet guests as the Landlord.

Oxygen ★ ★ ★ ★
The Doctor, Bill and Nardole arrive on board a deep space mining station. The only oxygen is provided by the smartsuits, network-controlled spacesuits which have orders to deactivate their organic component when the occupant can no longer pay for oxygen.

Extremis/The Pyramid at the End of the World/The Lie of the Land ★ ★ ★ ★
The alien monks offer apparently benevolent rule and help, but only to those whose supplications are made in love. Bill asks them to save the Doctor and ushers in a reign of lies and terror.

Empress of Mars ★ ★ ★ ★
As a spacecraft approaches Mars, NASA scientists are dumbfounded to read the message on the planet's surface: GOD SAVE THE QUEEN. British soldiers from the nineteenth century have been brought to the red planet by an Ice Warrior, who seeks to revive his queen, Iraxxa, and her hive.

The Eaters of Light ★ ★ ★
Second century Scotland. The Romans and the Picts are being destroyed by an alien that devours light. The Doctor must imprison it or it will feed on the sun and all the stars.

World Enough and Time/The Doctor Falls ★ ★ ★ ★ ★
Bill and the Doctor land on a spaceship so huge that time at one end travels more quickly than time at the other. Bill finds herself in a sinister medical facility which converts humans into Mondasian Cybermen; Missy and her previous incarnation, the Master, act as agents of chaos as the Doctor attempts to save the humans from the Cybermen.

Twice Upon A Time ★ ★ ★ ★ ★
Christmas special. Refusing to regenerate, the Doctor finds himself at the South Pole in 1986. Here he encounters the first Doctor, who also refuses to face his regeneration, and a Captain from World War I. The adventure takes both Doctors to the battlefields of the Great War and the starship *Testimony*. Both Doctors eventually accept that they must regenerate, and the thirteenth Doctor is expelled from her disintegrating TARDIS...

# Appendix Two

# Seven of the Best

If you want to sample the original series, a good place to start might be with one story from each of the Doctors. The following stories are among the best the series had to offer at the time of each individual Doctor:

**William Hartnell**
"An Unearthly Child"

**Patrick Troughton**
"The War Games"

**Jon Pertwee**
"Carnival of Monsters"

**Tom Baker**
"Genesis of the Daleks"

**Peter Davison**
"The Caves of Androzani"

**Colin Baker**
"Vengeance on Varos"

**Sylvester McCoy**
"Remembrance of the Daleks"